LION'S SHARE

VEIT ERLMANN

Lion's Share

Remaking South African Copyright

DUKE UNIVERSITY PRESS
Durham and London
2022

© 2022 DUKE UNIVERSITY PRESS
All rights reserved
Designed by A. Mattson Gallagher
Typeset in Quadraat Pro and Scala Sans Pro
by Westchester Publishing Services

Library of Congress Cataloging-in-Publication Data
Names: Erlmann, Veit, author.
Title: Lion's share : remaking South African copyright /
Veit Erlmann.
Description: Durham : Duke University Press, 2022. | Includes
index.
Identifiers: LCCN 2022020036 (print)
LCCN 2022020037 (ebook)
ISBN 9781478016328 (hardcover)
ISBN 9781478018964 (paperback)
ISBN 9781478023593 (ebook)
Subjects: LCSH: Music—Law and legislation—South Africa—
History. | Copyright—Music—South Africa—History. | Music and
race—South Africa. Linda, Solomon. Mbube (Wimoweh) | BISAC:
MUSIC / Ethnomusicology | HISTORY / Africa / South / Republic of
South Africa
Classification: LCC ML3917.S62 E75 2023 (print) | LCC ML3917.S62
(ebook) DDC 346.6804/82—dc23/eng/20220816
LC record available at https://lccn.loc.gov/2022020036
LC ebook record available at https://lccn.loc.gov/2022020037

Sometimes the past is the present.

Henry Maine: *Village Communities in the East and West.*
Six Lectures Delivered at Oxford. 1871

CONTENTS

Acknowledgments ix

Introduction 1
"We Do Not Speak the Same Language"

ONE Aspirations and Apprehensions 16
Toward an Anthropology in Law

TWO The Past in the Present 62
Copyright, Colonialism, and "The Lion Sleeps Tonight"

THREE Assembling Tradition, Representing Indigeneity 109
The Making of the Intellectual Property Laws Amendment Act 28 of 2013

FOUR Circulating Evidence 174
The Truth about Piracy

FIVE Which Collective? 232
The Infrastructure of Royalties

Conclusion 301
How To Speak the Same Language, or at Least Try To

Appendix 309
South African Copyright: The Basics

Notes 315
Bibliography 345
Index 371

ACKNOWLEDGMENTS

No book, no matter how innovating its author imagines it to be, is written on a blank slate. And while ideas are free, acknowledgment of at least some of the many people that shared their ideas with me and made this book possible is de rigueur. First and foremost, I must thank André Le Roux, former general manager of the SAMRO Foundation, and his wife Kgomotso for inviting me to an afternoon birthday celebration where I had the opportunity to participate in a very informative conversation about the music industry, copyright, and many other things I did not yet fully understand during my first reunion with Johannesburg after almost two decades of absence. Soon afterward, Owen Dean, the doyen of South African copyright law, did me the honor of attending my first (and still very immature) lecture on the subject of copyright at the start of my fieldwork—and still kept talking to me afterwards. So did Eve Gray, senior research associate in the Intellectual Property Unit at the University of Cape Town. I am also hugely indebted to Hanro Friedrich, the family lawyer of Solomon Linda's daughters and a key player in the seminal case against Disney discussed in chapter 2. He generously shared all of his files and correspondence about the lawsuit with me. Copyright lawyer, legal scholar, and music industry veteran Graeme Gilfillan likewise went out of his way to enlighten me on the more troubling aspects of the country's music-related collective management organizations (CMO), both past and present, and shared a wealth of documents on the history and current situation of SAMRO, Africa's largest CMO for music performance rights. Nick Matzukis, an entrepreneur, prog rock drummer, and lawyer, took the time to share a wealth of information about contract law in the music industry, which he knows more about than just about anyone else in South Africa. The 2013 book he authored, *South African Music Law, Contracts & Business*, has served as my trusted research companion from start to finish. I am also grateful for stimulating conversations I had with Joel Baloyi, law professor at the University of South Africa and former counsel at SAMRO. Law professors Jean Sonnekus (University of Johannesburg) and Gardiol van Niekerk (University of Pretoria) provided valuable information about their involvement with the Disney case.

Filmmaker François Verster generously offered background information about the making of his trailblazing documentary *A Lion's Trail*. Rob Allingham, a former archivist at Gallo and the foremost expert on South African discography, deserves heartfelt thanks for spirited conversation and sharing details about his involvement with the Disney case. Elizabeth Ntsele, the daughter of Solomon Linda, graciously invited me to her father's house to share memories and voice her dissatisfaction with the outcome of the case. Thanks are also due to her sisters Fildah and Delphi. My insatiable curiosity about the music industry never fazed Angus Rheder, head of the Anti-Piracy Unit (RAPU) of the Recording Industry of South Africa (RiSA). Not only did he show me where to get the best coffee in Tshwane, but he also let me tag along on several antipiracy operations, observe his forensic work, and introduced me to other enforcement organizations, such as the South African Federation against Copyright Theft (SAFACT). In a related context, I must thank the countless police officers at the Jeppe, Hillbrow, Lyttelton, Sunnyside, Khayelitsha, and Boksburg North police stations for graciously tolerating (or ignoring) the presence of an inquisitive researcher. Tremendous gratitude is also due to the state attorney of Gauteng for allowing me to sit in on a meeting with a police officer who had been involved in a highly questionable raid. Amanda Lotheringen, director of copyright and IP enforcement at the Companies and Intellectual Property Commission took time out of her busy schedule to provide me with important material on her government department's antipiracy policy.

Sipho Dlamini, CEO of the Southern African Musical Rights Organisation (SAMRO) from 2012 to 2018, took a huge risk by inviting me to spend a few weeks at his remarkable organization. This leap of faith was only outdone by the warmth and kindness with which many of the workers under his supervision patiently and cheerfully initiated the unwitting anthropologist into the slippery world of licensing and royalty collection. I will never forget the gentle demeanor of Stephenson Mhlanga, the energy of Alen

Gustafson, and the graciousness of Thobile, Kevin, Sibongile, Dimakatso, Agnes, and Agreement who unlocked the secrets of "match and link" and "grudge-purchases" to me.

Mandla Maseko of the Association of Independent Record Companies (AIRCO) loved engaging me in spirited discussion about the majors, Frantz Fanon, and oral poetry, throwing in a divine *braai* (South African barbeque) for good measure. Other key players in the music industry, like Jacques Botha at SAFACT, Gillian Ezra of the streaming platform Simfy Africa, and David Alexander of music publisher Sheer Music, graciously shared their views on everything from copyright, publishing, and freedom of expression.

Closer to my academic niche, I am indebted to Adam Haupt, professor of media studies and director of the Centre for Film and Media Studies at the University of Cape Town, for his critical acumen in dissecting South African hip-hop and the country's mediascape more generally. Caroline Ncube, copyright expert extraordinaire and a professor at the same institution, kindly visited one of the courses I taught as a Fulbright Scholar at the University of Cape Town and invited me to speak at an eye-opening conference on South African intellectual property law. Likewise, Tobias Schönwetter, director of the Intellectual Property Unit at the same institution provided insight and intellectual stimulation. I am eternally grateful to Dr. Desmond Oriakhogba, a lecturer at the University of Venda, who didn't even think twice before providing me with his vast collection of research materials on competition law and collective management organizations in the South African and Nigerian creative sectors. Dr. Chijioke Okorie at the University of Pretoria broadened my understanding of the legal aspects of multisided music platforms immensely by allowing me to read and comment on the proofs of her 2019 book *Multi-Sided Music Platforms: Copyright, Law and Policy in Africa*, now felicitously available in print.

Earlier versions of excerpts from the book have been presented at various institutions around the globe, including the Africa Open Institute for Music (Stellenbosch); the Alexander von Humboldt Institute for Internet and Society (Berlin); the Centre national de la recherche scientifique (Paris); Columbia University; Cornell University; Duke University; Goethe-University Frankfurt; Harvard University's Kennedy School; the International Library of African Music (Grahamstown); Oxford University; Rhodes University; Stellenbosch University; the University of Cape Town; the University of Siegen; and the University of the Western Cape. I am immensely grateful to Georgina Born, Michelle Cocks, Mamadou Diawara, Detlef Diederichsen, Adam Haupt, Patricia Henderson, Premesh Lalu, Louise Meintjes,

Stephanus Muller, David Novak, Emmanuelle Olivier, James Parker, Ute Röschenthaler, Erhard Schüttpelz, Carina Venter, Stephanie Vos, and Lee Watkins for hosting these events. Beyond conferences and invited lectures, almost daily interactions with my students at the University of Texas have been a constant source of inspiration. Conversations with Andy Normann about his work on South African hip-hop, infrastructures, and fugitivity have been particularly fruitful.

For over twenty years, I have had the privilege of holding the Endowed Chair of Music History at the Butler School of Music (University of Texas at Austin). Without the support of the anonymous donors who made this endowment possible, this book would not have been written. Oren Bracha, a prominent legal historian and professor at the University of Texas School of Law Austin, whose office is right across the street from mine, allowed me to take his upper-division course "Advanced Topics in Copyright," which gave me the opportunity to see and read the law in a completely new light. I also had the immense pleasure of hosting a 2015 symposium at UT Austin on "Music, Property, and Law." I am indebted to all of the speakers at this event, especially Olufunmilayo Arewa, Toni Lester, and Matt Stahl, for inspiration and encouraging debate.

Funmi Arewa, Graeme Gilfillan, and Caroline Ncube read and commented on all or parts of the manuscript. Two anonymous readers at Duke University Press also offered most productive insight and suggestions for improvement. Michele Faguet provided invaluable editing assistance.

My biggest debt, however, is to my beloved wife Christine, to whom this book is dedicated. I can only hope that its spirit will pay back at least some of what I owe to her while thinking in law.

Introduction

"We Do Not Speak the Same Language"

"We do not speak the same language." It was the conclusion to a law conference at the University of Cape Town in July 2019.[1] In a general discussion rounding off the proceedings, participants had been invited to reflect on the Copyright Amendment Bill—the latest attempt by lawmakers to remake South African copyright law. Much like the Intellectual Property Laws Amendment Act 28 of 2013 (hereafter Intellectual Property Laws Amendment Act) before, this legislation had sparked intense debate, with numerous trade associations, lawmakers of the opposition parties, nongovernmental organizations, and academics slamming the bill as what veteran copyright scholar Coenraad Visser, summing up the views of virtually the entire legal fraternity and more likely than not those present at the conference, as a "mess."[2] The verdict prompted me, in turn, as the only nonlegal scholar in attendance, to wonder out loud what the rejection of the bill might say about the rift between legal scholars and politicians, but more importantly about all of us—politicians, legal experts, and the academy at large. Hence Visser's one-liner: "We do not speak the same language."

How did we get to this point, and how does this book address this impasse? At a moment when South Africa's intellectual property system hangs in the balance—and the country as a whole appears to be in crisis—*Lion's Share* represents a modest attempt to engage the humanities and legal studies in a conversation about South Africa's ongoing project of bringing its aging copyright system in line with the profoundly altered cultural landscape of the country, and especially of the music industry, more than a quarter-century after the end of apartheid. I approach this task with a keen sense not just of each of these disciplines' lacunae in tackling this daunting task, but I am also acutely aware of the vacuum that exists between them and the scholarship on postapartheid cultural production in general. South African musical scholarship—broadly construed as encompassing sound studies, musicology, ethnomusicology, performance-oriented cultural studies, and music-related media and communication studies—took a major turn in the early 1980s. It is then, at the height of the struggle that would end about a decade later with the unbanning of the African National Congress (ANC), the release of all political prisoners, and finally, the swearing-in of Nelson Mandela as the first democratically elected president of the country, that I became part of a small group of scholars determined to set the study of South African music on a new course of what almost three decades later would be known under the name *decolonization*.[3] Historically, the study of South African music had been dominated by a set of colonial and apartheid concepts stressing the continuity of allegedly timeless tribal forms of association and cultural traditions. Urban and westernized practices, although ubiquitous from the beginning of the twentieth century at the latest, were considered as the mere product of acculturation at best, or, simply as aberrations and signs of degeneration and, consequently, were to be disregarded as objects of serious study. In contrast, the "radical rethink," as Christine Lucia calls the new approach pioneered in those heady days, and that over time came to be recognized as a genuinely South African "new musicology," prioritized quite a different set of parameters.[4] Instead of tribes, migrant laborers and black urban elites now became the nuclei of cultural production. And tradition increasingly emerged as a construction serving vested interests rather than being frozen in a mythical time before colonization and apartheid. But, above all, the new direction, in a move that, following Paul Gilroy, one might describe as a form of anti-anti-essentialism, also retained a certain idea of shared collective identities as a precondition of a new cultural politics, whether they are framed in nationalist terms, centered around working-class consciousness, or articulated in tropes of blackness.

This shift continued to stimulate a rich vein of postapartheid scholarship published in the immediate aftermath of the birth of the new South Africa. Apart from my own writing of the late 1990s, more recent work emerging from the early 2000s added important new insights into music and other expressive forms as significant sites of the construction of new identities beyond colonialism's and apartheid's dichotomies as well as arenas of contestation in which indigenous and other marginalized populations advance demands for justice, inclusion, and belonging.[5] Looked at with the benefit of hindsight, however, one might say that this new direction is not owed to the history of popular resistance to apartheid alone. It may also require us to adopt a new analytic—one in which struggles over subject formation and social reproduction increasingly follow a logic that is not unique to South Africa or, indeed, the Global South but is symptomatic of the massive reconfiguration of social relations occurring in late modernity everywhere. Two of these shifts are of particular relevance to the topic of this book. The first is a process in which culture—once thought of as a vital component of the imagination of homogeneous entities, such as the emerging nation-states of the nineteenth century—becomes a pivotal element in the making of what Andreas Reckwitz calls the "society of singularities." Late-modern culture, he argues, is no longer a subsystem in an all-encompassing system of instrumental rationality, as during the formative period of modernity, but is itself a global "hyperculture" in which virtually everything, "from Zen meditation to industrial footstools, from Montessori schools to YouTube videos, can be regarded as culture and can become elements of the highly mobile markets of valorization, which entice the participation of subjects with the promise of self-actualization." In other words, late-modern culture—that is, culturally endowed objects, subjects, places, events, and collectives—at its core is composed of singularities.[6]

Much of this may not be readily discernable in current South African affairs, not only because of the persistence of strong socio-moral imperatives keeping the singularization observed by Reckwitz in check but also because it is buried under a thick layer of official discourse conjuring national unity and social cohesion as antidotes to heterogeneity and fragmentation. The argument that I develop in this book, however, goes one step further. Instead of the fixation of past scholarship on questions of identity, I wish to foreground the growing significance that property and ownership play in the postapartheid order. Ownership, I argue, has turned from a marker of racial privilege into a pivot around which virtually every aspect of South Africans' public and private lives is centered. Of course, in the context of the early history of slavery and colonization, ownership, first and foremost, refers to ownership of one's own body.[7] Yet, as the struggles over the ownership of one's body and bodily labor intensified in the run-up to the so-called mineral revolution of the late nineteenth century and later on apartheid, ownership also came to comprise the control over an ever-shrinking range of other resources—above all land and water. Finally, by the time the democratic South Africa came into being and prospects for comprehensive land reform proved elusive, employment rates plummeted, the domestic market was flooded with cheap imported consumer items primarily benefitting a rising black middle class, and a new set of tenets operating under the name "black economic empowerment" for the first time attracted a mass following outside the ANC longing for "economic freedom," the conflicts over ownership entered a new phase.

Henceforth, the South African frontier is no longer defined solely by the epic struggles over colonial dispossession, land restitution, or the complex forms of collective belonging and identity these have afforded for centuries. Although artistic creativity and performative excellence have always been key elements of black anticolonial and antiapartheid politics, almost three decades after the demise of apartheid, ownership of one's creative work and, by extension, of a person's well-being and sense of self is emerging as a major impetus of social and cultural reproduction. And so, by asking how those older struggles have shaped the history of South African copyright and what impact the current efforts at remaking South African copyright described in this book may have on the future of cultural reproduction in the country more generally, I hope to show that copyright is more than just a major battlefield on which disputes over the ownership of works of creativity are being staged. It is, at the same time, a key site where notions of propriety, appropriation, culture, and selfhood intersect to the point of becoming indistinguishable from one another, where selves are made and remade in ever-changing configurations, where new commodities and markets of valorization and modes of accumulating "singularity capital" are created, and where a new pragmatics of citizenship is being forged.[8] The frontier has moved inwards, it seems, while becoming more dispersed in the process, drawing more people into new commercial circuits and ultimately hastening the drift toward the idiosyncratic, private, and insular as the defining features of the South Africa of the twenty-first century.

The signs of this corrosive shift and its expression in a discourse that South African journalists Rapule Tabane and Ferial Haffajee, as long ago as 2003, called "ID-ology" are hard to overlook. Although—or perhaps because—South Africa's Constitution has been celebrated as one of the most progressive and liberal in the world, offering far-reaching guarantees in regards to human and cultural rights, the country's political establishment struggles to stem the tide of a fractious politics of the particular that is not only irreconcilable with key premises of liberal democracy but whose reverberations in everyday life also threaten the very foundations of the new nation-state as the materialization of those premises. The list is long—

from various forms of vigilante justice allegedly rooted in "tradition" and customary law to the resurgence of ethnic divisions long deemed to have been engineered by the apartheid regime to the looting spree unleashed in July 2021 by followers of embattled former President Jacob Zuma protesting his incarceration in the wake of him having disregarded a subpoena issued by the Constitutional Court, the terrain of dissension in the last couple of decades has shifted dramatically. Even the law is getting caught up in the madness. While the tonality of the country's political discourse may have shifted from revolutionary to democratically legitimated "rights talk," the class-action suit has replaced the class struggle as the preferred medium for settling differences. Traditional leaders, nongovernmental organizations, social movements, corrupt politicians, and even crime syndicates take one another to court to make claims against one another or the state, often in ways that challenge key concepts of the rule of law.[9]

But this weaponization of the law is not limited to politics. Law's reach extends deep into the realm of cultural reproduction, raising urgent questions about the possibility of legal interventions to right past wrongs and the attendant need for a new theorization of the nature of conflict in postapartheid South Africa, all told. For all the talk about the imminent rise of a creative class complete with creative cities and a knowledge economy, postapartheid cultural producers are increasingly becoming resistant to narratives of the rainbow nation or the miracle of postapartheid transformation. Instead, they are finding themselves in a more ambiguous condition of fugitivity, here understood in the sense of a dialectic between the pursuit of the irregular, incalculable, or utopian and the aspiration for autonomy, security, and well-being in the given now that simultaneously embraces and refuses the mythologies of subjectivity grounded in national identity or in the individual of the liberal-democratic imagination.[10] Thus, while black cultural producers over the past twenty or so years have triumphantly reclaimed their rightful place at the center of the country's cultural affairs, the constitutional guarantees—of equality or freedom of expression, among others—that enable these endeavors of reparation, repatriation, and recuperation remain incomplete without the state delivering on the far-reaching socioeconomic rights recognized in the Bill of Rights.[11] In other words, human rights and liberal-democratic gestures of appreciation and recognition that fail to appreciably alter the conditions under which cultural producers may reap the material benefits of their creative labor can never advance racial justice. In fact, in the eyes of many of these cultural producers and large sections of the citizenry, they are perceived as a means to obscure the continuation of the structures of the past under a different name. That is why the late Johnny Clegg, musing about his career as one of South Africa's most distinguished musical voices against apartheid, missed the mark in blaming the poststruggle generation of so-called freeborns for being "totally gripped by a materialistic world."[12] Racial, social, and intellectual property justice are mutually constitutive of each other.

On the other hand, what complicates this turn to copyright law as the idiom of choice for translating claims to equality and ownership into a "ready means of commensuration," a "repertoire of more or less standardized terms and practices that permit the negotiation of values, beliefs, ideals, and interests across otherwise-impermeable lines of cleavage," is that novelists, filmmakers, dancers, visual artists, and musicians may end up reproducing the very racialized terms that have worked against them in the past.[13] If the ownership of one's creative work is increasingly becoming a touchstone for determining a person's success in having escaped the vicious cycle of poverty, stigmatization, marginalization, and more poverty, by the same token, it may also be read as a sign of that person having modeled themselves on the liberal credo of the propertied, competitive individual and markets as conditions of a free, prosperous citizenry. Drawing on Alexander Weheliye's insight that the "entry fee for legal recognition is the acceptance of categories based on white supremacy and colonialism," one might conclude that getting even by legal means does not reduce unevenness as much as it may exacerbate it.[14]

With few exceptions, much of this has so far escaped anthropological and musical scholarship. And not just South African. Elsewhere in the Global South, scholars likewise appear to be dragging their feet in recognizing the growing significance of the culture-copyright-ownership triad as a fundamental force shaping postcolonial cultural production in the twenty-first century more broadly.[15] But, legal scholarship, in turn, hardly fares any better. Here, it is not a lack of attention to copyright per se that is at issue. After decades of neglect during which copyright law was little more than an exotic niche topic languishing in the shadow of patent and trademark law, or was ignored altogether (a fact whose repercussions are still felt in the dearth of copyright experts in the South African judiciary), a small number of South African law schools now have LLM programs in intellectual property law and have become sites of cutting-edge scholarship and vigorous debate. The problem, however, with this upsurge is that with respect to copyright, much of this energy is somewhat disconnected from the world of cultural production. While the music industry, for instance, counts a fair number of legally trained executives among its ranks, academics with significant industry experience are far more difficult to identify.[16] Most South African legal scholars (in fact, African legal scholars in general) have yet to systematically engage with the theoretical and practical dimensions of the new forms and technologies of producing and circulating cultural goods, vastly expanded opportunities for capital accumulation afforded by digitization, and rapidly shifting aesthetic preferences and consumer tastes.[17] Last but not least, the study of copyright—and of law in general—in tertiary education still needs to disengage from the legacies of colonial legal thought and embrace the call for decolonization that has swept South African campuses under the banner of the #FeesMustFall student protests of 2015–2016.[18]

It is this uneasy, reciprocal silence that has motivated my work over the past decade and that this book seeks to break. *Lion's Share: Remaking South African Copyright* is an attempt to generate an interdisciplinary framework for thinking about copyright and cultural production in South Africa and the postcolony at large—and possibly even regenerate a dynamic, almost lost tradition of dialogue between law and the humanities more broadly—that now seems to have reached an impasse, stuck in entrenched positions, stale dichotomies, and outdated categories. To that end, the book offers an ethnographically and legally informed story about the actors, discourses, and fault lines shaping the policies, legislative initiatives, court cases, activist interventions, and public debates about a copyright law of the twenty-first century in a music industry that ranks among the tenth- to twentieth-largest markets for recorded music in the world, along with Brazil, Mexico, and Sweden. But here is the rub. While the book seeks to engage anthropologists and legal scholars in a deeper, substantive conversation about music and copyright law, it offers no proposal for how to fix copyright or how to align South Africa's ongoing efforts at remaking its copyright framework with the country's larger project of transformation and development. Nor is it a manifesto for or against any particular version of this project, be it an Access to Knowledge (A2K) paradigm, Creative Commons model, or the Africanization of copyright in the name of the philosophy of *ubuntu*. Others more qualified than me have put forward a rich variety of recommendations and blueprints for such undertakings.[19] Therefore, the subtitle *Remaking South African Copyright* is not meant to be prescriptive as much as it invites the reader to consider the project of renewing the country's aging copyright system from a more descriptive vantage—from the perspective of those who are embroiled in the long-drawn-out effort to restructure the statutes, institutions, industry structures, and practices at the heart of copyright.

But counterbalancing this studying-up perspective is also an approach in which the owner bias of copyright jurisprudence is decentered by studying sideways, in recognizing the agency of users, consumers, and the public at large in remaking copyright, be it by critiquing policy; developing alternative, nonproprietary models of cultural production; or just by undermining copyright by illegal means such as file-sharing or piracy. In other words, when talking about the current moment as one of remaking, I do not imply that South Africa's copyright mess is a problem that can be addressed by any single agent, from only one location, or on the basis of tidy precepts and visions of social order. Still less do I want to suggest that this mess is a uniquely postcolonial predicament resulting from the failure of developing countries to fully embrace core tenets of the Euro-modernist imagination, such as the rule of law, representative government, and free-market policies foremost among them. Rather, it is to query the underlying notion that disorder—a botched bill, a dysfunctional legislative process, divergent opinions, and even mutual incomprehension—can be contrasted with a world of legality and civic order, legal certainty, and social stability. The mess of the Copyright Amendment Bill and the Intellectual Property Laws Amendment Act, I argue, is part of a broader conundrum inherent in the present world order or, as South African–born anthropologists John and Jean Comaroff put it, of "a dialectic of law and dis/order, framed by neoliberal mechanisms of deregulation and new modes of mediating human transactions."[20]

Before anything else, however, the waning of certainties once held to be unassailable; constant and abrupt shifts in the most mundane aspects of our daily lives; the demise of cultural work as we knew it; the unsettling prospect of an entirely human-made, nature-free planet; and much more all call into question inherited concepts of order, rules, or method—indeed, what it means to know. But they also encourage us to explore new ways of dealing with the indefinite, unstable, and even unthinkable. In other words, remaking copyright entails more than redefining one or the other legal term, enlarging the scope of exceptions, designing newfangled categories of works, or creating as yet unknown exclusive rights. Such amendments merely work within the existing space within which arguments and debates about copyright can legitimately take place, but they do not consider the fact that the mess these amendments seek to untangle is intertwined with another mess, one that can no longer be accounted for by any reliable method or technique and that therefore calls for a different type of inquiry, a reset and going back to the drawing board, or an unmaking of received terminologies, analytics, and assumptions about what is knowable or worth knowing.[21]

The name I provisionally gather these efforts at unmaking and remaking under is the anthropology *in* law. Distinct from an older brand of anthropological inquiry into law called legal anthropology or anthropology of law, but also in (sometimes tense) conversation with more recent modulations, such as critical legal studies or critical legal race theory, I like to think of this approach as a novel way to frame the interdisciplinary study of law in which law's and anthropology's (or any other political, cultural, scientific) knowledges interpenetrate each other to a point where "speaking the same language" does not mean unconditional consensus, uniformity of codes, or what John Law calls the "singularity" of definitive sets of processes through which one may determine "discoverable entities" but an openness to a never-ending cycle of questions and answers.²²

Perhaps it is this openness that the African proverb that when asking questions, you cannot avoid answers refers to. Different, unexpected answers, as I understand it. Answers that you may not like and therefore provoke more questions such as the following: How do we make sense of the new power imbalances that have arisen in the democratic South Africa and that seem to displace or mask the persistence of older dichotomies, such as those between state power and grassroots forms of political and cultural practice? To what extent is the seismic shift in postapartheid politics from the militant rhetoric of *revolution* and *liberation* of the apartheid era to a more measured vocabulary stressing *rights* and *citizenship* reflected in, and perhaps also impacted by, the arts and the South African creative industries more broadly? Did the past twenty-some years of copyright reform align South African cultural life with the broader objectives of restorative and distributive justice espoused after apartheid? Or will the Intellectual Property Laws Amendment Act and the Copyright Amendment Bill perpetuate old divides and possibly even create new ones? What, if any, are the unforeseen effects of the reform process that resist being packaged into government betterment programs, political manifestos, academic paradigms, and legal prescriptions? And who will reap the lion's share?

It will be up to the reader to decide what additional questions might arise from reading the book and, especially, what answers they might generate that I did not think of while writing it. But here, at least, are some suggestions as to the possible lines along which the project of "speaking the same language" might proceed. First of all, *Lion's Share* is not a musical ethnography. Although the South African music industry forms much of the book's backdrop, musicians, musical genres, or musical aesthetics hardly matter. Nor do particular geographic regions or cities, demographic groups, ethnicities, or racialized groups figure prominently. In fact, the book is not concerned with the more traditional mainstays of ethnography—identities, communities, or spaces—to begin with. If anything, over long stretches, *Lion's Share* is about fragile, multiplex, asynchronous relations interlinking mundane, unexciting, and understudied techniques, procedures, classifications, forms, protocols, infrastructures, scripts, contracts, legal norms, and, yes, occasionally also music. And it is about how all these actors perform, mediate, and sustain legal norms and processes, identities, and spaces in uncertain, contingent ways.

But if the book is about relationships rather than music or any other a priori given domain, does law not also count as a domain—perhaps more than any other, delineated and insulated from everything around it? The short answer is that law may actually be the quintessential relational form that *binds* people, things, and actions through webs of rules, norms, rights, and obligations. But this assertion does not tell us much about how the law goes about weaving these webs. Nor does law's built-in relationality give us any indication as to the purpose of this weaving beyond strengthening normative ideas. To be sure, most legal practitioners and, perhaps, a substantial number of scholars, irrespective of jurisprudential affiliation, would probably subscribe to the functionalist notion that the purpose of the law is to somehow improve or otherwise better human relationships according to agreed-upon social and cultural norms. Consequently, they might also expect a book about the remaking of copyright in a country crying out for fundamental transformation like no other to offer, if not a new prescription for a different legal framework, at least some empirically grounded and theoretically informed sense of how these norms are intertwined with the broader sociocultural order that sustains and is constituted by them. Others, especially those in the academy, will vehemently contest this assumption, pointing instead to the role of law in encoding and legitimizing asymmetrical power relationships. As a result, they will consider any attempt at lending cohesion and credibility to law as a viable analytical category to be politically futile, intellectually bankrupt, or both.

The long answer to the question above—or the proverbial string of answers—may come as somewhat of a surprise. While indeed concerning itself with law as a set of relations, *Lion's Share* is beholden to neither of the above views. I do not conceive of law as a means to an end, where the end is for another discipline, method, or way of thinking to define—be it anthropology, sociology, or economics. Nor do I accept the notion that law can be reduced to ideology. Not only do both approaches fail to grasp the unprecedented complexity of cultural reproduction in the twenty-first century, but they also do not seem to have at their disposal the kind of theoretical and methodological toolkit required to engage the vastly changed circumstances under which anthropology might relate to law in a new way. What I call the anthropology in law is thus an attempt to sketch the outlines of such an approach. It departs from the notion that even as the law appears to ever-more-forcefully penetrate every recess of our public and private lives, throughout its long relationship to anthropology, it has always figured as another—its incorporation into anthropology's canon and condition of possibility being contingent on various strategies of marginalization, functionalization, and reification. To know law has been, and to some extent continues to be, subject to a peculiar, Janus-faced episteme. For example, during legal anthropology's formative phase, scholars such as Lewis Morgan, John McLennan, or Henry Maine posited that law's "relation to modern ideas," as the subtitle of Maine's classic *Ancient Law* words it, was always already dichotomous, opposing nineteenth-century scientific rationality to the irrationality of status and brute force.[23] But by the same logic, Maine also managed to frame the ascent of law toward reason as a process of evolution toward contractual relationships forged among reasonable actors. The new anthropology of law emerging in the 1980s in the wake of the decolonization of the colonial world likewise, if rather more tacitly, rested on an existing separation between the social as a space of power conflicts and disorder and anthropology's superior epistemic power to reveal the structure underpinning that space along with law's ordering capacity. Even the critical anthropology of the more recent past took long to arrive at an understanding of anthropology as every bit as culturally contingent as some of the signifying, cultural forms provided by the law to apprehend the world.

So, how can we anthropologically think *in* law? Many of the answers to these questions can be found in a commitment to what one might call joint ethnography—that is, a synergy of the methodologies of anthropological fieldwork and the attention to technicality, form, and process at the heart of legal practice. *Lion's Share* differs from other contemporary projects to reground the interdisciplinary study of law by attempting to disentangle the layers of law from the inside out in a search for compatibility and the pursuit of a new type of relationality. The anthropology in law I grasp for no longer assumes that law is a self-contained body of knowledge always prepositioned as an object of these disciplines' gaze. But conversely, it also relinquishes any pretensions to completeness and interpretive authority. In this way, it exemplifies, perhaps, more a performative process of building rather than an affirmation of an already existing relationship. Building on the rich body of experimental ethnographies that have appeared in recent years on topics and locations as diverse as South African social medicine, *ngoma* dancing, and pharmaceutical laboratories, I therefore draw together and constantly circle back among a wide range of material sources and discursive formats from statistics, policy documents, and legal briefs to royalty statements, audio recordings of parliamentary debates, crime dockets, and personal narratives.[24] Consequently, I deliberately eschew any claim to methodological uniformity, drawing eclectically on actor-network theory, science and technology studies, thing theory, critical development studies, organization studies, and many others. The aim of such an incestuous intermingling is to further the notion that an ethnography of the kind offered here can be anything but a tidy story. Understood thus, ethnography resembles what in the physics of light or acoustic waves is referred to as diffraction, a bending of waves as they move around an obstacle. In this sense, ethnographic diffraction allows the researcher to better attend to the interference that occurs when different and possibly even radically incompatible practices, epistemologies, and viewpoints come into contact with one another, producing unforeseen effects as a result. But for this to happen, both fields need to question some of their most ingrained habits. At a very fundamental level, one cannot but notice a profound discrepancy between the undercontextualized abstraction, formalism, and obstinate faith in the progress of legal reasoning on the one hand and anthropology's antiessentialist, antimodernist impetus to debunk legal categories such as "property" or "author" as ciphers for asymmetrical power relationships on the other. Where legal scholars may invoke received and largely exhausted categories of social analysis, anthropologists are all too prone to gloss over the nitty-gritty of legal doctrine and practice. As I will show in the following chapters, the attempt to remedy this sort of mutual paralysis and propose a model for folding together diverse epistemologies and methodologies does not necessarily entail relinquishing the gains made by either of these earlier developments or ceasing to think like a lawyer. For instance, dispute resolution, among the hallmarks of early legal anthropology, informs parts of chapter 2. In some way or another, most chapters also echo the concerns of the older law-in-action paradigm by shifting the emphasis from state law to the vagaries of litigation strategies—all the while decentering the courtroom as a normative space for conflict resolution and replacing it with a wider range of institutional settings and forms of social control. Still, other chapters address the subtle disparities between jurisprudential universals, international norms, and their local reinterpretations that animate current debates about justice. Finally, reverberating throughout the book is the signature achievement of critical legal studies of the 1980s and 1990s: reorienting our long and troubled preoccupation with law as a system of propositional enunciations toward law as a power-laden discourse.

Yet, for all the innovative ideas and critical attention to new contexts, social settings, structures of domination, and counterhegemonic practices, there is still one area, one constant, in the existing literature that seems irreconcilable with the larger project of an anthropology in law. Most ethnographic accounts relate legal developments and their relationship to the extralegal sphere as though they are already part of a small set of surprisingly simple and ready-made storylines, such as the emergence of global capitalism, the fetishization of the law as a panacea for everything from poverty to the HIV/AIDS crisis, the international homogenization of law, and so on. Rather than positioning these totalizing processes as the a priori of the quotidian, makeshift, unsought, and unpredictable events that incite the ethnographer's instinct, I question the very premise that the main purpose of attending to such events is to validate the totalizing nature of that which they are entangled with. The totality is just as transient, unpredictable, unstable, and, hence, worth of ethnographic study. At the same time, to practice an ethnography of copyright is not only to decenter law; ironically, it also compels us to take law more seriously as a protagonist of its own account of what the world outside itself is like and to recognize law's agency by meticulously attending to that which constitutes it—form, technicality, procedure. But, conversely, if law's entire raison d'être rests on an *is-ought* dichotomy between tidy facts and even tidier visions of what should be, my ethnography emphatically comes down on the messy side of the *is*.

Here, then, is what is in store over the coming pages. In each of the book's five chapters, I propose a different modality of pursuing an anthropology in law. The first is introductory and lays the groundwork for those that follow. In addition to offering an overview of some of the key issues in current South African copyright debates, I attempt to outline a future history of South African copyright in the context of the country's creative industries and introduce a series of conceptual tools to foreground the relational, networked nature of my anthropology in law. In chapter 2, I revisit the internationally celebrated 2006 settlement between the heirs of Solomon Linda and Walt Disney, Inc. for the latter's unauthorized use of the song "Mbube" in the blockbuster musical *The Lion King*. This account offers what is perhaps the first-ever in-depth look at how a case is put together by following the countless hoops and hiatuses it encountered on its way to resolution. While on the surface, the theoretical framework may hark back to a law-in-action paradigm, at a deeper level, it utilizes this case to probe the twin legacies of colonial and imperial law and their precarious continuity within postcolonial transformative justice.

Chapter 3 is about lawmaking, specifically the making of the Intellectual Property Laws Amendment Act. Having shadowed the Portfolio Committee on Trade and Industry and having worked through the resulting mountain of policy documents, draft legislation, minutes, and expert opinions, I examine the act's cultural imaginary and its production in the legislative process. Although the act has been roundly rejected as unworkable and potentially unconstitutional, my primary concern is not its perceived failings but the way it assembles the indigenous by undoing it. By turning indigenous communities into the authors of traditional cultural expressions, it creates a whole new rights-based domain of belonging, one that reproduces past categories of exclusion more than it creates new opportunities for inclusion.

Chapter 4 addresses the enforcement of copyright by so-called public-private partnerships involving a variety of state agencies, such as the South African Police Service (SAPS), and trade associations like the music industry's trade association Recording Industry of South Africa (RiSA) and the film industry's South African Federation Against Copyright Theft (SAFACT). The broader rationale of this strategy is to promote the public interest by protecting the rights of copyright owners. Having followed these organizations as they engage in education campaigns, police raids on suspected pirates, forensic analysis of infringing copies, and collection of statistical data, I question the public interest narrative as concealing decidedly unpublic industry strategies and the reproduction of the socio-spatial order bequeathed by apartheid.

In chapter 5, I offer a case study of the Southern African Music Rights Organization (SAMRO), one of South Africa's three so-called collecting societies for music-related rights, whose principal function is to collect royalties for the public performance of works owned by its members. Much like the other bodies I examine in this book, SAMRO imagines itself to be a staunch champion of copyright and a vital contributor to the country's economic and cultural well-being. However, many of the society's members and critics have vigorously contested this narrative by suggesting that its status as a de facto monopoly is detrimental to both their own interests and those of the public at large. Indeed, SAMRO has been embroiled in controversy and rocked by numerous scandals since its inception in 1961. Nevertheless,

I approach the conflicted nature of collective management organizations like SAMRO from a slightly different angle. Having interned in SAMRO's Licensing and Sales department for some time, I offer an ethnographic account of how the dissonance between private and public interest constituting SAMRO's very raison d'être is less the result of insufficient regulation than it is intrinsic to its internal modus operandi.

The book concludes with some brief reflections on the furor that greeted the Copyright Amendment Bill mentioned at the beginning and how it exposed the mutual incomprehension among lawmakers, legal scholars, and the broader public. Much like the Intellectual Property Laws Amendment Act before it, the bill is not only plagued with numerous issues, but it also tests the boundaries and possibilities of what it means to speak in law.

ONE

Aspirations and Apprehensions
Toward an Anthropology in Law

It is common knowledge that the cultural industries of the twenty-first century can no longer be divorced from the pervasive impact that increasingly restrictive copyright policies have on virtually every aspect of life. In her groundbreaking study, *The Cultural Life of Intellectual Properties: Authorship, Appropriation, and the Law*, Rosemary Coombe argues that in this "textually saturated, hypersignificant world . . . intellectual property protections are central cultural conditions of production, circulation, and reception."[1] Similarly, in her book *From Goods to a Good Life: Intellectual Property Law and Global Justice*, Madhavi Sunder suggests that "we must see intellectual property law as regulation of meaning and, in turn, of the social relations that flow from how we envision our world."[2] Deborah Halbert, for her part, believes that "pro-intellectual property interests have used the state to establish a legal regime that has moved well beyond the protection of copyrights, patents, trademarks, and other types of abstractions as a limited monopoly balanced against a public interest, to protecting these abstractions as a form of property to which an original owner must be given virtually absolute rights."[3] But at the same time, these authors caution, the tightening of copyright regulations excludes growing numbers of people from meaningful participation in culture, self-development, and even freedom. Sunder writes, "Participation rather than passive reception in the production of culture and science enables a democratic citizenry ready to question convention and to seek novel answers to problems, old and new."[4] Likewise, Coombe calls for an approach to copyright that prioritizes the potential of "activities of reiteration, recoding and reproduction"—in other words, of the sort of cultural practices that copyright claims to encourage while simultaneously limiting the space in which such creative activity might flourish.[5] And Halbert cautions that the new global political economy of intellectual property "has ramifications for the free flow of information, access to knowledge, and the future of innovation. Intellectual property has always been, but has now more visibly become, an issue of social justice."[6]

Coombe, Sunder, and Halbert are not the only ones critical of copyright's seemingly unstoppable drift toward ever more exclusionary policies, or what James Boyle, in reference to the enclosure of the English commons in the seventeenth century, famously termed the "second enclosure" of the intangible commons of the mind.[7] Powerful critiques have also emerged from a broad coalition of internet and information activists, artists, and cultural industry critics from the European Union and other advanced economies of the Global North—and increasingly the Global South as well. But the latter differ from the former in several respects. Although decolonial views there are beginning to seep into, if not everyday legal practice, the academy, serious scholarly attention to the articulation of the law and the sheer velocity and complexity of the creative practices and modes of cultural production, for instance, on the African continent is long overdue. And, what is more, where such interventions do exist one of the main hindrances impeding their critical potential is that they are frequently couched in established conceptual systems and languages that are beholden to the developmental state and nation building as preeminent sites of social and cultural reproduction. In fact, emerging decolonial legal scholarship often might be said to perpetuate the provincialization of Africa by failing to acknowledge recent interdisciplinary work, such as postcolonial studies or Afropolitanism that has profoundly altered the conventional view of Africa as a "residual entity" forever doomed to catch up with the rest of the world.[8]

Still, for all its shortcomings, this groundswell of advocacy for copyright of law as an agent of change toward a broad-based participatory culture is compelling, and I am largely sympathetic to the broader critical-transformative potential of this scholarship. There is, however, one caveat. *Lion's Share* is less about what should happen to make copyright more responsive to the interests of authors and consumers and more about taking stock of the complications and unforeseen consequences of copyright law even where transformative views appear to have taken hold already. Integral to this more open-ended approach is a concern with the processes, materialities, and techniques through which the postapartheid nation-state legitimizes itself and the law as motors of transformation and as guarantors of stability. At the same time this approach aims to highlight the taken-for-granted tropes, assumptions, stereotypes and essentialisms or what Michael Herzfeld calls "social poetics" that sometimes "deform" the self-representation of the state and sometimes are symbiotically articulated with it.[9] In this way I hope to be able to avoid the is-ought binaries that underwrite legal thought and much critical theorizing about law in the humanities and that tend to reduce interventions of the latter type to an either-or of success and failure.

This type of inquiry naturally raises a number of inconvenient questions in its wake. Has the impact of copyright protections on social relations become as total and detrimental as Coombe and Sunder claim? How is it that copyright law came to be invested with such omnipotence to determine who is able to create and recreate the world and who is not? Is the growing juridification of cultural commodity production on the verge of becoming one of the main sites of contention in twenty-first-century South Africa? Do cultural commodity production and the growing prominence of intellectual property (IP) law move toward a juro-cultural order where law and culture osmotically inflect one another? Will the commodity provide the images through which culture is at once confirmed and contested and where, in turn, the law ever more profoundly alters the meaning of vital moral and aesthetic concepts, such as the greater good, tradition, creativity, authenticity, or the public and private spheres? How does copyright render older forms of social order obsolete while fashioning novel ones almost from scratch? What discourses and material practices contribute to the stabilization of this volatile situation, and, conversely, what alternatives are available to copyright absolutism if any at all? How might South Africans revitalize copyright's promise—firmly anchored in its long jurisprudential history—of the good life and enable wider participation in culture?

In South Africa, perhaps more so than in the privileged Global North, these and many other questions that I discuss in this book hold enormous weight. But the debates among the country's lawmakers, policymakers, industry leaders, cultural producers, legal scholars, and IP law activists are as polarized as their sociopolitical context. For instance, some actors portray South Africa's evolving legal order as nothing less than a comprehensive project of transformative justice geared toward undoing the racial and economic imbalances of the past, and perhaps just as importantly, serving as a model and beacon of hope for the developing world as a whole. Indeed, the champions of this narrative—policy and lawmakers primarily associated with the country's governing African National Congress (ANC)—are able to point to a number of significant policy and legislative initiatives. In addition to having joined the Agreement on Trade-Related Aspects of Intellectual Property Rights (TRIPS) in 1995 and having passed the Performers' Protection Amendment Act 8 of 2002 (hereafter Performers' Protection Amendment Act), in 2006, the daughters of South African composer Solomon Ntsele Linda prevailed against Disney, Inc., and other media corporations on the infringement of their rights to Linda's song "Mbube" (revisited in chapter 2). Partly inspired by that seminal case, a *Copyright Review Commission Report* in 2011 urged a sweeping overhaul of the country's copyright policy.[10] Reflecting the commission's recommendations, two major statutory developments stand out: the promulgation of the Intellectual Property Laws Amendment Act 28 of 2013 (hereafter Intellectual Property Laws Amendment Act, discussed in chapter 3) aimed at the protection of so-called indigenous knowledge and traditional cultural expressions, followed by the introduction of a Copyright Amendment Bill into the National Assembly in 2017.

At the other end of the spectrum, in a rare show of unity, many artists and cultural producers, along with the legal fraternity, industry leaders, and IP law activists, take a more realistic, if not downright alarmist, view. Apart from constitutional concerns and questions about these measures' effectiveness and their compliance with South Africa's international obligations, these critics worry that the government's expectation that a reworked copyright system will thrust the country's flagging economy into a golden age of innovation and knowledge production, offering opportunity and inclusion to all its citizens, may be inflated. Among artists, in particular, there is a widespread sense that the copyright system only serves the interests of foreign-owned corporations and should be discarded entirely.

A good example of these jarringly divergent tales of aspiration and apprehension is a 2018 forum organized by the Legal Research Group of the ANC.[11] In opening remarks, Sadulla Karjiker, a professor of law at Stellenbosch University and incumbent of the prestigious Anton Mostert Chair of Intellectual Property, criticizes the fair use exceptions provided in the Copyright Amendment Bill then winding its way through Parliament. In order to counter the threat that Google and Amazon pose to copyright protections, he argues, it is futile to call for more sweeping exceptions, or to invoke the North-South divide as the cause of the country's IP woes. Instead, South Africans should be asking themselves why "South African authors should be receiving less protection than their counterparts elsewhere."[12] In fact, shifting the blame to the North-South divide amounts to nothing short of racism, for it suggests that "South Africans are not, and should not, be motivated by economic considerations when they create works" and that "they should create out of some *ubuntu* spirit" instead.[13] Proponents of a maximalist developmental approach, Karjiker continues, who argue that intellectual activity and creativity in the country's educational system is best stimulated by widening the scope of copyright exceptions are basically telling authors that it is not a worthwhile investment of their time to write textbooks, thus undermining the very thing they are purporting to incentivize. Ultimately, the failure—government's failure—to protect IP rights will turn South Africans into "perennial victims" of the exploitative conduct of others, forcing them to purchase know-how, expertise, high-tech goods, and other intellectual resources from Europeans and Asians, all the while lamenting that they have been ripped off.[14]

In the debate that ensues, several members of the audience disagree, echoing debates raging elsewhere in the Global South. South Africa should follow the examples of Brazil and India and "move towards an IP maximalist developmental approach," one person says for instance. Similar to the fair use policies of these countries, he ventures, the bill should include major exceptions as a way to rein in "multinational corporations that extract maximum value from the value chain."[15] Yet another person who introduces himself as a lawyer and consultant to the book publishing industry takes a contrary view more in line with Karjiker's point. With an alleged revenue of approximately R5 billion ($6.5 million) in 2018 and seven out of every ten books sold being for educational purposes, he maintains, this sector—which includes a growing subsector of indigenous language books largely produced by school teachers—will stand to suffer the most if broad exceptions are brought into play.[16]

Debates like this are symptomatic of the profound shift said to have occurred in postapartheid South Africa from a restorative-redistributive phase during the Mandela presidency to the openly probusiness, neoliberal policies espoused by his successors, Thabo Mbeki and Jacob Zuma. It is within this policy shift that both narratives continue to wield considerable rhetorical force. The digital revolution, the scourge of piracy, the exponential growth of mobile technologies, the deepening conflict over cultural rights, the rising concerns over privacy, or the vociferous demands for broad fair use exceptions are largely framed in dichotomous terms, counterposing a world of power imbalances against the rule of law. Thus, copyright is widely perceived as a Western (primarily US) imposition, designed to further enrich a small number of wealthy stakeholders, while the Intellectual Property Laws Amendment Act is praised for protecting the rights (and returns) of impoverished indigenous communities. This is also why many consider piracy a legitimate response to government and industry failures to combat unemployment or develop more user-friendly business models. And why many South African artists are deeply suspicious of the country's collecting societies, considering them relics of the apartheid era or rackets that deprive them of their hard-earned royalties, while publishers and record labels tend to cast these organizations in a more benign light as guardians of South African culture.

But these opposing visions of South Africa's copyright of the future are not only limited to specific constituencies and vested interest groups. They also mobilize growing numbers of South Africans in unpredictable and ambiguous ways around agendas and narratives that transcend IP law and are shaped by collective memories of the past, experiences of a stubbornly stagnant present, and hopes for a brighter future. Tradition and indigeneity, but also freedom, development, justice, and social cohesion are some of the ideas around which these imaginings cluster.

Apart from highlighting the uncertainties, incongruities, idiosyncrasies, and sprawling imaginaries pervading debates such as the forum above, there is another reason I deviate from Coombe's totalizing stance and its interpretative hegemony over questions of IP law in critical legal studies, postcolonial studies, and a variety of other critical interventions. I am compelled to ask: What is left of the once novel discovery that the end of the bipolar, post–World War II order in the late 1980s dramatically altered many facets of life around the globe when few still bother to empirically account for the way that order supposedly determines even the most localized and intimate aspects of our lives? Is there still any theoretical purchase, for instance, in the claim that "copyright and its ubiquitous infringement [and] piracy . . . are the categorical means by which governmentality . . . operates as cultural policy under the sign of neoliberalism"?[17] When things are supposed to happen under the sign of something else, are we not in danger of leaving the realm of fact and entering that of astrology, magic, and religion?

Countering this universalizing discourse, I place a strong emphasis throughout this book on infrastructures, documents, statistics, and classification systems, along with a close reading of the technicalities of legal practice, complete with countless acronyms and mesmerizing Latin phrases. Due to their very tendency to obscure local meanings and agency behind a veil of seemingly apolitical, technocratic efficiency these manifestations of the reproduction of global systems of governance are often undervalued or denigrated as alien to the ethnographic method. But subjecting them to closer scrutiny may actually prove to be useful for the anthropology in law, I propose, because these aspects perform part of the argument I advance about the making and remaking of copyright in situations that are more about process than substance, form than content. Finally, the focus on the mundane, unmarked, and what has been called "flat ontology" serves to convey the challenges of fieldwork in a "world of generalized ethnography" in which the "scratching of other pens" produces a surplus of data that always already seems to contain their own interpretation and that, yet, invite more interpretation regardless.[18] Likewise, the dissatisfaction with the grand paradigms of the socio-legal or critical legal studies variety is the reason why, throughout my account, there is an almost obsessive preoccupation with tracing nearly imperceptible connections between seemingly unrelated phenomena—why I privilege syntax over semantics and why protocols, databases, and commonplace objects like exhibit bags, crime dockets, and registration forms take center stage.

The fieldwork itself took place between 2010 and 2018 in a wide range of settings—from the parliamentary Portfolio Committee on Trade and Industry and Southern African Music Rights Organization (SAMRO) to the South African Police Service (SAPS) to the Recording Industry of South Africa (RiSA), and in more conventional spaces of legal inquiry, such as courtrooms, Hansard-type databases, and policy documents. In presenting the findings of these forays, I am guided by four broad claims. First, South Africa's copyright landscape cannot be considered in isolation from the larger historical and sociopolitical context of colonialism and apartheid. At the same time, however, the attempt to decolonize the country's copyright system may be undercut by two tendencies of postcolonial critique: the unwitting reproduction of a host of unexamined intellectual premises inherited from the colonial past and the contrary position that the non-Western world is a culturally exceptional realm of its own that can only be understood by those who inhabit it, through their own concepts and metaphors. That is why any effort to decolonize South African copyright is inadequate without some reflection about its colonial origins and aftershocks in what anthropologist Anna Tsing has described as "global friction: the awkward, unequal, unstable, and creative qualities of interconnection across difference."[19]

Second, the interdisciplinary study of law has reached an impasse. Despite their critical impact on how we now think about law, hegemonic academic disciplines, such as law and society, law and economics, and critical legal studies, remain too narrowly focused on the instrumentalist means-end logic rooted in eighteenth-century utilitarian philosopher Jeremy

Bentham's credo that "it is the greatest happiness of the greatest number that is the measure of right and wrong."[20] As a result, these disciplines may be ill-equipped to grasp the complex realities of the Global South. For linked with this instrumentalist rationale is a vocabulary that is derived from obsolete, mostly Eurocentric, notions of what constitutes the ends of copyright law. Perhaps among the most questionable of these effects is society. Others such as public interest, the common good, or the idea of wealth maximization, popular among law and economics scholars, though held as universally accepted values, too are products of the Enlightenment. An alternative or, better yet, an anti-anti-instrumentalist approach might therefore conceive of law more as a means without an end or rather a means without a *desired* end. This does not mean, however, that law's transformative agency should be disregarded altogether or that interrogating instrumentalism impoverishes our thinking about copyright law. Adopting an anti-anti-instrumentalist stance enriches it by considering law's effects outside the is-ought binary of legal instrumentalism.

Third, in order to revive the interdisciplinary study of law, I offer a model of inquiry introduced in the introduction as *anthropology in law*. Distinct from the anthropology of law and inspired by actor-network theory, this reboot is motivated by the desire to replace the dichotomy between the law-first and society-first approaches that have stymied the interdisciplinary study of law for decades with a more flexible view. Key to this endeavor is a different concept of jurisprudence as a pragmatic-performative theory of law. Instead of the conventional notion of jurisprudence as a philosophy of law in which one set of assumptions about the discovery of truth (philosophy) objectifies another field of truth-making (law), this alternative form of jurisprudence conceives of the way lawyers and nonlawyers speak about their respective disciplines in adverbial terms. Instead of speaking about law prepositionally, the anthropologist might have to learn to speak legally. That is, even where she may be reluctant to let go of the aim of providing systematic, representative accounts of the lived worlds of others (and ourselves, as we try to make sense of these worlds by living within them), she will need to rehearse a new way of knowing—one that occurs in the forms and idioms provided by law's knowledge, in the conventions of legal writing, the pragmatics and technicalities of legal practice, and in the materiality of its institutional settings.[21]

Lastly, this anthropological approach to the study of law calls for a new type of ethnographic sensibility aimed at a complete revision of the notion that human action, no matter how incongruous or irrational, results from and can be explained by some kind of social force outside of it. I question the idea that the focal point of an empirical inquiry into law is the effectiveness of legislation and judicial decisions in impacting patterns of behavior and bringing about meaningful change. Or, to put it another way, I challenge the notion that law is deemed to be effective when code determines conduct, when the projected output conforms to the input, and when the cause-effect relationship can be black-boxed. I further reject the conclusion that any failure of the law to achieve the desired effect—due to malfunctioning institutional structures, for example—necessitates opening up the black box. For while such moments of inspection of the black box may serve to justify a statutory amendment, a restructuring of the penal system, or calls for empirical social research, they hardly ever trigger a systematic review of the instrumentalist paradigm itself. Ethnographic inquiry, consequently, is reduced to mere unblack-boxing. In a nutshell, what preoccupies me is not *whether* law works but *how* it is able to translate a messy conglomeration of organizations and cultural practices into a linear narrative of transformation.

Shadows of the Past: Copyright, Cultural Reproduction, and Development

One of South African legal history's most persistent myths is that the law of copyright is not only apolitical at its core but that it was also peripheral to the colonial project and even survived the ravages of apartheid unaffected. For example, IP law is conspicuously absent from legal historian Martin Chanock's otherwise superb work on the making of South African legal culture, while ANC veteran and Emeritus Justice Albie Sachs even went on record claiming that apartheid never denied rights to IP.[22] In fact, a quarter-century after the end of apartheid, standard textbooks of South African IP law still routinely open with only a token nod toward the growing significance of IP for the country's emergent "knowledge economy," with far greater attention being given to international law and English common-law than to the colonial past that enabled them.[23]

Joined to this tradition of erasure like a Siamese twin is the idea that the history of South African creativity and cultural reproduction can be separated into two distinct spatiotemporal orders: a colonial mentality that considered creativity and cultural value to originate from individual effort on the one hand, and a native world of collectively reproduced, and thus unoriginal, tradition on the other. And while the former was seen as constantly evolving and, as such, a subject deserving of historical inquiry, the latter was deemed static and mainly of interest only to anthropologists. This tale of two orders endures in the current legal and socioeconomic imagination, where the relationship between these worlds is ambivalently figured as one of intrusion and integration, exclusion and inclusion. Thus, in the rare instances where it is discussed at all, the making of colonial copyright law, from crude beginnings in the Cape Colony's Act No. 4 of 1854 to the first modern statute, the Copyright Act of 1916, is usually framed as the expansion and consolidation of a core of British liberal ideas of property within a messy world of Roman-Dutch and customary law, where the absence of concepts of individual creative ownership coupled with a surplus of "traditional" works provided little incentive for creativity and innovation.[24] If anything is seen to be amiss in this picture of colonial copyright law, it is little more than the vague feeling that the law either failed to protect indigenous creative expressions because it "omitted" certain categories from the list of eligible works or, even more abstractly, that it was heedlessly adopted with little input from the colonized. According to this logic, it is, therefore, no surprise that much of the current policy efforts at remaking copyright is focused on filling this lacuna by incorporating "traditional" forms of creative activity into an unspecified economic and cultural mainstream.

But the lack of critical scrutiny is hardly exclusive to policymakers and legal theorists. Members of my own discipline too have long turned a blind eye to both the cultural implications of IP law and the legal implications of culture. As Coombe observes, while anthropologists were quick to denounce the sudden advent of the cultural commodity sign in the space of the Other as the harbinger of the pending loss of cultural identity prior to the 1980s, they rarely acknowledged the appearance of "our" signs in "their" world as potential sources of cultural identity. With few exceptions, we have neglected to acknowledge that once IP rights, such as copyright, attach to the commodity-sign, it is this convergence that becomes the space of colonization par excellence.[25]

In the South African context, this ambiguous juxtaposition of copyright and cultural commodity production is readily discernible in what John and Jean Comaroff call the "double gesture" central to the colonial project. The colony was not merely an extension of modern, metropolitan society. Rather than an unequivocal process of the colonial center imposing a ready-made cultural frame onto the colonial periphery, the metropolis itself was made modern by the colonial encounter. But while this gesture was based on the propertied, rights-bearing individual of mid-Victorian liberalism, the

South African equivalent was increasingly considered to be enmeshed in and shaped by a "culture of legalities" that ascribed two antithetical forms of subjectivity to the colonized.[26] The first was as citizens of a sociopolitical universe where *culture* was synonymous with *civilization* and thus promoted the inalienable right to own property in perpetuity, the right to reap the rewards of one's own labor, the almost messianic belief in free will as the basis for the exercise of individual freedom and civic duties, and so on. The second form that colonial subjectivity increasingly took as the nineteenth century wore on was as subjects of chiefs and members of tribes beholden to tradition and tethered to an essence of being that, though considered ineffable and inalienable, was codified in customary law regardless. But there is more to this double gesture. In the first type of subjectivity, culture was cast in the singular and involved a set of inexorable universal values and technologies of the self, such as education, a commitment to self-improvement through labor, or what Max Weber dubbed the protestant work ethic, and, most crucially, a canon of spiritual practices centered on a person's inner self as the creative core and repository of ideas about the world. The second kind of colonial subjectivity, however, was figured in more plural terms, as *cultures* and *legalities*. It is not just that missionary discourse gradually veered toward greater acceptance of the notion that Western culture had a corrupting influence on the intrinsic, God-given humanity of the so-called native, adding a new danger—the uber-assimilated native—to the already troublesome detribalized one. Culture in the plural was increasingly becoming conterminous with a supposedly benign, pastoral version of segregation designed to protect the native from himself *and* the whites, followed by all-out apartheid legality soon thereafter.

Thanks to a robust body of anthropological and ethnomusicological scholarship, the ideological roots of this split image of African and Western/universal economic and legal spheres can no longer be ignored. There cannot be the slightest doubt that this pluralism, much like the initial vision of the civilizing mission, was a liberal project to the core. As I have argued in my book, *Music, Modernity, and the Global Imagination*, the South African music industry was firmly integrated into the nascent colonial and global order from the day American and British minstrel troupes began performing to packed concert venues in the early nineteenth century; since the first South African organists and pianists started adapting and playing from hymnals and sheet music imported from the UK; and both British and local presses published the scores of a new generation of black South African composers. Most of this was seen as offering proof that the metropolis would not only "bring the light"—the title of a work by the late nineteenth-century composer John Knox Bokwe—to a benighted continent but usher in a novel way of refashioning subjectivity in terms of the property relations governed by the rights and rules set out by colonial law. But the integration of South African cultural production into global markets also had another lesson in store. Traveling in the opposite direction, from South Africa to the heart of empire, black choirs touring the UK were frequently abandoned by their white agents and thrown to the wolves of London's West End, where they learned that the liberal credo of the possessive individual did not apply to them. As one pioneering member of this emergent global industry caustically put it in the bovine imagery of his ancestral Basutoland, "civilization" is something the "natives" have "caught hold of by the tail, and not by the head."[27]

By the time colonial conquest was complete and the Union of South Africa came into being in 1910, the liberal project developed an even bleaker streak, in no small part because it also became an anthropological project along the way. In the 1930s, a small group of politicians and intellectuals associated with the liberal Institute of Race Relations, including its president Alfred Hoernlé and his anthropologist wife Winifred, dreamt of defusing South Africa's racial tensions by rekindling what they took to be Hegel's notion of the liberal spirit. Faced with growing pressure from an ever more intransigent white electorate, and fearing that the growing radicalization of "detribalized Natives" would thwart the project of "strong and wise leadership of Natives by Natives," Hoernlé pictured a constellation of culturally homogenous African societies.[28] Insulated from both the universalist-humanist ideology of the missionaries and the rapaciousness of the racist state, these societies would then interact with white society in the "liberal spirit" of "respect for social groups other than one's own, for cultures other than one's own, for sentiments and traditions other than one's own."[29]

This "fundamental consensus" between diehard segregationists and culturalist liberals shaped cultural politics between the 1920s and 1940s and is perhaps nowhere more apparent than in the emergence of the music industry as South Africa's core creative sector at the time.[30] It was during this period that the passage from assimilationist to culturalist strands of liberal thought was neatly mirrored in the work of two key musicological figures—Percival Kirby and Mark S. Radebe. In 1919, Kirby, who was a music inspector in the Natal Education Department prior to teaching music at the University of Cape Town and the University of the Witwatersrand, stated, "For the present, the musical training of the Native will have to proceed along European lines."[31] However, by the 1940s, he argued for "the deliberate recognition of indigenous music by all educationists."[32] Radebe, one of Kirby's first black students, echoed his mentor's change of heart. Inspired by the "pluralism" preached by Hoernlé and his ilk, Radebe praised the record companies for preserving traditional music, "our most treasured cultural inheritance."[33] At the same time, however, he worried that these companies might "look at it from a commercial point of view only" by discarding or otherwise modifying "certain features which are not of commercial value." To counter such commercialization, Radebe called for a "Bantu movement of Natives" who would "get out into the country to study pure Native tunes."[34] Different strokes for different folks? Respect for black culture, royalties for whites? Or as Joseph Shabalala of Ladysmith Black Mambazo and *Graceland* fame would comment decades later to US folk singer Pete Seeger, "When the word 'traditional' is used about a song, it means that the money stays in New York."[35]

Clearly, the history of colonial copyright and the evolution of the South African creative industries are two sides of the same coin. But it is not through mere negligence or the imposition of international law, such as the Berne Convention, that colonial copyright policy failed to recognize the interests of the colonized. Rather, the dynamic is subtler and hence less readily apparent.[36] It was through colonialism's double gesture, I contend, that culture became the primary marker for identifying and managing vastly dissimilar interests by legal means. If culture in the colonial imagination served as the foundation and justification for defining identities, it has remained a highly unstable construct that, over the course of the past two centuries, has proven to be a major site of contestation. Copyright was one way in which this instability was kept in check. Although generally averse to attaching any of its key categories, such as author or work, to specific identities beyond nationality or date of death, copyright was fundamental to securing the hegemony of culture by papering over the cracks in the double gesture at the heart of colonial legality.

But culture is not the only compromised idea that clouds our ability to "see intellectual property law as regulation of meaning and, in turn, of the social relations that flow from how we envision our world," to reiterate Sunder's earlier injunction.[37] If there is any term in the South African juro-political glossary that is at the same time more ubiquitous and more ambiguous, it is *development*. In fact, in its varied colonial, apartheid, and postapartheid inflections, it is probably the South African master narrative par excellence and, as such, needs to be briefly addressed here (I will revert to it later in this chapter). Like *culture*, *development* is rooted in centuries of inequality, and like *culture*, it tends to function as its own referent, being immune to any further attempt at serious scrutiny. Thus, in order to disentangle the circularity of *development* discourse and to fill in the void left by the startling inattention of legal scholars and many anthropologists to the industries that constitute the essence of copyright protections, some hard economic talk is necessary, beginning with one of the most enduring myths informing discussions of post-transition South Africa: second economy.

Ubiquitous in media, government publications, and academic conferences alike, the term *second economy* is central to the idea that South African society can be divided into two spheres: a powerful formal economy that comprises the industrial, mining, financial, and service sectors, and whose stability rests on a steady supply of wage labor alongside a modicum of social technologies like insurance; and an informal, third-world sector that is structurally disconnected from the former and marked by high levels of unemployment and poverty that affect nearly half of urban and rural populations. From 1996 to 2001, as both the government's Reconstruction and Development (RDP) and Growth, Employment, and Redistribution (GEAR) strategies dramatically raised growth rates but failed to eradicate inequality and mass poverty, public policy rhetoric shifted from an emphasis on national reconciliation to a macroeconomic focus on the integration of the informal sector into the powerhouse of the formal economy.

The corporate sector enthusiastically embraced this new philosophy as the confirmation of a long-held belief in the power of markets to awaken the entrepreneurial spirit lying dormant in the informal economy.[38] In contrast, the response of political economists was less affirmative. Poverty, they argued, is not an aberration produced from within this "second economy" as much as it is systemic, caused by structures of inequality endemic to an economy that has already been integrated for centuries.[39] There may be some merit to this argument, but by casting poverty and unemployment as mere byproducts of the fluctuations of the formal economy, these critics still reproduce the binary rhetoric of disconnection and integration inherent in the "second economy" axiom while simultaneously neglecting to examine the "underlying assumption that this larger system into which people need to be integrated will necessarily function to their advantage."[40]

This lacuna is particularly evident in policy studies on employment in the creative industries. For instance, in 2017, the South African Cultural Observatory (SACO), a research project of the Department of Arts and Culture, published a series of five reports on South Africa's creative and cultural industries that charted the socioeconomic impact of areas such as cultural trade within the BRICS group, the macroeconomic context, festivals, and the situation of ownership and employment. The last topic, in particular, exposes the self-perpetuating, self-referential function of the second economy narrative and its place in the overarching ideology of development. While the authors of the reports found that in 2015, cultural occupations—which include people working in sectors traditionally categorized as cultural or creative, such as fine arts, performing arts, film, libraries, music, craft, and so on, as well as more commercial sectors like design, architecture, advertising, and computer programming—comprised 2.5 percent of all jobs in the country, they also noted that the number had declined from 2.93 percent in 2014. Likewise, in 2015, the international trade in cultural goods experienced significant declines in exports (16 percent) and imports (25 percent) from the previous year. While the reports attributed this downturn to the country's declining GDP growth rate in 2015, they also acknowledged a silver lining. Higher levels of education or formal qualifications, they found, may have had a significant demographic impact within some cultural sectors. For example, in 2015, the audiovisual and interactive media and design and creative services sectors were found to be respectively 41 and 43 percent white, with 54.9 percent in the former group and 66 percent in the latter having completed tertiary education. Finally, the reports reiterate the findings of earlier studies that show that the country's creative industries, in terms of GDP and employment, are clustered predominantly in the provinces of Gauteng, Western Cape, and Kwazulu-Natal.[41] Consequently, one of the policy recommendations put forth by the authors of the reports is "to promote competitiveness, informal-formal sector linkages, employment, and export opportunities" through the creation of so-called hubs or clusters.[42]

The point of the above is not to assess the reliability of these figures, much less challenge the broader imperative of public support for the creative arts. Rather, it is to illustrate how the ideology of development—along with its satellite concepts economic growth, second economy, and employment—revolves around an image of South African cultural production as an emerging component of the formal economy that has the potential, given proper policy choices, to improve the livelihoods of second economy, informal sector cultural producers simply by absorbing these producers into the national economy. There are several problems with this narrative. First, it appears to take for granted that the rise of the South African cultural industries is merely an effect of deindustrialization, filling the void left by declining employment opportunities in the country's key industrial sectors—mining and manufacturing. Furthermore, it disavows the history and present experience of a large segment of artists. For the better part of the twentieth, if not the nineteenth century, the wellspring of cultural reproduction has not been self-sustaining rural communities governed by principles of reciprocity and equitable access to common resources. Rather, much like the majority of South Africa's poor, the country's artists have long been absorbed in commodity relations, albeit in ways that have made them more dependent on bundles of livelihood strategies than the minority of white industrial workers whose racially privileged position earned them the comforts of a family life centered on the male wage-earner and household head. This historical burden endures in contemporary South Africa, where millions are doomed to a perennial state of limbo. Caught in alternating cycles of unskilled industrial employment and unemployment, almost half of the population is wholly dependent on what anthropologist James Ferguson refers to as ad hoc networks of "survivalist improvisation."[43] Another way to describe the South African economy—especially its cultural sector—might thus be in terms of what Jane Guyer calls "platform economy." An alternative to both free-market economics and its critique by political economy, the term might serve as a vantage point from which to rethink emerging economies, such as South Africa, by combining historical, institutional, cultural, and neoclassical theory into a more malleable framework that accommodates idiosyncrasies and deviations from the ideal market of the neoclassical imagination.[44]

At the same time, the fictitious second economy happily absorbed by the larger economy, overlooks the possibility that the creative industries might not, in fact, herald a new dawn of universal employment as much as they put the final nail in the coffin of what used to be known, at least in the developed industrial economies of the Global North, as a "proper job"—complete with a stable monthly income, social benefits, and a roof over one's head.[45] There is no doubt that job scarcity and job insecurity are endemic to the creative industries, but to assume that this is just an unfortunate yet surmountable epiphenomenon or a transitional phase is more wishful thinking than it is based on solid evidence from similar industries elsewhere. In fact, employment in South Africa's creative industries—or at least in its music industry—may soon go the way of its US counterpart. Instead of the promise of individual autonomy and freedom from alienation symbolized by the romantic figure of the artist-genius, today's unsalaried, uninsured, and socially unmoored creative worker may actually be the model worker of tomorrow, prefiguring the precarity of *all* labor in postindustrial societies everywhere.[46]

Which brings us, finally, to the big question of this section, if not the entire book: What does the whole debate have to do with copyright? As a quick review of some pertinent documents reveals, the mythology of the second economy is deeply inscribed in current copyright and IP policy. Thus, the 2004 *Policy Framework on the Protection of Indigenous Knowledge through the Intellectual Property System* adopts the integrationist rationale of the second economy philosophy by setting up a dichotomy between "local ecosystems" and "local communities" on the one hand and "national economies" on the other. Accordingly, given that "indigenous peoples depend on traditional knowledge for their livelihoods," legal protection and the commercialization of such knowledge is expected to not only benefit individuals and communities but also the national economy.[47] Similar, if not more direct, language also informs the presentations made by government officials to lawmakers deliberating the Intellectual Property Laws Amendment Act (discussed in more detail in chapter 3) that resulted from the policy. In their entirety, these policy objectives are not only based on unsupported claims about the scope of the local ecosystems evoked, but the idea that indigenous people depend on traditional knowledge for their livelihoods too also seems rather myopic in view of the fact that traditional knowledge is a highly mobile category of commodity that traverses local boundaries and is enmeshed in extensive interindustry networks spanning several sectors.

In sum, development or second economy, are, sensu stricto, not concepts that denote a specific goal or set of political and economic strategies. Rather, with their static binaries, such as modern-traditional, state-community, community-individual, none of which adequately describe the lived reality of cultural reproduction in twenty-first-century South Africa, they constitute what Ferguson calls an "interpretive grid" through and in which argumentation takes place, diverse positions and interests may be arrayed, and worldviews articulated and rendered meaningful.[48] Thus, for most South Africans, development is, on one level, a trope that enables them to narrate their collective aspiration for a more just society. But at the same time, it may also serve as a lens through which categories, such as state, economy, or IP law, are brought into alignment with much larger imperatives stemming from nationalist ideology or the logic of global capitalism. In the next section, I will show how these conceptual barriers resonate with the justification prevalent in copyright theory: legal instrumentalism.

Breaking the Grid: The Fallacies of Instrumentalism

Given the broad thrust of the argument I have laid out in the previous pages, it should come as no surprise that this book makes no claim to comprehensiveness. Not only is the scope of covered topics hopelessly limited, in contrast to the problem-solving, input-output logic of the consultancy report, the impact study, or the legal policy review, but my primary concern is also not to bring policy visions, however well-intentioned, in line with everyday realities on the ground. Rather, *Lion's Share* is resolutely nonprogrammatic and unapologetically nonprescriptive. I do not join the chorus of doomsayers, particularly those of the poststructuralist persuasion, who dismiss modern copyright law as rooted in the Romantic ideal of the author as the source of creativity ex nihilo or what Michel Foucault famously called the "author function," which impedes the free circulation and manipulation of ideas.[49] By the same token, I am averse to portraying law as an irredeemably technocratic discourse that conceals the continuation of hegemonic structures under the guise of a new set of orthodoxies such as good governance, pluralism, the rule of law, civil society, or democracy. If anything, the book's preferred gesture is one of precaution, similar to that outlined by Michel Callon, Pierre Lascoumes, and Yannick Barthe in their book *Acting in an Uncertain World*, as a form of abstention. Instead of offering a prescription for action, the book itself comprises an "active, open, contingent, and revisable approach."[50] In that spirit, *Lion's Share* offers a perspective that resists reducing the complexity of legal policymaking to a zero-sum game or to a success/failure or is-ought binary. Although most chapters address one failure or another, the overall focus is more on the way discourses of success and failure create their own reality by obscuring a more ambiguous state of limbo between stability and instability rather than on the failure per se.[51] Law, politics, society, or technology—domains we usually take for granted as real, existing, and clearly demarcated terrains of action—are seen as states of affairs that reach a level of temporary stability not *in spite* of the ruptures and failures of a poorly implemented plan but *because* of them. The key question of an anthropology in law, then, is not how to provide legal scholars interested in the causes of suboptimal policy results with details about how to overcome these failures. It is, rather, as Tania Murray Li phrases it, to first ask which practices and assumptions are required so that law may "translate messy conjunctures, with all the processes that run through them, into linear narratives of problems, interventions, and beneficial results."[52] Monolithic narratives that frequently accompany the success/failure binary, such as voluntarist concepts of human action or theories of domination, resistance, or false consciousness, offer scant guidance in this regard. Additionally, by examining the opposite end of the means-end chain, this book identifies the specific conditions of possibility that must be present within the reality stubbornly refusing to conform to law's ends for law to justify its own interventions.

Above all, however, I seek to provide an alternative to what Austin Sarat and Thomas Kearns call the "great divide" between a "constitutive" view of law as socially constructed and an "instrumentalist" concept of law as the necessary precondition for social order.[53] Examples of the former abound in critical legal studies, for example, the hypothesis that IP law "is an authoritative means and medium of cultural politics in which the social is itself articulated" or the idea that law has the "capacity to forge authoritative understandings of social relationships."[54] The instrumentalist side of the great divide is rooted in the American pragmatism of the late nineteenth and early twentieth centuries, which has become known as legal realism. The founding theorists of legal realism held that law should be more than a set of logical rules devoid of any sense of broader purpose beyond maintaining its own internal cohesion. Rather, as Roscoe Pound wrote in 1908, as a means to an end, law "must be judged by the results it achieves, not by the niceties of its internal structure."[55] Legendary Justice Oliver Wendell Holmes, one of legal realism's chief architects, concurred, asserting that the real justification for the rule of law is "that it helps to bring about a social end which we desire" and that it is "for science to determine, as far as it can, the relative worth of our different social ends."[56] Finally, singing from the same hymn book, in 1921, Benjamin Cardozo stated that among the greatest forces shaping judicial change is "the power of social justice which finds its outlet and expression in the method of sociology."[57]

Most realist and postrealist legal scholarship, however, neglects the fact that whether as the origin or telos, both the constitutive and the instrumentalist view of law see society functioning as a discursive a priori by being construed as "*already composed as a single whole.*"[58] As a result, the forms through which people account for the world they live in and act upon (forms that include law) are supplanted by an explanation that locates the real source of such forms and agency elsewhere—in society. Yet, according to the same functionalist logic, these forms may also allow for the opposite claim: namely, that it is pointless to unmask such forms as ideology precisely because they are part and parcel of how the social order already functions. Either way, society remains something of the elephant in the room. Its status as a major analytical construct in legal theory, and the instrumentalism that enables it, has never been more uncertain. A century after Pound, Holmes, and Cardozo, and following decades of debate about the death of the social and the demise of objectivity, this kind of scientism rings peculiarly hollow. This is particularly true in those regions of the world where the idea of the social is a distinctly Euro-modernist import that either fell on deaf ears or was deemed ill-suited for its application there.

And yet, instrumentalist logic remains deeply inscribed in copyright jurisprudence. According to William W. Fisher, there are four theories that shape copyright policy.[59] The first and most popular theory posits that lawmakers should be guided by the principle that the end of property rights is the maximization of wealth. One of the more prominent manifestations of the maximization rationale is the law and economics school of thought pioneered by neoclassical economist William Landes and Judge Richard Posner. In their pithy formula, the central issue in copyright is how it might "maximize benefits from creating additional works minus both the losses from limiting access and the costs of administering copyright protection."[60] The chief legal mechanism for achieving this balance in the allocation of resources is by granting authors the exclusive right to make copies of their work and market these copies at prices that are typically higher than in a competitive environment. In the absence of copyright protection—in large part resulting from high levels of infringing activities such as piracy and inadequate enforcement—authors will be unable to recoup their costs of expression and ultimately be dissuaded from creating new works.

Although the law and economics paradigm currently dominates copyright theory globally, there are three further rationales. The second of these is based on the notion that copyright is a natural right that entitles an individual who utilizes resources believed to be unowned or held in common, such as ideas and facts, to claim ownership over the fruits of their labor. While South African jurisprudence may emphasize this sweat-of-the-brow approach to a greater extent than other Anglo-American legal traditions, it too has a utilitarian component. This aspect is most noticeable in the concept—usually attributed to the famous proviso in John Locke's labor theory—that the enjoyment of a property right resulting from one's labor is legitimate only if it does not harm another person's efforts to do the same. Hence, the originality requirement for copyright eligibility under which a work is protected only if it has been independently created does not prevent another creator from claiming protection for a work that was created concurrently.

The third approach Fisher mentions is that private property rights are bound up with universally held concepts of personhood. Derived from Kantian and Hegelian transcendental philosophy, and thus more prominent in the German- and French-speaking legal world, this theory assumes that an artifact like a musical work is the expression of an individual will, fulfilling a vital role in the satisfaction of a fundamental human need. While the instrumentalist thrust of this approach may appear less pronounced than in the utilitarian, incentive-based argument, it elevates the intended telos to a higher level—first by grounding it, like the natural right theory, in human nature, and second by shrouding it in an aura of intellectual volition rather than labor.

Finally, the last of the four approaches is rooted in the idea that copyright should help foster a just and attractive society, thereby shifting the emphasis from an objective concern with an optimal, market-driven allocation of resources toward subjective features, such as well-being. The advantage of this theory of "social planning," as Fisher calls it, is that it stimulates collective deliberation about the features deemed essential to an attractive society: the happiness of consumers, the availability of a wide array of ideas and works, full access to these resources, the opportunity to fully participate in the production of cultural meaning, and so on.[61]

Not all of these theories have found equal application in South African copyright justifications. While a handful of scholars might identify with law and economics, it is safe to assume that the bulk of South African scholarship subscribes to a combination of the incentive and social planning theories.[62] Be this as it may, in the remainder of this section, I present my own case for a noninstrumentalist theory of copyright, and how such a theory might enable us to better grasp the obstacles faced by current efforts to remake South African copyright law, and what alternatives might be available to overcome those challenges. In so doing, I focus primarily on the ends part of the teleology—on concepts such as public interest, common good, social welfare, wealth maximization, and, again, development. These goals differ significantly from one another and, while at times being utilized interchangeably, they are associated with distinct schools of legal thought.

To begin, I argue that instrumentalism is a double-edged sword. In the broadest sense, it is a "threat to the rule of law," to quote the subtitle of Brian Tamanaha's insightful book *Law as a Means to an End*. Instrumentalism's rise to near-total hegemony in the 1970s, Tamanaha argues, has left the law with a bleak vision: a Hobbesian "war of all against all within and through law."[63] Ironically, although these wars are waged with utmost ruthlessness, combatants do not necessarily envisage themselves as pursuing their particular interests at the expense of the common good. On the contrary, in justifying the pursuit of their utilities, they invoke a whole cluster of interchangeable ideas coursing through the Western legal and political imagination over the last two centuries: Adam Smith's "invisible hand" advancing the public good when individuals pursue their own private interest, social Darwinism (survival of the fittest), or the liberal ethos that whichever definition of the common good prevails is the product of community consent.[64]

The fact that instrumentalist thought can serve different masters is perhaps nowhere more evident than in South Africa. In addition to frequently finding itself at odds with deeply entrenched moral absolutes rooted in indigenous tradition, instrumentalism here also clashes with the widespread resentment of any unrepresentative, technocratic form of power that does not immediately manifest in better living conditions for the country's poor. Worse still, abuses of power immediately conjure up memories of the apartheid judicial system—an indisputable tool of domination that placed "the stamp of legality on a legal framework structured to perpetuate disadvantage and inequality," according to Pius Langa, the first black justice on the newly established Constitutional Court.[65] However, as the growing number of memoirs by former judges and lawyers—perhaps a bit too self-serving at times—show, antiapartheid activists also used the courts as strategic locations to fight political battles when all other arenas for the lawful articulation of dissent had been closed off.[66]

While apartheid law has been rightly debunked as a sham, and though we must honor the bravery of those who fought against apartheid *by means of* colonial and apartheid law, we cannot disregard the ongoing reverberations of instrumentalist thought's double-sidedness in two intertwined areas of postapartheid legal discourse and practice. The first is the debate that arose around the concept of "transformative constitutionalism" introduced in 1998 by Karl Klare. As a reading of the South African Constitution that embraces the fundamental commitment to rule-of-law constraint, this brand of constitutionalism also proceeds from an understanding of adjudication as enabling intellectual and institutional practices commensurate with a new culture of justification that subjects every exercise of power to judicial review. Within this ambiguous configuration of legal constraint's normative force and the experienced reality of adjudicative practice, Klare suggests there is room for a "more politicized" concept of the rule of law and adjudication engaged with and committed to the idea of "establish[ing] a society based on democratic values, social justice, and fundamental human rights," as stated in the constitution's preamble. But Klare is careful to distance himself from too narrow an interpretation of this concept of transformative adjudication along the lines of more traditional categories, such as "social democratic" or "revolutionary," and instead prefers to speak about a "postliberal" reading of the constitution. Such an ostensibly "apolitical" reading would not only prove just as political as postliberal interpretations, but it would also allow for a serious conversation about South Africa's broader legal culture and how it might further an "empowered" model of democracy.[67]

It goes without saying that Klare's constitutionalism contrasts sharply with classical liberal positions. For example, Anthea Jeffery, head of policy research at the Institute of Race Relations, a long-standing bastion of liberalism, has voiced one concern shared by many liberals. She notes that several provisions in the constitution undermine the guarantees of individual liberty, potentially enabling an omnipresent, centralized state that controls every aspect of individual behavior. Thus, the application of direct horizontality in the Bill of Rights allowing the rights of a private individual to be enforced against another might mean that any state official could enforce these rights against any individual. Similarly, so-called socioeconomic rights might pave the way for the ruling party to implement its idea of social engineering, such as the current "National Democratic Revolution."[68]

Clearly, there is more to the newfound zeal for constitutionalism and its endless possibilities for transformative politics. Another area—the second major theater where instrumentalist thought's double-sidedness is in full view—is the growing litigiousness within South African politics. As numerous commentators have noted and a cursory reading of what is left of the country's independent press confirms, the new South Africa is no stranger to the war of all against all within and through law. The terrain of dissension has shifted markedly. As many former comrades figuratively (and sometimes literally) traded the bazooka for the bar, and sites of popular struggle moved from street to statute, the country has increasingly become engulfed in a general state of lawfare or what John and Jean Comaroff have termed a "fetishism of the law"—a rampant instrumentalism that invests the law with the magical capacity to shape every conceivable type of relationship in its own image of order and security.[69] Its catchy ring notwithstanding, the term is perhaps less useful for the kind of anthropology in law that I attempt in

Lion's Share because it partakes of its own discursive fetishism in reifying intricately interwoven, messy political, cultural, and legal processes into a simple binary between rights and revolution, law and lawlessness as the master narrative for postcolonial subjectivities.

Society, Development, and the Public Interest:
Mythologies of Copyright

Moving beyond legal fetishism, there is another area where South African legal instrumentalism endures, which I discussed earlier in a different context: the rhetoric of development. Clearly, in a country where a huge number of schools lack basic resources like books or indoor plumbing, the wholesale rejection of some kind of forward-looking perspective—some sense of what law might contribute toward the restructuring of a country whose social fabric has been in tatters for centuries—is simply not an option. At the same time, however, we should not lose sight of the fact that South African legal discourse figures development as an end of law that is so broad that it is almost devoid of meaning. The field of law and development studies is a good example of the difficulty of providing a clear sense of what development might mean within instrumentalist legal thought. As Tamanaha has shown elsewhere, after scholars initially adopted the basic tenets of modernization theory, which held that the transfer of core elements of the rule of law, such as a regime of contract and property law or basic human rights to developing countries, would almost automatically guarantee development, a sense of disillusionment set in beginning in the 1970s.[70] The discrepancy between the empirical reality of those countries and what some law and development theorists called the "legal-liberal" model became all but impossible to ignore.[71] Consequently, law and development studies moved from a universalist to a relativist stance. Rather than insisting on law's primacy in shaping development policy, scholars now acknowledge that the "center of gravity in each society rests upon its unique historical, cultural, economic, political and material mix" while also recognizing the "derivative nature and secondary influence of law" within it.[72] In theory, this move into what is ultimately the cultural pragmatics of development appears to provide a blueprint for greater involvement of local actors in solving a country's development challenges. However, in reality, many current theories addressing law's contribution to development reflect more of a neoliberal, top-down corporatist bias even as they purport to champion the recognition of historical or local specificities. Thus, whenever a minimalist version, or what Michael Trebilcock calls a "procedurally oriented conception," of the rule of law is invoked, it is black boxes such as transparency, predictability, stability, and enforceability that are being foregrounded and not corporate interests.[73]

Unsurprisingly, South African jurisprudence on copyright's concept of development is divided along similar lines. Some theorists draw upon conventional incentive justifications and law and neoclassical cost-benefit analysis, positing the global market as the normative space for the realization of South Africa's development agenda through the alignment of the country's IP policy with international law or the rejection of major copyright exceptions, among other things.[74] Others favor a softer, more contextualized approach that prioritizes national or regional interests within a broader pan-African context. For instance, lamenting an IP culture that feeds African policymakers' "relatively stable, globalist, protection and harmonization-centric IP narratives," the editors of a pioneering collection entitled *Innovation & Intellectual Property: Collaborative Dynamics in Africa* stress the need for counterbalancing strategies focused on "open development" and "nationally or locally contextualized IP realities and imperatives."[75] At the very least, they further suggest, such strategies would require a major reset of two of the most entrenched positions shaping current IP discourse on Africa: the undervaluation of Africa as a site of innovation and creativity and the failure to recognize the contribution of current IP policies toward facilitating such innovation.[76] One example of how such narratives of African deficiency and legal failure are reproduced is the all-too-ready acceptance of conventional IP metrics centered on the number of patents issued in Africa as a measure of innovation. But this practice does more than simply distort the record of the more marginalized and often most resilient African inventors; it also disregards the possibility that in some instances, these very patents may be creating bottlenecks impeding collaboration.[77] Another example is the present-day currency of the term *innovation* and its intricate relationship with other IP justifications. Traditionally associated with patent law, *innovation* is increasingly emerging as an umbrella term that allows IP policymakers to subsume other types of property rights protected by sister doctrines like copyright (more commonly understood to promote creativity) under overarching theories centered around entrepreneurship, progress, and prosperity. After all, unlike the unrestrained exuberance of artistic creativity, innovation appears to have a more sober, practical dimension to it—signifying a clean break with the past while clearing a path toward a useful future. In short, once designated as innovation, creative behavior appears more compatible with the demands of global capitalism. Still others, finally, invoke human rights as a rationale for a more developmental approach. Although the South African Constitution does not provide for IP rights as a human right per se, and the country has yet to incorporate IP-related provisions of international instruments such as the International Covenant on Economic, Social and Cultural Rights into domestic legislation, the right to freedom of expression and the right to work protected by s 16 (1) and s 22, respectively, may support the case for an "equitable balancing of creator and user rights" cognizant of South Africa's emergent economy and its agenda of promoting small- and medium-sized enterprises.[78]

The impact instrumentalist thought has on postapartheid IP and copyright law reform is, however, most pronounced in and compounded by the way in which the idea of development is invoked in justifying policies predicated on the concept of the second economy discussed above. According to this rationale, the reader will recall, development has to be understood as a "normative sequence of national economic development" in which a rural and largely agrarian economy will transition to an urban, industrial economy first, followed by a full-blown "knowledge economy" later.[79] In this scheme of things, so-called rural development has always played and, according to current policy documents such as the Comprehensive Rural Development Programme, will continue to play a subsidiary role as an ambiguous space of both deficiency and potential for growth. The problem with this type of development discourse is that by subsuming the country's fractured economic system under an unilineal trajectory, it loses sight of the specificities of different economic sectors, such as the decline of long-term industrial employment as a strategy substituting for waning agrarian livelihoods or the sociocultural microdynamics of rural households. In fact, as a significant body of scholarship over the past two decades has consistently shown, national economy discourse not only led to development initiatives that are ineffective and overly inward directed toward individualistic and voluntaristic approaches. It also ended up bypassing large sections of the population to the point where equitable rural development has simultaneously become the very opposite of being a precondition for the path of national economic development and, as I will show in chapter 3, a pretext for an IP policy fixated on reimagining communities rallying around ideas of shared and communally owned "traditional knowledge."[80]

If, then, development discourse tells us next to nothing about the purported developmental benefits of South Africa's vision of a future copyright framework that leaves behind the ghosts of the past, those ghosts may yet continue to haunt the reformist agenda in the form of some of the conventional justifications inherited from the colonial past, such as the public interest, arguably the most frequently cited goal of copyright protections. Public interest justifications are notoriously unspecific, as are attempts to appropriate the idea for decolonial projects. Much like the previous issues, the debate operates on binaries such as the discrepancy between global and national public interest.[81] Critiquing this dichotomy, some African legal scholars endeavor to fashion a "global counterdiscourse," for instance, by establishing a parallel between the historical roots of regional networks of cooperation such as the Africa Group of the World Intellectual Property Organization (WIPO) and anticolonial movements.[82] This dichotomy suggests several things: First, it attributes an oppositional position to the nation-state vis-à-vis the homogenizing global, which obscures the reality of many African countries rather than naming it. Second, the global-national binary is the product of an imagination that views the global as homogeneous because we wish to contrast it to the local.[83] A better way to describe the connection of African states to the global political economy might be as what James Ferguson calls "global shadows." These are not simply spaces of absence, however, as terms like *shadow economy* or *shadow army* suggest. Rather, "highly selective and spatially encapsulated forms of global connection combined with widespread disconnection and exclusion" are what define Africa's place in the world order. And it is within this combination that new enclaves, new nonnational economic spaces, and even new forms of government by NGOs emerge.[84]

Another example of how the universalizing concept of public interest may collide with postcolonial reality is the litany of colorful, albeit largely received, terms such as *the public sphere* or *civil society* that much of the literature on present-day African publics written by legal academics blindly recites without giving much thought to their meanings. Such terms are not only culturally and historically contingent constructs with wildly divergent meanings; they are often antithetical to one another. Despite, or perhaps precisely because of its ubiquity in South African political discourse, the term *civil society* has become eviscerated to the point where it serves less as a viable analytical category and more as a stand-in for much larger, and as of yet unspoken, collective desires.[85] For example, at the height of some of the most heated debates in the period between 1994 and 1996 leading up to the certification of the South African Constitution, the Constitutional Court, after an initial moment of hesitation when it sought to enlist the support of Parliament and "civil society" for deeply unpopular legislation protecting same-sex marriage and *against* the death penalty, held steadfast in its decision to declare the former constitutional and strike down the latter.[86] Another example is the assertion that discussing South Africa's future is less about considering the continued presence of power structures inherited from the colonial past and more about following a narrative that frames the country's historical trajectory and social structures in terms of a "colonialism of a special type." This South African exceptionalism is problematic because it conflates the public with the nation. The same is true for the remaining terms. Because of the lack of definition and awareness of their situatedness, they are all rather ill-suited for the kind of reality where there is neither one coherent "public space" nor "any single organizing principle" but a "plurality of 'spheres' and arenas, each having its own separate logic."[87]

The larger point, however, that I wish to make about these chimeras of African publics is not whether they are transplanted Western concepts; if vibrant indigenous forms of public sphere are in place on the continent and elsewhere in the Global South; or whether, indeed, the Western liberal ideal is even viable for a future, developed Africa. Rather, I am interested in the logic according to which the interwoven narratives of public interest and development, while ostensibly offering a more grounded antithesis to the aloof, distribution-phobic rationality of law and economics scholarship, is actually largely consonant with it and how, consequently, this logic lends credence and continuity to the notion that some generic concept of development and the public interest are two sides of the same coin. For instance, pointing to the perceived limitations of liberal incentive theories in furthering the goals of developing countries, some critics turn to Nobel laureate Amartya Sen's philosophy of development as freedom, suggesting that it provides alternatives to universalizing IP discourse and is thus more attuned to African forms of public interest.[88] In the book mentioned at the start of this chapter, Madhavi Sunder follows Sen in arguing that the ability to innovate and create is a fundamentally human value. Yet, in contrast to conventional copyright jurisprudence, where this capacity is said to fully come into its own only at the end of the means-end chain—that is, when works enter the public domain—for her, that freedom constitutes a vital condition of development from the outset. As Sunder goes on to explain (invoking Walt Disney's unlawful appropriation of South African composer Solomon Linda's song "Mbube" along the way), "Development requires far more than meeting basic needs and enhancing GDP. . . . Development as freedom requires improving each person's capacity to make choices and meaningfully participate in political, economic, and cultural life."[89] But development does not end with the opportunity to create, innovate, and share ideas. It has implications for other freedoms, too—not least, the freedom to secure one's livelihood.

This is where Sunder's analysis runs into some inconsistencies and fails to provide answers, at least for the purposes of this book. What is the broader political and economic framework in which this vision of development as freedom is most likely to flourish and serve the public interest in one fell swoop? Sunder's discussion of a "fair culture" and its difference from Creative Commons guru Lawrence Lessig's call for a "free culture" might provide us with some clues.[90] Whereas Lessig believes that a free culture may help to counterbalance the tendency of maximalist IP policies to stifle innovation, ultimately leading to market failure, Sunder takes issue with this idea because it lacks a clear articulation of the cultural dynamic it presupposes and, perhaps more importantly, because of its overall libertarian thrust. Lessig, she notes, "fails to acknowledge people's unequal capacity to exercise the freedoms that law provides." In addition, his vision of freedom gives short shrift to other values, such as government subsidies for the creative practices and knowledge production of economically disadvantaged communities.[91] Ultimately, though, Sunder's countersuggestion of a fair culture is equally ambivalent—a fragile combination of state intervention, the politics of recognition, and the liberal trust in the market's ability to give everybody, even niche creators, a chance to succeed.

Meanwhile, University of Cape Town–based legal scholar Caroline Ncube pursues a similar strategy of leveraging copyright for a larger project of (re)distributive justice, albeit by recruiting a slightly different set of interrelated—perhaps even irreconcilable—ideas such as the "representative individual" of liberal economics, the calibration of the interests of creators and consumers on the basis of democratically legitimated majority decisions, or the communitarian ideals of *ubuntu*—the idea that being human is contingent on collective relationships. Each comes with its own set of complications. The notion of the representative individual, for example, is difficult to take at face value both for methodological and philosophical reasons. Following Ncube's reading of Lok Sang Ho's ex ante rule, if the public interest is the outcome of policy decisions that are made after all special interests have been eliminated and that best cater to an "imaginary person," who is represented by this mythical figure?[92] Is it "anyone," as Ho claims? Or, rather, is this person a placeholder that in reality represents the rational utility-seeking subject that is so near and dear to law and economics scholarship and whose actions miraculously add up to wealth maximization? Conversely, does this alleged uber-rationality necessarily imply that all individuals act rationally? Finally, might the representative individual simply be a convenient fiction allowing economists to provide microfoundations for the sort of aggregate behavior redolent of Adam Smith's "invisible hand?"[93]

Things become even hazier when ubuntu enters the mix. Despite having left deep traces in South African constitutional and case law, the concept is a rather iridescent one, its place in the country's jurisprudence anything but settled.[94] While some critics deny its compatibility with core liberal ideals, positing a fundamental contrast between Western concepts of human dignity rooted in individual rights and ubuntu's emphasis on family and community, others emphasize its flexibility and incorporation of individuality. Which begs the question of why the concept is even needed when courts can function just as effectively on the basis of conventional, liberal principles, as elaborated in Hegel's *Philosophy of Right* or the work of some of his modern-day successors.[95] Still, others embrace ubuntu by pointing to its close connections to "living" customary law and its ability to both collectively shape long-held moral values, such as "freedom" and "equality," and embody key notions of substantive law, such as "good faith" in contract law or "reconciliation" in criminal law. Lastly, some have expressed concern that ubuntu is just another word for vox populi. Or, to put it another way, there is a real danger of ubuntu encouraging conformity with majority values that supposedly reflect a "way of life," an "African worldview," or a "dominant value in traditional African culture," to quote a few telling phrases from recent judicial opinions.[96]

Although Ncube's intervention, like that of other scholars, remains at a level of abstraction well beyond what an ethnography of law might tolerate, she does offer a series of concrete policy measures that provide vivid testimony of the intensity with which the leading copyright minds seek to carve out for copyright law (and perhaps, by extension, private law in general) a more prominent role in strengthening such a model of distributive justice. Yet, while many of these proposals, familiar to readers well-versed in Creative Commons and A2K (access to knowledge) philosophies, are worthy of greater attention, what interests me more is how ubuntu-like these measures really are and how they might intersect with the now-discredited Lockean, incentive-oriented bias that necessitates an ubuntuist inflection of copyright jurisprudence in the first place. To begin with, one cannot overlook the fact that many ubuntu-inspired policy recommendations are largely couched in essentializing categories—cultural or otherwise. For instance, in order to meet the interests of the now amalgamated African ubuntu/liberal Western public, Ncube envisages a system of constitutive registration sensitive to diverse motivations of creativity that would allow authors who are *not* driven by commercial concerns to opt out of the copyright system altogether. This would make more public domain works available—works, one can only speculate, that would then go on to nurture the ethos of altruism and reciprocity at the heart of ubuntu. Intriguing as it may be, the proposition merits closer scrutiny in the context of a soon-to-be-postindustrial South Africa. Not only does it display a strong proclivity toward antiutilitarian, German Romantic ideas, but more surprisingly, perhaps, it echoes Marcel Mauss's well-known gift/commodity dichotomy and its current reincarnation (or, more often, misreading) in the shape of crowdfunding, sharing economy, or personal autonomy narratives.[97] It is also reminiscent of efforts to portray African creative practice as motivated by an innate vitality, especially in those regions of the continent where copyright protection is sparse, without paying equal attention to the dire conditions under which artists there are forced to labor and where commercial interests *are* uppermost on their minds as a result. In this way, ubuntu might actually not lead to more equality but perpetuate the legacy of the disavowal of property and its contemporary resurgence in the kind of "taking-as-giving" benefit-sharing schemes that are increasingly touted as ethical alternatives to conventional IP protections for traditional knowledge.[98]

Another example of how the theory of an ubuntu-infused public may cover up its tacit, liberal underpinnings is the idea of a tiered copyright system based on different revenue levels. According to Ncube, such a system would facilitate the entry of works into the public domain at an earlier time than allowed by current copyright law. For example, in tier 1, a work would be protected for a nonrenewable period of, say, ten years; while in tier 2, after an initial duration of one year, the work would be renewable for a maximum duration provided it does not fall below a certain revenue threshold. Here consumer choice—in other words, market rationality as the governing principle of social relations and final arbiter of cultural value—does more than just determine the fate of copyright protection *as an individual right*. The agency of rational market participants vanishes behind a veil of mysterious emotions and personal impulses. Consider the case of gospel. While there is no reason to doubt the religious fervor of countless gospel choirs, with its more than 50 percent market share, South African gospel is an industry as commercial as any other, and its artists are second to none in occupying key positions in the music industry and in enforcing their rights under conventional copyright protections.[99] Stated another way, the noncommercial author who altruistically furthers the public interest does not exist apart from or prior to the self-serving, market-oriented author. In the economics of copyright, greed and generosity are mirror images of each other. One is the discursive possibility of the other.

Clearly, the ubuntuist notion of a public good based on the domestication of unrestrained market rationality is born from the same emphatically owner-centric premise that dominates conventional copyright law. More troubling still, this notion is also embedded in a number of clichés that feed on Western fantasies of social order and social welfare mapped onto the postcolonial world. The invention of the social in Europe during the late nineteenth and early twentieth centuries—the idea that poverty or crime were not moral issues but social ones that required social solutions—and the welfare programs and institutions that emerged in its wake and are now held to be threatened by neoliberalism, never took hold in the colonies. In South Africa especially, as an earlier generation of anthropologists believed, the social was primarily a question of black labor migration and the attendant breakdown of traditional African social structures. Yet instead of neutralizing the moral impact of this process and the threat it posed to white supremacy by absorbing the impoverished masses into some kind of social dispensation, the colonial, and later apartheid, state pursued a diametrically opposed vision of the social—namely separate development.

To reiterate, my point here is not a normative assessment of whether or not ubuntu provides a viable justification for an alternative concept of the public good. Rather, I question what is at stake in contemporary efforts to Africanize definitions of the public good. It is difficult to avoid the impression that ubuntu posits a strange circularity of thought. A copyright reform, or so the argument goes, that aligns the concept of democratically legitimated majority rule with the distributive justice rationale of ubuntu and in which Western and African philosophies of the public good mutually inform each other would garner copyright a "cultural legitimacy" that it lacks in its current liberal guise.[100] The point is hardly Ncube's alone. Writing about the Roman-Dutch sources of South African contract law, Andrew Hutchison, for instance, advocates an "infusion of African values" into existing South African contract law to fashion a "more individualized sense of ubuntu" or "contractual ubuntu."[101] Thus, legitimacy is attached, nota bene, to the very regime of property relations in place since the dawn of colonization. The net effect of ubuntuist interpretations of the public interest, one might conclude accordingly, is less that they offer a corrective to liberal-individualistic copyright law and more that they entrench it even further by naturalizing it.

Returning to the hegemony of developmentalist discourses in South African legal theory, the point of the above is to highlight the tensions, discrepancies, and obstacles encountered by efforts to craft a more locally attuned version of the public interest, and how in that process, one of the most fragile premises of copyright instrumentalism is made even more precarious once it is adapted to the developing world. Whichever the difference between the rationale and the significance ascribed to one or another social end, the ethnographer's misgivings that theirs is the same means-to-end logic that also defines Anglo-American law in toto are not easily dispelled. The local, regional, or African element in developmentalist/public-interest discourse merely figures as yet another cog in law's instrumentalist machine, further bolstering its authority to make claims about human agency to shape the future rather than advancing the public interest as such. All assertions to the contrary, then, both instrumentalist and contextualist views may obscure the fact that efforts to reduce the uncertainty inherent in the gap between legal policy prescription and empirical development practice, through more detailed institutional planning or more efficient management procedures, do not yield more development but merely more illustrations of law's instrumentality.

The instrumentalism that underwrites both the universalizing rule-of-law and the relativist-contextual view brings me to the final and most important objection to legal instrumentalism. I argue that although the consequentialist logic of copyright jurisprudence may satisfy the policy-oriented style of legal reasoning de rigueur in US (and possibly also South African) law schools, it would not fare so well in an environment that prioritizes reflexivity and the historical and cultural contingency of human action—that is, in a setting committed to the idea of ethnographic work. A good way to illustrate this is by revisiting what has become known as the "gap problem" in socio-legal studies. Although by now mostly obsolete, in its heyday, gap studies functioned like those troubleshooting guides for distraught consumers trying to fix their malfunctioning devices.[102] As such, the concern with the discrepancies that occur when the shift from the *is* to the *ought* of instrumentalism fails to produce the desired social outcome is more than the bête noire of socio-legal scholarship, forever haunting scholars' realization that instrumentalist claims cannot but fail in the face of reality. It is also its condition of possibility.

But at another level, the gap problem is also an entirely self-inflicted wound that refuses to heal over. The gap only becomes an issue with the assumption of an existing stable policy framework that activates the input-output mechanism in the first place. Hence, socio-legal studies' claim to offer a missing piece of the instrumentalist puzzle by describing the perceived gap between law in the books and law in action, and how this gap is articulated in everyday social and cultural practice, is not grounded in ethnography as much as it is a function of the black-boxing of the means-end relationship at the heart of instrumentalism's eternal recurrence of the is-ought binary.

What does this mean for an anthropology in law? What are some of the conceptual hurdles that we must overcome in reframing the law-society nexus along more elastic lines? Previous generations of anthropologists have not shied away from attempting to solve this conundrum. Early in his career, for instance, South African–born legal anthropologist Max Gluckman famously contradicted Henry Maine by arguing that there is no need for anthropology because all societies are based on contractual relationships ab ovo. But in his mature work, he spoke more about "absorbent" and "multiplex relationships" between law and society.[103] Likewise, Clifford Geertz recast the law/nonlaw dichotomy, with slightly more rhetorical flourish, as a "hermeneutic tacking between two fields."[104] Finally, the intrusion of culture into the hallowed sphere of the law is why the authors—one a professor of law, the other a cultural anthropologist—of one of the field's classic works suggest that there is a contrast between official legal discourse and lay litigants' perspectives on the law. While the former is primarily concerned with rules whose application transcends social differences, laypeople often invoke personal values, social relations, and broad conceptions of justice in seeking legal remedies for their grievances.[105] This disjuncture, the authors point out, forms the basis of the "uniquely joint nature" of their work: to study the ways that ordinary people relate to the American legal system. The best path to understanding these ways, however, is not by focusing on popular discourse per se but on the way it relates to the world of legal rules. In other words, Conley and O'Barr propose an anthropology of legal discourse, consciousness, and meaning—an exercise in the art of interpretation.

One last point about legal instrumentalism: For all the critical energy socio-legal studies, legal anthropology, and critical legal studies have expended on opening the legal black box, the concept of a black box itself seldom comes under scrutiny. It is beyond question that decades of such scholarship yielded an enormous amount of insight into both the workings and failings of the law. Just as this insight has tremendously broadened our perspective of the law as enabling, disrupting, and even destroying entire worlds, from the most local, microcosmic, and face-to-face to the most encompassing and complex sets of relationships. And it is also thanks to critical legal studies that the notion of the law as a self-evident and autopoietic realm of practice offering privileged, putatively authoritative access to particular sites of cultural reproduction—whose notorious volatility it is called upon to regulate and stabilize—has become utterly implausible. Last but not least, no longer possible is the idea that law precedes the structures, practices, and ideologies constituting the music industry, giving them form and meaning before the practices themselves become opportunities of meaning production and the mediation of social relations. Yet, despite all of this, the image of law as a mousetrap, no less than the tacking and the shadow-of-the-law approaches, appears to have run out of answers. As anthropologist and legal scholar Annelise Riles writes, "The task of relating law and anthropology as disciplines, or law and society as social forms . . . has now lost its rhetorical force. . . . Manipulating one dichotomy after another, the scholar has the sinking sense that all the possible positions are prefigured."[106]

Or are they? Do we really have nothing new to say? Are the social sciences forever doomed to open the black box of legal policy's means-end machine whenever it runs afoul of the reality it is meant to shape? How might ethnography continue to offer an additional layer of reflexivity to account for the dynamics of increasingly convoluted, all-encompassing systems of global copyright protections and its effects on the ground in South Africa?

Hosts and Valences: Ethnography and Anthropology in Law

One of the chief motivations for writing this book is the firm belief that there *are* alternatives. If we want to overcome the formidable obstacles that the prominence of instrumentalist thought in international and South African jurisprudence has put in the way of an alternative account of the country's copyright policy and practice, a complete reset of the determinist, binary gridlock is not only possible, it is also imperative. To that effect, I seek to mobilize a concept of ethnography that operates entirely outside both the gap problem and the law-society dichotomy. Of course, the allure of ethnography as a magic fix for the issues of academic discourses and disciplines widely believed to have become acquiescent to the status quo because of their affinity to technocratic and economistic rationality is nothing new, either in anthropology (which invented the method) or in legal studies, which increasingly embraces it alongside other disciplines in the humanities and social sciences. Socio-legal studies, critical legal studies, and even law and economics scholars have all, in one way or another, made use of ethnographic methods—as a rhetorical device to insert other voices into monologic narratives; as the source of supposedly richer, qualitative data; as a counterweight to top-heavy, rule-oriented discourse; as a way to tap into less readily accessible layers of legal practice and consciousness; and so forth.[107]

In this book, however, I gesture toward a slightly different ethnographic project. Among the most persistent myths about ethnography is that it addresses *other* places—an island, unknown village, or lost tribe—in short, the kinds of locations that are too small and peculiar to warrant the attention of those interested in the big picture, humankind, or the merely quantifiable. If this sounds a bit like a parody of what ethnography might have meant at the beginning of the twentieth century (or indeed still means to many of the legal practitioners who wondered what exactly it is I am doing), it is to underscore the point I made in the introduction about relations rather than a priori determined locations, domains, or identities that predestine the ethnographic enterprise as the most appropriate way of making sense of the state of copyright in our present moment. If there are no privileged locales of pursuing legal ethnography, a makeshift forensic lab tucked away in a nondescript office building, a police van taking a squad of police and complainants on an antipiracy operation, or an imposing committee room in the nation's Houses of Parliament may all exist on an equal footing with more traditional venues, such as the courtroom or the law office as legitimate sites to decipher the South African copyright universe. Beyond questions of the proper fieldsite, then, my ethnographic efforts are centered on a humbler and, at the same time, more ambitious goal. It is to draw people, things, and law into new alignments and to think about new configurations among disciplines that too often bypass each other. Concretely, by eclectically borrowing from actor-network theory (ANT), science and technology studies, thing theory, critical race theory, policy studies, critical development studies, infrastructure and information studies, and organization studies, I hope to forge a new sense of connectivity—even inspire a commitment to linkages, synergies, convergences, and correspondences as productive, ethnographically identifiable forces in their own right. This emphasis on the relational aspects of human practice eschews the widespread absorption in contemporary, poststructuralist, and postcolonial discourse with depth, identity, and difference as signposts directing human action toward stability and safety in an increasingly uncertain and unpredictable world. It is for this reason that it might be tempting to retreat from ethnography altogether—or at least come up with a different word for this strange venture. If they were not so unwieldy, one might even invent new terms for this ethnography of connections, such as *nexography* or (reviving a time-honored moniker) a *symbolic ethnography* that throws things together.

What, then, are the pragmatics of a noninstrumentalist ethnography of copyright law? It should be clear by now that in my view, the task of the ethnographer is *not*, as the authoritative *Blackwell Companion to Law and Society* tells us, "to overcome the resistance of law to more nuanced analysis on the ground, among real people" by recording "on-the-ground personalized experiences of the law." For a book to qualify as an ethnography fit for the twenty-first century, more is required than reciting pieties such as "exploring alternative voices" and the "willingness to listen and take seriously critiques of own's own perspective," or extolling the virtues of fieldwork, focus groups, and "semi-structured" interviews.[108] We need to push the ethnographic method beyond the catalog of so-called qualitative methods that define the anthropologist's professional habitus, such as the abhorrence of quantification; the reservations against objectivity; the fetishization of immersion, first-hand experience, and participant observation; the romanticization of the give-and-take of fieldwork; and so on. Even more importantly, we need to rethink the critical posture that a younger, post-Geertzian generation of anthropologists who rose to prominence in the 1980s have adopted by insisting that the poetics of ethnographic representation is closely related to power relations beyond the control of those who are the subjects of our accounts and that therefore necessitates a relativist authorial stance on the part of the ethnographer.

In this vein, consider the issue of property—ordinary or intellectual. According to Riles, anthropologists have struggled to extricate themselves from a tradition in which property is "always an implicit or explicit marker of a disciplinary relationship between anthropology and law." In the hands of anthropologists, she argues, property is an artifact that serves as a "stand-in for the relationship of law to anthropology as anthropologists wish to see it."[109] For instance, in the widely quoted anthology *Property in Question: Value Transformation in the Global Economy*, Katherine Verdery suggests that anthropology's key objective is to ask "through what sorts of social struggles" actors strive "to carve individual ownership rights."[110] Seen through this lens, it would appear to make sense that relations of ownership become objects of ethnographic inquiry primarily as already existing targets of critique and not as factors that are brought into existence by the ethnographic project in the first place. But the irony of this society-first approach is that it enables anthropologists to "seek critical distance from property relations" by pointing to property's instrumental uses.[111] And, of course, it also disregards the law of property as an object of ethnographic description in its own right.

Further following Riles, an alternative point of departure toward a new ethnographic paradigm might be to altogether disengage the study of law from the dogma that law is little more than politics by another name and to focus more on lawyers' own practice of relating means to ends through a "chain of cases and arguments about those cases in which the ends of one analytical practice become the means of the next." Similarly, legal theorists would also do well to reconsider their at times amateurish appropriation of anthropological constructions of things, such as other people's property, as a means to foreground it as a given object of absolute, immutable rights. Such a rapprochement might then lead to a shared analytic that recognizes property "as a chain of relations of means and ends of anthropological and legal knowledge, each recycling the ends of the other's knowledge into means of its own."[112]

In this book, I want to amplify Riles's argument by developing a more fine-grained version of this image of a chain of means and ends relations. *Lion's Share* joins an emerging conversation within law and the humanities whose primary objective is to delineate the terrain for a new, postdisciplinary type of inquiry in which ethnography comes up against a myriad of worlds that already contain within themselves the description of their own rules and practices. This experience is, for instance, what constitutes the real ethnographic "discovery" in Bill Maurer's study of Islamic banking and "lateral reason."[113] And it is this same insight that informs Riles's *The Network Inside Out*, an ethnography of international human rights organizations, as well as her later work on the finance industry.[114] However, it is in Bruno Latour's study of French administrative law, *The Making of Law: An Ethnography of the Conseil D'Etat*, that the idea of law as a form of auto-ethnography finds its perhaps most captivating expression thus far.[115] I will return to Latour's work and the key tenets of ANT throughout this book, limiting my comments here to just a few introductory remarks about two concepts of particular legal salience: attachment and passing. According to Latour, to speak of a connection or attachment between law and society is to posit that agency is not an innate ability of either law or the social to engender attachments but the result of attachments. "Far from being what should provide the *source* of explanation of those phenomena, what we loosely call 'the social' is rather the *result* of what has been produced by types of connection . . . that are established by scientific, religious, political, technological, economical or legal connectors."[116]

The second concept, passing, denotes the stages something must go through to bridge a series of discontinuities. Elsewhere, Latour gives a particularly engrossing example of this: moving from a soil sample taken from the Amazon rainforest to a graph representing the advance of the savannah. Unlike in science, however, where the subject matter passing across these divergent ways of circulating reference is objectivity, Latour claims that law's passes are unique in that they have no other objective and do not transport anything other than law's own existence. Unfortunately, this narrowing of law to a feedback loop of enunciations without external referents leads him to renounce the possibility, and indeed necessity, of any meta- or intranarrative—sociological or otherwise. To allow for such a discourse, another brief excursion into the world of physics may be permitted: Isabelle Stengers's discussion of what she calls the "state function" of modern epistemology. This is the notion that an objective account of reality, such as the movement of falling bodies, amounts to nothing short of the description of the conditions and status of all the items involved at a given moment. But since the velocity of a falling body changes from one instant to the next, describing its state cannot deliver an objective description of its movement. And while one may well describe this movement—as Galileo famously did—by measuring and conceptualizing its instantaneous states as resulting from a "dynamic equivalence between cause and effect" (where the velocity is defined as the effect of its past and also the cause of its future), modern physics after Lagrange went one step further.[117] Where Galileo was content to describe an equilibrium in relation to a cause or event, Lagrange absolutized the state function as a model of referencing an object world that is no longer contingent on any external factor.

The purpose of this small detour is this—once the relational aspect is excluded from the description of instantaneous states, and rational mechanics becomes the absolute measure of objectivity spreading to other fields, such as sociology, economics, or, for that matter, law, the fiction of a noncontingent world leads to the misconception that if only "we could fully describe an instantaneous situation (the neuronal brain, or even a society), we could deduce its behavior over time."[118] That is why an ethnography of law must always insist on a notion of law as a contingent event that is not and should not be reducible to a given state. Instead of fixating on things like society, global capitalism, or neoliberalism as states that allow the researcher to elucidate their impact on the law, a more productive approach would focus on the tangible pathways along which a doctrine, statute, judgment, policy, or business model must travel in order for the social-legal nexus to become one of reciprocal self-determination. The fundamental gesture of such an ethnography is thus an itinerant one—of grasping things en route or "circling back," to quote Riles.[119] Such an ethnography eschews fixed points of reference, last causes, founding principles, and unique sources of agency. Rather, it presents agency in a form that allows us to identify force fields and terrains of tension and how to model these into a theory of human action as always fluid and contingent. For this reason, the primary task of ethnographic description may consist more of capturing these fleeting moments in terms of what some languages call the middle voice—that is, a mode of address in which the emphasis in conventional subject-object-centered epistemologies on the doer behind the deed makes way for a concern with the quality of the fluctuating alignments and nonalignments between them.

A new terminology is key to this undertaking. There is no shortage of candidates: *articulation, affordance, coproduction,* and *transduction* are some of the more prominent terms currently in circulation. I will briefly parse some of these here before introducing my own terminology. *Affordance* enjoys wide currency among media and communication scholars who have sought to develop more flexible, less techno-determinist models of human interaction. Broadly, affordance presupposes the prior constitution of technologies, independent of the communicative processes and agency of those who use them. It is a function, then, of this interaction being situated in and conditioned by its specific niche. For example, a dog sees a chair not as an object that serves a number of purposes but rather as a jump-onto-thing and not much else besides. Although then, it stops short of deploying a full-blown concept of causality, affordance still implies the operation of a cue-like, though somewhat weaker, link between opportunity and actuality. Like affordance, *coproduction* too boasts an illustrious pedigree dating back to the formative period of science and technology studies. Yet, the core argument of coproductionism, as Andrew Pickering phrases it, that "the world makes us in one and the same process as we make the world" suffers from the same dilemma that also troubles affordance.[120] Finally, there is *transduction*. Originating in genetics, the term was introduced into anthropology by Gregory Bateson (who was originally a student of biology) and more recently applied to ethnographic method by MIT anthropologist Stefan Helmreich. A transductive ethnography, Helmreich writes, would be a "mode of attention that asks how definitions of subjects, objects, and field emerge in material relations that cannot be modeled in advance."[121] My choice of terminology shares Bateson's ecological conception of consciousness as a relational phenomenon rather than a thing located in the brain. And, like Helmreich, I borrow eclectically from the vocabulary of the humanities and sciences. But more importantly, I take Helmreich's modeling of ethnography—a kind of zigzagging between different species, material practices, and cultural forms—as an invitation to query the image of the lone ethnographer immersing herself in local life, extracting meaning from hidden structures and self-reflexively monitoring her inner self, and constantly on the lookout for potential breakdowns of the subject-object relationship she so carefully groomed over years of ethnographic fieldwork.[122]

Lastly, for the sake of completeness, brief mention must also be made of Niklas Luhmann's figuration of the relationship of law and society in terms of contingency. In his first major work on law, *Kontingenz und Recht* (Contingency and Law), the legally trained sociologist argues that the growing complexity and contingency of social relations is accompanied by new forms of law's regulatory function.[123] Instead of a pragmatist rationale that grounds law's social efficacy in its ability to fulfill a given policy, such as fighting poverty or injustice, Luhmann argues, law's genuine function is more of a formal, systemic kind. Law produces a higher-order form of quasi-normative contingency that enables it to reduce or stabilize social contingency by coordinating with it. Although this is certainly a weaker formulation than James Gibson's affordance, in the sense that the formation of these orders is a matter of autopoiesis, it too holds on to the prior existence of two separate domains and, hence, the instrumentalist notion of law as a means to an end.

Here, at last, is the first term that I will frequently be using, both as a noun and a verb: *host*. Of course, when speaking of a host, one immediately thinks of its counterpart, the guest. But I follow Michel Serres for whom the French equivalent *hôte* is a much more ambivalent term, encompassing both *host* and *guest*. In a wonderfully evocative chapter of his *The Parasite*, the French theorist of intermingling bodies writes about Lafontaine's fable of the town mouse and the country mouse and wonders what happens to relationships of exchange (in this instance, between the rodents and the landlord) when the parasite enters the equation.[124] For Serres, the parasite is not a new being but the complete blurring of boundaries: between host and guest, subject and object, cause and effect. But does this mean that there can never be a shared ground for a new postdisciplinary dialogue? Or, to put it more formally, does the parasitical blurring of boundaries render any attempt at establishing a relationship between legal scholarship and anthropology futile from the outset? Do such town-mouse, country-mouse moments of ambiguity always run the risk of eluding description altogether, destabilizing the very idea of ethnography as more than just knowledge of the singular and the contingent?

To offset this risk of mutual paralysis, I will occasionally use a cognate term of hosting—*valence*. In its adjectival form—*polyvalent* especially—*valence* has recently acquired the rather unfortunate connotation of a sprawling interconnectivity of free-floating signifiers randomly docking to any number of signifieds. But the meaning of *valence* I am interested in derives from chemistry, where it denotes quite the opposite idea. When chemists speak of valence, they are referring not to an arbitrary number of combinations between hydrogen atoms and other atoms in forming chemical compounds but a maximum number. To take an example of contemporary salience, in CO_2, the formula for carbon dioxide, carbon always has a valence of two. Similarly, in methane (CH_4) it has a valence of four, and so on. (Incidentally, there is also a parallel linguistic concept according to which the number of bonds an intransitive or transitive verb form with a noun or pronoun constitutes its valence.) Without overstraining the analogy, but also without excluding the possibility of different valences changing over time, one might say that the term *valence* achieves two things for the ethnography of law. First, it makes it more difficult to assume a naturally given causal link between law and the social. Second, it enjoins us to describe one domain according to the combination it enters into with another domain purely in terms of connectivity rather than essence, meaning, or location. It is, in this sense, that the word resonates strongly with one of law's cardinal features, faint memories of which reverberate in a long-forgotten word said to be at the origin of the word law: *leg-*, to collect. To speak of law's valence, then, is to give preference to its connectivity over its alleged dominance; to cast it as something that is collected rather than as that which collects; to locate its agency in the ability to create multiple bonds instead of only one—all of this a far cry from law's hermetic formalism but even more so from law and society studies' unidirectional intrusion of the social into law. It is, as well, a radical departure from Max Gluckman's holistic model of "absorbent" legal concepts permeated by principles derived from the social totality, as well as an alternative to Geertz's "hermeneutic tacking between two fields."[125]

In many ways, my unconventional reinterpretation of host and *valence*—doesn't every unusual task call for a new terminology?—is akin to one or the other key objective of ANT. One of the most misunderstood claims of ANT is that it attributes agency to humans and nonhumans alike. Lost in the uproar over this conflation is the more important point that agency is never the product of a sole actor. Whatever else might be said about ANT—and we will explore some of its wrinkles at various points in this book—it offers, at the very least, a way out of the binaries undergirding socio-legal studies by positing that traditional disciplines like sociology or anthropology are of little use in accounting for some other phenomenon by exploring its social dimension. Rather, the task is to reprogram our knowledge machines in such a way that the means-ends relationship in our methodologies is reversed. What prevents us from resetting our research agendas as social scientists or legal scholars so that causal relationships are no longer beholden to the model of the state-function but bound to ideas of mutuality, feedback, and affinity? Instead of assuming that legal policy produces stable social, cultural, or political outcomes, why can't our methods operate on the premise that it is policy that stabilizes itself by invoking these outcomes?

Speaking Prudently, Speaking Legally

Of course, in a country like South Africa, it is not an option to outright reject some kind of constructive perspective—some sense of what law might be able to contribute toward the restructuring of a country whose social fabric has been in tatters for centuries (not least because of its laws). Hence, the whole point of my critique of instrumentalism and the associated need for a different kind of ethnography is not to belittle the former's significance in forcing an urgent conversation about the aspirations and moral grounding of South African copyright of the twenty-first century. It is, rather, to nudge copyright jurisprudence from its utilitarian telos toward always keeping a close eye on the tension between the claims that are made on behalf of copyright law and the reality of its effects. Language and rhetoric are crucial to this effort. Earlier, I hypothesized that it is futile to speak *about* law, suggesting instead that the only possible discourse pertaining to law is adverbial speech. Perhaps in place of a proposition or content, a *clef de lecture* or interpretive key that marks a given enunciation as pertaining to law is all it takes to understand it: "What you are about to read is law, not politics, anthropology or fiction."[126] The question, then, is not whether by studying the social construction or the politics of IP law, scholars outside the law might miss the point but whether in speaking across disciplinary divides they apply the right key. For instance, adequately representing the scientific process while also situating it in some social or historical context is not a contradictory operation as long as the historian or sociologist of science respects the specific epistemic boundaries that separate history and sociology from science. In like manner, the anthropologist who speaks well of the law should acknowledge the latter's rigid formalism, numbing emptiness, and stubborn aloofness as sui generis legal means serving legal ends. In fact, Latour believes that the anthropologist may even speak about law and society entirely in law's own metalanguage, provided we learn to think of society not as a given domain but as a way of connecting heterogeneous phenomena socially, much like law binds together such phenomena legally. Only then will we begin to understand that linking, interweaving, and knitting already constitute the law *as* law. Or, as Latour argues in his later work, hitting the right key, respecting the "precise ontological tenor of the value" that matters to those we speak about, is the best way to do ethnography of law.[127]

On this last, I beg to differ. Ontology no more gives us a sense of the totality of the law than a tenor stands in for a mixed choir. Nor does respecting law's ontology by speaking legally mean that the ethnographer should abstain from critique altogether, in the manner espoused in Latour's account of the Conseil d'Etat, which in the eyes of some commentators amounts to nothing short of a blanket exculpation of legal formalism. The point is that there are two kinds of critiques. One, which could be called normative, merely reproduces the logic of what it questions. The instrumentalist hypothesis inevitably leads to this type of criticism. But then there is another type of critique, a practical critique in the Foucauldian sense, or what I prefer to call a performative critique. This critique is not concerned with an ontology that reveals the essence of a given domain or practice but one that is attuned to the processes through which actors and practices bind to each other in constantly shifting configurations. The object of this type of critique is best described as a moving target, or as Foucault has suggested, an "instrument-effect," that is, an unintended effect that is simultaneously the cause of something else.

Lion's Share leans toward the latter, more modest critique. If we subscribe to Cato the Elder's dictum that beyond the ability to craft elegant speeches, rhetoric is an art that requires *vir bonus, dicendi peritus*—a good man skilled in speaking—then why not envisage an ethical, well-spoken ethnography of law? It will be up to the reader to decide to what extent this book succeeded in this goal. For my part, I cannot claim that I brought this humility with me into the field when initiating this project; rather, it was brought to me. One of my earliest insights while doing fieldwork was the discovery that most musicians I met desired not less but more, or rather better, protection. The task, then, was to devise a new way of articulating something that many musicians, lawyers, policymakers, and music industry agents were already talking about with great sincerity and a profound sense of urgency. The question was how to come up with an ethnography of copyright law that lives up to the challenge of both skillfully enunciating its subject matter while also charting a practical, ethical course. The answer to this question is: through a new understanding of jurisprudence as *phronesis* or prudence.

It is unfortunate that in modern parlance this Aristotelian term has acquired a certain conservative, if not pejorative, ring and is frequently invoked by policymakers and special interest groups to defend the status quo. But in the ancient world, *prudence* was seen as a form of reason better attuned to the appropriate *and* the imaginable within specific local contexts. Thus, it was viewed not only as irreducible to categorical imperatives, rules of logic, or universal laws but also conducive to debates about what is morally desirable. Phronesis, one might say, was an art of the contingent and the contextual—an improvisatory, performative art.

It is this more capacious sense of jurisprudence that I am after in this book, probing its usefulness for confronting the challenges and perils facing copyright law in the postcolonial world. At first glance, prudence appears to be at odds with the input-output logic of instrumentalist legal thought. For the prudent actor is always on the alert, never trusting that the rule determines the outcome and constantly on the lookout for pitfalls and imponderabilities. Yet, as Robert Hariman points out, prudence at the very least also requires that the performer recognize the range of variations a rational plan of action or script may afford. Stated differently, faced with situational constraints, traditional values, embodied knowledge, and other obstacles to pure rationality, prudence takes on a calculative dimension and becomes a "standard of rationality devised for a performative context."[128] But there is also a less prognostic side to prudence that does not exhaust itself in the mere implementation of rational rules and principles but operates instead within a contingent sphere of action. Such performative prudence, as Hariman calls it, is not only difficult to account for since, like practical reason, it generally evolves in context. But it also requires effective use of existing norms and conventions. As such, it might be said to correlate with the constitutive view of law. The contrast between this type of rationality and more formal reasoning cannot be any more pronounced. Establishing the validity of a logical proposition requires none of the balancing acts above. Prudence does.

The parallels between performative prudence and the type of inquiry pursued in this book are not difficult to discern. To the extent that prudence is a guide of action that must comprise more than the rules ensuring the continuity of action, and given that this "more" is realized in performance, an account of such prudent action must necessarily include a description of those performative moves that cannot be reduced to either structure or rules. To be sure, practically and conceptually mastering the logic of an event by following its performative unfolding may require periodic adjustments to its constraining factors as they occasionally assert themselves. Yet, such accommodation to the persistence of rules always consists of more than mere tactics in what otherwise remains a thoroughly rule-governed event. An approach might be said to be prudent when it refuses to dissolve the idiosyncratic, irrational, discordant, or just different into mere aberrations of a broader rule or system. Speaking prudently, as Michel Callon argues in reference to the fundamental difference between ancient concepts of logic and rhetoric, "implies relationships of entanglement between propositions and their referents; it acts on the ontology of the entities to which it refers."[129] But this does not suggest that the prudent writer should ignore structures, conventions, or entrenched ideologies altogether. On the contrary, it is in speaking prudently—about economics, politics, or law—that such constraints may be seen for what they are: achievements of performative action rather than enabling conditions.

TWO

The Past in the Present
Copyright, Colonialism, and "The Lion Sleeps Tonight"

"Come to my father's house on Khanyile Street," Elizabeth Ntsele said.

She had grown up in this house in the Zola area of Soweto, one of four daughters of famed composer Solomon Ntsele Linda and his wife, Tobi Regina. I first visited the house in 1987 to interview Regina about her deceased husband's life and music. Linda, whose work I was familiar with from my research on a variety of South African musical traditions, was hailed as the pioneer of a genre of male choral and dance performance called *isicathamiya* and as the composer of one of its most popular tunes: "Mbube."[1] However, this time, I came with a different purpose: I wanted to present Elizabeth and her sisters Fildah and Delphi with a recording of that memorable meeting with their mother, together with a photo I had taken of her during the interview. But more importantly, I also wished to learn more from the sisters about the legal action that had been brought in the early 2000s on their behalf against the Walt Disney Company for having exploited their father's song in the derivative work "The Lion Sleeps Tonight" without their permission.

Arriving at the four-room matchbox house on one warm spring afternoon of 2013, I was immediately struck by how little had changed since my last visit. Elizabeth's son and his family were now living in the house, and although there was a carport and a TV and DVD player adorning the living room, an air of poverty still hung over the place. It was as if Solomon Linda might walk in at any moment like the lawsuit never happened. Nothing has changed; indeed, Elizabeth grumbled. "We're still struggling, even now." When news of the settlement broke, "the neighbors changed, and

FIGURE 2.1 Regina Linda, 1987. Photograph by the author.

the community as a whole changed. I was in a hell when I was living in this house, they were knocking, they wanted to kidnap my keys, they say I'm a millionaire, I must give them money." A millionaire? Although a trust fund was set up for the three sisters, Elizabeth continued, "We don't know the name of the trust fund. We don't know the amount of the money we got from Mr. Disney. Even now we don't know."

Why had Solomon Linda's daughters been unable to achieve a sense of closure, let alone inclusion, more than a decade after the case was closed and royalties had been flowing into their bank accounts until 2017, five years after "Mbube" entered the public domain? Why did Elizabeth and her sisters seem to have such little faith in liberal justice? And why did the law appear to have the power to undo decades of blatant abuse at the hands of the rich and famous but seemed utterly inept at making its logic, integrity, and detachment reach into the moral and cultural worlds of those it purported to protect? To put it in even starker terms, can copyright law—that supreme creed of the so-called self-possessive individual of the liberal imagination—undo the injustice it may itself have engendered? Can copyright law usher in a new era of creativity, inclusiveness, and well-being? Or was the case about something else altogether? Thus musing, I returned to the world of look-alike business parks, malls, police stations, and courtrooms that had become my field site for eight years.

The Walt Disney Company is one of the world's largest entertainment conglomerates, priding itself on "entertaining, informing, and inspiring . . . people around the globe through the power of unparalleled storytelling."[2] But with a turnover of around $34 billion in 2000, the house of mouse also seems to view the globe as more of a hunting ground, its army of lawyers at the ready to crack down on any T-shirt vendor who dares to use an unauthorized depiction of Mickey Mouse, Captain Hook, or Winnie the Pooh.[3] As for the inspirational part, since its inception in 1928, many Disney films have been anything but. Racist, xenophobic, and sexist imagery and sounds abound in films such as *Aladdin*, *Jungle Book*, and *Pocahontas*. Meanwhile, *The Lion King*, the highest-grossing traditionally animated feature film of all time, is permeated by supremacist and social Darwinist thought, as for instance in the theme song "The Circle of Life":

> It's the circle of life
> And it moves us all . . .
> 'Til we find our place
> On the path unwinding
> In the circle
> The circle of life[4]

But sometimes the circle is broken, and life is more than a never-ending struggle for survival where the fittest come out on top. Or so it may seem. On February 15, 2006, eminent South African copyright lawyer Owen Dean of the leading intellectual property law firm Spoor & Fisher announced that an obscure black family in South Africa had settled a dispute with Disney over copyright infringement of the rights in "Mbube." As a licensee of Abilene Music, a publisher that owned the rights to a derivative of Linda's original work called "The Lion Sleeps Tonight," Disney was liable for the use of "Mbube" in South African screenings of *The Lion King* without permission from Linda's heirs.[5] The main points of the press release are as follows:

> It is confirmed that MBUBE is an integral part of THE LION SLEEPS TONIGHT which was derived from it.
>
> Solomon Linda has been recognised as a co-author or composer of THE LION SLEEPS TONIGHT and it has been acknowledged that MBUBE was the foundation of the worldwide success of THE LION SLEEPS TONIGHT.
>
> Solomon Linda's heirs will receive appropriate compensation for past and future uses of THE LION SLEEPS TONIGHT.

The precise details, in particular the monetary arrangements, are to be kept confidential and an obligation is placed on the parties to the settlement to ensure that such confidentiality is achieved both by their own doings and those of their associates.

Compensation for past uses of THE LION SLEEPS TONIGHT will shortly be paid to the Executor of the Solomon Linda estate. It has been arranged that he in turn will pay the proceeds over to a trust which is in the process of being formed and that this trust will administer the funds, as well as undertake the collection of future royalties on behalf of the heirs. The heirs' trust will be responsible for the payment of monies from time to time from its assets to the heirs.

The release ends on a hymnic note. "I'm not a radical," Dean declares there, "but we have to accept that creative people were done down during the apartheid era, often entering deals they'd never have countenanced if they'd had access to education, lawyers and money. In a way, I would liken their situation to those who lost land because of apartheid. People who were essentially rightless then can now go back and demand restitution."[6]

By all appearances, the settlement is something like the big bang of the postapartheid copyright universe. For the first time in the history of copyright, a plaintiff located on the fringes of the global music industry defied one of the world's largest media conglomerates notorious for its aggressive copyright stance. Three poor, black women in smoke-choked Soweto had put the mighty Disney in sunny California in its place. Or, as the New York Times aptly headlined, "In the Jungle, the Unjust Jungle, a Small Victory."[7] Meanwhile, more theoretically oriented observers celebrated the "Mbube case," as I will hereafter casually call it, as a shining example of the integrity of the South African legal system and its enduring ability to come to the defense of the less fortunate. Other commentators welcomed it as a reminder of just how critical intellectual property rights are for the future of South Africa's creative industries and the country as a whole.[8] And even the South African government got in on the act, touting its financial support for the legal proceedings as a major step toward securing the intellectual property rights of South African musicians.[9]

This chapter offers a slightly different reading of the case. Now that the champagne celebrations have long passed, it might be useful to reconsider it from a more prosaic, less triumphant perspective. As South Africa's music industry is at a critical juncture and the country's copyright policy is hanging by the thread, the controversies about ownership, race, culture, and justice that animated the struggle against apartheid reignite with fierce urgency. In my view, the settlement and the fact that it quickly became interpreted as evidence of the power of liberal justice to redress racial inequity cannot erase the profound implication of copyright law in the colonization and subjugation of people of color in South Africa. The elevated status the case holds in South Africans' collective imagination and visions of a better future is not because justice triumphed over racial injustice. On the contrary, the case has become a touchstone for gauging how far the country has progressed toward some form of restorative justice precisely *because* it was infused with race through and through. To put it even more crisply, in rejecting race as a category for determining creatorship, personhood, and ownership, the case reinstated it. By working with race and not just against it, the case bestows on copyright law—and by extension the state and even the music industry—the legitimacy and discursive authority it needs to function as a crucial vehicle for aligning visions of freedom and economic equity with postapartheid race-neutrality. But at the same time, this acceptance risks forestalling more sustained scrutiny not only of copyright law's colonial roots but also the persistence of the very colonial concepts and structures the democratic order set out to undo.[10]

The chapter is divided into four parts. In the first, I narrate the genesis of the case from a variety of texts and discourses about Solomon Linda and his song's journey across a number of bewilderingly complex sites of cultural production and ownership. But these discourses, I suggest, are of more than just anecdotal interest. They are powerful resources for turning colonial stereotypes about black South African personhood, creativity, and ideas of belonging into categories and concepts that become legible to the postapartheid project of copyright reform and transformative justice more generally. In the second part, I turn to a more conventional, technical reading of the case, offering a close-up view of the convoluted body of texts, legal procedures, and translations that had to be enrolled in order for the case to move forward. The purpose of this combination of doctrinal analysis and a law-in-action paradigm and the fact that it follows, rather than precedes, the contextual analysis in the first part is twofold: First, it is meant to reverse the familiar order of cultural, socio-legal, or anthropological inquiries, where seemingly objective legal arguments often figure as little more than ideology and as raw material for richly textured stories about something else—society, culture, the economy, or the politics of race as the true forces shaping law. Alluring as this type of critical scholarship is in many ways, it is trapped in its own ideological cage; there is an implicit claim that engaging legal technicalities on their own terms is futile, precisely because their sole function already is to conceal technocratic power behind an impenetrable veil.

The second reason for prioritizing the technical aspects of the case prior to a discussion of its sociocultural ones is to expand on Annelise Riles's argument, mentioned in chapter 1, about the agency of legal form.[11] Rather than a mere vehicle of more important forces, recentering the technical as the protagonist of its account opens the analysis to a larger inquiry into the multiple intersecting agencies involved in legal practice and the production of legal knowledge. In contrast to some of the rather monocausal models offered by socio-legal studies—and to a certain extent also critical legal studies and critical race theory—this approach does not prioritize any single agent in determining the operation and effects of law, be it economic incentives, power politics, or racial formations and scripts. And instead of revealing the hidden political dimension and cultural *content* of the legal text, it is the analysis of that text as *form* that compels us to reexamine our culturalist preconceptions as humanist scholars. Culture then, in this inverted perspective, emerges as a field of human practice that can no longer claim interpretational sovereignty over other fields but becomes itself the subject of legal interpretation, reformulation, and remaking.

In the third part of the chapter, I examine the case in light of the growing interest that intellectual property law is experiencing among scholars of critical race theory. The fourth and final section takes us back to the beginning, to the question of closure—or, rather, the absence of closure—in the context of copyright law's moral valences.

The Making (and Unmaking) of Solomon Linda

Beginning, then, with the genesis of the case, we turn to rock music—to *Rolling Stone* magazine, to be precise. The biweekly is not generally known for paying much attention to music outside the Northern Hemisphere.[12] But in May 2000, at the tail end of the world music boom of the 1990s, it ran a remarkable story entitled "In the Jungle: Who Owns 'The Lion Sleeps Tonight'?" This is its opening paragraph:

> Once upon a time, a long time ago, a small miracle took place in the brain of a man named Solomon Linda. It was 1939, and he was standing in front of a microphone in the only recording studio in black Africa when it happened. He hadn't composed the melody or written it down or anything. He just opened his mouth and out it came, a haunting skein of fifteen

notes that flowed down the wires and into a trembling stylus that cut tiny grooves into a spinning block of beeswax, which was taken to England and turned into a record that became a very big hit in that part of Africa.[13]

The author of the article is Rian Malan, a well-known figure in South African journalism. In the dying days of the apartheid regime, Malan caused a minor stir with *My Traitor's Heart*, an award-winning, gut-wrenching account of the hardships of ordinary and some not-so-ordinary people living under apartheid.[14] Yet, while the book was translated into over ten languages and found receptive audiences across the globe, some of his other projects did not fare so well. Between 2001 and 2003, the former crime reporter and rock guitarist published a series of articles claiming that the leading cause of death in South Africa was not the HIV/AIDS virus and that health professionals were cooking the statistics in order to obtain more international funding. True or not, the allegations blended in well with the sobering mood of the post-Mandela era and the HIV/AIDS denialism of Mandela's successor, Thabo Mbeki.

Malan is a master of his trade: provocative claims, hard-hitting phrases, and glib metaphors are his trademark. Sandwiched between a portrait of "girl sensation" Britney Spears and the latest on Metallica's lawsuit against Napster, "In the Jungle" serves up a dark tale of duplicity, greed, and dashed hopes, all in *Rolling Stone*'s signature cadences that blend together coolness and rawness, gripping detail and grand mythologizing. Its narrative thread is spun around Malan himself as a lone hero on a mission to hold accountable a cabal of powerful US music industry captains who have shamelessly and unlawfully exploited the Lindas for decades. The endeavor takes him into some well-trodden territory of South African and US musical history. But he frequently also strays into the realm of fantasy, where colonial stereotypes and other figments of the South African white imagination still run free—and where a journalist has access to a dead person's mind.

But let us follow the story one episode at a time. Solomon Linda, Malan would like us to understand, is the very embodiment of that strange figure of the copyright imagination known as the author. Originating from within his brain, without the assistance of any mediating technologies or preexisting ideas, the haunting skein is a miracle—an apparition from nowhere, not unlike the dreams that several decades later would inspire Joseph Shabalala, Linda's musical heir and leader of Grammy Award–winning Ladysmith Black, to compose his mellow strains in the "Mbube" mold. In other words, "Mbube" is solely owed to Linda's diligence or what in South

African copyright jurisprudence is commonly referred to as the "sweat of the brow," while Linda, in turn, is the romantic antithesis of the uninspired native of the colonial imagination, content with reproducing tribal tradition. In a word, he is the ideal, racially and socially unmarked, subject of the postapartheid imagination.

But he is also something different altogether. "Mbube," we learn, is not only a "ditty" that came to the thirty-year-old Linda spontaneously in 1939 during a recording session at Gallo Recording Studios, South Africa's first record company; it is also stylistically indebted to the "syncopated spirituals" introduced to South Africa by Orpheus McAdoo and the Virginia Jubilee Singers.[15] McAdoo was born to slave parents in Virginia and, after emancipation, attended Hampton Institute, the first chartered institution for former slaves, before he took the Virginia Jubilee Singers to Australia and South Africa, where they toured for a record seven years in the 1890s. By the time McAdoo's novel sound had seeped into remote rural areas decades later, Malan writes, Linda worked "bits" of the "Orpheus-inspired syncopation thing" into a more elusive tradition called "Zulu songs" performed at weddings. "Mbube," we are told, is the product of this juncture of African American and South African indigenous traditions—a homecoming of sorts of the sounds of forced relocation to the African soil.

Initially, the spirituals did, indeed, form the core of McAdoo's repertoire and were celebrated by white liberals as eloquent proof of what the so-called civilizing mission might do for South African natives. But in his last years in South Africa, McAdoo also sought to cash in on the rag craze sweeping the American South since the mid-1890s, before enjoying global popularity as vaudeville or syncopated music about a decade later. While the term *syncopated* entered the musical lexicon in the 1890s to denote the offbeat phrasing characteristic of early blues and jazz, syncopated music was distinct from the jubilee tradition in structure, performance style, and, especially, context. During the last years of the nineteenth century, the sounds of piano ragtime became a staple of the vaudeville stage alongside demeaning images of black bodies harkening back to earlier blackface minstrelsy. As a result, ragtime was not only frowned upon by the educated black elite but also became the preferred target of Southern white racial vitriol. And while this mixing of slavery's sorrowful sounds with frivolous vaudeville fare was not uncommon in early-twentieth-century African American showbusiness, to mention the jubilee songs, as the spirituals are properly called, in one and the same breath, together with syncopation, is a serious misreading of the history of African American music, if not a racial affront tout court.

As for the parts of McAdoo's music amalgamated into Zulu songs, there is hardly any reliable evidence to suggest that by 1939 it was the model for the kinds of performance practices now generally referred to as *isicathamiya*, other than a remark made to the present writer by a veteran of isicathamiya: "Our oldest brothers, the first to sing *isicathamiya*, were the Jubilee Brothers. That was in 1891."[16] Be this as it may, by the time "Mbube" had become one of the most profitable items in Gallo Africa's catalog, selling around one hundred thousand copies between the 1940s and early 1950s, Linda was not only considered the undisputed king of what would henceforth be known as *mbube* music, he took on yet another persona. Linda, Malan tells the perplexed reader, became the Elvis Presley "of his time and place."

From romantic author, to "Zulu tribesman," blending "spirituals" and "syncopated music" into a heady mix of "Zulu songs" popular with migrant workers, to the South African Elvis, the conceptual positioning of Solomon Linda in Malan's essay is a pastiche of epic, orientalizing proportions. How can one square the image of a man as a self-possessing, hard-working, inventive individual with the notion that his work is simultaneously embedded in a history of denial of those very qualities to McAdoo's enslaved ancestors? How can the same man then slip into the role of yet another controversial figure whose legacy wavers, to this day, between the King of Rock and Roll and the King of Cultural Appropriation? The answer, I believe, is not found in the real Solomon Linda but in the positioning of Malan's text within the politics of rainbowism of the Mandela presidency—that is, the foundational myth of the New South Africa where color connotes less racial difference than it symbolizes cultural diversity.

Moving on to the aftermath of that momentous 1939 recording session, Malan's rhetorical flourishes take a sharp turn toward the acerbic and cynical—to the "long, hidden genealogy" of "The Lion Sleeps Tonight" in the US, to be precise. Sometime in or around 1950, singer-songwriter Pete Seeger teamed up with Alan Lomax, a folklorist, record collector, and one of the most prominent ethnomusicologists of his era. Both men happened to be left-leaning intellectuals who shared a deep interest in the common people and their music. Lomax assembled a vast collection of recordings of the likes of Muddy Waters, Lead Belly, and other blues greats, while Seeger worked with Woodie Guthrie, another leftist bard probably best remembered for his "This Land is Your Land" anthem. After Seeger received a copy of Linda's recording of "Mbube" from Lomax, he and his band, the Weavers, turned the song into something American audiences might recognize as a folk song in the Guthrie mold, sans the talk of socialism and revolution.

They moved a few notes around, changed Linda's original title to the vaguely English-sounding "Wimoweh," and, voila, out came the first in a long line of covers that would travel the world. But this renaming was only the first step in the erasure of the song's origin and meaning. Next, the Weavers landed gigs at upscale venues, such as New York's Village Vanguard, followed in July 1950 by the assignment of the rights to their version to Folkways Music Publishers, founded by Moses Ash in 1948 and taken over in 1950 by Howard Richmond, founder of the Richmond Organization, one of the largest music publishers of its time. Eventually, by the time Gordon Jenkins, an arranger for Frank Sinatra, Billie Holiday, Louis Armstrong, and other 1950s musical icons, puffed it up into a big-band version, "Wimoweh" had regained a quality it never possessed—the "barbaric splendor of the Zulu original."[17]

In hindsight, however, "Wimoweh" was little more than a stopover on the ascent of "Mbube" as one of the world's most-covered songs. For in 1961, a band of high-school graduates called the Tokens were signed by RCA Victor to record another adaptation of "Mbube." Penned by songwriters George Weiss, Hugo Peretti, and Luigi Creatore—all industry veterans who had worked with the likes of Jimmy Rodgers and Elvis Presley—the song was titled "The Lion Sleeps Tonight." Unlike Seeger's "Wimoweh," however, which was more a cover of "Mbube" than an adaptation, Weiss and his co-authors completely reshaped "Mbube" from a call-and-response structure into a classic Tin Pan Alley, 32-bar AABA format, complete with a bridge and the "haunting skein of fifteen notes" that ends Linda's 1939 recording as the hook. And to top it all off, they also added lullaby-like lyrics about a lion that, contrary to its natural habitat in the savannah, not only sleeps in a village but in the "quiet jungle" to boot. After its release in July 1961, "The Lion Sleeps Tonight" quickly rose to the top of the US charts before reaching number one in November and eventually topping the charts everywhere else in April 1962—ahead of even the Beatles' latest hit. Hundreds of covers followed well into the 1990s, before "The Lion Sleeps Tonight," aka "Wimoweh," aka "Mbube," in 1994, became part of Disney's *The Lion King*.

One may argue about Malan's sarcastic remark that the sudden popularity of "Wimoweh" in the US, much like the American folk music revival of the 1950s and 1960s in general, was the result of Seeger restyling himself from a "banjo-picking comrade on a mission" into someone who "had managed to filter the stench of poverty and pig shit out of the proletarian music and make it wholesome and fun for Eisenhower-era squares." But what is indisputable—and what Malan conveniently glosses over—is the fact that the 1950s was also the era of the civil rights movement in the United

States, the anticolonial struggle on the African continent, and, crucially, the antiapartheid movement in South Africa, which drove scores of black musicians into exile in Europe and the United States—such as Miriam Makeba. Already a celebrity in South Africa recognized for her deft combination of folkloric fare and African jazz, Makeba became the subject of intense scrutiny following her arrival in the United States and her first appearance at the Village Vanguard in 1959. Initially, the press feted her as an exotic "African tribeswoman" and a welcome "import" from South Africa.[18] But after she married Black Panther Party activist Stokely Carmichael in 1968, she was by turns painted as a dangerous agitator by the FBI and a paragon of a black, cosmopolitan identity by African Americans and white liberals. An argument might therefore be made that American audiences, ready to turn over a new leaf in the country's troubled history of racial inequality, were torn between reassuring images of an alluring yet domesticated Africa on the one hand and a continent about to take its rightful place as an equal member of the family of nations on the other.

The combination of splendor and barbarity Malan claims to have detected in "Mbube" and its derivatives is, to this day, one of the most stubborn stereotypes about the African continent and, indeed, much of the postcolonial world. But it is not limited to music, nor is it simply a fringe idea. Rather, as Edward Said argued long ago in his classic *Orientalism* with regard to the British and French colonization of the Middle East, it is a "style of thought based upon an ontological and epistemological distinction made between 'the Orient' and (most of the time) 'the Occident.'"[19] But this difference is not per se concerned with a "correspondence between Orientalism and Orient, but with the internal consistency of Orientalism and its ideas about the Orient (the East as career) despite or beyond any correspondence, or lack thereof, with a 'real' Orient." In other words, by making statements about the Orient—such as its "barbaric splendor"—the West not only seeks to assert authority over the Orient or, for that matter Africa, it *authors* itself as the West.[20]

But the orientalist self-authorization is also the condition of possibility and result of a wide range of semiotic, material, and, crucially, legal practices that have denied authorship, control, and ownership to those coming under the sway of the orientalist episteme. Whether in the late-nineteenth and early-twentieth-century world exhibitions and their repugnant displays of indigenous bodies, or the exploitative recording practices of so-called race records in the United States, Western self-making has historically been intertwined with white claims of entitlement to the stories the colonized tell about themselves—and, to add insult to injury, with the idea that this appropriation was in their best interest because it preserved the heritage they supposedly lacked.

All this does not mean, though, that Malan single-handedly prepared the ideological ground for the events that unfolded when "Mbube" fell into the hands of much more powerful forces than Peter Seeger and his songsters and whose commercial and legal aspects I will now review in more detail. Nor should we forget that antiracist, antiorientalist views were articulated in the United States and in South Africa, not least by Solomon Linda himself who, in some of his songs, for instance, decried what he and many Zulus had long perceived as the destruction of their social world, exemplified by the dwindling role of Zulu kingship.[21] Rather, the rise of Malan's story to prominence as the master narrative of the undoing of Solomon Linda from one of the most iconic figures of South African musical history to a nobody who died penniless on October 8, 1962, calls for a more nuanced perspective. "In the Jungle," I argue in a Laclauian vein, became hegemonic not because—or, not only because—it shone a glaring light on the chasm that separated the cut-throat world of the US music industry from Malan's Solomon Linda but because it narrated it in such a way that it became serviceable to the project of postapartheid justice of neutralizing ongoing social and cultural antagonisms by shifting attention elsewhere—in this case, onto the US music industry.

Picking up from where we left off in the early 1960s, we follow Malan in his quest for answers about money. "What might all this represent in songwriter royalties and associated revenues?" he wonders. While Linda and his family continued to live in abject poverty, "What happened to all that loot?" This is where Malan's writing pivots to a different register. Instead of the tribal grandeur and the raucous self-confidence and "brain-rattling intensity" of the South African Elvis Presley that he had bathed Linda in, Malan treats his readers to a biting account of how a motley cast of US music publishers and other industry figures divided among themselves the estimated $10 or $15 million in royalties earned by "Mbube" during its half-century run as the biggest-selling tune to ever emerge from Africa—and how those very industry figures dodged Malan's questions about the "loot." All of this is then interlaced with poignant descriptions of Solomon Linda's descent into illness and obscurity and Regina and her children's lives in a house with no running water and no jobs or other visible forms of income.

My critique of Malan's text should not be construed as deflecting from the service its author has done not only in bringing to light one of the most scandalous abuses of a black South African composer in history, but also to Linda's daughters personally. But questions remain. For instance, why does Malan focus his ire solely on the "Americans"? Why does Gallo Africa—the label that first recorded "Mbube" and, as described further below, was the first to hoodwink Linda into a disastrous assignment—come off surprisingly well? "No one forced Linda to sell 'Mbube' to Eric Gallo . . . all the deals were perfectly legal," Malan writes toward the end of his article.[22] And did Regina really not derive an income from her husband's song? The article was an instant success all the same. Ecstatic comments from around the world came pouring in, expressing outrage. "Mr. Weiss has got to take a deeper look into his soul and do the right thing." "These men . . . and any others associated with such obvious and outright plagiarism must find it hard to sleep at night." "I'm appalled that Weiss cannot admit defeat with all your proof!" "My first and only thought is outrage and disgust at these 'white' men who have not just profited nicely, but received obscene amounts of money for what was never theirs to lay claim to."[23] The "Americans," for their part, were not amused. In letters to Rolling Stone, Folkways owner Howard Richmond, for instance, took issue with Malan's "myopic perspective," which denigrated "the good efforts of many people who succeeded in establishing the valid Wimoweh copyright." He continued: Only by having achieved copyright recognition for the Weavers version had it become possible to "restore" copyright to "Mbube," which Gallo had long ago abandoned.[24] And while Weiss himself never weighed in, Seeger berated Malan for his "inflated adjectives" and for ridiculing him as the "scion of wealthy New York radicals," when, in fact, he had once loaned his penniless father, musicologist Charles Seeger, five dollars to buy milk for his infant brother Michael.[25]

Reversionary Interest: From Colonial Statute to Postcolonial Precedent

> Provided that, where the author of a work is the first owner of the copyright therein, no assignment of the copyright, and no grant of any interest therein, made by him (otherwise than by will) after the passing of this Act, shall be operative to vest in the assignee or grantee any rights with respect to the copyright in the work beyond the expiration of twenty-five years from the death of the author, and the reversionary interest in the copyright expectant on the termination of that period shall, on the death of the author, notwithstanding any agreement to the contrary, devolve on

his legal personal representatives as part of his estate, and any agreement entered into by him as to the disposition of such reversionary interest shall be null and void, but nothing in this proviso shall be construed as applying to the assignment of the copyright in a collective work or a licence to publish a work or part of a work as part of a collective work.

The paragraph is the proviso of s 5 (2) of the British Copyright Act 1911, also known as the Imperial Copyright Act 1911 (hereafter Imperial Copyright Act). The act was the outcome of a long, drawn-out process of legislative reform with the primary goal of harmonizing British copyright law with the Berne Convention of 1886 (the first international copyright treaty) and straightening out a chaotic history of legislation that governed copyright with twenty-four parliamentary acts and a slew of decrees and regulations. Most importantly, however, the act represented an attempt at striking a balance between the interests of the domestic book market seeking protection from the importation of cheap, pirated copies and the growing pressure placed on the imperial government by self-governing and increasingly self-confident dominions, such as Canada and Australia, to create a uniform legal and commercial framework that afforded their own burgeoning book markets the same protection as in the metropolis.[26]

As for the reversionary interest provided in s 5 (2), it is perhaps one of the more eccentric examples of the Janus-faced nature of copyright's colonial roots. Nicknamed the Dickens clause, the proviso originates in Charles Dickens's long-running battle against the "piratical" serialization of his works in what he called the "most consummate national blackguard in existence"—America.[27] But his work was also pirated in South Africa. Prior to his anti-American crusade, Dickens prevailed in the country's first reported copyright case against the Port Elizabeth–based *Eastern Province Herald*, which had printed a serialized version of his *Great Expectations* without his permission.[28] So riled was Dickens by the appropriation of his work that he even offered to renounce his long-held abolitionist views if Southern US states passed new legislation providing better protection for foreign works.

Time will tell whether the name of a man of great artistic genius albeit dubious ethics should grace a provision that at least once upended the colonial master-servant relationship and if the Dickens clause should be renamed the Linda clause instead. In the interim, the Imperial Copyright Act 1911 continues to cast a long shadow over the postcolonial legal world to this day. While countries such as India sought to distance themselves from the

British copyright framework, others maintained a certain degree of loyalty to British tradition under the guise of international norms. In Canada, for instance, s 5 (2) continues to be referenced by authors wishing to file termination notices. Some critics, however, have rather mixed feelings about the provision and fear that owners, given the tenuous nature of their ownership interest, may be "disinclined to invest resources toward the exploitation of works nearing the reversionary threshold."[29] As for South Africa, the act was incorporated lock, stock, and barrel into domestic law by the South African Patents, Designs, Trade Marks and Copyright Act 9 of 1916. But in 1965, the copyright portion of that act was repealed by the Copyright Act 63 of 1965, which, in turn, was repealed by the act currently on the books: the Copyright Act 98 of 1978 (hereafter Copyright Act). As of January 1, 1979, then, little if anything was left of the Imperial Copyright Act—except the provisions of the rights of ownership. For although the 1965 and 1978 Acts did not provide for the "reversionary interest" contained in s 5 (2) of the Imperial Copyright Act, they did uphold the status quo whereby the proviso of s 5 (2) is still applicable to works made under the 1916 act. Translating all this into plain English, in contrast to most other countries outside the British Commonwealth, copyright in "Mbube" should have reverted to Solomon Linda's heirs in 1987, twenty-five years after his death, with the term expiring in 2012, fifty years after the author's death. Or, to put it in even more jarring, bread-and-butter terms, instead of living in a bare-bones township house and eating mealie pap and chicken feet day in day out, Regina Linda and her family could have already been living comfortably on the proceeds of "Wimoweh" and "The Lion Sleeps Tonight" for decades.

By the time Malan was researching his article, the Imperial Copyright Act had long faded from most lawyers' view and, consequently, his efforts to see justice served invariably came up empty.[30] But no sooner had "In the Jungle" come out that the tide would turn. For the moral furor unleashed by the article did not go unnoticed in South Africa—especially at the Gallo headquarters. Although the label is barely mentioned in the article, Gallo executives worried that Malan's findings would undermine the company's efforts to refurbish its image as a bulwark of apartheid culture. Furthermore, the unwelcome news jeopardized its drive to recapture that portion of the African market it had lost after the apartheid government assumed power in 1948, and in which it held the rights to more than 90 percent of recordings made in Southern and East Africa. Lastly, the prospect of being dragged into the moral morass revealed by Malan's story posed a risk to the public perception of Johnnic Entertainment, Gallo's parent company, as a major Black Economic Empowerment corporation and a key player in the new Growth, Employment, and Redistribution strategy of the Mbeki administration. As a result, Malan received an invitation to meet with Geoff Paynter, general manager of Gallo Publishing; Gallo archivist, Rob Allingham; and Johnnic CEO, Paul M. Jenkins, to design a strategy aimed at averting a major PR disaster. As Malan filled the participants in on his findings, Jenkins reportedly jumped up from his chair, exclaiming, "That's it. Let's go after the Americans."[31]

Shortly after the meeting, Owen Dean, an attorney at the prestigious South African law firm specializing in intellectual property law, Spoor & Fisher, received a phone call from Paynter. "Your mandate is to find a way, and to do everything possible, to enable the children of Solomon Linda, the composer of a song called 'Mbube,' which subsequently evolved into the international hit song 'The Lion Sleeps Tonight,' to derive some financial benefit from the considerable revenues generated by the popularity of 'The Lion Sleeps Tonight.' You should recommend any reasonable course of action which you can conceive and we are willing to finance it even if it means conducting litigation abroad."[32] Prior to Paynter's instructions, Dean had been involved with the Motion Picture Association of America and had served as director of SAFACT, the South African Federation Against Copyright Theft. It is in this context that Gallo became one of his most important clients and that he also acted on behalf of Disney. He was thus ideally placed to take on Paynter's brief. But more than Dean's network of contacts and experience in the entertainment industry, it was his intimate knowledge of South African and colonial copyright history that proved to be a major asset for Gallo. In his doctoral dissertation entitled *The Application of the Copyright Act, 1978, to Works made Prior to 1979*, Dean had argued that the development of South African copyright law from crude beginnings during the Dutch occupation of the Cape to the current Copyright Act was fraught with difficulties.[33] The transitional provisions governing the passage from statute to statute, repeal to repeal, especially created a host of problems that threatened the continuity of the law and diminished the desire of copyright owners to enforce their rights. Yet, despite this history of discontinuity, Dean concluded, the law of copyright in South Africa had reached a stage "where at least the road ahead is relatively straight and travelers equipped with a map can find their way." And since in copyright, "as in life in general, the past cannot be brushed aside or altered with the stroke of a pen," it would be imprudent to perpetuate the uncertainties of the past by introducing entirely new legislation. "Copyright, like people and the society in which we live, is to a large extent a captive of the past."[34]

Written not only six years prior to the first democratic elections but also decades before what feels like the eternity it has taken the South African legislature to embark on a major overhaul of the country's outmoded copyright statute, these lines appear to reflect a peculiar ambiguity between discomfort at the tyranny of precedent inherent in the Anglo-American legal tradition on the one hand and acquiescence to the apartheid copyright regime on the other. But in what must be one of the great ironies of South African legal history, it is this very ambivalence that set in motion a truly transformative, precedent-setting chain of events, not unlike the one unleashed by Ali Baba when he stumbled upon the infamous caves of the forty thieves. Buried in a statute enacted nearly a century ago by the Parliament of the imperial power, a section named after one of the world's greatest novelists, who had little sympathy for readers in the Cape Colony and openly colluded with the slave-holding American South, would be resurrected in providing relief to the surviving daughters of a composer born just one year before South Africa gained independence from Britain. But caveat lector: To better understand this convergence of the past and the present, imperial law and postapartheid justice, I will adopt what is called a standard FIRAC (facts, issue statement, ratio, analysis, and conclusion) approach, where the analysis progresses from the facts of the case to the legal issue and the rule to the application and conclusion. Hence, there will be no ready-made critical readings or sophisticated deconstructions. Instead, this account will be the kind of material that ethnographers, accustomed to more scintillating fare, loath like no other—paragraphs upon paragraphs of regulations, pages and pages of correspondence, and reams of royalty statements. Worse still, it will move at an excruciatingly slow pace, maneuvering through almost imperceptible nuances of legal jargon, often pausing at unexpected moments, changing course midway, and frequently returning to square one along the way.

Let us backtrack, then, and resume the story in 1950, in the middle of the chain of events that began in 1939 and ended in 2006. To refresh the reader's memory, it was in 1950 that Pete Seeger adapted "Mbube" into "Wimoweh" and, as is standard music industry practice, immediately assigned its copyright to Folkways Music Publishers, Inc. on July 10, 1950. (A later version of "Wimoweh" was registered under Paul Campbell—a pseudonym for Seeger and the Weavers—on December 21, 1951.) On January 2, 1952, Folkways granted a license for "Wimoweh" for Southern and East Africa to Gallo; Gallo then returned the favor by licensing the world rights of "Mbube" to Folkways. A decade later, the reader may also remember, "Wimoweh" was joined by another adaptation of Linda's original work, "The Lion Sleeps Tonight." Here, too, the authors assigned the recording and public performance rights of their adaptation to a relatively unknown publisher (and eponym of the Tokens) called Token Music Publishing Company on October 17, 1961. Later that year, on November 6, Token transferred and assigned all rights in "The Lion Sleeps Tonight" to Folkways.

All of this would not be particularly noteworthy were it not for the simple fact that prior to 1952, Gallo did not yet own the rights to "Mbube." It was only on January 14, 1952—two weeks after Folkways licensed "Wimoweh" to Gallo—that Solomon Linda assigned "all his right, title and interest in and to the copyright (including all mechanical [the right to reproduce a work from a so-called master] and performing rights) of my arrangement of the traditional folk-song" to Gallo, following up with similarly worded assignments for "Mbube" and the B side "Ngi Hambiki" on February 26, 1952.[35] Adding to the confusion, on April 9, 1952, Linda executed yet a third assignment, this time describing "Mbube" as a "composition composed by me."[36] In the space of fewer than three months, then, "Mbube" not only went from an "arrangement" of a "folk-song" to a "composition," Gallo in what appears to be a classic example of *nemo plus iuris* (no person may transfer more rights than they hold) entered into an agreement with Folkways about rights to "Mbube" it did not actually own at the date of signature. Folkways, never far behind when appropriating soi-disant folk-song in the name of preservation, likewise licensed to Gallo the Southern African and East African rights in a derivative work ("Wimoweh") of "Mbube" without actually having received permission from Solomon Linda as the owner of the original work.[37]

But this is just the beginning of a saga in which the rights to "Mbube," "Wimoweh," and, later, "The Lion Sleeps Tonight" would eventually split into two macrogeographic territories, entangling Folkways, Gallo, and several other publishers in an inextricable transatlantic web of incongruous publishing and subpublishing agreements, sublicenses, and US legal battles. We will follow these intercontinental voyages closely because their inconsistencies tell us a great deal about the jockeying that routinely takes place behind the backs of unsuspecting authors living on the margins of the global music industry and copyright law's own complicity with it.

The first broadside was fired in the fall of 1961 by Folkways. Having acquired the rights to Seeger's unauthorized adaptation of "Mbube" in 1950,

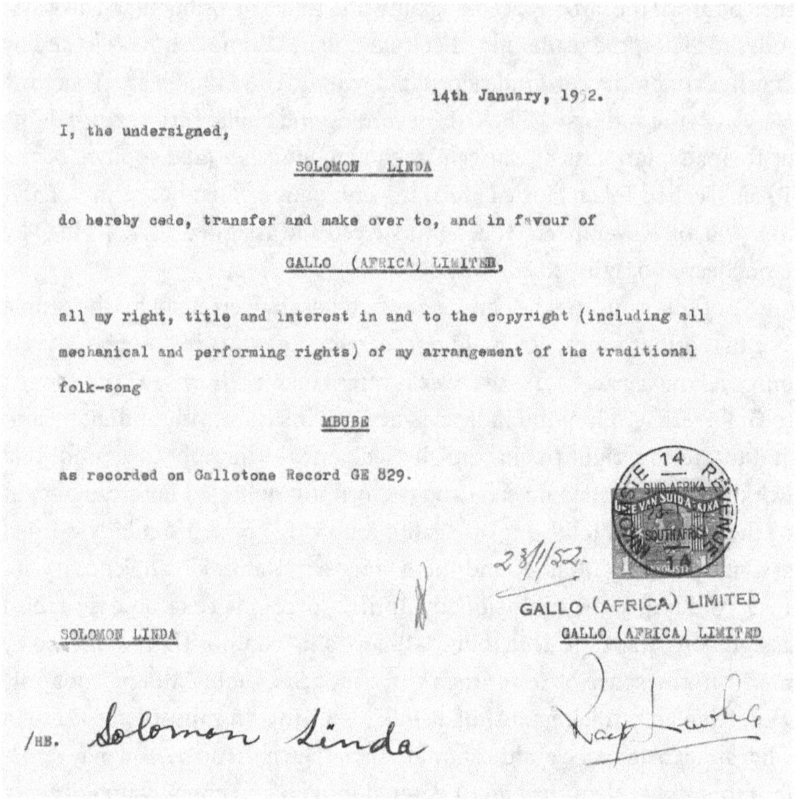

> 14th January, 1952.
>
> I, the undersigned,
>
> SOLOMON LINDA
>
> do hereby cede, transfer and make over to, and in favour of
>
> GALLO (AFRICA) LIMITED,
>
> all my right, title and interest in and to the copyright (including all mechanical and performing rights) of my arrangement of the traditional folk-song
>
> MBUBE
>
> as recorded on Gallotone Record GE 829.
>
> SOLOMON LINDA   GALLO (AFRICA) LIMITED
>
> /HB. Solomon Linda

FIGURE 2.2 Assignment of "Mbube" to Gallo, January 14, 1952. Photograph by the author.

it comes as no surprise that at the precise moment that "The Lion Sleeps Tonight" started its ascent to the number one slot on the *Billboard* Hot 100, Folkways accused Token of infringing its copyright of "Wimoweh." It was no accident either that Token immediately surrendered, ceding its worldwide rights as publisher of "The Lion Sleeps Tonight" to Folkways. Although the dispute would erupt again almost thirty years later under slightly different circumstances, the skirmish is of particular interest to this account for two reasons. It established, for the first time, the lineage leading from "The Lion Sleeps Tonight" and "Wimoweh" all the way back to Linda's original composition. If the musical nature of this line of descent may be obvious enough even to the uninitiated listener, its dubious legal status did not escape Dean's attention. In the opinion he wrote for Gallo, he argues that while the assignment of copyright in "The Lion Sleeps Tonight" to Folkways rendered the latter's claim of infringement redundant, it did not alter the fact that at the time of its writing, "The Lion Sleeps Tonight" constituted an unlawful reproduction or adaptation of "Wimoweh," which in turn was an adaptation of a substantial part of "Mbube." In short, "'The Lion Sleeps Tonight' is an unauthorised *indirect* copy of 'Mbube.'"[38]

The second reason why the Token-Folkways assignment is significant is that it brought Gallo back into the fold, as it were. In gaining copyright recognition for the Weavers version, it recognized the copyright to "Mbube," enabling Gallo to normalize its exploitation of the work. And so, between 1961 and 1970, Gallo and Folkways entered into a string of license agreements that, although partly incongruous, essentially boil down to two key points. First, Folkways finally recognized the fact—already hinted at in the 1961 Folkways-Token deal—that "Wimoweh" is derived from "Mbube." Second, the two publishers divided up the "Mbube" cake along broad territorial lines, with Gallo controlling the Southern and East African rights and Folkways those of the rest of the world. Similar agreements govern the Southern African and worldwide rights to "The Lion Sleeps Tonight."

Birds of a feather flock together? Spurious as it may seem, all this horse-trading was perfectly within copyright owners' exclusive rights and, as such, of no immediate consequence to the question of reversionary interest. That is, until 1983 when disaster struck again. By that time, the initial twenty-eight-year term of the US rights to "Mbube"—Gallo had also registered "Mbube" in the United States on April 9, 1952—had expired. But rather than seeking better terms for her copyright, Regina—on the advice of her lawyer—assigned it to Folkways on March 30, 1983, for the paltry sum of one dollar![39] And since history, according to Karl Marx, repeats itself first as tragedy then as farce, in 1992—two years after Regina's death—her daughters also renewed the assignment. A flimsy document of just two paragraphs, Regina's 1983 assignment bears close scrutiny. It is the proverbial fly in the ointment, a veritable ghost in the machine that would go on to haunt Dean right up to the 2006 settlement. Would the assignment be valid? Would s 5 (2) override it? I will return to both of these agreements frequently because their wording gives rise to rather divergent interpretations of the exact nature of the rights transferred to Folkways. But before continuing with my summary of Dean's opinion, it is necessary to take a small detour via what, at first glance, might appear tangential to the broader drama, but upon closer inspection turns out to be an all-too-familiar tale of the cognitive dissonance between white liberal sympathy and black aspirations, which has hampered African American and South African musicians throughout much of the history of recorded music. At its center is an unusual, if somewhat overlooked, figure—Raymond Tucker. To an older generation of antiapartheid activists, Tucker is no stranger. During the heyday of the antiapartheid struggle, he was one of a handful of admirably resourceful lawyers who worked to undermine the repressive legal system by its own means—by adroitly exploiting the contradictions between official lawlessness and what little remained of the rule of law.[40] Along with attorneys, such as Geoffrey Budlender, Sydney Kentridge, Christopher Nupen, and George Bizos, he represented (often pro bono or at reduced fees) antiapartheid heroes like Nelson Mandela, Tokyo Sexwale, Robert Sobukwe, and Winnie Mandela. And unlike the majority of lawyers who turned a blind eye to the everyday travails of ordinary black South Africans caught in the labyrinthine system of pass and labor laws, Tucker, for many years, spent every Saturday morning at the offices of the human rights organization Black Sash advising people on the few rights that were left to them. Says veteran legal scholar John Dugard, "He was a strict adherent of the traditions and ethical standards of his profession . . . guided by professional modesty and not avarice in the charging of fees."[41] Or was he?

Tucker had been acting on behalf of the Linda family, transferring the royalties on "Wimoweh" to South Africa some twenty years after Seeger, in a Damascus road moment, had instructed Folkways to do something for the Linda family. On receiving the good news, the ailing Linda promptly asked Seeger to send the money to the Union of Southern African Artists (USAA), an organization founded in 1952 by the impresarios Alf Herbert and Ian Bernhardt that brought black and white artists together in open defiance of apartheid's assault on the arts.[42] However, it is far from clear whether any funds ever made their way into Linda's bank account prior to Tucker appearing on the scene. Some authors and contemporary witnesses have provided conflicting reports about USAA's role in the transfer of funds to Linda. One of them was Harry Bloom, script writer of the musical *King Kong* staged by USAA to much cross-racial acclaim in 1959. A lawyer by training, Bloom had been tasked with handling the transfers to Linda, claiming that the first check from New York was presented to Linda at a ceremony that coincided with the foundation of the Union in 1952—ten years prior to Linda's letter to Seeger![43] Complicating Bloom's narrative of USAA's beneficence even further, Pat Williams, lyricist and coauthor of *King Kong*, reported that by the time Linda received his payments, black performers already had begun harboring "bitter feelings of artistic and financial exploitation."[44] The payments that can be established with some degree of certainty, however, are

ASSIGNMENT OF COPYRIGHT

FOR AND IN CONSIDERATION of the sum of One ($1.00) Dollar and other valuable considerations, the receipt of which is hereby acknowledged, Regina Linda, c/o Raymond Tucker, 901 Pritchard House, PRITCHARD Street, Straat, Johannesburg, Republic of South Africa, hereby sells, assigns, transfers, and sets over unto Folkways Music Publishers, Inc., 10 Columbus Circle, New York, N.Y. 10019, its successors and assigns, all of her right, title and interest in and to the musical composition entitled:

MBUBE
Words and Music by Solomon Linda
Eu 281531, May 7, 1952
RE 66-071, September 8, 1980

including, but not limited to all rights, copyrights and copyright rights therein and thereto in the United States of America, and all renewals and extensions thereof now existing, or which shall hereafter come into existence, and all claims, demands and causes of action thereunto appertaining.

IN WITNESS WHEREOF, the undersigned has caused this document to be executed this 30th day of March 1983.

Regina Linda

Sworn to before me this 30th day of March 1983.

FIGURE 2.3 Assignment of "Mbube" to Folkways, March 20, 1983.
Courtesy of Copyright Office, Library of Congress.

for a period between 1985 and 2004, a good twenty years after Tucker took over the transfer of royalties from Bloom, and during which the daughters received $25,854.38 or 12.5 percent of the earnings on "Wimoweh" from Folkways.[45]

Of course, for an international pop staple such as "Wimoweh," this is a mere pittance that should have raised eyebrows with any legal expert. And indeed, in July 2001, the Law Society of the Northern Provinces received a complaint by the sisters, alleging that Tucker had severely neglected his fiduciary duties by not properly accounting for the transfers from the United States and by charging excessive fees for his services. Worse still, he had talked Regina and her daughters into signing the notoriously unfair Folkways assignments, whose legal and commercial implications they clearly were not in a position to understand, given their insufficient command of the English language. Outraged, Tucker denied any professional misconduct, claiming that he never had any professional dealings with the Linda family "beyond facilitating the receipt of moneys for their benefit from the United States." He also had reason to believe that the "spurious and vexatious" complaint had not been initiated by the daughters themselves but that someone had "put them up" to it.[46]

At this point, the slightly unnerved reader may very well question the purpose of delving into the twists and turns of yet another tale about the (involuntary?) connivance between white corporate greed and white liberal generosity. What is the point of laboriously unraveling this knot of wills, licenses, and cross-licenses entangling "Mbube," its offshoots "Wimoweh" and "The Lion Sleeps Tonight," and a coterie of rights holders in South Africa and New York when the agony and injustice inflicted on the Linda family was in plain view? But the point of this brief digression from Dean's opinion is to reiterate that an ethnography of the kind attempted here should feed on as many contradictions and incongruities as possible in order for it to keep passing. For an ethnography of law to succeed, the anthropologist has to constantly account for the effect seemingly peripheral issues, such as an ethics complaint or the choice of a lawyer, have in further destabilizing what is already a highly contentious and, more often than not, emotionally charged affair. And, indeed, as the case lumbered from one calamity to the next, the tussle over Tucker's alleged malfeasance, the potentially duplicitous 1983 and 1992 assignments, and the (belated) royalty payments made by Seeger would haunt Dean right up to the end.[47]

Continuing, then, with our review of Dean's opinion, we will move straight to the final conclusion, the recommendations. A most idiosyncratic

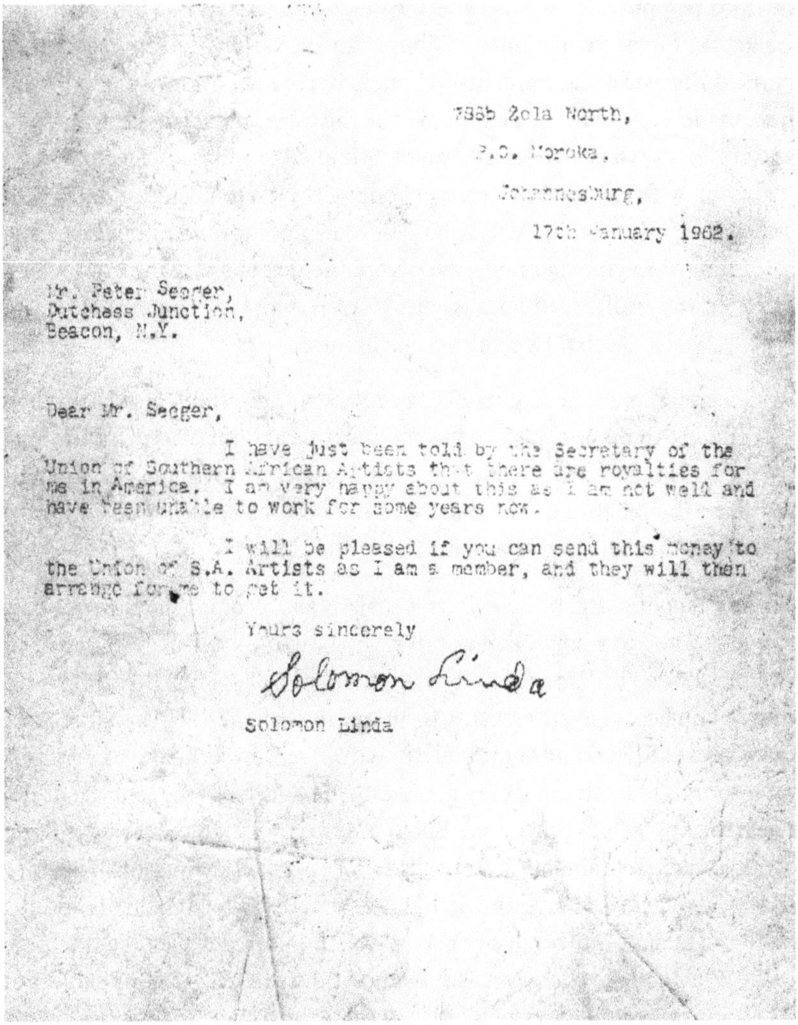

FIGURE 2.4 Letter by Solomon Linda to Pete Seeger, January 17, 1962. Photograph by the author.

and delicate category of legal writing in its own right, Dean's recommendations are striking for their restraint. There is no blazing call to arms here, no angry accusations of wrongdoing, and no "vengeance is mine . . . saith the Lord." Instead, it is all about what is practical and, so it seems, in the interest of the involved parties. Linda's daughters, Dean advises, should assign the Commonwealth copyright to Gallo, subject to "appropriate equitable financial arrangements." This would not only consolidate the split copyright of "Mbube," but it would also simplify relations with Folkways by enabling Gallo to enforce its copyright of "Mbube" and its various derivatives in other parts of the world and claim infringement and damages from persons who have made copies of Linda's song. While the assignment was clearly aimed at transferring the US renewal term of "Mbube" to Folkways, Dean goes on to reason, it did not include the reversionary interest protected under British and, by extension, South African law. Moreover, at the time she executed the assignment, Regina had not yet acquired the reversionary interest, which only became available in 1987, twenty-five years after her husband's death. "In the final analysis," Dean closes his opinion:

> The assignment by Regina Linda could only have transferred the copyright in Mbube which she owned at the time and this was probably only the copyright for the renewal term of American copyright. . . . Accordingly, the balance of the copyright in MBUBE, besides the American copyright, remained vested in Gallo at that time.

The story could easily end here, Dean's analysis and recommendations roughly corresponding to what one might think of as an old-boys-club solution: an attempt to keep it all in the family by elevating the daughters' standing from that of unpaid domestic servants to somewhere slightly above that of poor relations at the lower end of the table. As we will see further below, this roughly corresponds to the terms of the 2006 settlement as far as the renewal of the reverted copyright is concerned. But at the same time, the outcome of legal action is never certain, however brilliant the doctrinal analysis or skillful the lawyering. There is always a major hiatus—in fact, a whole chain of ruptures and near-failures—that must constantly be monitored if the case is to proceed. What happens between the pleadings and the trial phase is subject to an elaborate system of statutes and rules of court. There is an entire choreography that must be followed in order to go from the notice of motion to the particulars of claim and on to the discovery and the pretrial conference. What was the likelihood that a court would accept Dean's reading of s 5 (2)? Was there sufficient precedent in support of this argument? Who would be the plaintiffs, and what would be their standing? What about funding?

These and other issues surfaced time and again, threatening to undermine the very ability of the law to produce results in a case that is just as much about statutes as it is deeply embedded in South Africa's political economy. Small wonder, then, that the uncertainty surrounding the correct interpretation of s 5 (2) or the legality of the 1983 and 1992 assignments had to be kept at a minimum by selecting a cast of actors and drafting a plot that might provide a certain measure of stability to the proceedings. However, in order to probe these risk-reducing strategies, a shift into a different analytic register beyond doctrine is required—one that will entail a careful description of the linkages connecting law and politics, law and economy, law and morality. We will now jump ahead two years to catch up with the case in 2002, as it entered its next phase: the treadmill of interviewing plaintiffs and witnesses, securing birth and marriage certificates, consulting with other lawyers, and the drafting of the particulars of the claim.

By 2002, Gallo's initial enthusiasm for funding the case had not only waned (it would evaporate entirely a year later for reasons I will address further below), the 1983 and 1992 Folkways assignments, in true revenant fashion, staged an unsettling return, this time by casting doubt on the likelihood of the courts setting them aside under s 5 (2). Determined to press on after a renewed analysis of the assignments, Dean revised the conclusion of his 2000 opinion by offering a slightly different interpretation of the phrases "all of her right, title and interest . . . including, but not limited to . . . all renewals and extensions thereof now existing or which shall hereafter come into existence."[48] The expressions "interest" and "shall hereafter come into existence" caught his attention in particular. The most common meaning of *interest* refers, of course, to a person's stake in a matter whose enjoyment is postponed. For instance, it may refer to the sum of money paid for the use of someone else's money or to a piece of leased land whose full use reverts to the owner once the lease expires. More ominously, it may also recall the so-called futures or derivates that were partly responsible for the near-meltdown of the global financial markets in 2008. In this case, though, *interest* bears a slightly different meaning, which is hinted at in the phrase "hereafter come into existence." Under the Folkways assignments, Regina's acquisition of the reversionary interest in "Mbube" would have automatically triggered the transfer of the copyright she previously assigned to Folkways. Accordingly, Dean concludes, if Regina's rights could not have encompassed the reversionary interests because they had not yet devolved on her at the time of the assignment, a counterargument could be made. At the time of Solomon Linda's death, the right to acquire the reversionary rights devolved on his widow as part of his estate in the form of an "interest." According to this view, then, the phrase "interest . . . which shall hereafter come into existence" could be construed as implying the right of future acquisition of the copyright. At the same time, Dean cautions, the chance that this interpretation would be accepted in the South African (or, for that matter, British) court was slim.[49]

These shifts may appear subtle—too subtle, perhaps. But intricacy is the law's home planet. It is minute distinctions rather than sweeping generalizations, minuscule nuances of interpretation rather than stark statements of truth and untruth that the law transports as it weaves its net of valences. This is nowhere more apparent than in another piece of legal writing: the opinion Dean commissioned from Jean Sonnekus, a law professor at the University of Johannesburg specializing in property and succession law. Like Dean, Sonnekus begins his analysis by making a subtle distinction between copyright and interest. However, he adds one crucial point. Under South African law, he argues, the expectancy of a "future interest" can never be included in a person's estate, only "real," existing assets, whether these are tangible or immaterial property, such as a copyright. Consequently, the reversionary interest mentioned in s 5 (2) can only consist of the copyright vested in the author's estate, whereas the exploitation—the "interest"—of the copyright is "postponed" for twenty-five years.[50]

But this is where the problems are just beginning. Because s 5 (2) is silent on the exact definition and content of the reversionary interest, it was left for the courts and experts to choose between two possible scenarios. In the first interpretation, confirmed in a long series of decisions and expanded on in a wealth of commentary, it is the copyright itself that forms the inherited asset and not some uncertain future interest in the copyright. Hence, Regina would have automatically acquired the right to claim performance from the executor on Solomon's death in 1962, even though the exploitation of that asset would have been severely restricted by the twenty-five-year term prior to 1987. It is obvious that this interpretation leads to the rather quixotic situation of two distinct owners of the same copyright: the assignee (Folkways) as the rightful owner of the copyright and the heir (Regina) as holder of the reversionary interest, unable to exploit it even though she may dispose of it at any time. The above line of reasoning, Sonnekus goes on to suggest, is confirmed even if one assumes a second, opposite scenario in which the reversionary interest contained in s 5 (2) had not vested as a copyright but merely as an interest in the copyright. The conundrum with this alternative interpretation is immediately apparent. The reversionary interest in the copyright would have to form part of the estate of the deceased author in order to bring its administration in line with the law governing the administration of estates. As Linda died intestate, Regina would have inherited the reversionary interest only. The copyright itself would not be accounted for as an asset in the estate and, hence, would not be reflected in any normal liquidation or distribution proceedings. It would simply surface as an unaccounted asset in the hands of the executor after twenty-five years: a perfect cat-and-mouse game!

Thus, we are back to square one: two owners of the same copyright. To get out of this quandary, Sonnekus argues, it makes sense to assume that during the initial twenty-five years between the author's passing and the beginning of the reversionary period, only one holder of the reversionary copyright exists: the assignee of the US copyright, Folkways. At the same time, the sudden appearance after twenty-five years turns the reverted copyright into an unaccounted asset that, under South African law, can only be distributed to the heirs through the office of the estate's executor. It is the executor—and only the executor—who is not only entitled but *obligated* to transfer all assets of the estate to the rightful owner, "be it the heir or the transferee who acquired the interest in the intervening years by agreement with the heir."[51] Again, translated back into this case, the executor of Linda's estate would have to transfer the reversionary interest to Regina (or her daughters) on condition that they had not, in the meantime, divested themselves of it by assigning it to Folkways. This, however, as should be amply clear by now, is exactly what both Regina and her daughters did.

There is, however, a silver lining to all of this, both for Folkways and the Linda heirs. As Sonnekus notes, even if Linda's daughters were to contest the legality of the 1983 and 1992 assignments because they were entered into under duress by the other party; because the one dollar that was paid was far below the actual market value; or because no proper legal opinion was obtained in the matter, it is a generally recognized legal position that anyone can buy or sell assets at a certain future point in time. Failure to perform the transfer at the agreed-upon time, however, will merely constitute a breach of contract but will not void the agreement as such. On the downside, the assignee would have to wait for the twenty-five-year interim period to lapse before they can exploit their new acquisition. The bright spot for the Linda daughters, in turn, is that they are entitled to the interest, that is, royalties, collected by Folkways and paid to Gallo from around 1983.

The children of the late composer, Sonnekus closes his opinion, "probably cannot lay claim to the copyright to the composition if the widow had assigned the reversionary interest or the reverted copyright." He continues: "This holds good even if the agreement of assignment was entered into before the first twenty-year period had lapsed."[52] In other words, since Regina Linda had assigned the copyright to "Mbube" to Folkways, the likelihood that Elizabeth, Fildah, and Delphi would win a case by invoking s 5 (2) was virtually nil.

And so s 5 (2) remained a major drawback, forcing Dean to try a different tactic. As always in civil cases, the first order of business was the choice of a suitable plaintiff. The question is anything but trivial, as it implies legal and, above all, psychological repercussions well beyond the case itself. On the face of it, it would have made sense for Linda's daughters to institute proceedings. As impoverished township residents suing powerful media moguls, they were guaranteed a high degree of sympathy. What is more, as heirs to Solomon and Regina, they also had a "direct and substantial interest" in the subject matter of the litigation, the most basic requirement for *locus standi*. Or should Gallo Africa be the plaintiff? After all, not only had the publisher commissioned Dean for an opinion, it had also increasingly come under pressure to refashion itself as a driving force of black economic empowerment, not to mention that it was rumored to be in the crosshairs of the South African Revenue Service for tax evasion. Last but not least, its parent company Johnnic had deep pockets.[53]

In the end, neither of these options would come to pass for two reasons. The first is the distinct possibility that once the copyright to "Mbube" automatically devolved to Linda's heirs in 1987, such reversionary interest would immediately be passed on to Folkways by dint of the fateful assignments Regina and her daughters executed in 1983 and 1992, respectively. The second is that appointing someone as plaintiff who may not even be the copyright owner might fail to meet the "direct and substantial interest" test. Most importantly, though, there is no mention in s 5(2) of the interest in a work reverting to the heirs of the author directly, to begin with. Instead, it is their "legal personal representatives as part of his estate" to whom the interest devolves. Without a legal representative, there would, then, be no plaintiff to bring the proceedings. Of course, it does not take a Nobel Prize winner to realize that in the 1960s, at the peak of the apartheid era, most black South Africans lacked the wherewithal to leave a will, much less appoint an executor of their estate. For better or worse, intestate succession according to the rules of customary law was the norm. There were thus two hurdles. The first was to locate the files of Linda's estate and augment it ex post facto with the recently surfaced asset of the reversionary interest; the second, to find an executor to administer the Linda estate and decide how the reversionary interest would be handled if and when it became available. It is worthwhile to follow the trail of applications, statutes, and judgments that had to be recruited in order to bridge the yawning gap between the statutory rights vested by s 5 (2) and the simple matter of standing of the actual flesh-and-blood individuals approaching the courts to repossess what was rightfully theirs.

The story goes something like this: For the better part of the twentieth century, South African law provided that the intestate estate of a "native" or black person, unlike the estates of whites administered by the master of the High Court, had to be administered by a magistrate. Accordingly, after a successful search for Linda's estate file, the Johannesburg magistrate appointed Stephanus Griesel, a chartered accountant, as executor of Solomon Linda's estate and, hence, as the legal representative to whom the reversionary interest in "Mbube" would devolve in terms of s 5 (2). There was yet another hurdle to overcome though. In *Bhe and Others v Khayelitsha Magistrate and Others*, two extramarital daughters, both minors, had sued the magistrate of Khayelitsha (a township in Cape Town) for having appointed the grandfather of the girls as executor of their deceased father's estate.[54] On the face of it, the magistrate's decision was perfectly in line with the Black Administration Act 38 of 1927 (hereafter Black Administration Act) that an intestate estate was to be distributed according to "Black law and custom" and that, hence, the system of male primogeniture at the heart of customary laws of succession applied. But by 2004, the case had reached the South African Constitutional Court, which, in a majority decision, declared the provisions of s 23 of the Black Administration Act and the principle of male primogeniture to be incompatible with sections 9 (equality) and 10 (dignity) of the Constitution and invalid ab initio.

The ruling touches a sore spot on a social body still bruised from centuries of racial abuse, raising a host of issues from the place of customary law and the legal status of customary marriages in the new democratic order, to property transfers such as the *lobolo* (bride price) traditionally involved in such marriages, to children's rights. While some welcomed the judgment as sounding the death knell of one of colonial rule's last vestiges, others were less affirmative. In a rare show of unity, progressives and traditionalists alike warned of the consequences of tampering with indigenous forms of sovereignty. To do so, they argued, might raise the specter of unrest in what they euphemistically described—in lieu of plain patriarchy—as the country's "traditional communities."[55] In actual fact, however, the judgment is far more ambiguous about the possibility of developing the ossified, colonial version of customary law into a more adapted living law in conformity with the Bill of Rights. The "inherent flexibility of the system of customary law" and the value of ubuntu, the justices held, are worthy of constitutional protection in their own right.[56]

The next issue is jurisdiction. Dean had long harbored doubts about Gallo's commitment. Indeed, in April 2004, Gallo reneged on its pledge to unconditionally fund the case, ostensibly because Nu Metro, a South African cinema chain that, like Gallo, was part of the Johnnic empire, was a licensee of Disney. The idea first mooted at the crucial 2000 meeting with Johnnic CEO Jenkins to go after Disney thus reached an impasse. With *The Lion King* having netted the Burbank giant close to $1 billion and Gallo dropping out as a potential instructing client, chances were that the case would be doomed from the beginning. Worse, Disney did not even have a place of business in South Africa, and the South African court had no jurisdiction over a foreign entity. What Disney did have, however, was the South African rights to more than 250 registered trademarks, most notably in staples of popular culture like Mickey Mouse and Donald Duck. Thus defeated on the funding front, Dean once again changed tactics. Because these assets made Disney extremely vulnerable in South Africa, he decided to pursue a fairly common strategy to found jurisdiction of the South African court. Called *ad fundandam jurisdictionem*, it entails seizing property by virtue of a summons or other judicial order for the purpose of bringing a defendant to trial.

There were advantages and disadvantages to this route. One of the benefits, Dean figured, was that launching action in South Africa would be far less costly than in the United States. On the downside, the damages that would potentially be claimable from South African defendants would be significantly smaller because South African courts can only award damages suffered in South Africa. Still, he reasoned, if the plan to establish jurisdiction in South Africa was successful, more ample and reliable funding from other sources might eventually materialize to take the case to the world stage. As it turned out, Dean's gamble paid off. In June 2004, an ex parte application was granted to the newly appointed executor and plaintiff S. Griesel to attach some 250 registered trademarks and, interestingly, the copyright of *The Lion King* owned by Disney Enterprises, Inc.[57] Needless to say, Disney alias Abilene responded swiftly by filing an application to set aside the court order, advancing several familiar pleas. Their South African attorneys, Adams & Adams, argued that Griesel had no standing because he was appointed executor by the Johannesburg magistrate rather than the master of the High Court. Furthermore, he also failed to fully disclose material facts relating to the 1983 and 1992 Folkways assignments. Last but not least, Disney was not a contributory infringer responsible for the sale of infringing copies of "Mbube" by various South African record labels and movie distributors. The application was dismissed mainly on procedural grounds, and the case moved to the all-important pretrial conference.

On July 22, 2005, a fax from Tugendhaft Wapnick Banchetti and Partners landed on Owen Dean's desk. Disney Enterprises, Inc., it stated, wished to propose a "full and final settlement before the aforementioned parties, the plaintiff and the heirs in the estate of the late Solomon Linda." Specifically, the attorneys went on to state, the defendants were prepared to pay circa $24,000 in terms of an arbitration case between Folkways and Weiss & Co. over the renewal rights in "The Lion Sleeps Tonight;" an additional $37,500 representing 25 percent of royalty income received by Abilene for "The Lion Sleeps Tonight" in the Commonwealth countries between 1999 and 2005; and an advance of $75,000 recoverable from future royalties on the song for the duration of copyright to "Mbube."[58]

Predictably, team Dean was not having any of it, responding with a barrage of thinly veiled threats and counterclaims instead.[59] Not only had the case generated a great deal of publicity detrimental to the defendants' reputation, Dean wrote, but things could also easily escalate to potentially catastrophic levels if they failed to make the offer applicable worldwide. To wit, his client had received offers from numerous solicitors eager to replicate the South African proceedings in places such as Paris and Hong Kong, both sites of hugely profitable Disneyland theme parks.[60] Furthermore, the defendants should not be in any doubt that his client was determined to put his money where his mouth is. Since the South African government had taken a keen interest in the matter and was prepared, if necessary, to go the extra mile in "gaining recognition for the international worth of South African culture," his client's funding was virtually unlimited.[61]

As for the specific demands, Dean proceeded to systematically refute some of Disney's more eccentric justifications for the "full" offer. By now, the reader will be familiar with the most important of these. First, there is the issue of standing, already in dispute in the pretrial phase. Contesting Disney's claim that the magistrate simply had no authority to appoint the executor and, as a result, S. Griesel not only had no standing to bring proceedings against their clients, but also the reversionary interest in terms of s 5 (2) did not vest in him either, Dean pointed to Bhe. The justices may have struck down the Black Administration Act, he wrote. But the court also held that only those "Africans with sufficient resources, knowledge, education or opportunity to make an informed choice" were able to extricate themselves from the regime of colonially fabricated "customary law" by making a will. Hence, in order to "avoid dislocation," the justices allowed for an interim phase during which estates currently being wound up should continue to be administered under the old apartheid legislation. In other words, Griesel's appointment as executor by the magistrate was lawful. Additionally, his client would also be happy to pursue the matter before the Constitutional Court if necessary.[62] Another counterclaim, equally well-known by now, concerned the validity of the 1983 and 1992 agreements between the heirs and Folkways. Even in the unlikely event that those agreements proved legitimate, Dean was confident that the executor was acting in terms of a statutory devolution of the copyright in him and, hence, was unaffected by any prior agreements. Finally, one should also add the issue of originality to the list of claims and counterclaims. Allegations disputing the originality of a work are de rigueur in copyright proceedings, even though they are rarely advanced this late in the game. Because the first two 1952 assignments to Gallo refer to "Mbube" as an "arrangement" of a "traditional folk-song" or "traditional tune" and only the third assignment uses the word *composition*, the defendants argued, these differences in wording placed "serious doubt on the originality of the musical work."[63] Undeterred, Dean countered that his client would be ready to lead evidence from an "eminent" musicologist, a "Zulu" (and, as such, a presumably a credible witness) who had conducted an independent study of the origins of "Mbube" and found that the song was, indeed, Linda's original work.[64] Hence, to refer to the song as "traditional" was "divorced from the facts of the matter." In conclusion, to settle the matter, the defendants would need to pay $1,000,000 (R10 million) in damages as well as $1.6 million in return for waiving a claim for past damages and to cover his client's costs. Furthermore, in addition to payment of 25 percent author's royalty on any future uses of "The Lion Sleeps Tonight" throughout the world, his client would require the acknowledgment that Solomon Linda is the author of "Mbube."

To recapitulate, thus far, we have followed a fairly well-trodden path, routinely taught in law schools the world over and traveled by countless lawyers seeking solutions for their clients. We were confronted with a situation in which the descendants of Solomon sought relief against a perceived infringement of their father's copyright of "Mbube." Next, we examined the law: What does the statute say? What is the duration of the copyright for a work composed in 1939? This was followed by the development of a legal strategy that included, inter alia, establishing the validity of a statutory provision—s 5 (2)—thought to be unenforceable. We also observed the unfolding of a process in which even the most basic elements underwent subtle, albeit substantial, transformations. For instance, there is a progressive narrowing down of the facts into "facts of the case," a distilling into primary components, as well as a successively more rigorous delineation of the place of these facts in the broader strategy. The Folkways assignments, for instance, began as a major contractual stumbling block but vanished almost entirely at the very end. Conversely, while the need for an executor was not even mentioned in the initial opinion, it became a constitutional issue and a major sticking point right to the end.

Much of this resembles the concern with law as a set of materialities and practices that can be studied empirically rather than merely on the basis of doctrinal analysis. This law-in-action approach, as it is sometimes referred to, has its rewards. By depicting the case in the step-by-step manner of the previous pages, we avoid the risk of mistaking the social for the explanation of the legal. Instead of a priori granting the social explanatory power over the legal, we simply ignored the social. And rather than reinstating the social, we will now shift to a different register and return to where we began—to discontinuities.

Is There Race in This Case?

Now that my readers have been initiated into the inner workings of the Linda case, looked over the shoulders of attorneys and barristers, and observed in an almost passé, law-in-action fashion the unfolding of the action, they may wonder whether there is really nothing more to all this abstraction, incessant referencing, and rewriting and retrieving, completely detached from anything external. How is it, the anthropologist, for instance, wonders, that this potpourri of actors, narratives, and texts comes to form such an unbroken chain? What are the valences that compound all these moments of nineteenth-century British literary history, South African legal history, and the global entertainment industry into a handful of terms and paragraphs? And what about the big picture: the social background, politics? Might there be a sturdier, more material way of grounding all of this interconnectivity and intertextuality in something concrete—something one might call an extratext? Surely, there has to be an unofficial version to the story told by and about statutes, opinions, wills, and contracts. Perhaps a story a la Malan about shady lawyers and music industry executives. But, first and foremost, if the hiatus between the law and industry abuse, negligence, or finessing is so blatant, why not state the obvious and talk about race? After all, race was written into the legislative history of s 5 (2) ab ovo, and the plaintiff was literally conjured up from the lingering mists of customary and apartheid law. And would anyone seriously dispute the notion that music in South Africa—much like its counterpart in the United States—contributes "substantially to the vocabularies used to construct race?"⁶⁵ Is further proof necessary to establish that the scores of musicians who signed away their rights for a mere pittance were hoodwinked by unscrupulous publishers and producers?⁶⁶

The fact of the matter is, from front to back, all the Imperial Copyright Act refers to is authors and assignees. This stands in marked contrast to the torrent of colonial and apartheid law regulating ownership of tangible property on the basis of race, such as the infamous Native Lands Act 27 of 1913 (hereafter Native Lands Act), enacted three years before the Imperial Copyright Act was incorporated into South African law. While the declared rationale of the act was to reduce the abilities of so-called natives to purchase, hire, or acquire from any person other than a native land outside areas designated as native, no such marker of class, ethnic, or racial identity is used in the copyright law. Might copyright law, then, have been one of the last sanctuaries of race neutrality—an exemplar of the perseverance of the rule of law in the face of legalized oppression and segregation? Or might it be little more than a facade concealing some hidden racial dynamic? Instead of openly espousing the politics of racial segregation long part and parcel of South African life, this form of race-neutral legalism might be seen as operating by exnomination, a kind of proxy for racist assumptions through which the white minority naturalizes its privileged status by not referring to itself by its name and identity and by using the seemingly racially unmarked term *author* in its place. In this way, *author*, in practice, implies "white author."

Despite this implicit osmosis of law and colonial rule, one cannot quite so easily skim over copyright's complicity with racial oppression, however. While it is true that the system of large-scale dispossession and disenfranchisement, put in place from the moment the Dutch East India Company set foot on South African soil in 1652, effectively barred black South Africans from becoming market participants on anything but a rudimentary level, it is more difficult to advance a parallel argument about the capacity of black musicians to enter the music market on an equal footing with whites by way of copyright protections.⁶⁷ Racially based hindrances to market participation are, however, thrown into sharp relief when examined in conjunction with copyright's cousin, the law of contract. Although more comprehensive studies of contracts in the South African music industry have yet to appear, it is safe to assume that racially discriminatory industry practices—such as the various assignments signed by Solomon Linda and his family—are more the product of a systemic articulation than they are sporadic aberrations flying in the face of a supposedly color-blind system of private law.[68] Prior to the twentieth century, colonial contract law was governed by core ideas of Roman-Dutch law, which stress subjective intention and equity. Yet, during the early decades of the Union of South Africa the law of contract experienced a marked turn toward English doctrine and the limits it imposes on the role of courts to enforce contracts, however inequitable. But, as Martin Chanock observes, this shift, along with the heated controversies surrounding it, obscures the role the concept of contract increasingly played "as a master tool of discipline and rule within the society as a whole."[69] Using labor contracts in the gold mines and debt as examples, he shows how consensus ad idem was simply absent in most contracts involving black South Africans. Elsewhere, until at least the mid-1900s in the manufacturing, service, and especially agricultural sectors, paternalistic relationships were the norm.[70] And in the music industry such relationships are common even today. Take, for example, Geoff Paynter's response to Owen Dean's suggestion that Gallo had to atone for past wrongdoing. After having received a $1,000 payment from the United States, Geoff Paynter invoked one of the most insidious stereotypes of black musicians as shiftless spendthrifts, Linda "went AWOL from work for months and partied wildly in Kwazulu on the proceeds, before humbly returning to Gallo and begging for his job back (which he got!)."[71] Is a more glaring example of the continuity of this kind of paternalistic thinking possible than its parallel with the following response by a white settler to emancipation in the Cape in 1838? "But in what do the most favorable reports, and [the ex-slaves'] highly creditable conduct consist? Is it in their deserting a life of industry for a life of indolence, or is it because those who have had the best of masters, and were the best treated, have behaved themselves the most ungrateful, in leaving their aged masters without any assistance?"[72]

In the absence, then, of a more complete idea of music contracts in South African copyright history, it might be helpful to briefly parse the rich body of critical scholarship that has sprung up in recent years around the history of copyright law and African American music. This literature is structured around three paradigms: The first centers on the long line of decisions that failed to recognize key aesthetic principles of black musical production. As Olufunmilayo Arewa and Kevin J. Greene have compellingly pointed out, US copyright—and much of twentieth-century copyright law doctrine in the rest of the world—was visually prejudiced toward sheet music as the sole medium of fixation, thus effectively silencing the sonic, improvisatory, or experiential elements crucial to blues and other African American expressive genres. For example, in registration and adjudication contexts, sound recordings have long been, and continue to be, considered inferior to written evidence—commonly referred to as lead sheets—in determining substantial similarity, negatively impacting predominantly African American forms such as jazz and hip-hop as a result.[73] A related argument is that US and Western copyright law simply could not recognize other forms of authorship that do not meet the basic requirements for copyright subsistence, such as originality. Because the blues reflected an aesthetic of repetition and revision, copyright law denied blues musicians the same status of inspired prodigies that it accorded white artists.

Unlike the first paradigm, which describes the discriminatory effects of copyright law *ex negativo* by focusing on the protections it did *not*, or only reluctantly, afford to black musicians, the second paradigm assumes a more direct, causal link between copyright and exploitative music industry practices. For instance, in contrast to the current 1976 Copyright Act, protection under the 1909 Copyright Act was only available to works that had either been published with proper notice or registered. This means that a great many works created by authors during the formative era of twentieth-century African American music were registered under the names of their managers or promoters.[74] Other common abusive industry practices include the unconscionable sale or transfer of copyright to the record company or, more subtly yet equally damaging, the racialized marketing strategies of record companies utilizing genre categorizations such as "race music" or "rhythm and blues," which restricted black musicians' ability to cross over into genres dominated by their white counterparts. Until well into the 1950s, US record companies routinely prevented black musicians from breaking into the pop market before having secured a firm foothold in the "black" market. Meanwhile, white musicians "borrowed" from "black music" at will. But the effect of such categorizations also extends beyond marketing.[75] Because musical genres, as David Brackett observes, operate on the principle of general "citationality," the legibility of a genre in racialized terms is contingent on a certain kind of feedback loop. The conventions of the genre must continually be cited; the genre as much as the racial category it is said to represent is "performatively constituted by the very expressions that are said to be its results."[76] Last but not least, there is also the psycho-moral dimension of the disparate treatment of black artists and, by extension, the communities in which they are embedded and in which their works are invested with meaning.[77]

The third paradigm is grounded in a slightly different line of thinking about copyright's racial legacy. While critiques of unequal contract negotiations, doctrinal inefficiency, and economic power differentials are important, in *The Color of Creatorship: Intellectual Property, Race, and the Making of Americans*, Anjali Vats draws upon critical race theory to argue that these critiques "shy away from historically and ideologically situated explanations of how and why economics fails to produce equity and inclusion in the intellectual property context."[78] Current understandings of intellectual property law in terms of romanticized notions of (US) citizenship and creatorship, she contends, constrain the manner in which the intersection of race and creativity can be studied, managed, and adjudicated. Therefore, to dismantle the "racial episteme" that consistently protects the intellectual property interests of white people and devalues those of people of color, copyright scholars should aim to uncover the "racial scripts" that enable the exclusion of people of color by calling upon dominant ideas of personhood, creativity, and national identity without explicitly invoking racial categories at the same time. On this view, then, "the outcome of individual legal cases involving creators of color is less important than how doctrinal standards were forged through epistemically raced concepts of citizenship."[79] The persistence of racial scripts is the reason why positive outcomes cannot undo a history of racial injustice. Even instances such as the famed (or infamous?) "Blurred Lines" case in which Marvin Gaye's estate prevailed against Robert Thicke and Pharrell Williams for their infringement of Gaye's "Got to Give It Up" prove that a copyright system invested in Euro-American concepts of creatorship and offering people of color little more than tools that pit them against one another does not produce racial justice but merely serves to "shore up protection for *whiteness* itself."[80]

Much of Vats's reasoning, along with the interventions of other copyright scholars framed in the tenets of critical race theory, resonates with the emphasis in subsequent chapters of this book on South Africa's three-decades-long efforts to refashion copyright in more racially equitable ways and, importantly, how this broader antiracist thrust frequently founders on the persistence of old racial divides and reproduces the very colonial and Western-modernist categories it seeks to deconstruct. Yet at the same time, the concept of racial scripts as deployed by Vats is difficult to reconcile with the idea at the heart of an anthropology in law that the making of specific legal, social, cultural, and economic worlds is always embedded in multiple forms of agency. In critical race theory, it seems, agency only resides in the script. What is more, critical race theory not only disavows individual agency—say Owen Dean's fight against Disney—as inconsistent with more organized antiracist practices, it considers effective reform of intellectual property law from within futile from the outset, even where it periodically benefits people of color, "because it is too deeply intertwined with racism and racial capitalism to be redeemable."[81] On that logic, and mapping the argument on South African postapartheid justice, the only conclusion possible is that what little progress, if any, may have been made in isolated instances such as the "Mbube" case only serves to entrench the copyright system's invisible racial bias even further by giving it the appearance of race neutrality.

Vats's concept of copyright, then, has a certain jack-in-the-box quality to it; once opened, all it reveals is copyright law's irreversible racial bias or script. But in contrast to law's instrumentalist logic, Vats and other critical race scholars are not satisfied with simply fixing a broken system. Because copyright law is fundamentally unsuited for shaping the future of creativity along more racially equitable lines, it should be replaced by a different decolonial or fugitive logic. Looked at more closely, this argument does not imply the total rejection of inclusion or recognition, though. Fugitivity, Vats argues, is "metaphorical shorthand for the need for constant vigilance about the underlying racial investments of the state and publics as well as an epistemological break with the seductive forces of law, even when they seem appealing."[82] Thus, in the final analysis, as Vats grapples with delineating a "space for committing to continuing antiracist and anticolonial struggle," the reader is none the wiser as to what concrete forms of agency, creative practice, and subject positions might emerge from within this space. From an anthropological perspective, agency—whether destructive, as in Vats's racial script, or fugitive—is never monocausal but always relational. For that reason, there are also no spaces of agency that are either entirely destructive or constructive. To tell stories about agency means to linger in the zones of indeterminacy and intersection between competing and even antithetical, irreconcilable agencies. Just as a racially scripted set of legal norms can produce remedial and transformative outcomes, fugitivity is not always bliss. In this sense, as part of this book's gesture toward an anthropology in which neither law nor any other form of knowledge production can assume the existence of an object prior to the inquiry, the final section of this chapter will return to where the story began: my visit to Khanyile Street, to Elizabeth Ntsele's jeremiad, and what it might tell us about law, morality, and missed opportunities for carving out spaces of antiracist agency.

The Moral of the Story

"It is the merit of the common law that it decides the case first and determines the principle afterwards." Thus wrote legendary Justice Oliver Wendell Holmes Jr., one of the pioneers of philosophical pragmatism and legal realism in 1870.[83] What he meant by "principle" is ideas such as justice, equality, fairness, or righteousness. These, Holmes and other pragmatists, such as John Dewey, held, are mere effects of procedure. A just outcome is right not because it was derived from unalterable principles but because it was reached by following legal process.

Elizabeth is unlikely to ever have heard of the learned judge. But the consequentialist notion that just procedure automatically leads to justice, surely, would strike her as absurd. "We don't know the name of the trust fund," she had said. "We don't know the amount of the money we got from Mr. Disney. Even now we don't know." How can there be justice, she seemed to imply, when you don't even know the remedy for the wrong you suffered? How is one supposed to have confidence in the justice system when you have never met most of those who administer justice before? In other words, for her, justice works the other way around: it is moral norms that must guide legal process. By contrast, Owen Dean might concur with Holmes's dictum. In his eyes, the principles—justice for Solomon Linda's heirs, fairness, or racial equality—had been reached by following legal procedure indeed. Beyond a "landmark piece of litigation" whose outcome exceeded his wildest dreams, the settlement ensured, in "true fairy tale fashion," that the sisters "ought to live happily ever after."[84] So what caused this disconnect between Elizabeth's unhappiness and Dean's confidence that justice had been served? Instead of rejoicing in the financial amends or at least savoring Disney's recognition of the moral harm that had been inflicted on their father and past generations of South African composers like him, why do the sisters still feel used? What exactly were the gains they expected and did not reap? Or is it about something else altogether, and Elizabeth was simply trying to lead this naïve mlungu [white person] down the garden path?

It is only subsequent to my 2013 visit with the sisters that I learned about the war of words that had broken out almost immediately after the first deposits showed on the sisters' bank statements; a war in which Elizabeth had found a receptive ear for her grievances in the tabloids and that continued as late as 2019 when Disney released a remake of *The Lion King*. In essence, those grievances boiled down to two points. The first is that the trust fund that had been set up was misappropriated by Spoor & Fisher, Dean personally, the executor, and the trustees. The second claim was that the lawyers involved in the case had charged excessive legal fees. Both claims were rejected by Dean. Not only was there no foundation whatsoever to the daughters' claim of misappropriation, but also the suggestion that the lawyers, who "went out on a limb for the family" by launching the litigation without funding, should have waived their fees was unreasonable.[85] But then, there was also the secrecy the proceedings were shrouded in; the fact that the plaintiff was not the daughters but Stephanus Griesel; that the trustees were selected from a group of people, some of whom the daughters had never met; that the settlement amount was never disclosed; or, that in a move that can only be called cynical, the trustees reassigned the reverted copyright to Gallo—that is, the same publisher whose shameful treatment of Solomon Linda will forever be indelibly etched into the annals of the South African music industry.[86] To be sure, it does make perfect sense that the copyright in "Mbube" revert to the executor of the estate and not the daughters. After all, it was the law. And it also made sense in view of the complications created by the 1983 and 1992 assignments. For had the copyright devolved on the daughters, it would have immediately triggered the transfer to Folkways. Likewise, from a business perspective, even the nondisclosure agreement may be understandable to an extent, given the likelihood of others jumping on the bandwagon and taking similar action.[87] And finally, much the same might be said about the role of Gallo in the postsettlement phase. Although Gallo and Dean looked back on a long, if at times strained relationship, as evinced, for instance, by the former's decision to backtrack from its initial offer of funding the case because of a potential conflict of interest with Johnnic as a shareholder of codefendant's Nu-Metro cinema chain, chances of getting another publisher to administer the rights to "Mbube" for a mere six years must have been slim.

All of this, the inscrutability and detachment of the world of law and the dealing and wheeling of the music industry, was clearly beyond the daughters' grasp. What they are aware of, however, is how these alien worlds impinge on their daily lives in subtle and, just as frequently, in not-so-subtle ways that manifest in closed doors, withheld wages, unkept promises, or lectures on how discipline and hard work alone guarantee a better life. One way to unpack this confusion of hurt feelings, misgivings, accusations, and counter-accusations, therefore, is to see it as emblematic of the long history of efforts by well-meaning white liberals to seek justice for underserved black communities and how these efforts frequently founder on hugely diverging concepts of moral order, economic well-being, and legality held by such communities. At the same time, they reveal how contexts of extreme inequality, violence, and oppression have the potential to generate expectations and interpretations of events as banal as a string of contractual agreements, millennial expectations of a multimillion-dollar bonanza, or historic as a legal fight won against one of the world's largest media conglomerates that cannot be more discordant, eccentric, or just plain fictitious. Consequently, the ongoing drama raises larger questions about the discursive and moral hegemony in judging South Africa's success (or lack thereof) in overcoming the injustices of the past. But as a corollary of the attention to discourse, an ethnography of the sort attempted in this book must also provide a sense of how the back and forth of allegations, press releases, or, for that matter, grievances aired to a passing anthropologist might add up to something larger, no matter how legally sound, self-righteous, incoherent or manifestly untrue they may be otherwise; something that is as much traceable in the rhetorical and behavioral minutiae of the postsettlement fracas as it is interwoven with the structural, semiotic, and material coordinates of postapartheid politics. This approach, then, is not about what in an older type of anthropology used to be called "structures of signification." Nor do I suggest that we should simply be reading social and cultural practices, such as suing people who have used your music without your permission or lying, as texts. What I am interested in is more what Clifford Geertz called the "informal logic of actual life"—the combination of parameters that must be in place to produce a certain structure of feeling; a shared sense of, if not of justice, rightness in situations where even a modicum of unanimity about things such as an obscure provision in a long-forgotten statute, powerful actors in the global cultural industry, and the life-world of a family of South African township residents seems almost impossible.[88] And as a corollary of such a logic, I wish to attend to the way those parameters must be continually monitored and recombined in much the same manner a set of Lego bricks of various shapes, colors, sizes, and types are combined to build a house, castle, or tower that does not collapse at the first gust.

The Legos metaphor—which I borrow from Latour—may appear trivial.[89] But as I argue, it prevents us from reducing the congeries of lawyers, statutes, unscrupulous publishers, narratives, and moral norms to a zero-sum game in which the gains and losses of one side are balanced by those of the other side; where, in other words, the fluctuating relationships between the legal and the social or the legal and the moral have already settled into a stasis where each side becomes a domain onto its own. And so, imagine a series of Legos bricks, one labeled legal or LAW brick, another named cultural or CUL brick, and still others bearing the inscription MOR (moral) or ECO (economic). The LAW brick might be a will, an affidavit, a statute, a trial, and so on. The CUL type of brick might comprise things like racial categories or citizenship. The MOR brick, for its part, includes a set of religious practices or assumptions about the nature of equality. Next, picture some kind of building or structure made from these differently shaped, differently colored bricks. Depending on the category and number of bricks, the building will either be identified as a legal, cultural, or moral one, however heterogeneous the bricks themselves are. But this identity does not tell us much about the stability of the structure, which depends on the specific nature of the attachments among its constituent parts.

The question thus facing the anthropologist wanting to disentangle the postsettlement imbroglio is not how legally sound Dean's reasoning or brilliant his litigation strategy was. Nor is it the anthropologist's role to ascertain how righteous or coherent the indignation and various declarations of the Ntsele sisters are—after all, as Geertz remarked apropos another rigamarole elsewhere on the continent about theft, compensation, and the law, "There is nothing so coherent as a paranoid's delusion or a swindler's story."[90] It is what happens to an assembly of different bricks that is constantly changing its contours as the bricks are rearranged, added, or removed. Will the structure collapse, leaving a gaping hole between a cluster of LAW and MOR bricks? What if a missing CUL brick was suddenly replaced by a completely different one, such as a politics (POL) brick? Will the lifetime of the building be prolonged? As every six-year-old and every bricklayer knows, the bond that ties the bricks together is key to the overall statics of a wall or structure. Or, to put it in more abstract terms, again paraphrasing Latour, the legal or the moral "is not the name of any one link in a chain, nor even that of the chain, but it is that of the chaining itself."[91]

To get a better sense of this chaining, we might begin with what I called the ECO brick and take a closer look at the monies that supposedly never materialized and the allegedly exorbitant legal fees. As mentioned above, one of the terms of the settlement agreement was that a trust fund—later dubbed the Solomon Linda Trust Fund—be established and administered by the sister's family lawyer, Hanro Friedrich; the executor of Linda's Estate, S. Griesel; general and financial manager at Spoor & Fisher, Glen Dean (no relation with Owen Dean), and Nick Motsatse, the newly appointed CEO of the collecting society Southern African Music Rights Organization (SAMRO). According to the deed of trust, these individuals were given the "widest possible powers and authority" "firstly to pay the costs and expenses of the TRUST and its administration, including TRUSTEES' remuneration and income tax." In addition, the trustees were empowered to "pay so much, if any, of the net income of the TRUST to one or more or all of the persons named hereunder ("the INCOME BENEFICIARIES") as the TRUSTEES in their discretion may deem reasonable or desirable from time to time, in supplementation of their own incomes, if any, should it be necessary . . . to maintain themselves, as also any persons legally dependent on them, or any of them, at a reasonable standard of living within the discretion of the TRUSTEES."[92]

"Reasonable standard of living." The phrase warrants close scrutiny. Unfortunately, accurate figures documenting the flow of money between 2006 and 2012 are hard to come by. However, according to information leaked to the press, correspondence among the various parties involved, a large (albeit incomplete) collection of bank and royalty statements, and, especially, the 2008 liquidation and distribution accounts in the estates of Solomon Linda and Regina Ntsele, several scenarios are conceivable. (All amounts are in US dollars using average exchange rates for 2008.)[93] According to the latter, the two accounts combined contained cash and assets worth c. $603,000—ca. $580,000 in Solomon's and ca. $140,000 in Regina's. Of the former, some $457,000 came from damages paid by the main defendants Disney and Abilene Music and codefendants David Gresham Entertainment, David Gresham Records, and Nu Metro Home Entertainment. Twenty-three thousand dollars was paid by Abilene as a result of an earlier US arbitration award, and ca. $127,000 was paid by the Department of Arts and Culture in support of the legal action. The liabilities, apart from various estate duties, administration costs, and executor's fees, amounted to ca. $358,000, a staggering $345,000 of which alone were attorney's fees—$240,000 for Spoor & Fisher and the experts and advocates they engaged, and $105,000 for Hanro Friedrich Attorneys.[94] Elsewhere the legal costs are given as ca. $233,000. Either way, the daughters' net income from the trust during the initial two years from 2006 to 2008 amounted to somewhere between $245,000 and $370,000. Not factored into this calculation are the proceeds from Disney's and Abilene's offer to add an additional five years of royalties, extending the period to 2017, as well as royalties from sundry uses after 2008 totaling $30,000.[95] By contrast, a far more favorable accounting is offered by Cullman, who estimates that each of the daughters had received up to $250,000 over the life of the settlement deal until 2013.

Whichever calculation one goes by, these figures hardly lend credence to Dean's theory of a happy ending, though, where the Linda daughters "will be able to sustain themselves economically into the future."[96] To be sure, they had refurbished their existing homes or, in Elizabeth's case, purchased a new house in Protea North, one of the slightly more upscale neighborhoods of Soweto. But the likelihood that three middle-aged, black women in poor health, only one of which was in regular employment, would be able to live for another twenty-plus years on whatever was left of the income after 2012 seems remote. Conversely, though, Elizabeth's rant does not quite render the whole picture either, as it conveniently papers over the cracks in the carefully crafted image of the victims cheated out of what was theirs all over again, such as the fact that a bar Fildah had bought at the cost of R 1 million had gone bankrupt; that relations with the trustees had deteriorated to the point where all of them resigned from their positions; or that Disney and Abilene had offered to extend royalty payments for another five years beyond 2012.[97] Using the Legos metaphor one more time, it thus stands to reason that the ECO bricks Dean and the sisters marshaled to prop up their diverging moral edifices failed to provide lasting stability to a project that from the start was rife with misconceptions, false starts, and inflated expectations from the outset but that also brought before our eyes the contours of a future transformative copyright regime in which legal procedure and principles might form a more perfect union after all.

And thus, despite all the hyperbole, half-truths, misjudgments, and rancor, as an anthropologist, I suspend final judgment. I hesitate to dismiss the possibility entirely that there is something more to the laments, insinuations, and self-serving rhetoric according to which the daughters "love money more than tradition" that makes them legible as cultural form, beyond the merely idiosyncratic and judgmental.[98] In closing, I instead want to argue that the disconnect between legal reason and moral imperatives—white or black—mirrors the way South Africans grapple with the injustices of the past and the uncertainties wrought by their stubborn continuity in the present. The inability of either Dean or the sisters to string together from disparate elements (or bricks of Legos if you prefer) a compelling and universally accepted narrative about right and wrong is owed to the persistence of old divides. The postsettlement moral reckoning pursued by both sides not only entails different memories, traditions, and rhetorical registers, its ability to achieve discursive hegemony, too, is not the same for the Ntseles as it is for Malan, Dean, and Disney. The aftermath of the settlement is a prime example of the state of the postapartheid politics of reconciliation that, after initial moments of rainbow pluralism, quickly deteriorated into a stasis of ostensibly irreconcilable visions of moral order, sharply contrasting notions of justice, and, of course, vastly unequal living conditions and capabilities to overcome them. In contradistinction to the aspirational tone that continues to reverberate through the postcolonial copyright sphere, the story of the lion that awakens from its slumber did not rekindle a politics that instead of insisting on the integrity of legal process and moral absolutes as the measure of all things finds points of contact and mutual recognition as sources of a different, stronger, and more equitable system of copyright protections than the one in place since the dawn of colonialism.

If more recent developments both in the legal arena and popular culture offer any indication of the persistence of the past in the present, one need look no further than two seemingly unrelated sequels to the Mbube drama: the hotly contested Copyright Amendment Bill and Cullman's documentary film *The Lion's Share*. The former, directly inspired by the Mbube case and following a recommendation by the 2011 Copyright Review Commission, in s 23 provides that "assignment of copyright in a literary or musical work shall only be valid for a period of up to 25 years from the date of such assignment." In a generous reading, the provision may be said to reflect sincerely held concerns about the competitiveness of authors working on the margins of the industry and their capacity more generally to profit from an unexpected renaissance of their works twenty-five years later. But similar to critical interventions on the subject of termination rights elsewhere on the African continent, it can also be read as a gesture of appeasement; an attempt at neutralizing the wide-spread resentment of the music industry by contrasting the "author-centric deontology and economic consequentialism" at the heart of the star system with a concept of "creative autonomy" rooted in "talent."[99] More problematically still, the provision might also place undue limits on parties' freedom to contract, thus undermining the very liberal foundations large sections of which the bill also rests on.

Cullman's *The Lion's Share*, on the other hand, is not troubled by such jurisprudential niceties. Instead, the film takes the viewer back to where the whole saga began, plunging headlong into the postsettlement moral quandaries of—Rian Malan.[100] Much like in François Verster's *A Lion's Trail* before it, here too the real story being told is about Malan. It is Malan who frames the sequence of events from its early beginnings to 2018 as though it was his autobiography, interspersed with cameo appearances by Owen Dean, Glen Dean, Hanro Friedrich, Geoff Paynter, Paul Jenkins, Nick Motsatse, and Rob Allingham. And it is Malan who sets the tone right from the beginning. "I love blacks and I feared them," he says. "But I was a coward. . . . I let them [the sisters] down." "Above all I want absolution from the sins of my forefathers and I want to be loved, okay." As for those allegedly let down, as usual, they only have their say toward the end, reiterating their allegations of misappropriation and hurt feelings about having been treated like children. The final word, however, is again Malan's, who bookends his self-flagellation and bouts of white guilt with a piece of analytical insight of the kind even a passing visitor might come up with. "Given our history in South Africa it's possibly inevitable that it actually ended this way. I mean, the fact of the matter is that South Africa is a country where people of various races don't know each other very well, don't trust each other, and where almost any dispute is inclined to become immediately racialized."

Sometimes the past is the present.

THREE

Assembling Tradition, Representing Indigeneity
The Making of the Intellectual Property Laws Amendment
Act 28 of 2013

Cape Town, February 16, 2010. The suffocating heat of the summer has subsided; only a few clouds are visible in the sky, and a gentle breeze is blowing from the direction where majestic Table Mountain overlooks South Africa's legislative capital. In the Houses of Parliament, a sprawling complex at the southern edge of the old city center, the National Assembly is gearing up for the first term of the 2010 legislative period. Members check-in at the entrance; the flag of the new South Africa flaps gently in the wind; the smell of curry, beer, and coffee wafts in from the takeaway cafes nearby; and the homeless who have spent the night on the park benches along the fence surrounding the area gather their modest belongings before being whisked out of sight by police.

Is this the beating heart of a thriving constitutional democracy, the visitor muses? The temple of the rainbow nation, the people's Parliament, where the rule of law triumphs over the law of the jungle? Or is parliamentary democracy just the continuation of settler colonialism with a new livery—a masquerade obscuring the continued structural violence of racial capitalism underneath a rhetorical veneer of human rights, constitutionalism, multipartyism, and equitable development? And who and what does this parliament represent, anyway? The interests of the powerful? Or the legions of unskilled, unemployed, unauthorized South Africans—the un-people?

Part of the answers to these questions may be found just steps away, in a building further down from the Parliament on the corner of Government Avenue and Adderley Street. Long known as the Slaven Loge or Old Slave

Lodge—and now renovated as a museum named the Iziko Slave Lodge—it is here that the slaves held by the Dutch East India Company were locked up at night and where, subsequently, the British Legislative Council of the Cape laid the foundations of a very different, though no less brutal, order of representation. One of the first and most notorious of the body's many ordinances is the so-called Hottentot Proclamation of 1809, aimed at controlling the mobility of the indigenous labor force, collectively referred to by the derogatory term *Hottentot*. Under the guise of a contractually agreed upon period of "apprenticeship," the decree required that these individuals should have a fixed "place of abode" and carry a pass whenever they left their master's farms. Adjacent to the Slave Lodge and right behind the Houses of Parliament is a park that likewise bears vivid testimony to the country's tumultuous history. Commonly referred to as the Company Gardens, it was a farm in the 1650s that provided the ships of the Dutch East India Company voc with produce and fresh water. By the time Britain took control of the Cape in 1806, the area had developed into a botanical preserve for the scientific study of indigenous species and an urban playground for the colonial elite—a metaphor of good governance and a metonymy of the laws of nature and the laws of humankind.[1] In the new South Africa, the Gardens serve as a tourist attraction and national heritage site featuring statues of colonial figures like Cape Governor George Grey and mining magnate and imperialist Cecil Rhodes gesturing northwards: "Your hinterland is there."

Compressed into an area of fewer than twelve acres, the Gardens are an extraordinary illustration of the intersection of global trade, colonial domination, science, and British culture over three centuries of South African history. But equally significant, the Slave Lodge and the Gardens serve as tangible reminders of the making and unmaking of both indigenous and nonindigenous identities—from the natural order of chattel slaves to colonial subjects; from the forcibly subdued to the emancipated, yet second-class, so-called native to the free, self-regulating individual of the new South Africa; from the slaveholder to the colonial administrator to the democratically elected politician. It takes little more than a passing familiarity with South African history, of course, to realize that these shifts were of the utmost brutality and most radical discontinuity. However, what remains largely hidden from view are the more subliminal legal continuities from the colonial to the postcolonial era. For example, although the Hottentot Proclamation was repealed in 1828 when British settlers in the Cape experienced a significant shortage of free labor, the effects of the decree are still felt today. From the Master and Servants Act 15 of 1856 and the Native

Lands Act to the Black Administration Act and the apartheid-era Group Areas Act 41 of 1950 to present-day municipal vagrancy ordinances, being indigenous was and still is, in part, synonymous with reduced mobility, insecurity of land tenure, and insufficient legal protection of both tangible and intangible property. In fact, as I argue in this chapter, it is the legacy of these restrictions that produced and continues to reproduce the indigenous as a category of difference and exclusion.

To understand this, we must retrace our steps and return to the Houses of Parliament. But it is not to attend solemn state-of-the-nation addresses or listen to rousing speeches about state capture or land reform in the New Assembly Hall (destroyed by fire in January 2022), built to accommodate the tricameral Parliament created by the apartheid regime in a last-ditch effort to shore up its rule. Rather, we will be frequent visitors to a less eye-catching part of the complex: Room E249, to be precise. Like the assembly hall, E249 features warm wood panels, colorful intarsia that matches the striped tan carpets, and two blocks of green leather benches facing each other, like in the British Houses of Parliament. As such, it is one of several rooms where portfolio and ad hoc committees are briefed on white papers, deliberate legislation (about forestry, the sugar industry, gambling, and so on), fine-tune legal definitions, and hold public hearings or question government officials. But on February 16, 2010, the Portfolio Committee on Trade and Industry is holding its first meeting on the Intellectual Property Laws Amendment Act. The making of this act is the subject of this chapter.[2]

Engine Rooms of Parliament?

MPs proudly refer to committees as the engine rooms of Parliament. The nuts-and-bolts association of the phrase reflects a long history of political thought in which the image of a well-oiled government machine served to rationalize a sociopolitical order marked by full-blown relations of capitalist-industrial production and deep divisions of class, race, and gender.[3] And while it may contrast sharply with the often carnivalesque atmosphere of the assembly and its perennial points of order and danses macabres by Economic Freedom Fighters MPs donning the aprons and hard hats of South Africa's underclass of maids and construction workers, in the era of industry 4.0, the machine metaphor seems oddly out of place. At the same time, however, the broader idea that technology provides the model for political intervention is alive and well, forcing us to realign our thinking about the space of the political at a time when that space is no longer delineated by the nation-state and its institutions but by global networks, partial spheres, and the technologies articulating and circulating through them.[4] Alas, emerging work in the ethnography of legislative or other public rule-making bodies offers scant guidance here.[5] For although richly detailed, some of these works are beholden to an anthropological tradition of critiquing the familiar and the taken-for-granted of the Western political imagination by defamiliarizing it as distant and inscrutably idiosyncratic. The deference owed to peers in the British House of Lords, for instance, reminds Emma Crewe of the "Hindu caste system, with clerks holding the sacred priestly knowledge and peers seen as warriors."[6] In like fashion, and despite cautioning against contrasting law's unique epistemology with that of science or politics by setting its peculiarities "against an unquestionable background, like masks from diverse origins on the white wall of a primitive art museum," Bruno Latour cannot help casting himself in the role of the "naïve" observer, "entirely ignorant of legal method," and hampered by "incomprehension."[7] More problematic yet, the object and very raison d'être of these institutions—law itself—hardly ever come under scrutiny. Lawmakers are largely depicted as operating within structures and networks always already constituted as political, independent of the legislative process.

There is, however, one aspect of the parts-and-labor image of parliamentary committees that might be salvageable for this chapter. It might draw attention to the almost artisanal character of lawmaking by breaking away from both the old, yet remarkably persistent, Marxian view of the state as the "committee for managing the common affairs of the whole bourgeoisie" or the mythology of the seamless, just-in-time world of policymaking in the third machine age.[8] The work of the portfolio committee described in this chapter is both a tightly structured mechanism translating a messy world of collective identities and claims of belonging into the cold language of the law and a leaky, high-maintenance, potentially dysfunctional, and, yet, remarkably malleable and absorbent assemblage capable of accommodating cultural difference and idiosyncrasy. It is this more realistic image of the making of the Intellectual Property Laws Amendment Act that forms the starting point of the argument I pursue in the pages that follow.

Over the past several decades, the world has witnessed the slow but steady consolidation of indigenous knowledge as a new subject matter of either intellectual property or sui generis rights. Here, I seek to disrupt the prevailing narrative that indigenous knowledge represents something of a new frontier and that the law, in mapping this terra incognita, opens a conceptual and governable space where indigenous knowledge and intellectual property law figure as two regimes of truth—two stories, neither of which can be told without evoking the other in the same breath. In contradistinction to this voluntarist interpretation of legal rationality but also against classical theories of the public sphere and communicative action a la Habermas and Rawls, it is the routine, humdrum nature and the decidedly unexotic, low-key dimensions of committee work that allow us to better interrogate law's blind instrumentalism. It is by attending to forms and processes rather than presumed essences, institutionally dispersed power instead of individual agency, technical minutiae before grand political visions, and contingency instead of normativity that the logic and logistics of lawmaking become visible and that the coupling of indigenous knowledge and intellectual property law is grasped as part of a process in which various forms of indigenous subjectivity and objects of knowledge are not a priori given but the result of the qualities, capacities, and knowledges attributed to or claimed by various actors entangled in complex constellations of political power, scientific knowledge, and legal technicalities. The assemblage of minutes, protocols, and PowerPoint presentations that will hopefully emerge from this type of ethnographic inquiry may more faithfully reflect the promise and challenges of liberal governance in a postcolony as diverse and divided as South Africa than a mask on a white wall.

Drawing on the substantial body of documents and audio recordings generated by the committee during this period and based on several visits to its meetings and interviews with experts and other commentators, I narrate the work of the committee in chronological order, dividing the three-year process from the introduction of the bill in 2010 to its adoption by the National Assembly in 2013 into three phases. After an initial period of about half a year, during which the focus was on the government's IP policy, the committee engaged in intense deliberation and hosted public hearings and workshops over more than a year. The process ended with a relatively brief wrap-up phase of redrafting and fine-tuning definitions. The goal of this linear structure is less to impute a temporal logic to the evolution of the act than to allow the concatenation of legal technicalities and technologies of lawmaking to come to the fore in all their nuance and subtlety, thus forwarding an ethnographically informed theory of legislative practice in the context of the sticky encounter between the clean-cut world of policy and the messy reality of democratic-representative politics and indigenous cultural reproduction.

The bill was drafted by Esmé du Plessis, a patent attorney and partner at Adams & Adams, one of the leading IP law firms on the African continent and a longtime member of the Standing Advisory Committee on Intellectual Property to the Minister of Trade and Industry. It was subsequently redrafted by MacDonald Netshitenzhe, director of commercial law and policy, in the same department. Alternately hailed as pioneering and denounced as unworkable, the act in its current form inserts a host of novel provisions into the country's existing Performers' Protection Amendment Act, Trade Marks Act 94 of 1993, Designs Act 195 of 1993, and, most extensively, the Copyright Act. Key to this endeavor and in keeping with the broader theme of this book, this chapter emphasizes two fundamental amendments in the scope of copyright protection and authors' rights. One is that protection subsists in various traditional, indigenous, derivative indigenous, and indigenous cultural terms or expressions; the second is on authors' rights being vested in the indigenous community.

I use the terms *assemblage*, *representation*, and *indigeneity* to highlight the parallels, ruptures, and slippages among legal, political, and anthropological forms of knowledge and the authority they afford legal experts, politicians, or for that matter, anthropologists to speak for and/or about indigenous people. A term such as *indigenous community*, therefore, describes less an existing social or cultural reality than a project of discursive bricolage. Excavated from the rubble of a ruinous history and combining the most disparate and unlikely of cultural and natural elements, and circulating these elements through a range of technologies of representation, including law, the rules of parliamentary procedure, and expert knowledge, the term reflects diverging epistemologies and serves different material interests. It allows the portfolio committee to constitute and legitimize itself as the representation of the indigenous body politic even where the views of the oldest and most vulnerable indigenous population, the San—descendants of the country's first inhabitants of over 150,000 years—are not taken into account. For the copyright expert, on the other hand, the indigenous community is little more than an anomaly flying in the face of some of the core tenets of the liberal imagination, such as the rights-bearing, private-property-holding individual. Finally, the indigenous community presents a dilemma for the anthropologist. On the one hand, they may be wary of the idea as a painful reminder of anthropology's history of complicity with colonial models of social being around which indigenous people were summoned to assemble in ways that, precisely, negated indigenous views of what is in-born. But on the other hand, they may consider a commitment to indigenous people seeking redress for abuses of their traditional knowledge practices by refashioning themselves in terms of the politics of recognition as essential to what it means to be an anthropologist.

The complexity and imponderability of this construct will preoccupy us throughout this chapter. But before we take our seats in E249, a word about its valences in current political philosophy, cultural studies, and anthropology is in order. In the former, it appears, the idealization in classical sociology of gemeinschaft as the counterproject or the sublimation of the modern gesellschaft deemed to have gone astray is experiencing something of a revival. Yet, this resurgence of the communal and its manifestation in what Andreas Reckwitz calls the "hyperculture and cultural essentialism" of late modernity is less surprising than it may seem.[9] The combined effects of globalization and deregulation alongside the retreat of the welfare state in the advanced economies of the North did not, as many commentators hoped, herald the triumph of democracy, human rights, and multicultural tolerance but quite the opposite. Over the past twenty to thirty years, everywhere, from the US and the EU to Japan, has witnessed the resurgence of varied forms of nationalism and rising levels of racist, anti-Semitic, and Islamophobic violence and, in parallel with it, a revival of the idea of community as a vehicle for reconstructing shattered subjectivities in the twenty-first century in both popular and academic discourse.

In the broadest sense, those discourses insist on community as the ontologically primary locus of social and cultural reproduction. Within anthropology, in particular, this mediating function of community also helped to ground the ethnographic enterprise itself, often by imputing a homology of identity and place even where such equivalence is being torn asunder by globalization. Does the rhetoric of community, then, serve as a convenient remedial discourse distracting from the havoc being wreaked on polities small and large by the deterritorializing effects of global markets by inserting a softer, "resonant" sociality between the locally embedded individual of earlier times and the larger political and economic systems of the current moment?[10] Should we think of community more as a form of ad-hoc polity entangling our increasingly peripatetic lives in all-encompassing commodity relations and "societies of singularities," or more bleakly, circumstances of "bare life," and "necropolitics?"[11] And as a means to attribute cohesion and connection, especially in those historical and contemporary settings of large-scale (forced) dislocation, migration, multiple residential locations, and fluctuating workplaces, might this rhetoric be little more than a device for enlisting a wide variety of interests and causes in projects of decidedly uncertain communal import?

In South Africa—and perhaps other relatively stable liberal democracies such as India or Indonesia—the relationship between "community" and other kinds of belonging, like formal citizenship made available through far-reaching constitutional guarantees and progressive policy prescriptions, appears to be similarly, if not more, unpredictable. Here, ideas of social organization rooted in primordial collectivities have been inscribed in the country's DNA from the beginning, making it a prime example of the Janus-faced character of "community" discourse, utterly out of place in some contexts, including the Intellectual Property Laws Amendment Act, and productive in others that transcend barriers of race, class, or ethnicity. One example of this ambiguity is the long shadow the revisionist, neo-Marxist historiography and political economy of the 1980s and 1990s continues to cast on current debates about the way out of the social and economic quagmire the country has found itself in from the early 2000s. Having critically rejected apartheid ideology and having been locked in fierce (and frequently rancorous) competition with liberal constructions of South Africa, this school of thought—to which my earlier work is indebted—had made class the single most important category of social analysis.[12] But somewhat more fluid forms of social relationships clustering around racial, ethnic, and other communities defined by shared cultural experiences and practices never disappeared altogether. If no longer dismissed as false consciousness, as in orthodox Marxism, they are sublated, in true Hegelian fashion, in a dialectic of class and race.

Much of this scholarship, like the memory of South Africa's past it so magisterially charted, by now has sedimented into the country's cultural archive. But its telos—a more united South Africa providing justice and opportunity for all—is alive and well, finding expression in community as one of its rallying points. To be sure, significant aspects of the current political and legal order continue to be shaped by various inflections of ethnic or nationalist sectarianism and strong affective bonds to custom and cultural identity that may sporadically erupt into violence barely tempered by a precarious or, as some would argue, developing balance of constitutionally guaranteed rights, minority rights, and customary law.[13] At the same time, because of the rapidly progressing deindustrialization of the country, along with the decline of class-based forms of association following in their wake, invocations of community have increasingly come to comprise a diffuse mix of highly ephemeral personal relationships and groupings—as clouds of warm sociality or shared taste, as heavily fortified suburban neighborhoods, or as social movements coalescing around whatever issue du jour ignites their reformist passions. Between them, however, all these aggregations—or better, perhaps, disaggregations—of the social cast doubt on the viability of community as both an analytical concept for the postcolony, let alone a legal category for determining authorship.[14]

To give a concrete illustration of what I mean by this lack of viability, and before we examine the legislative process in considerable detail, I would like to take the reader on a brief excursion to a place far removed from the august halls of Parliament, one in which the idea of a community has been and still is being held to be a major factor of social and cultural reproduction: the *platteland*, the rural hinterland of South Africa. Generations of anthropologists have told us that in these parts—and to a lesser extent, in the urban environment—strong networks of moral obligations governing relations of reciprocity, patronage, and respectability have served as "social capital" offering resources to aggrieved individuals or groups seeking cooperation or making claims against other members of the network in order to mitigate the effects of poverty.[15]

A generous reading of the act might concede that it is itself a form of social capital; a collective resource offering legal protection to social protection as it were; or to put it in Robert Putnam's canonic definition, "features of social life—networks, norms and trust—that enable participants to act together more effectively to pursue shared objectives."[16] But on closer inspection, it appears that there may also be a "dark side" to social capital, as du Toit and Neves show in their study of the role of social protection at the margins of the "formal" economy.[17] While, in theory, social capital not only depends on networks of reciprocity but also helps to create those networks in the first place, the outcome is not necessarily an equal one. On the contrary, there is mounting evidence that these networks are, if not breaking down completely, progressively coming under pressure due to multiple external factors and also as a result of internal social differentiation caused in no small part by rapidly evolving intrahousehold gender and intergenerational relationships.[18]

On balance, then, the idea of an indigenous community that is rooted in and sustains equitable relationships and a sense of shared ownership of a set of traditional resources and practices, and its corollary in the hoped-for benefits accruing from their integration into the economic mainstream, appears to be more wishful thinking on the part of lawmakers than it is based on solid empirical evidence. And so, it is against this hypostatization of supposedly self-evident categories, such as the "indigenous community," that I reposition indigeneity as a fragile assemblage of twenty-first-century strategies, material practices, and rhetorical tropes that indexes as it enacts a politics of belonging that enables indigenous people to form various kinds of attachment to place, time, and expressive practices. The core question of this politics is twofold. How does the rhetoric of indigeneity enable the liberal-democratic state to channel claims for recognition and inclusion advanced by the country's most underserved populations, such as the San, into a vision of a postrestorative, postreconstruction South Africa that increasingly prioritizes the alliance of the rule of law and the laws of the market over the pursuit of social and cultural justice? Related to this question is the set of concerns at the heart of this book's methodological theme—the critique of legal instrumentalism. What if, instead of seeing the act as ill-conceived—in other words, by arguing in familiar instrumentalist fashion from the output end of the instrumentalist logic where the end justifies the means—we start from the beginning, from the input side? How might certain, usually unspoken, a priori that may lie buried in the concept of indigenous communities and the knowledge over which they seek jurisdiction serve as podiums for legal claims not just about that knowledge itself but, more importantly, also about law's interpretational sovereignty in defining it? How do these a priori enable or constrain specific understandings of the material aspects of tradition, identity, citizenship, or even land tenure? And how might the objects of such claims, in turn, react back on some of those a priori of legal knowledge in ways that might upset such sovereignty?

The Returns of Policy

Empirical inquiry into the workings of the postcolonial state in Africa, Jean-François Bayart reminds us in his pioneering *The State in Africa*, "passes through a narrow door."[19] My door, or rather the first of several doors I invite the reader to pass through in this chapter, is policy. Having settled, then, into our seats, we join the committee as officials from the Department of Trade and Industry brief them about the government's decision to introduce what from now on will be referred to as the Intellectual Property Laws Amendment Bill (B8-2010). The presentation consists of four parts. With the aid of a PowerPoint presentation, the officials begin by walking the MPs through the bill's history, from its 1999 origin in the government's Policy on Indigenous Knowledge Systems (IKS) to its eventual adoption by the cabinet in 2004.[20] This is followed by a short discussion of the findings of a regulatory impact assessment, weighing the costs and benefits of the proposed legislation. In the remaining two crucial sections, the MPs are first given a rough overview of the international debates surrounding the protection of traditional knowledge through intellectual property systems—from the 1976 Tunis Model Law on Copyright to the Intergovernmental Committee on Intellectual Property and Genetic Resources, Traditional Knowledge and Folklore of WIPO established in 2000—before the presentation ends with a discussion of eight policy objectives:

> To provide a legal framework for the protection of the rights of IK holders
> Empower communities to commercialise and trade on indigenous knowledge [IK]
> To bring IK holders into the mainstream of the economy
> To improve the livelihoods of IK holders and communities
> To benefit the national economy
> To conserve the environment
> To prevent misappropriation/bio-piracy
> To prevent exploitation without recognition[21]

The reader may find all this obvious. After all, who would seriously object to the protection of indigenous communities and their knowledge? Who would put their political career at risk by denying the need to ameliorate the living conditions of the country's marginalized population? And what politician would not want to make a stand for environmental conservation? Yet, as the ensuing discussion shows, the MPs transpose the policy goals to quite a different discursive register. Rather than the international policy context or the regulatory assessment, they home in on a flurry of colorful terms that dot the slides: *tradition, respect, sustainability, misappropriation, benefit-sharing, livelihoods,* and, of course, *indigenous community.*

> Marian Shinn (Zimbabwean-born journalist and member of the opposition Democratic Alliance (DA): "How can it be determined who the originator of the indigenous knowledge was, whether this could be a person or a community?"
>
> Ndabakayise Gcwabaza (veteran of Umkhonto we Sizwe, the armed wing of the ANC): "Whilst it would be proper to acknowledge the origin of traditional music or any kind of creative work, we should not go so far as to penalize the person who had used that knowledge, precisely because in the South African Constitution we spoke about freedom of association. This suggests that, for example, Johnny Clegg was free to associate with the Zulu musical tradition, in the same way that an African poet could associate with Afrikaans poetry."[22]

Sarel Marais (businessman) (DA): "So Johnny Clegg would no longer be able to write songs anymore, but would have to refer to the community from which his songs may have originated? Suddenly I cannot do what I am anymore, because I must go to a community. Who is this community?"

Tim Harris (DA): "What about traditional music? Had the committee considered this important issue given that a lot of indigenous music went to the West where others made a fortune exploiting it commercially? Had Solomon Linda's song 'Mbube' not existed for centuries and was it therefore not an original work eligible for protection? And what is the meaning of tradition anyway? Would it not be more appropriate to talk about indigenous culture, as it succinctly captures the impact of colonial oppression?"

Yet others take the conversation into patent law and the plant kingdom, specifically addressing two of South Africa's most iconic species. Hoodia gordonii is a succulent plant that, from time immemorial, has served as the source of water, food, and energy in the country's arid northwestern region and for a short while was touted as an appetite suppressor and antiobesity drug. Rooibos is a shrub that grows only in the Cederberg region north of Cape Town and is consumed around the globe as a tea rich in antioxidants, calcium, and iron.

Bhekizizwe Radebe (ANC): "It is well known that African resources had been long exploited by the colonial powers. So whose intellectual property is rooibos?"

Alan Jeftha (member of the Standing Advisory Committee on Intellectual Property): "Unlike champagne, sherry and port, South African rooibos producers have been on the receiving end where rooibos had been registered as a trademark in the U.S.A."

Sarel Marais (DA): "Many items that the bill seeks to protect do not belong to a specific individual or group but rather to South Africa as a whole, for example, rooibos. Moreover, it grew wild."

No, another member across the aisle retorts: "It belongs to the indigenous community of San who have inhabited the region for millennia."

Clearly, the government's attempt to frame its policy objectives against a background of taken-for-granted parameters, such as economy, environment, communities, or rights, does not immediately translate into the terms through which the MPs view their world. Theirs is more a hodgepodge of moral and cultural concerns and, as democratic politics go, its valences in the unpredictable encounter with local ideas and sensibilities. But if MPs consider the moral valences of indigenous knowledge to be beyond dispute, what about its legal valences? How can the moral be made legible to the law? And how can the state, in turn, stage itself as a moral authority mediating between these sensibilities and the coldness of the law? What role do the intricacies of IP protection play within these processes? What theoretical models are available to think through the interplay of policy and parliamentary process beyond the obsession in conventional policy studies with efficiency and smart policymaking? How does one translate something as ephemeral, amorphous, and elusive as an *ihubo* war cry or a *kiba* dance into the object of rules and regulations?

In *Seeing Like a State*, James Scott describes legibility and simplification as central problems of modern statecraft. By creating a standard whereby complex local practices can be monitored and transmuted into a legible and administratively convenient format, he argues, the state is able to shape the social worlds in its care according to its agenda of "improvement." Scott identifies four conditions that account for the catastrophic failure of many such "well-intentioned" projects of social engineering—administrative simplifications that enable the reordering of society and nature; a "high-modernist" confidence in science and technology as key elements in economic growth and the mastery of nature; an authoritarian state that uses its coercive power to put this ideology into practice; and, lastly, a prostrate civil society that lacks the ability to resist this strategy.[23]

Of course, South Africa is not an authoritarian state, and civil society there is anything but docile. Nonetheless, some aspects of Scott's gloss of the developmental state as a great simplifier may fit the fixation in South African state policies on grand transformative schemes—and their frequent running aground on the quicksand of global markets, local cultural sensitivities, and rampant corruption. At the same time, however, the idea that simplification is the central mechanism of panoptic state power and that state-initiated projects of social transformation can either succeed or fail is, well, too simple. The power of the state bending social relations into a shape it considers desirable does not (at least primarily) reside in its ability to shrink the order of things down to its lowest common denominator but in quite the opposite. Agency—the power to turn heterogeneity into homogeneity, uncertainty into predictability, a multiplicity of voices into a singularity of purpose—is never inherent in any one actor alone, be it the state or an obscure policy document. It requires the intertwining of a multitude of actors in a never-ending process of aligning competing prerogatives, rationales, and moralities through what Michel Callon calls "interessement" or, roughly, in-betweenness.[24] Like all attempts at fashioning coherence by translating the terms of one domain into those of another, making creative practices such as *kiba* or *mbube* assignable to the law is not a question of how tightly such translations are structured.

This premise calls for a different style of inquiry into policy. Following the work of scholars in critical policy studies, the committee presentation might more fruitfully be viewed as a performance: a reiteration of established routines, prescriptions, and forms whose ability to "push" policy through an impossibly complex system of institutional spaces and jurisdictions is contingent on maintaining a delicate balance between the unsettling "hosting" and the stabilizing "valence" functions of these routines and forms.[25] Hence, the focus here will be on the way policymaking always revolves around itself in self-reproducing, self-serving cycles; on how success and failure, order and disorder are not diametrically opposed but coproduce one another; and how policy, much like a needle on a broken record, reproduces an unintended "sound" during each rotation.

Beyond this, the disconnect between the government's presentation and the committee's impassioned, if somewhat haphazard, reaction might also speak to a profound antinomy stemming from the nation-state's endeavor of accommodating difference within the framework of liberal governance and universal rights on the one hand and the resurgence of the local and ethnocultural on the other. The history of IP for indigenous knowledge is a case in point. In its summary of that history, the government appears to pursue two goals. First, it connects its policy to a narrative of historical continuity and renewal. The policy, the officials seem to suggest, is part of a larger reform effort at restoring the country's ties with the international system of policy diffusion largely severed during apartheid. At the same time, it underscores the postapartheid state's dual claim as the legitimate heir to the antiapartheid struggle and the driving force of IP policy innovation on the entire African continent.[26] Second, the briefing serves to garner parliamentary consent to what is ultimately a state-driven and, in part, exclusionary global system of regulation marked by significant conceptual discrepancies and sharply divided interests between the West and the Global South. But it is precisely by positioning itself as a champion of both South African indigenous property rights and the international IP system that the government gets caught in a bind. On the one hand, it must present a narrative in which cultural difference does not undercut law's claims to universality. Conversely, in foregrounding the material conditions under which indigenous knowledge and cultural expressions have historically been marginalized—conditions rooted in that very international system— the government must also take care in eschewing questions about law's complicity in facilitating those very structures of marginalization.[27] This triangulation of international law, the birth of the indigenous movement, and not least the reluctance of many, if not most, African countries to recognize indigenous minorities operates by means of a series of subtle translations through which seemingly minor semantic nuances act as powerful mediators in the emergence of a global system of indigenous intellectual property protections.[28] These translations appear to move back and forth along a continuum stretching from national interests at one end and indigenous claims at the other; from holistic to compartmentalized models of indigenous intellectual property protections; and from the objects of intellectual property to its metaphysical dimension.

The idea that some form of protection of traditional knowledge practices, either by intellectual property or sui generis legislation, might offer a solution to some countries' so-called indigenous problem has been floated since the 1950s as independence movements in Africa and Asia gathered pace. Central to this struggle for national sovereignty was a cultural strategy. To counter the calls for secession increasingly being voiced by the nascent indigenous movements within the emerging nation-states, the new governments embraced the idea that one of the most productive ways to quell these movements was to protect "folklore" by simply subsuming it into these countries' cultural heritage.[29] First debated at the 1967 Diplomatic Conference in Stockholm, the subject of folklore was subsequently incorporated into the 1976 Tunis Model Law, followed by the Convention of the African Intellectual Property Organization of 1977 and the so-called Model Provisions drafted by a working group of UNESCO and WIPO experts and attached to the Universal Copyright Convention of 1985. Looking back on this initial phase of crafting an international rights regime for the protection of indigenous intellectual property, the universally accepted view appears to be that in the nearly two decades it took to get from Stockholm to the 1985 Universal Copyright Convention, a significant step forward has been made in recognizing indigenous peoples' demands for the protection of their heritage. More specifically, the Model Provisions are credited with paving the way for a new philosophy that prioritizes sui generis approaches over conventional copyright protections increasingly deemed ineffective.

But despite these and other disparities pertaining to conventional copyright law requirements, such as duration, originality, and fixation, these early covenants share a fundamental tension among different types of entitlement. Thus, the Tunis Model Law squarely casts the state in the role of the guardian or "competent authority" that owns and is responsible for the regulation of "works of national folklore."[30] But at the same time, it provides for exceptions for noncommercial uses by a public entity. The UNESCO-WIPO Model Provisions, in contrast, while offering national legislators the option of designating a "competent authority" to administer authors' rights, vest full ownership of what by then had come to be labeled "expressions of folklore" with the "aboriginal or other traditional communities."[31] However, for all its improvements, the Model Provisions are not free from ambiguity either. They too leave unresolved the Tunis Model Law's apparent dissonance between commercial utilizations subject to authorization and uses by national or other public bodies that, although not commercial in nature and thus exempt from having to obtain the communities' permission, may still violate the sacred or secret nature of such expressions protected under other norms, such as customary law.

Further challenges to an already brittle mosaic of rules and agreements emerged in the 1990s from a rather unexpected quarter—the environmental movement. From as early as the 1970s, conservationists were instrumental in drawing attention to the erosion of the world's biodiversity. But only by arguing that the rapid expansion of patent and plant breeders' rights to genetic resources was detrimental to the developing world were environmentalists successful in finally closing ranks with Australian and North and South American indigenous movements long engaged in an analogous struggle for cultural survival and the restitution of ancestral lands. Thanks to this broad coalition of indigenism and environmentalism, rights discourses around expressions of folklore and traditional knowledge gained new momentum, ultimately leading to the all-important 1992 Convention on Biological Diversity. Although the convention focuses on patent rights, it also binds member states to respect the traditional knowledge of indigenous and local communities, obtain the consent of those communities prior to exploiting such knowledge, and equitably share the benefits derived from its uses. One of the earliest, perhaps most compelling academic contributions to the debate is James Boyle's *Shamans, Software, and Spleens: Law and the Construction of the Information Society*, which introduces the concepts of "cultural environmentalism" and "cultural raw materials."[32] Later, though, critics such as Madhavi Sunder would take issue with Boyle's defense of the public domain, pointing to the Janus-faced character of "development" and the protection of "traditional knowledge." While talk about culture as "raw material" established traditional knowledge as a political and legal category, "the same metaphor may also inadvertently obscure the *inventiveness* of traditional knowledge. Reifying the public domain may have the unintended effect of congealing traditional knowledge as 'the opposite of property,' presenting poor people's knowledge as the raw material of innovation—ancient, static, and natural—rather than as intellectual property—modern, dynamic, scientific, and culturally inventive."[33]

Still, the recognition of a close relationship between biodiversity and traditional knowledge—and implicitly, the protection of the very indigenous communities that sustain them—marks a turning point in the transition from the compartmentalized, IP-centric Tunis Model Law and the ambiguities of the Model Provisions toward a more organicist view of indigenous culture as an integrated system of interwoven and mutually enabling practices that include expressions of folklore and distinct—and for the most part, historically disparaged—forms of knowledge production. The growing convergence of environmental and indigenist concerns preoccupied the international community for the remainder of the 1990s and well into the twenty-first century, leading to a seminal UNESCO-WIPO World Forum on the Protection of Folklore in 1997 in Phuket, Thailand. This was followed by a string of regional fora and roundtables held under the auspices of WIPO, and, eventually, the establishment in 2000 of the aforementioned Intergovernmental Committee on Intellectual Property and Genetic Resources, Traditional Knowledge and Folklore as the first standing WIPO forum for the discussion of issues around expressive culture. Although the committee provides a platform for developing countries to push back against the West's blockade of even the most basic protections by advancing a strong moral claim to redress the wrongs of colonialism, it yet has to produce a legal instrument. Little wonder, then, that over the past two decades, the controversies of the 1970s and 1980s over the ownership and administration of rights or the difference between a holistic view of traditional knowledge and its protection under separate IP doctrines keep flaring up. Wary as ever of any form of outside intrusion, primarily indigenous delegations from former settler colonies favored a combination of some type of holistic philosophy and indigenous ownership, whereas the European Union and some African and Middle Eastern countries insisted on what one report termed "the principle of national sovereignty of States over their resources."[34]

In 2005, the slow but inexorable drift toward merging folklore and traditional knowledge in some comprehensive system of protections entered its third and decisive phase when WIPO members agreed on the Revised Provisions for the Protection of Traditional Cultural Expressions/Expressions of Folklore. Apart from coining the term *traditional cultural expressions* (henceforth TCE), the document breaks new ground in three ways. Unlike the 1985 Model Provisions, it, for the first time, explicitly ties the regulation of TCE to customary law as the normative regulatory framework, regardless of whether the origin of these expressions is attributed to a community or an individual. Second, in addition to nation-states and traditional communities, the revised provisions recognize any indigenous communities as holders of TCE. Thirdly, and perhaps most crucially, by using "expressions of traditional knowledge" and "expressions of folklore" interchangeably to refer to traditional cultural expressions, WIPO realigned the valences of folklore. As Marc Perlman astutely observes, in devaluing the affective or aesthetic properties of folklore, WIPO imagines TCEs as "carriers or embodiments of *information*."[35] As such, this shift might signal the second coming of the old imperial order in new garb: an order where the kingdom of custom enables and is seamlessly co-opted into the empire of global capitalist circulation with its abstraction, random fungibility, and portability of goods, services, and people. Or, according to Benjamin Lee, if cultures of circulation can be identified by the objects circulating through them, they are not reducible to these objects. Instead, "circulation interacts with the semiotic form of the circulating objects to create the cultural dimensions of the circulatory process itself."[36]

The above is not meant to belittle the violence a term such as *folklore* has done to the expressive practices of colonized people in South Africa and elsewhere. At the same time, one cannot quite discount the fact that apart from coinciding with South Africa's reentry into the arena of global IP politics and the resurgence of South African politics of custom, the rebranding of folklore as information may reveal the aspirational character of the policy more than its practical import. A close reading of the second part of the policy brief—the eight policy goals mentioned earlier—provides a possible explanation for this. Read against the backdrop of the history of the protection of folklore and traditional knowledge in international law, these goals appear to be based on a series of dualisms. The first is the contrast between a national core and its periphery implied in the goal of bringing traditional knowledge holders into the mainstream by making them "benefit the national economy." Undoubtedly born from the historical experience of the black majority's exclusion from the nation that emerged in 1910 and subsequent mass removals to the wastelands cynically designated as homelands, the notion that this process also witnessed the coming into existence of two separate economies—a national economy and some non-economy or "second economy"—is mistaken.[37] Rather, what facilitated the politics of marginalization was a unified economy, albeit one in which black people's place and sole right of existence were less as market participants of the liberal imagination and more as actors within what Jane Guyer calls a "platform economy."[38]

Underpinning this economy, as Peter Drahos argues in relation to indigenous knowledge in Australia, is an "extractive property order." Secured by a system of institutions and a set of rights and rules, such as IP law protecting individual productivity and property, this order has traditionally excluded indigenous people, subjecting them to "institutionalized insecurity for their assets" by concentrating power in the hands of an elite. According to Drahos, it is because of this concentration that "extractive intellectual property" law is unable to engender a property order that advances indigenous development. Furthermore, this extractive order also contrasts with a system that considers knowledge innovative, prizing connection over extraction as a means toward generating new knowledge. During the colonial era and well into the present moment, Australians have pictured indigenous people and their knowledge as somehow situated in an economic no-man's land. In truth, however, these knowledge practices are inextricably interwoven with what Aborigines call "service to country." Hence, aboriginal knowledge systems for Drahos are not so much holistic as they are connectionist, in the sense that they foster richly layered experiences that, in turn, nurture the social relationships underpinning the performance of indigenous knowledge.[39]

The parallels with South Africa are not difficult to appreciate. Colonial views of indigenous knowledge and traditional cultural expressions have for centuries been informed here by an imaginary that considered the latter not only devoid of economic value but inimical to progress and development tout court. But as a growing body of work illustrates, indigenous knowledge practices might more fruitfully be viewed as forming part of the country's service sector or even health sector.[40] As such, like many traditional cultural expressions, they not only perform vital cultural but also, more crucially, social care work. There is, of course, a great deal of overlap between these two sectors. But the main point about this paradigm shift is that these practices have not only been incorporated—albeit on vastly asymmetric terms—in the mainstream already, but they also have historically fulfilled and will likely continue to play an important part in restoring South Africa's severely damaged socio-psychological fabric. Much like aboriginal fire technologies and forms of fire management are vital to the maintenance of Australia's socio-ecological systems, many South African indigenous knowledge practices and traditional expressive forms are embedded in economic structures and forms of immaterial labor typically geared toward the manipulation of affect in the reconstruction of a shattered precolonial world *and* the reproduction of the capitalist order.[41] This is in tune with a conception of economy that, instead of assuming even access to resources and the capacity to grasp opportunities purportedly afforded by "market economies," embraces "entanglements, the coexistence and intricate enmeshment of old and new, the plausibility of differential rates of entropy, predatory dismantlement, retooling, and the continual ferreting around to find the loose ends, spaces, small abandonments, and sudden juxtapositions that can be seen as 'apportunities.'"[42]

The second dichotomy in the policy goals is a distinction implicit in the term *misappropriation*. Lacking historical, local, and legal specificity, it offers no concrete prescription for legal or social action. Rather, like *cultural appropriation*, it is symptomatic of a deeper malaise troubling what Bruno Latour calls "political ecology" and its inability to speak to the larger concerns central to emergent social movements in South Africa and around the world by bridging the widening gulf between nature and politics.[43] The weakness of environmental movements, he suggests, illustrated by the sluggishness of the leading industrial nations to tackle climate change, stems from political ecology's desire to silence any effort at questioning the absolute supremacy of Science over politics. Science, in the uppercase, is an epistemology completely divorced from the way the sciences, in the lowercase, work in real life, Latour contends. Pointing to Plato's cave analogy, Latour argues that for over twenty-five centuries, Science's pretension to deliver irrefutable truth about "things as they are" has dictated the rhythm of all things human. In other words, Science has accomplished the rare feat of having politicized "the sciences through epistemology in order to render ordinary political life impotent through the threat of an incontestable nature."[44]

The South African reverberations of this politics of nature, in inverted form, are clearly felt in the science wars that have been raging on the country's campuses from the early 2010s. Running parallel to the debate about intellectual property protections for traditional knowledge and other issues of cultural and cognitive justice, a universalist vision of science has struggled to assert itself against an aggressive science phobia framed as decolonial scholarship. The origins of this polarization are traceable to the late 1970s when many Africanist historians and anthropologists, disillusioned with nationalist and socialist narratives of modernization and development, began to focus more on history from below, rural communities, ethnicity, and cultural continuities. Naturally, this shift entailed greater attention to local or indigenous forms of knowledge, ultimately resulting in a new analytical construct called "colonial science."[45] Additionally, given the broader context of the debate, there could also be no denying that the politicization of the sciences was a colonial undertaking from the outset. Whether as social Darwinism, scientific racism, *volkekunde*, or, indeed, anthropology, nineteenth-century colonial understandings that cast indigenous cultural practices as natural and, hence, immutable formed an integral part of the justification of colonial conquest and the shoring up of white power. Colonial politics and local knowledge converged in the chimera of what British natural philosopher Joseph Priestley in 1791, celebrating the French Revolution and the idea of "universal peace," called an "empire of reason."[46] Local knowledge and Western logos united in giving birth to an empire of a more material sort where the social would replicate the natural order and vice versa.

This process was by no means devoid of friction. Historians appear to be in broad agreement that most colonial field scientists, such as geographers, anthropologists, or botanists, considered Africa a living laboratory offering untold opportunities for in situ experimentation and the use of science to develop the continent in accordance with the so-called civilizing mission. But it is equally true that many scientists working in the colonies were also conflicted figures with divided loyalties. Half agents of the colonial state whose research arose from the need to make Africans' knowledge serviceable to the larger project of imperial governance, half advocates of universal reason, their findings were often doubly disconnected from the epistemic worlds and practical experience of white farmers and cattle breeders on the ground. In a strictly political sense, then, it is this synergy of nature and culture that manifested in the emergence in the early nineteenth century of what Saul Dubow calls the "acquired indigeneity" of English-speaking settlers. These settlers, Dubow contends, were concerned about forging a distinct national, South African form of indigenism, at once opposed to imperial overrule and distinct from the more unapologetically British identity espoused by subsequent waves of settlers flocking to the Cape. The knowledge of the land and its people afforded by colonial naturalism and its close links with the emerging colonial nationalism, or so they thought, imbued them with a "custodial or proprietorial sense of ownership" on par with that of the autochthonous population.[47]

In *Africa as a Living Laboratory*, Helen Tilley takes a diametrically opposed view. The concept of a "colonial science," she writes, is problematic because it is centered on at least four dualisms. First, it posits that "Western" science developed in isolation within Europe. Second, "colonial science" was somehow a category of knowledge distinct from Science in the uppercase. Third, parts of "colonial science" misrepresented "real" science, and, fourth, indigenous bodies of knowledge were rendered inherently incommensurable with "Western" science and ultimately obliterated by colonialism.[48]

While the recognition of ambiguity and the absence of convenient dualisms may offend those for whom nuance equals the betrayal of pure decolonial doctrine, a new breed of scholarship has begun to question the tendency among many champions of indigenous knowledge to merely transpose the broader frame offered by decolonial scholarship—facts are values, nature is culture, the social is racial, and so on—into the register of identity politics, without, at the same time, interrogating the terms and dualisms inherent in such a critique.[49] Contesting the false dichotomy that all ways of knowing, including the sciences, are either belief or knowledge as a "significant impoverishment of debate on the possibilities for postcolonial (or decolonial) scholarship in South Africa," this body of work offers a wealth of studies that unpack the complex entanglement of natural history, colonial history, indigenous and scientific knowledge practices, heterogeneous interests, epistemologies, and methodologies and their intersection with a variety of political, economic, and historical factors playing out on a global scale at an ever-accelerating pace.[50]

There are three lessons to be learned from this joint, albeit vastly unequal, production of knowledge by colonizers and colonized and the racial politics it would go on to foster until well into the present moment. First, it highlights the need to query the essentialism inherent in the category of indigenous knowledge. While knowledge may be autochthonous, it hardly ever exists ab ovo. Second, it is from the identity politics of nature that the policy goal of preventing misappropriation derives its moral valences. Practices that in an older vocabulary were euphemistically referred to as cultural exchange, and in most cases were and still are not punishable offenses, have now become a direct assault on cultural identity tout court. But the same politics also has its legal valence. Just as intellectual property law has become a key site for stabilizing traditional knowledge as a type of distinct knowledge, here the construction of this knowledge as the utterly incompatible Other of Science, and, as such, forever vulnerable to misappropriation, serves to buttress intellectual property law's black-boxing of tradition as occupying a "neutral space, where history and politics informing the term remain in abeyance."[51]

Similarly, while in laying claim to their traditional knowledge as property, indigenous people do more than expose the instability and inadequacies of intellectual property law in vesting property rights in that knowledge, the prevention of misappropriation through intellectual property systems, in turn, might be said to destabilize the very struggles of indigenous people for self-determination and entitlement. As Jane Anderson argues, intellectual property statutes that seek to protect indigenous knowledge differ from intellectual property law in general in the sense that the latter does not distinguish any of its categories in terms of cultural identity. But to establish a connection between knowledge and identity and to specify certain forms of practice, like traditional knowledge, as unique forms of property, the law must create a special position. That position is a cultural one. Culture becomes the "primary trope for identifying and explaining the unique concerns that are brought to intellectual property law by indigenous people."[52]

But note the conditional *might* in the paragraph above. As Rosemary Coombe has pointed out, the legal valence of *cultural appropriation* is a double-edged sword. While ostensibly lending credence to nationalist programs of the preservation and protection of a nation's cultural patrimony, the term also exposes the fallacy, pitfalls, and political counter-effects of this "special position." The rhetoric of cultural nationalism, Coombe tersely suggests, "bears traces of the same logic that defines copyright."[53] As the West exported its concept of "culture" to the rest of the world and nations or indigenous people were figured as authors of various cultures, this gesture of recognition was limited to objects of property, such as prominent monuments or artifacts of "superior" or "unique" aesthetic value. Knowledge and forms of indigenous expressions were not included. Even though in South Africa and elsewhere intellectual property–like or sui generis statutes seek to provide ownership rights in expressions, there is the real danger of such provisions to perpetuate past injustices and to destabilize the very struggles of indigenous people for self-determination and entitlement they are meant to support. In short, and although stated many times before, it bears repeating that the history of indigenous struggles has been a Janus-faced process offering few assurances for an identity-oriented politics that provides a stable foundation for protecting indigenous knowledge. On the one hand, the very idea of indigeneity has become a tool of identity formation. By successfully grounding the idea in a range of concepts, such as tradition, community, environment, or ethics, and contrasting them with the modernist nation-state's failure to formulate a universal vision of social order, indigenism was able to provide indigenous movements with a sense of "moral certitude."[54] At the same time, by embracing the language of human rights to pursue its agenda of self-determination and cultural survival, the global indigenous people's movement also had to come to terms with another conundrum. To assert its collective rights, it had to channel its demands through the labyrinth of international human rights organizations and its complex system of legal instruments, conferences, and NGO consultants, all of which, in one way or another, are committed to the principles of liberal individualism.[55]

Finally, the third dichotomy that shapes the policy follows from the protectionism of the former, anti-misappropriation stance. The idea that state policy should empower communities to "commercialise and trade on IK" presumes the prior existence of a divide where indigenous knowledge is cocooned in some trade-free zone from which it hatches into a free-trade one, empowered by a state that sees itself as a custodian of cultural diversity.[56] This storyline—itself echoing "second economy" dogma—obviously disregards the fact that South Africans have exchanged their knowledge and cultural expressions for thousands of years, thus giving rise to the very practices that are suddenly deemed in need of commercialization. More significant still, it also overlooks a subtler dynamic at the heart of cultural processes in the twenty-first century—a dynamic that is more than just the intrusion of markets into a sphere once orientalized as traditional, ideal, immaterial, or transcendent and from which indigenous culture must be protected. A dynamic, too, that has little to do with the picture of indigenous people as somehow destined to provide the raw material for the Western aesthetic imagination even as they languish in a state of cultural deprivation as passive consumers of Western cultural goods. Rather, as numerous scholars have pointed out, this dynamic culture in the Global South is conceived as an open-ended process in which "human subjects and cultural objects, produce, reproduce, and refashion each other."[57] One example of this "culture cycle," as UNESCO's *Framework for Cultural Statistics* calls it, is the blurring of lines between producers and consumers, performers and audiences. Consumers become cultural producers and content coproducers by valorizing and certifying standards of "taste" set by other producers or, in turn, creating new consumers through "feedback processes by which activities (consumption) inspire the creation of new cultural products and artefacts."[58]

Clearly, the call for commercializing IK and TCE implies competing valences for indigenous subjectivity and agency. On the one hand, it interpellates indigenous people to represent themselves to one another and to the state in the terms offered by the policy, thereby objectifying and ultimately domesticating them by, once again, containing them within the confines of their presumed collective identity, now legitimized by the act. But ironically, the cultural commodity also enjoins indigenous subjects to conceive of themselves as individuals. Indigenous producers are encouraged (empowered) to model themselves on the inspired, risk-taking cultural entrepreneur of the creative industries as ethnopreneurs, with consumers finding themselves forever engaged in a quest for individual selfhood mediated by ethno-knowledge and vernacular artifacts.

Lastly, mention must be made of a few issues conspicuously absent from either the 2004 IKS policy or its presentation in the opening session of the committee. First, the policy document was never made available to the MPs, thus leaving them with a rather sketchy picture of what exactly is meant by the term *national economy*. Despite extensive crossdepartmental consultation and the fact that officials responded to a question from one of the backbenchers about the anticipated benefits of the legislation's economic contribution by briefly singling out the health, agricultural, craft, and tourism sectors, the policy document itself fails to provide a comprehensive, detailed, and empirically grounded assessment of those benefits. A regulatory impact analysis commissioned by the presidency prior to the introduction of the bill did, however, identify "significant risks and challenges associated with the Bill." The likely commercial benefits for communities, it found, were "difficult to quantify, and may not be achieved on a significant scale."[59] Moreover, contrary to the drumbeat of indigenous creativity, the policy is surprisingly tongue-tied on the projected impact of the proposed legislation precisely in those spaces customarily invoked as preeminent sites for development, regeneration, or urban renewal—in other words, creative clusters like Newtown or Maboneng in downtown Johannesburg, or the Red Location cultural precinct in Port Elizabeth. Instead, what the government seems to envisage is traditional knowledge holders and creators of TCE who are happily ensconced in rural areas, and by drawing on an inexhaustible wellspring of ancestral knowledge, contribute to the national economy all the while remaining disconnected from the national economy just enough to justify the narrative of integration.

The opposite is, of course, the case. Traveling from Johannesburg, Durban, or Cape Town to any area situated in or near the former "homelands," one is immediately confronted with a world where centuries of forcible colonial "integration" have created a condition that might be best conceptualized as a form of "adverse incorporation."[60] This is a world where a combination of de-agrarianization, unemployment, crime, HIV/AIDS, and drug abuse led to dramatically reduced opportunities for smallholder farming, and where close to 90 percent of households are unable to survive on their own crop. But it is also a world of diversified livelihood strategies comprising, in addition to long-standing, albeit declining, male long-distance migration, intraregional migration, or rural densification in which growing numbers of people engaging in petty commerce or competing for ever-rarer jobs, shuttle between rural, culturally inscribed social networks and small towns, such as Mount Frere in the former Transkei region of the Eastern Cape. Situated in a seemingly pastoral landscape, Mount Frere is anything but idyllic. It is, as Andries du Toit and David Neves write in their landmark essay "In Search of South Africa's Second Economy":

> at one and the same time, a neglected hinterland and a crossroads shaped by tight connections with other places. . . . The busy N2 bisects the town, and freight-hauling juggernauts and cars rumble endlessly through. Present everywhere along the bustling main drag is the branding of corporate South Africa—Vodacom, Shoprite, Vicks, FNB, Cell C, Pep Stores, KFC, Castle Lager, Oxo and Boxer. Stalls line both sides of the main road, sometimes two deep, selling consumer goods, clothes, food and public cellphone access. The cosmopolitan make-up of this informal retail fringe gives the lie to the notion of Mount Frere as a far-flung rural outpost unconnected to the globalising world; business is conducted here by local people as well as Ghanaian, Senegalese, Zimbabwean, Chinese and Pakistani traders.[61]

In short, the economy imagined by the drafters of the bill, rather than being unintegrated, has already been part and parcel of the national economy for decades if not longer. And as such it hardly constitutes the kind of rural breeding ground for TCE and indigenous knowledge implied in the integrationist rationale of the underlying policy.

Another objective that did not feature in the presentation is what the 2004 policy document refers to as "cultural values." In the first sentence of the executive summary, one of the main drivers of IKS policy is stated as the affirmation of "African cultural values in the face of globalization." This, the summary continues, is a "clear imperative given the need for a positive African identity."[62] Even though the disparity between these values and globalization may be slightly overblown—given the formidable international presence of African music, for instance—it does enable policymakers to justify interventions in culture in the name of the public interest and, by the same token, to turn culture into a "resource for identity maintenance."[63] The absence of this rationale from the presentation is, therefore, all the more noteworthy, as it appears to signal a broader shift in post-Mandela cultural politics toward the "expediency" of culture and the wholesale espousal of market relationships as a means of determining cultural value.[64]

A further lacuna resulting from the policy's extraction-centric gaze is the absence of any substantive discussion of the distributive aspects of the policy framework. Riding the SMART policy (specific, measurable, attainable, realistic, and timely) wave touted by a global consultocracy of new public management ideologues, it appears that as early as 1996, some policymakers were eager to redirect the debate about how best to transform the apartheid state from a concern with equitable demographic representation in its institutions toward the efficiency of its public service sector in implementing the government's new GEAR (growth, employment, and redistribution) strategy. Contrary to its name, however, the expansion of employment opportunities not only disproportionally favored the upper echelons of the public service sector, the redistribution through a combination of land restitution and black economic empowerment initiatives failed to produce the desired effect of broad-based redress of past imbalances.[65] Even more important for present purposes, the strategy might be read as one further step toward the erosion of the government's commitment to diversity and human well-being as sui generis cultural needs recognized by UNCTAD and UNESCO. Thus, one searches the policy document in vain for words like *democracy*, the *public*, or *citizen*—all staples of the liberal-democratic imagination in which individual property rights, equal access to public resources, and self-determination mutually constitute one another.

To summarize, the government's IK policy clearly generates its own discursive bubble. Like the development it touts as its ultima ratio, the policy not only constructs indigenous knowledge or misappropriation as particular kinds of objects, but it also creates, to paraphrase James Ferguson, an epistemological frame around those objects in terms of which they may be interpreted and rendered into the language of policy. In this way, policy becomes a prisoner onto itself, confined within the narrow parameters of its own dichotomies. Steeped in outmoded socioeconomic and cultural categories, it is virtually impossible to judge it by any criteria other than its own. A fragile assembly or, to use Zygmunt Bauman's apt phrase, "retrotopia" of simultaneously retrogressive and forward-looking goals, it is unable to set out a practical agenda for transcending past and present injustices.[66]

Expert Systems: Disembedding Indigeneity

October 18–19, 2010. Parliament is in its fourth term, and the committee, after months of buzzing with marginalia and trivialities, seems to have reached an impasse. With the ANC-led coalition coming out in support of the bill's communitarian thrust and the oppositional Democratic Alliance taking a more conventional, copyright owner–centric stance, the party lines are firmly drawn. But the MPs will not only have to come to an agreement about some of the key provisions of the bill, they also have yet to engage with its finer points in more than a tangential fashion. With the ball thus squarely in their court, the critical question is: How a bill can be molded into a statute that at one and the same time mirrors party politics and the interests of members' constituencies, stands up to judicial review, and is in line with South Africa's treaty obligations? But for the ethnographer, who has patiently read countless minutes and silently followed hours of debate about tea, Zulu guitar music, and the cultural differences between Ndebele- and Zulu-speaking knowledge holders, the larger question hovering over all this is epistemological in nature rather than moral, political, or normative: By what device, rhetorical gesture, protocol, or logic do all these diverging actors and interests become hostable by and in the law? What connectors are required to bring them into some form of association? And how might such associations be made durable to outlast the next meeting, the next term, the adoption by the full assembly, or just the test of time?

Enter the expert. The committee had invited half a dozen legal scholars, members of the National House of Traditional Leaders, and representatives of a broad spectrum of copyright-related trade associations, collecting societies, and private individuals to speak to the submissions they had sent in prior to the hearings. The verdict is devastating. While acknowledging the urgent need to protect indigenous knowledge, speaker after speaker comes forward listing the bill's innumerable flaws. In the roughly fifteen submissions, four main areas of contention stand out: (1) The bill does not provide for sui generis legislation; (2) it is potentially unconstitutional; (3) it is unworkable; and (4) some of its definitions regarding the subsistence of copyright are inconsistent.

For instance, Professor Sihawukele Ngubane, chairperson of the Academic and Non-Fiction Authors' Association of South Africa (ANFASA), worries that instead of providing protection for traditional knowledge and cultural expressions by crafting new legislation, the bill inserts provisions into the host acts that might be incompatible with the fundamentals of these acts' subject matter, potentially compromising their integrity. What Ngubane seems to suggest may perhaps be illustrated by s 28A (1) as amended about the originality requirement of conventional copyright, whereby copyright subsists in independently created works. The section reads as follows:

> Subject to the provisions of this Chapter [2A], the provisions of this Act shall, except in so far as is otherwise provided in the said Chapter, *and in so far as they can be applied*, apply to traditional works [emphasis added].

In plain terms, if a provision of the Copyright Act cannot be applied to a traditional work because that work fails to meet the originality requirement—as all traditional works inevitably do—then the requirement may simply be ignored. Mind-bending inconsistencies like these move Joel Baloyi, then secretary and counsel at the Southern African Music Rights Organization (SAMRO), to join the chorus of critics recommending that the government return to the drawing board and introduce a sui generis bill, taking into consideration "other appropriate global initiatives," such as the discussions at WIPO, the African Regional Intellectual Property Organization, and recent legislative reforms in India and elsewhere.

Meanwhile, Owen Dean, chairperson of Spoor & Fischer, submits that by "clothing traditional knowledge as intellectual property and seeking to protect it as a species of intellectual property," the bill will encounter "serious and unacceptable problems" in the context of South Africa's international treaty obligations, such as the national treatment requirement of the TRIPS agreement, which provides that South Africa must provide subjects of other member countries the same copyright protection it affords its own subjects. The bill, he states, "does not provide for this and thus places South Africa in breach of the TRIPS Agreement." Furthermore, he argues, there is a real chance that the bill will also run afoul of the South African Constitution, most notably the "property clause," s 25 (1), prohibiting "arbitrary deprivation of property." But the bill, Dean contends, does just that. It provides that the protection of traditional works previously in the public domain be henceforth "owned" by communities and the commercial exploitation of these works controlled by a National Trust Fund, without any provision being made for the funds derived from such exploitation to be actually paid out to any community. Arguably, then, the bill wants to have it both ways. "Having in a sense granted rights in such property to a community, with the one hand, the Bill then removes such right from the community and places it in the hands of the Fund, with the other hand."

Dean's constitutional concerns are shared by Nicol Faasen, spokesperson of the Publishers Association of South Africa (PASA). The bill, he cautions, might well become the subject of constitutional challenge, as Article 27(2) of the Universal Declaration of Human Rights states that "everyone had the right to the protection of the moral and material interest resulting from any scientific, literary or artistic production of which he was the author." Moreover, he wishes to register his extreme disappointment that despite PASA's positive and constructive participation in the drafting of the bill, none of its proposed amendments were taken into consideration. Worse yet, there was no national consultation. Nor had the full approval of those who stand to gain from the bill, that is, the elusive traditional communities, been obtained.

As the hearings wear on, other experts get into the practicalities of administering the legislation. Thus, representatives for SAMRO and the South African Music Performance Rights Association (SAMPRA), collecting societies for performance rights and sound recordings, respectively, decry the bloated administrative structures that must be established for dealing with traditional knowledge. To wit, the bill provides for no fewer than four bodies: a national council, national databases for the recordation of traditional knowledge (henceforth TK) and traditional cultural expressions, a national trust, and a national trust fund. On top of this behemoth, s 28C (8) also provides that each community must formulate a protocol, preferably based on the UNESCO-WIPO Model Provisions, that identifies the community and sets out the terms under which indigenous works may be licensed to third parties. Noble as the ideas behind these institutions may be—from representing the indigenous communities, documenting TK, and promoting the commercialization of TCE, to administering funds flowing from such commercialization—they have one thing in common. They will create "complete and utter chaos," SAMRO's CEO Nicholas Motsatse warns. Specifically, it is the provisions of s 9 relating to sound recordings that would complicate the negotiation of royalties at the heart of the modus operandi of collecting societies the world over. These provisions would introduce into the process a swarm of parties, like the copyright owners and users of literary works, cinematographic films, broadcasts, published editions, and computer programs that "clearly have no direct or indirect interest in a copyright in sound recordings."

Another stumbling block is the categories of eligible works. Here, s 2 (1) introduces "traditional works" as a new category and defines it as "a literary work, an artistic work or a musical work which is recognised by an indigenous community as a work having an indigenous origin and a traditional character." As is well known, one of the most critical, globally recognized criteria for a work to be eligible for copyright protection is that such a work, in the phrasing of the host Copyright Act, is "reduced to a material form." But here is the rub: While the bill incorporates the materiality requirement for "traditional works" into s 2 (2), in subsection 2 (2B) that follows, it also adds the phrase "or communicated to the public." But this additional condition for satisfying the fixation requirement—nonexistent under the current Copyright Act except for sound recordings—only adds to the confusion by leading to situations where several scenarios may be envisioned for the subsistence of copyright in "traditional works," one as quixotic as the other. The first scenario would involve a work that has neither been "reduced to a material form" nor "communicated to the public." While it seems reasonable to assume that a great number of "traditional works" created in indigenous communities do fall into the first category of never having been "reduced to a material form"—and, as such, will continue to be denied protection under conventional copyright law—the proposed alternative path via a "communication to the public" right will likewise do little to make such works eligible for copyright. One of the reasons for this cul-de-sac—and this would be another scenario—is that even in the rare instance where such "communication to the public" were to occur, it is unclear who the public is. Assuming, ANFASA notes, that in South Africa's racially and ethnically divided climate, the indigenous community from which the work in question originated, in addition to being the author, frequently also constitutes the public the work is communicated to, the effect would be a situation in which author and public, absurdly, are one and the same and where, accordingly, an author's internal communication amounts to communicating with the public.

More than the poor drafting, twisted logic, and uninspired smallness of it all, however, what draws the harshest criticism by far are the key requirements for the subsistence of copyright. Beyond originality and fixation, the definitions of authorship and ownership, speaking as they are to some of the most contentious issues of identity and belonging, are paramount. Predictably, most submissions waste no time in attacking the definition of the author head-on. Thus, the spokesperson of the Dramatic, Artistic and Literary Organization takes issue with the concept of "traditional community" as the author and first and sole owner of the copyright. According to s 1 (1) (j), that community is:

> any recognizable community of people originated in or historically settled in a geographic area or areas located within the borders of the Republic, as such borders existed at the date of commencement of the Intellectual Property Laws Amendment Act, 2011, characterized by social, cultural and economic conditions which distinguish them from other sections of the national community, and who identify themselves and are recognized by other groups as a distinct collective.

The terms *indigenous* and *traditional*, the spokesperson says, are not only used interchangeably to qualify the word *community*, but they also do not have the same meaning. "The Greek community in South Africa would arguably qualify as a *traditional* community, but obviously not an *indigenous* community." Actress and writer Gcina Mhlophe—the lone artist present at the hearings—adds another example:

> Let us assume an author wishes to write a book telling a traditional Zulu children's tale. Which Zulu community is entitled to lay claim to the story? The entire KwaZulu-Natal region? But what about the Zulu people in the Eastern Cape; do they have less of a claim? And what if the writer actually wrote the story as told by a Ndebele story-teller, which would then have slight Ndebele nuances when compared to the original Zulu version. Does this divest the Zulu people of their claim? And what if the Ndebele story-teller was from Bulawayo and not from Nelspruit?

Mhlophe's point is amplified by Anjuli Maistry, an attorney working for South Africa's oldest and largest human rights law clinic, the Legal Resource Center. The definition of *indigenous community*, she argues, rejecting the homology of place and community implied in the definition, as "any community of people living within the borders of the Republic, or which historically lived in the geographic area located within the borders of the Republic," is out of step with reality. Communities do not define themselves spatially. Boundaries constantly expand and contract depending on many factors. In fact, s 1 (iv) of the Restitution of Land Rights Act 22 of 1994 defines community as "any group of persons whose rights in land are derived from shared rules determining access to land held in common by such group, and includes any part of such group. In other words, "communities define themselves through social and political organisation at layered levels and through shared customary laws, values, identity and mutual recognition of culture."

But the lack of clarity in the definition of *traditional community* and its divergence from established copyright norms also provides an opening for Nkosi Vtuthuko Khuzwayo, deputy president of the Congress of Traditional Leaders of South Africa (CONTRALESA), to tout his version of the traditional community. A major player in the South African politics of ethnicity and self-proclaimed "cultural custodian" and "key to rural development," CONTRALESA is better known for its deft combination of custom and capital. It successfully lobbied the ANC-led government for reneging on its long-standing hostility—hardened during the liberation movement's struggle against Bantustan despots such as Lucas Mangope—toward any form of chieftaincy while simultaneously being heavily invested in distinctly untraditional, high-stakes ventures, running the gamut from mining and telecommunications to the financial sector.[67] Fittingly, Khuzwayo requests that the bill be written so that it reinforces the "progressiveness" of indigenous communities, but its definition of the indigenous community also includes the "allegiance" to the "hierarchies" within these communities.

The inconsistencies in the definition of *indigenous community* are further compounded by a phrase such as "social, cultural and economic conditions." Taken together, these terms appear to suggest that such communities are primarily organized along racial and ethnic lines and, as such, may include the Zulu or Xhosa, members of the Church of Nazareth, the Pan-African Congress, or for that matter, the fans of the Orlando Pirates soccer team—all predominantly black, ethnic, and economically disadvantaged communities.

After just two days of hearings, with countless inconsistencies and drafting errors pointed out, crucial terms shown to lack clarity, and the concept of the indigenous remaining more elusive than ever, the chasm between the members of the governing party and the opposition had widened to the point where virtually the entire legal fraternity found itself aligned with the opposition, and only CONTRALESA cast its lot with the ANC. Clearly, the fate of the bill hung in the balance.

The press eagerly seized upon this torrent of criticism as yet another example of government ineptitude and the ANC's willingness to undermine the rule of law by pandering to the sectarian, retrogressive interests of the chiefs. Yet, things are not quite that simple. Not only does the South African Constitution grant the politics of ethnicity and custom considerable latitude via the recognition of customary law, but lawmaking in liberal democracies is, more generally, also subject to a dynamic inherent in the broader discontinuities of modernity, which the British sociologist Anthony Giddens has identified in his book, *The Consequences of Modernity*. Modernity, Giddens argues, is the result of two conflicting mechanisms interacting with one another: the "lifting out" of social relations from "local contexts of interaction," or "disembedding mechanisms," and the "reembedding" of those disembedded social relations in local conditions of time and place. Giddens distinguishes two such disembedding mechanisms: "symbolic tokens" and "expert systems."[68] For the purposes of this chapter, it is the latter mechanism that proves particularly useful in unpacking the subtleties of lawmaking in the second, or what I call the definitional, stage of the committee's work discussed further below. Following Giddens, I take expert systems to be forms of organized knowledge that structure our material, social, and cultural worlds in ways that remove us from our immediate experience of these worlds while simultaneously demanding that we have confidence in experts' ability to accurately render a given state of affairs in order to realign it with that experience.[69] Examples of such relationships of trust may include the belief in the reliability of the technologies we depend upon in our daily lives; the expectation that the validity of expert knowledge is independent of the local, temporal, and personal circumstances in which it is produced or meant to become operative; the sense that the anonymity, and supposed impartiality, of statistics somehow provides a picture of reality that at least partly corresponds to the culturally encoded particulars of one's lived situation; the respect for scientific findings as an objective measure for managing the most intimate aspects of our lives; and last, and most crucially for my argument, the confidence that the opaque terminology of lawyers is not some secret code but a means toward the ends of justice.

Of course, such relationships are never stable, especially in contexts of extreme volatility where the expert's say-so frequently clashes with deeply entrenched notions of truth, morality, and social order. As such, these moments of instability and distrust require constant monitoring, certification, and the availability of opportunities for engaging in and sustaining forms of direct communication—or what Giddens calls "facework."[70] The examples Giddens gives of such facework—people passing one another on a sidewalk and other encounters with strangers that require the manipulation of subtle techniques of trust-building—have a certain scripted, performative aura. Although committee meetings may be kept on track by a delicate, facework-like balance of protocol, improvisation, and passionate engagement, such facework may fail in the face of the larger tugs of war between embedded politics and disembedding market relations in the world beyond E249. It is to a particularly telling case of such a breakdown of trust in expert systems that I will now turn.

Intermezzo: Benefit Sharing and the Politics of Recognition

Minority group rights are a delicate matter in South Africa, presenting the anthropologist with a set of challenges that, though familiar from other indigenous struggles elsewhere, are exacerbated by the sheer complexity of South Africa's racial past and present. It is among the San and other Khoisan-speaking people that these challenges are perhaps thrown into sharpest relief. Historically underprivileged and underrepresented, the San were the first to experience the uncertainties of being indigenous in the postapartheid order and being conscripted into the global drama of traditional knowledge and intellectual property law at the same time. More specifically, I argue, it is the fluid nature of indigenous rights and of indigeneity more broadly that compels the San to constantly walk a tightrope. Faced with a state that, like most African countries, argues that all black Africans are indigenous and, accordingly, refuses to adopt international indigenous rights or First Peoples frameworks in addition to limiting the definition of *indigenous* in the Constitution and elsewhere to customary law and people speaking Bantu languages, the San must espouse what some anthropologists have called "indigenous modernities"—displays of self-consciously fashioned forms of authenticity, the organization of collective forms of representation legible to the state and NGOs, and unfavorable benefit-sharing schemes in the exploitation of patent rights.[71] The latter avenue—though not directly concerned with provisions pertaining to traditional cultural expressions—is of special interest as it illustrates the inconsistencies and pitfalls that legal interventions, like the act under discussion here, are likely to run into once it becomes operative.

In this section, I will take the reader through the various stages of this story, focusing especially on the conflict over the patent rights in *hoodia*—the plant that so excited the MPs during their first meeting—and the benefit-sharing agreements entered by several pharmaceuticals and the San. Although the story has been told multiple times, it is worth recounting here in some detail, as it may illuminate in greater depth the strategies and contradictions shaping lawmakers' understanding of indigeneity as a basis for protecting traditional cultural expressions.

The curtain rises sometime in the early 1960s, at a time when most African countries reached their independence while, in glaring contrast, the apartheid regime was in its zenith. It is also during these years that the efforts of the regime to drive back the increasingly successful liberation movements in the remaining colonial possessions of Southwest Africa (now Namibia), Angola, and Mozambique coincide with the global hype over *hoodia*'s alleged appetite-suppressing properties.[72] In 1963, the state-run Council for Scientific and Industrial Research (CSIR) launched a project aimed at ascertaining the suitability of wild foods for the South African Defense Force in its antiguerilla operations, and in the course of that search stumbled upon the *hoodia*. It took two more decades for researchers to determine the molecular structure of the species in 1986 and an additional decade to file a patent application for the use of its active components in 1995. But no sooner had the patent been granted than a veritable rush for the green diamonds of the South began, starting with a licensing agreement between the CSIR and a small British company called Phytopharm in 1995, followed by agreements with US pharma giant Pfizer in 1998 and—after Pfizer pulled out in 2003— with nutrition, hygiene, and personal care multinational Unilever in 2004. The latter deal, especially, and the promise it held of marketing *hoodia* as an additive in so-called functional foods, made the new postapartheid government take notice. With an estimated global value of $65 billion, the government saw Unilever's project as an opening for making significant inroads into the functional foods market and tabled plans for the construction of an extraction facility in the Western Cape accordingly.

But the government had reckoned without the host, the San. In 2001, particulars of the CSIR-Phytopharm deal surfaced when *The Guardian* ran a story accusing Phytopharm of biopiracy. As Rachel Wynberg and other activists of an NGO called Biowatch South Africa told reporters, CSIR researchers had led the company to believe that the San had "disappeared" and that, hence, no claims of patent ownership or benefit-sharing were to be expected. Moreover, CSIR also neglected to obtain the informed consent of the San to use their knowledge of the potential health and nutritional benefits of the plant. *Guardian* journalist Barnett: "While the drug companies were busy seducing the media, their shareholders, and financiers about the wonders of their new drug, they had forgotten to tell the bushmen [i.e., San], whose knowledge they had used and patented."[73] News of the deal spread like wildfire, spawning a vast amount of critical literature and journalism on biopiracy, biodiversity, and, of course, the plant itself. But also a resurgence of the San—not as they see themselves but as they are perceived through "imperial eyes," as a discourse or, worse, brand.[74] Forever the noble savage, the San are interpellated to offer the world what the trailer of the 1980 blockbuster movie *The Gods*

Must be Crazy calls a "serious and revealing look at civilized man." Popular culture aside (I will return to the role of popular culture in the context of San efforts to reclaim self-determination in a later section of this chapter), Barnett's article persuaded CSIR officials to share a portion of the revenues received from the joint ventures it had formed with Phytopharm and Pfizer with the San—specifically, 6 percent of all royalties received from the sale of *hoodia*-based products and a further 8 percent of the milestone income it received from Phytopharm when certain benchmarks in its research and product development period were reached.[75] But more questionably, the agreement also specified that any intellectual property resulting from CSIR research would remain vested in the research institution and that the San have no right to claim ownership of the patents or products derived from them.

The CSIR-San agreement was anything but an act of benevolence, though. Preceding it by more than a decade was a sequence of extraordinary developments in intellectual property law, human rights law, and in world and South African politics more generally. The series of events starts with the 1992 adoption of the Convention of Biological Diversity by the United Nations and the coming into effect of the TRIPS agreement in 1995. Intersecting with these seminal moments was the end of apartheid rule and the election of Nelson Mandela as the first president of the democratic South Africa in 1994, followed, in short order, by the implementation of GEAR and an ambitious Reconstruction and Development Programme (RDP). Running parallel to these initiatives, the country also witnessed the rapid dismantling of the last vestiges of apartheid law and, along with it, the first tentative steps toward new policies aimed at improving the lives of the country's oldest indigenous communities, most prominently, perhaps, the signing of the 2002 !Ae!Hai Kalahari Heritage Park land and settlement agreement that restored some one hundred thousand acres to the ǂKhomani San and Meir communities. At the same time, however, it must be acknowledged that many of these measures evolved in tandem with international events, such as the United Nations' First International Decade of the World's Indigenous Peoples or the emergence of a whole string of indigenous land restitution policies in countries like Australia, Canada, New Zealand, and the United States. Closer to the topic at hand, the era also saw the 1996 establishment of the Working Group of Indigenous Minorities in Southern Africa (WIMSA), which supports San communities in Angola, Botswana, Namibia, and South Africa; and as a corollary, the founding of the South African San Council.

By 2008, Unilever's plans to develop *hoodia* came to a sudden halt. One may speculate about the reasons for this development: Was it because of security and efficacy concerns, as the company claimed? Or was it the growing muscle of San communities—the fact that the San were anything but isolated and traditional—that posed a threat to Unilever's bid to capitalize on the group's alleged extinction? Biodiversity scholarship tends to ascribe the collapse of the benefit-sharing arrangement to the synergetic effects of unrealistic expectations, corporate greed, lack of unity among political actors, and, first and foremost, poorly executed policy. Disillusioned by the over one-decade-long experiment, Rachel Wynberg and Sarah Laird, for example, conclude: "The objectives that law and policy on access and benefit-sharing are meant to serve, are rarely achieved." "No 'grand bargain' has actually been possible."[76] And indeed, by the time Unilever pulled out of its partnership with the San, the deal had only netted the latter a mere $70,000—a far cry from the exalted hopes for a new dawn complete with schools, small-business ventures, and expanded social services.

Deplorable as it is, my intention in revisiting the hoodia saga is to query the policy-centric, legal-instrumentalist perspective itself and the way it holds onto questionable, though fashionable, concepts of indigeneity and tradition. Some of these recall Eric Hobsbawm's and Terence Ranger's well-known invention of tradition hypothesis or Gayatri Spivak's concept of strategic essentialism. But in a discussion of San and Nama identity politics, Steven Robins rightly contends that these are irreconcilable with South African postcolonial identities and that anthropologists, in particular, are to be faulted for subscribing to a paradigm in which the "West" is seen to have a consistent and convincing history, whereas "all the subaltern can aspire to are fragmented fables, origin myths, invented traditions and staged ethnicities." In view of a brutal history of genocide and dispossession, he goes on to argue, the attempts of the San and other indigenous minorities to recover their identities must be read as an "act of recuperation and memory."[77] In her book *Reinventing Hoodia: Peoples, Plants, and Patents in South Africa*, Laura Foster similarly suggests that the whole process injected new confidence in the San. But, she also cautions, it is important to explore new forms of belonging beyond those envisioned by property rights and benefit-sharing agreements.[78]

Definitions: Amending the Amendment

May 31, 2011. We have returned to our accustomed visitor seats in E249 and listen to the MPs as they reflect on the blow dealt by the public hearings in October and November 2010 to B8-2010, laying to rest the notion that it would move to a vote in the full National Assembly anytime soon. For the past couple of weeks, the committee has heard parliamentary legal adviser Charmaine van der Merwe reviewing the critical comments offered during the hearings and the responses to those comments by the Department of Trade and Industry. Members were also given a presentation by the chairperson of the Companies and Intellectual Property Commission, the regulatory body within the Department of Trade and Industry tasked, inter alia, with accrediting copyright collecting societies, overseeing a copyright tribunal, and administering the registration of copyright in cinematograph films, and other aspects of copyright law. While these officials all reaffirmed that the bill was breaking new ground, they were also unanimous that multiple areas of uncertainty remained and that, ultimately, the committee may be faced with only three choices going forward: to amend, redraft, or withdraw the bill entirely. While the latter option met with a rather subdued response, the decision on what further steps should be taken to amend or redraft the bill preoccupied MPs for several more weeks, laying bare the constraints and the power of expert systems in simultaneously masking and creating new realities.

> As more amendments are likely to be forthcoming soon, one member suggests, "if these have more substance than the bill itself then a redraft might be better."
>
> The chairperson agrees: "The intent should be to engage with a bill on an organic basis. However, the point might be reached where redrafting was more of an option."
>
> But who would oversee either approach? "The Department [of Trade and Industry] should provide the amendments made in response to issues raised to date," the previous speaker argues.
>
> Chairperson: "The Committee has already decided to employ consultants and some names of leading experts, including academics and figures in the industry, have already been put forward."
>
> What about the demographics of these experts? "I want a representative panel of experts encompassing gender and race," the chairperson declares. "I will not have three all-male, white advisors."
>
> "Experts are needed on the technical matters," member Harris balks. "But the committee is doing a disservice to the other experts who would advise the Committee and who are not present."
>
> It could become "disastrous" if every political party in this parliamentary committee meeting wanted to bring in experts, each with a

different opinion, responds Joseph Selau, his colleague from the ANC. He is immediately contradicted by Mr. Gcwabaza: "The parties have a right to call experts whenever they want to," he says. "At the same time, however, these experts are people the Committee decided should consult the entire Committee, regardless of party."

At this point, the legal advisor, van der Merwe, intervenes. She understands that the management committee had decided to request the presence of the two people that were at the meeting. "Due to the complexity of the bill, and because of the variety of expertise that was needed, they might need a diverse panel to provide expert opinion."

"But would any lawyers be among the selected experts?" another MP asks.

"The committee needs to understand they are not in a meeting of lawyers, but in parliament," Selau reasons. "Therefore, they should ultimately come up with a report that could go before Parliament for adoption."

Clearly frustrated with the pace of the proceedings, Harvard-educated lawyer, self-declared libertarian, and member of the oppositional Inkatha Freedom Party, Marco Oriani-Ambrosini, in a rare moment of direct confrontation between members, gets into a heated argument with the chairperson. "The committee needs to deal with issues pertaining to the law as lawyers," he says, pointing to the potential violation of the Constitution and international obligations. Like the expropriation of works that have been in the public domain by the state, these are complex issues that demand a legal opinion.

"But you are not seeking clarification and have to be more concise in your questioning," the chairperson interrupts him.

"I cannot shortcut the complexity simply because you want to do something without the complexity," Oriani-Ambrosini fires back. "Do you want me to ask silly questions to get silly answers?"

The altercations continue for another round of meetings, with the division between a pro-expert, disembedding-prone stance and a more embedded view reflective of South Africa's fractured political and cultural landscape remaining visible throughout. But by June 9, the committee finally resolves that the bill be redrafted by a task team involving the parliamentary legal advisor, state law advisor, and the legal advisor to the Department of Trade and Industry and that additional input be sought from a select group of experts.

The list of those experts is worth examining in more detail. In addition to five eminent law professors from universities in the Western Cape Province and one practicing lawyer, it includes the director of the Intellectual Property Division at the World Trade Organization; a member of the NGO Natural Justice, which had sounded the alarm on hoodia; and a representative for the Geneva-based (but now defunct) International Centre for Trade and Sustainable Development. Several aspects of this selection stand out. Although by 2010, South Africa had become home to a vibrant, well-organized sector of traditional healthcare providers offering services in a wide range of fields from prenatal care and male circumcision to alternative medicine, no practitioner of traditional knowledge was invited to join the task team. Furthermore, few, if any, of the selected legal experts appear to have had any professional experience of working with and within San communities or, for that matter, any other community. Finally, most are white males who have either graduated from or work at the University of Cape Town and who are not only spatially and culturally distanced from those communities but whose entire professional ethos is predicated on that detachment.

But the closed-shop atmosphere of this fraternity is not the only disembedding factor determining the bill's destiny. Fast-forwarding another couple of weeks to July 25, 2011, we witness another key feature of expert systems—the attempt to gain incontestable sovereignty over competing knowledge claims by deploying what one might call, following Karl Maton, techniques of epistemological condensation.[79] Such techniques involve a range of strategies, such as the recontextualization of the voices of others; the incorporation of other voices into one's own speech by quoting or acknowledging the source of such voices; the open denial of alternative viewpoints; the endorsement of other positions as true; or the use of emphatic forms ("I do believe"). Other mechanisms that may generate condensation include graphic formats like bulleted lists and flow charts, framing devices such as bracketing and redacting, or data processing technologies like spreadsheets, glossaries, and taxonomies.[80] Taken together, these techniques allow experts to strengthen the semantic density of their knowledge claims by compacting a large quantity of seemingly unrelated and simple symbols into smaller units of meaning, such as abbreviations, keywords, or definitions. Consequently, the more symbols are condensed, the stronger the semantic density and epistemic authority of a claim and the less likely the chance that such claims may be challenged by nonexperts. Finally, while the use of techniques of condensation is mostly associated with expert systems, hi-fi environments of communication, and sophisticated technologies of inscription, its opposite, epistemological rarefaction, tends to be prevalent in settings that favor low-fi, face-to-face communication among laypeople and that are not primarily aimed at asserting epistemic power.

Law is, of course, no exception to this dynamic, as condensation strategies are ubiquitous in a wide variety of legal writing. One area where condensation is especially noticeable is in the naming conventions governing the structure of statutes, the best-known being the division into sections, subsections, and clauses, and here, especially, the definitions that frequently make up the first section.[81] The significance of these naming conventions cannot be overestimated when elucidating the condensation strategies at work in a setting like the meetings of our portfolio committee. It may be stating the obvious that the drafting of legislation is a notoriously messy business, constantly vacillating between time-honored conventions, the whims of the political actors involved, and the cold expertise of seasoned attorneys working in government departments and Parliament. But even during the most unstructured of moments in the committee's deliberations, it is the imperative of form that always asserts itself. For example, over the entire two years of its work, the committee time and again returned to the licensing fees and distribution of royalties envisaged for the proposed National Trust Fund and the problems these might cause for the proper tagging of the bill. Instead of the formidable practical challenge of distributing royalties to amorphous communities, what appeared to worry parliamentarians most was the possibility that by transferring knowledge from the public domain to the state and by collecting fees for the use of such knowledge by third parties, such fees might more accurately have to be considered a tax and the bill an appropriation bill accordingly. And so, it bears reiterating what I have argued throughout. The preoccupation with form, playing out over weeks and months of seemingly fastidious quibbling, is more than a mere sign of institutional inertia deflecting from the more substantive issues before the committee. Formal language, terminological precision, and procedural continuity are productive forces that have tangible effects on the distribution and legitimation of power and the meanings people attribute to the web of relationships they find themselves in, often against their own will.

To illustrate, let us turn to the series of meetings between July 25 and mid-September 2011 in which the definitions of key terms such as *traditional* and *indigenous* move center stage. The former, recall, had figured prominently—and at times concurrently with *indigenous*—in the bill from the beginning as "traditional communities," "traditional knowledge," "traditional culture," "traditional context," "traditional music," "traditional cultural expression," or "traditional work." Having just returned from a conference at the WIPO head office in Geneva, the task team (now rechristened, in the parlance of international politics, working group) asks that the committee debate the legal advisors' suggestion to split up the earlier draft's concept of "traditional intellectual property" into two categories: "hereditary" and "derivative" intellectual property. And to clear up the confusion around the simultaneous use of *traditional* and *indigenous*, the working group further recommends that the latter term be used exclusively with respect to an "indigenous expression of culture or knowledge," an "indigenous community," or "indigenous origin." The recommendation begs the question: Why the need for new terminology? The rationale of these amendments, the chairperson of the group elaborates, stems from several issues that would arise if some of the provisions in the first draft pertaining to the basic requirements of copyright remain unchanged. For example, whereas the first draft only awarded protection to "recent" works by introducing the category of "hereditary" IP, works that have been passed down from generation to generation would also be protected. Likewise, in the bill's first incarnation, a "traditional design" cannot be "traditional" and "not form part of the state of the art" at the same time. But while under the proposed amendment, hereditary IP rights attach even without the design "not forming form part of the state of the art," derivative IP would have to comply with this requirement. Or take the example of ownership and transfer. Under the old draft, the National Trust Fund would be the owner of "traditional" knowledge, impeding the self-governance of communities. To mitigate this risk, the group advises that a tripartite distinction be made between hereditary IP owned by the community (or its representative), derivative IP owned by the author/creator, and, in the case of an unknown author/creator, IP owned by the trust.

Although much of the foregoing defies ready comprehension, and, as subsequent commentators have been quick to emphasize, may well doom the act to failure at some point in the future, the committee does not feel the slightest inclination to debate this new wording in any depth, preferring, instead, to rehash some of the same points already discussed for over a year. Leaving it to future committees—or the courts themselves should the act ever come into effect—to unravel the terminological knot the MPs tied themselves into, it might be more fruitful to examine how legitimation codes manufacture silent consent. For instance, one reason for the committee's willing acceptance of the new classification of eligible works may lie in the way the group pitched the proposed amendments to the meeting by using sophisticated forms of what one might call diagrams of authority. The group frames its work as a flow chart followed by a list of "minor issues" and "major issues" that are further broken down into "resolved" and "still unresolved" issues.[82] Each issue is then put in relation to basic copyright requirements, such as eligibility and ownership, and its place within the relevant sections in the host acts that are affected by the new language. But what is so remarkable about something as mundane as a PowerPoint slide? What distinguishes the group's way of getting its point across from all the diagrams and fancy fonts academics or salespeople use to win over audiences at conferences and trade fairs? The way, I believe, that the group resolves the issue of the interchangeable terms *traditional* and *indigenous* rests on a number of subtle shifts whose logic is not rooted in some unmediated truth or the ability to condense such truth in a single concept but in a sequence of traceable steps. Put another way, epistemic authority is not realized here by inductively or deductively substantiating what is external to the method being used but by foregrounding the method itself. The content, if you will, of the slides is not an argument *for* or *about* something as much as it is a demonstration of the reliability of the argument itself. Apart from producing semantic density, the group's presentation rehearses the input-output mechanism underlying legislative work by self-reflexively opening, if only for a moment, the black box of bureaucratic rationality—and then immediately closing it again afterward. "We have done our homework," the group seems to reassure the committee. "Trust us, we are the experts, and we know best."

At a deeper level, though, one might also think of resolution as a beginning rather than an endpoint. Or, better still, as what actor-network theorists refer to as a mediator—something that does not reconcile or even sublate contradictions as much as it invests them with renewed agency for setting in motion another round of debate for another shot at resolution. In other words, as much as the shift toward expert knowledge appears to bear out the criticism frequently leveled at the developmental state's affinity for a managerial style of governance and the depoliticization following in its wake, it also opens a space for politics. In settings like our portfolio committee meetings, expert knowledge does have a significant impact in foreclosing the possibility of working through a problem politically, ultimately leaving lawmakers with nothing but the text (in the deconstructionist sense where x means y and y is just another text) as the only way to keep the legislative process moving forward—and, indeed, to have law. Yet the intertextual chain that ensues from and reproduces condensation also becomes subject to contestation at every turn.[83] In fact, the substitution of *traditional* with the *heritage/derivative* binary might simply be viewed as weakening semantic density and as an invitation to the committee to query expert knowledge through efforts at rarefaction. The discussion between the MPs and the drafters on July 25, 2011, aptly illustrates the wave-like motion of law and politics, of alternating condensation and rarefaction pushing against each other.

> Harris (DA): "The draft is a vast improvement from what was previously produced." Still, it "would require individuals to not only read the discrete sections in the four bills related to IK, but the entire body of intellectual property." This might be complicated for the layperson's understanding, especially for indigenous communities.
>
> Advocate Alberts of the opposition party Freedom Front Plus (FF++) concurs: "Because the law is protecting people that are poorer and in rural areas, understanding is important." In fact, a recent conversation with WIPO officials about the matter had made him aware that "South Africa was at a threshold to make history." If the country were to create a separate law, it would be "making history by creating a new protectable interest as was the case with copyright in England 200 years ago."
>
> Meanwhile, when pressed on his opinion of the amendment, Advocate Johan Strydom, legal advisor to the Department of Trade and Industry, insists that he is not a policymaker and is reluctant to discuss matters of policy. Nonetheless, he is concerned about the future process of the legislation, reminding members that it is "important that a policy or political stance be adopted on the future approach to the bill."
>
> Taking a related line, the chairperson of the working group feels that the discussion about terminology "has become a sort of existentialist argument" and, as such, "is better suited for philosophers than the experts." Ultimately, though, she hastens to add, law is a complex matter, and an end to the discussion and a vote on the redraft are essential for the bill to pass.
>
> To this, however, the Parliament's legal advisor adds a note of caution. If the committee decided to do further redrafts, she suggests, the bill could not become a new principal act. It would need to reject the bill in toto and start a new one. In addition, the legislation is a continuation of a policy that had been approved by the cabinet. If this is rejected, the whole policy must also be reconsidered.

The specter of failure appears to steer the conversation into calmer waters: procedure ("continuation of policy"), form ("law is complex"), context ("understanding," "protecting people"), and transformation ("make history") are balancing each other out. Strong and weak semantic densities are intertwined. Condensation and rarefaction are at a standstill—at least for now. But in the second week of September 2011, with little more than two weeks to go until the National Assembly's final adoption of the bill, the legitimation skirmishes flare up again. In three lengthy meetings, members take on another gem: *folklore*. Associated with early nineteenth-century German Romanticism, the term had been, if not purged from IP terminology, downgraded to a mere synonym of the more acceptable *traditional cultural expressions* in the Revised Provisions for the Protection of Traditional Cultural Expressions/Expressions of Folklore adopted by WIPO in 1985, granting its members the right to use "other terms in national or regional laws."[84] Although some members found the term too restrictive and suggested that it be replaced with *traditional works*, the drafters had left the definition of *folklore* unchanged because it was not included in the host Copyright Act and, in a flagrant misreading of the revised provisions and contrary to numerous African countries using the term in their respective legislation, because discarding the definition would effectively distance South Africa from the internationally preferred terminology.[85]

Ultimately, however, this wrangling over an arcane, pejorative term is about more than technicalities. The fact that it resurfaced as a subject of debate in 2011 at all is nothing short of stunning because it reveals the persistence of the profound chasm between state-centric and community-oriented rationales of TCE protections and, congruent with this divide, the continued significance of broader claims of national identity and the right to speak about and for indigenous cultural practices. Recall that during the early stages of its journey through the institutions of global governance, the protection of folklore was thought of as a crucial component of the wider project of modernizing the newly independent nations, particularly in Africa. Accordingly, US representatives and UNESCO officials suggested that "Africa's problem" could be tackled by a combination of reshaped trade and intellectual property policies and an emphasis on education. But the latter entailed more than just a massive expansion of institutions of basic education or large-scale literacy campaigns. According to African delegations at the UNESCO 11th plenary session in 1960, it would have to include the unconditional and complete recognition of "African values" and "national heritage."[86] This stance stems, of course, from what Partha Chatterjee calls a "blocked dialectic" at the heart of anticolonial nationalist politics.[87] Paraphrasing Chatterjee, one might say that the accession of the new nation-states to the system of global governance and its intellectual property instruments, such as the Berne Convention, was not solely the result of pressure from the former colonial powers. It was the more profound, unquestioning acceptance of universal reason that prevented these states from dismantling a "framework of knowledge whose representational structure corresponds to the very structure of power nationalist thought seeks to repudiate." The dilemma, then, that follows from this "forced closure of possibilities" is how the nationalist agenda can "succeed in maintaining its difference from a discourse that seeks to dominate it." The answers given by early nationalist leaders from Senghor to Kenyatta—and, I would contend, the ANC-led postapartheid governments—are overwhelmingly in the realm of culture. Then, as now, a "truly modern nation in Africa or Asia would combine the superior material qualities of the West with Eastern spiritual greatness and African ancestral wisdom."[88]

Thus, if the notion of folklore espoused in the Intellectual Property Laws Amendment Act is rooted in the blocked dialectic of nationalist thought, the indigenist approach, with its emphasis on community-controlled safeguards against cultural appropriation, might indeed appear to be diametrically opposed to the nation-state's pretensions to cultural sovereignty over its diverse populace. On closer inspection, however, both tacks share the prominent role given to cultural rights to advance their respective, albeit diametrically opposed, claims to sovereignty. Having been excluded from the nationalist agenda and progressively failing to achieve political self-determination, especially on the African continent, the only difference between the indigenous movement and the nation-state lies in the former embracing a more capacious, holistic understanding of culture—not as a folkloric appendage signaling difference amid acquiescence to universal norms but as indispensably interwoven with the movement for a new, planetary regime of rights and protections comprising culture and nature, humans and other living beings.

In closing this section, a few words are in order about the alternative private member's bill tabled by Wilmot James (DA) and the further fate of the act. Drafted by Owen Dean, James's bill reflects the consensus of the submissions debated the previous year that a sui generis approach would be more desirable than the intellectual property framework adopted in the bill favored by the committee. In the end, James's bill was unsuccessful, and B8-2010 was adopted by both houses of the National Assembly and published in the *Government Gazette*. But, as of this writing, the act still awaits the president's signature to become operative. Meanwhile, opinions about it remain divided, with some applauding it as an example of the "positive protection of traditional cultural expressions by intellectual property rights" and others decrying it as a "cumbersome and ineffectual way of achieving the objective of protecting TK."[89] Whatever the flaws or merits of the act, the debate about the proper protection of indigenous knowledge and TCE is guaranteed to continue for many years to come, and it remains to be seen what alternative models, if any, will eventually emerge. Leaving, then, the portfolio committee, the assembly, and the president to their own devices, I will end this chapter and explore alternative ways of protecting traditional cultural expressions, freeing the discussion about indigenous communities from the narrow confines of the nation-state's legal templates and institutions.

Aesthetic Citizenship

Consider the following three scenarios. In 2005, Sony and South Africa's oldest record label, Gallo, joined forces to take one Johan (Joe) Theron to court on charges of infringement of several songs in their catalog. Besides being South Africa's porn king (he is the publisher of *Hustler* magazine), Theron is the director of the label Sting Music and the executive producer of the wildly popular *Africa Umoja*, a musical stage play featuring a blend of township music and "traditional" choreography.[90] Theron, the complainants alleged, in the show had used three well-known songs without permission: "Thula Baba," adapted from a lullaby in the public domain by Bertha Egnos, director and composer of the equally popular musical *Ipi-Ntombi*; "Nomathemba," composed by Joseph Shabalala, leader of Grammy Award–winning *isicathamiya* group Ladysmith Black Mambazo; and "Siliwelile," composed by Mthunzi Namba, Lindelani Mkhize, and Jabu Hlongwane. Until a settlement was finally reached in 2013, the suit dragged on for years, with Theron (incorrectly) insisting throughout that all three tunes were of "African origin" and had no known authors.

In 1995, Pops Mohamed released a set of two CDs entitled *Sanscapes One* and *Sanscapes Two*. The set is the result of a collaboration with the !Gubi Tietei family of the Omaheke Region in Namibia and is part of a benefit-sharing agreement with the San brokered by the lawyer Roger Chennells and overseen by WIMSA.[91] Prior to *Sanscapes*, the Benoni-born Mohamed had carved out a career by performing with the likes of Abdullah Ibrahim, Kippie Moeketsi, and other icons of South Africa's vibrant jazz scene until he embarked on a mission in the mid-1990s to save traditional music from the "pop-stars streaming in from abroad" by suffusing it with "modern sounds and rhythms to appeal to a wider audience."[92] Other than the somewhat obscure *Sanscapes*, the first commercially successful demonstration of this new direction was the 1997 album *How Far Have We Come*, followed by the soundtrack to *The Return of Sara Baartman*, a 2003 film documenting the tragic life of a young Khoikhoi woman with steatopygia who was enslaved and exhibited in Europe as the "Hottentot Venus," and whose mortal remains, preserved at the French *Musée de l'Homme* for over two centuries, were only returned to South Africa in 2002.[93] Both the CD-set and the soundtrack draw on the recordings of the Tietei family in combination with a pastiche of "smooth jazz" and xylophone, mbira, kora, and ambient sounds, all of which, the liner notes to *Sanscapes* tell us, convey a "real sense of empathy for the Khoi-San."[94]

In 1993, Skyline Film and Television Productions released *Distant Echoes: Yo-Yo Ma & the Kalahari Bushmen*, a documentary about the visit of world-renowned cellist Yo-Yo Ma with the Ju/'hoansi people of the Nyae Nyae Conservancy in Namibia. The trip, he tells the viewer, is a personal journey, a quest for "our common humanity." Playing the cello for a captive audience of Nyae Nyae residents and learning to play a San harp, he concludes, have taught him that music is a "universal language." "The cumulative power of the trance dance is as great as a Beethoven symphony or a Stravinsky ballet."[95]

What do these three episodes have in common? Aesthetic prospecting, infringements of copyright, or something else altogether? Under the provisions of the Copyright Act, Theron's adaptations are a clear infringement of Sony and Gallo's rights in the three works mentioned. As such, they serve as a painful reminder of the long history of unlawful appropriation of black creativity, especially by those who claim to have the best interest of African tradition at heart. As for the remaining two examples, the precise nature of the appropriation is harder to define. But although the details of Ma's arrangements with the Nyae Nyae community and the benefits of Mohamed's collaboration to the !Gubi Tietei family are unknown, there is every reason to question the purported noble intentions behind these musical encounters across sharply drawn social and cultural divides. For what is at stake here is more than the possibility that by failing to credit the musicians appearing on *Distant Echoes*, Ma may have violated their moral rights in claiming authorship. Serious questions are also raised by the way that both men's claims may be contradicted by their own logic. Their projects, I contend, are an exercise in ethical-aesthetic judgment, where value is attributed based on their potential to host different platforms of identification. Thus, when

Ma praises Ju/'hoansi music as "beautiful" and on par with Beethoven and Stravinsky, it is to enhance the appearance of the putatively primitive so it may fit in with an imaginary global ecumene of shared aesthetic values. More than that, the move allows Ma to position himself, in Bourdieu's sense, as a cultivated cosmopolitan whose activities and aspirational messages about humanity's common ground may well boost his social and symbolic capital but otherwise leave Ju/'hoansi with little ability to choose the concrete conditions under which they may inhabit that communal space. Much the same might be said about Mohamed's desire to insert himself into an aggrieved community's struggle for recognition and inclusion through feelings of compassion without acknowledging the individual artists living in that community. For example, when the liner notes to *Sanscapes* construe benefit-sharing as a natural fit for the San because they are "by nature" a "sharing society," would this not suggest that San intellectual property rights claims to their indigenous knowledge and TCE are necessarily unnatural?[96] Ma's universalist and Mohamed's slightly more relativist stance, then, form part of a technology of valorization that provides ethical legitimacy to the appropriation of San music through unidirectional gestures of recognition, expressions of empathy, and affirmations of commonality. But at the same time, to be effective, this technology presupposes an irreducible singularity and otherness against which the relative worth of the original may be gauged.

In this last section of the chapter, I invite the reader to think through possible alternatives to IP protections for indigenous knowledge and traditional cultural expressions. Several such alternatives have been suggested for quite some time and, other than sui generis legislation, include customary law, soft law, and, perhaps most promisingly, what has become known as traditional resource rights.[97] It is the latter concept that I want to expand on by connecting the conversations about intellectual property law, decolonial knowledge, and indigeneity that have informed this chapter with the vibrant scholarship from the recent past about aesthetics, ethics, and creative justice and its relationship to ideas of personhood, belonging, and what I call aesthetic citizenship. In coining this term, I do not intend to add yet another flavor to the potpourri of citizenships that since the 1990s have made the rounds across anthropology, sociology, and political science, including cultural citizenship, biological citizenship, discursive citizenship, epistemic citizenship, ecological citizenship, netizenship, or artistic citizenship, to name but a few.[98] While the last term may well seem a good fit for the alternative forms of belonging that might arise from and sustain a multiplicity of attachments and possessive relationships to culture, I maintain a critical distance from the adjective *artistic* for two reasons. For one, I want to confront the romantic fetishization of the individual artist as creator in tandem with the modernist myth of the work of art as the preeminent site of meaning-making. Following from this, I introduce the concept of aesthetic citizenship to forward a more capacious sense of cultural reproduction. Instead of the image of the passive consumer, I foreground the collective agency of audiences in coproducing aesthetic value by attending—mindful of the meaning of the ancient Greek term *aisthesis*—to the perceptual, material dimensions of audience behavior.

In many ways, the turn to the cultural in theories of citizenship is indebted to the growing sense of discomfort with classic conceptualizations of citizenship as a formal status defined by a set of rights and obligations and to the effort to draw attention to the more substantial aspects of citizenship as tied to specific cultural practices, identities, and civic qualities embraced by an ever more diverse citizenry in post–Cold War Western liberal democracies as the foundation of more malleable concepts of citizenship. Among the earliest and most influential of these interventions is Charles Taylor and Will Kymlicka's unapologetically liberal defense of minority rights based on the recognition of cultural difference.[99] Yet, as critics of this pluralist approach have pointed out, instead of tackling issues of economic, cultural, and political hegemony, it limits the question of more inclusive forms of citizenship to a perceived lack of rights, thus ultimately promoting a conception of democratic pluralism in which the Other can be "understood conversationally, antiessentially, ironically, as mere difference."[100] As an alternative to this post-ideological notion of cultural citizenship, these critics have developed sophisticated frameworks within which to explore the tensions increasingly coming to the fore between the formal rights of citizens as members of modernist nation-states and highly localized, innovative, and flexible systems of collective affiliation and civic life interweaving the biological and the biographical, the public and the private, the ecological and the expressive.

South Africa has been part and parcel of these debates from the outset. Its rise from centuries of white minority rule coincided with the explosion of cultural citizenship scholarship in the West during the 1990s.[101] In the most general sense, postapartheid South Africa supports both a liberal-pluralist (rainbow nation) and a republican (*ubuntu*) concept of citizenship. But a crucial difference exists in how culture is factored into these categories. In accordance with the constitutionally mandated goals of unity in diversity and redress for past injustice, the country recognizes special rights for cultural communities through legislation governing customary marriages, structures of traditional leadership, communal land rights, language rights, and the like. Provision is also made for so-called Chapter 9 Commissions such as the Commission for the Promotion and Protection of Cultural, Religious and Linguistic Communities. As such, these rights not only straddle the divide between the material and the cultural aspects of South African lives, they must also be in concordance with the equality section 9 (1) of the constitution.

But, at the same time, culture has historically figured and continues, in many ways, to be viewed as a category of exclusion. From the early nineteenth century, British colonial discourse imagined culture in two distinct yet interdependent ways. In the first meaning, culture was an achievement, the result of humanity's ability to create itself by placing humans above nature, including our own. But this culture, held to manifest itself in the superior technologies, laws, arts, and moral values of the colonizers, reached its apogee as transcendent, human Culture (in the uppercase) only because it was distinct from a multitude of indigenous cultures (in the lowercase) rooted in timeless ethnic and racial essences. South Africa's efforts to dismantle apartheid's legacy of racialized communities and to create new opportunities for civic engagement across racial and ethnic divides notwithstanding, both Culture and cultures remain important, though largely hidden, ordering principles in restorative projects and the ideology of nation-building. Concretely, they manifest in what Adam Habib and Kristina Bentley refer to as "nativist" and "civic" models of redress and how these models imagine and address the citizenry. While the former requires the state to "represent" the population "proportionally" according to race or ethnicity, the latter is primarily concerned with poverty alleviation and economic equality. Accordingly, the forms of citizenship that may be said to correspond to these models are those rooted in cultural difference in the nativist case and in "human," nonracial Culture in the civic example.[102] A third type, finally, of cultural citizenship that has increasingly attracted attention is Afropolitanism. Conceived as a project of defamiliarization and deprovincialization, Afropolitanism is a lived practice and scholarly orientation that seeks to shift the center of gravity of traditional forms of analysis and interpretations of Africa from a fixed place of marginality, victimhood, and absolute Otherness toward one of mobility, connectivity, and metropolitan worldliness.[103]

Ultimately, though, these various reworkings of citizenship are of limited use for developing alternative visions of indigenous citizenship and the protections they may afford to indigenous knowledge practices and traditional cultural expressions. Despite the emphasis on the tactical, deterritorializing nature of such civic practices, these reinterpretations all too often rely on a narrative that either pits liberal-democratic citizens' rights against the "pragmatics" of citizenship or casts normative, disciplinary forms of citizenship in opposition to "negotiated," "discursive" ones.[104] In what follows, therefore, I will explore ways of collective attachment to expressive forms and practices that do not necessarily involve their commercialization, subordination to the developmentalist rationale of the nation-state, or proprietary rights protection. Equally, though, I also resist any notion that indigenous people's struggles for self-determination are well served by grounding allegations of cultural appropriation in some putative essential identity that makes these claims legible to the law in the manner envisaged by the act. In fact, I am concerned that in the context of the postapartheid politics of ethnicity, the prevention of cultural appropriation by legal means and its justification through some version or another of anti-anti-essentialism or benign ethnic nationalism will merely reproduce the very liberal premises of possessive individualism that led to the current stalemate in the first place.

The idea that there might be some correlation between aesthetics and a cluster of norms that bestow on—or deny—a person the status of a citizen of a country or community is as old as art itself. In recent years, though, the debate has taken on new urgency as cornerstones of the liberal-democratic order, such as voting rights, social grants, and human rights have become the subject of fierce contestation over the incorporation and rights of immigrants, refugees, or ethnic, religious, and other minorities that do not meet the full set of criteria defining citizenship proper. Much of this controversy oscillates between two premises—an autonomist and a functionalist view of art and the artist. According to the first hypothesis, the aesthetic is situated in a world of its own, divorced from the merely pleasant, practical, or political. On the functionalist view, by contrast, the aesthetic has always been at the service of a purpose beyond the sensory gratification art is said to afford. But as such, art and the artists that produce it typically reproduce or "represent," as Jacques Attali might put it, the prevailing order, in turns eulogizing authoritative figures, instilling a sense of common identity and shared values, or providing images of exemplary civic engagement and upliftment.[105]

But there is also a third way, according to which aesthetics bears an affinity to ethics within itself. It is this deeper meaning of art as both a repository and a school for the cultivation of ethical conduct that informs a series of studies on artistic citizenship that have appeared in the aftermath of the ethical turn in the humanities during the 1990s. For instance, in two identically titled collections on "artistic citizenship," the authors seek to forward a "civic-social-humanistic-emancipatory" project by enlisting a wide range of educational, institutional, and philosophical perspectives on the meaning of creativity at the intersection of the private and the public spheres in liberal democracies of the twenty-first century.[106] Thus, for Randy Martin, the explosion of community-based arts organizations geared toward all sorts of social projects and services, from assisting children at risk to the enhancement of school scores, serves as an example of what he calls the "paradox" of artistic citizenship inherent in socially conscious creative activity. On the face of it, such publicly visible activity might be judged as the classic embodiment of the ideal of ethical engagement. But at the same time, the artist who is doing good—rather than merely being "good" at their art—might be taken to merely conform to normative expectations of the artist as an exemplary representative of their country or community, thus also potentially alienating them from the private sphere of their creative endeavors. To bridge this gap between making art and judging art, between private expression and public responsibility, Martin appears to have a Kantian concept of judgments of taste as a *sensus communis aestheticus* in mind. This common aesthetic sense, Kant wrote, entails the "power to judge that takes account (a priori) of everyone else's imagination . . . in order to compare one's judgment, in our thought, of everyone else's way of presenting [something], in order as it were to compare our own judgment with human reason in general." In other words, because taste consists in the ability to judge the way that moral ideas are made sensible, its true propaedeutic lies in "developing our moral ideas and in cultivating moral feeling."[107] At the same time, Martin goes on to state, Kant excludes artists from the community that is engendered by "disinterested" judgments of taste because they are by definition "interested." Asked to remain silent about the terms and conditions through which their art works in the world, artists thus remain partial citizens, left with but one choice to become full artistic citizens—to search in themselves for the authority "by which we are obligated to one another."[108]

Martin's concept of artistic citizenship intersects with some of the ideas explored by Wayne D. Bowman. Like Martin, Bowman stresses authority and duty as the defining features of artistic citizenship. "The rights and privileges artists enjoy do implicate responsibilities—to those within one's practice . . . and to society more broadly." To this extent, artistic citizens are "stewards of individual rights and freedom on one hand, and agents of civic education on the other."[109] But there are differences in the way the artist's autonomy and obligations relate to the idea of citizenship in a more general sense. Here, Bowman distinguishes two conflicting models of citizenship—the civic-republican and the liberal-individualist. In the former, the emphasis is on active involvement in collective forms of decision making and, hence, on individual agency and a person's rights and obligations as being closely intertwined with a strong sense of one's identity and belonging to a specific community. In the liberal-individualist view of citizenship, by contrast, rights, entitlements, and privileges are more the result of contract-like agreements under which a person accepts a limited number of obligations impinging on their private life in return for a maximum of individual liberties in the public sphere. Accordingly, such a person is typically less invested in citizenship as a central determinant of their identity and more open to extending citizen status to others willing to opt into the social contract.

The fundamental question that follows from this distinction between the civic-republican and liberal-individualist view of citizenship for Bowman is one of ethics: "How does citizen status relate to one's personal, ethical convictions about the kind of person it is good to be and the kind of society required for its realization?" How can we conceptualize the arts and artists as engaging people in "deliberations about how individual rights relate to broader public interests?" What are the complex relationships between artists' rights and freedoms on the one hand and artists' responsibilities on the other? Answers to these questions, Bowman goes on to argue, cannot come from the two approaches to ethics prevalent in the Western philosophical tradition. Both the notion at the heart of duty or deontic ethics that righteous action is determined by its compliance with an absolute moral norm and the consequentialist-utilitarian idea that the propriety of an action is gauged by its consequences are concerned with determining a rational course of action—what it is *right to do*.[110] And while these two positions may be part of ethics, the subordination of individual freedoms to duties makes both equally unsuited for developing the idea of artistic citizenship. Rather, claims to such citizenship must be grounded in some version of (neo) Aristotelian virtue ethics, that is, in personal integrity and the ability to pursue right courses of action by recourse to "habitually developed, character-based ethical dispositions." Instead of setting abstract norms or moral codes as the sine qua non of ethical behavior, virtue ethics asks what kind of person it is *good to be*. And unlike rule-governed notions of ethics, virtue ethics rests on a form of practice that does not "consist in the execution of prescribed duties but in action that is optimally responsive to the unique demands of the situation at hand."[111]

The idea of ethics as practice is crucial for artistic citizenship insofar as creative endeavors can be construed as "potent ethical resources." But to become meaningful as a distinct form of ethical practice, these endeavors must be distinguished from other modes of human activity, such as technical, rule-governed activities or mere behavior. Unlike these, Bowman suggests, artistic practices are centrally concerned with habits and values that serve goods that are "*internal* to the practice." And in contrast to mere technical activities where the end is external to the practice and the relationship between intention and end is judged in terms of efficiency, the ends of artistic practice are often indeterminate and, hence, subject to deliberation. That is why the vibrancy and, indeed, the very existence of art as a living practice depends on the extent to which its intrinsic goods are not eclipsed by those external and not constitutive to it. Thus, between them, personal responsibility for the vitality of common artistic practices and nurturing "in oneself the habit of changing habits . . . in light of ethical deliberation about how best to live" is what lies at the heart of artistic practice. To be an artistic citizen "is to be a certain kind of person."[112]

Bowman's thoughts help carve out a space for articulating indigenous aesthetic practices and concepts of belonging in ways that destabilize the static ideas of personhood and citizenship imagined by the act's core category of the indigenous community. But herein also lies a danger. While on the one hand, Bowman may simply be rehashing Kant's point about morality as aesthetic judgment's propaedeutic, on the other hand, he almost seems to fall back on a pre-Kantian notion of art as appreciated solely, in Kant's words, when "we like it as a means," when it is "something useful."[113] Bowman writes: "Perhaps we might say that an artistic citizenry *exemplifies* lives lived ethically and responsibly, in pursuit of the kinds of goods I have here described . . . as virtuous." But as useful as the artist as a paragon of ethical behavior may be to "society at large," this expediency may reproduce the very hierarchical relationships between the artist and audience that an artistic citizenry is meant to overcome in the first place. Little wonder, then, that the ideal artistic citizen would be one whose practice is embedded in "older" forms of cooperation and community—such as the "indigenous community" invented by the present act.[114]

On the face of it, the parallels between Bowman's two forms of citizen ethics and the relationship between IP rights and the public interest seem obvious enough. Indeed, in the eyes of many legal theorists, the essence of copyright rests on a "default ethical vision" ab initio.[115] If, for instance, the limitations imposed on exclusive rights under the liberal-individualist model of citizenship are held to be reconcilable with the consequentialist notion that such restrictions ultimately serve the public good, the civic-republican model is based on strong moral norms that recognize the benefits to the public without any protracted consequentialist argument required. Other aspects of copyright that might be said to mediate between deontic and consequentialist ethics include the notion that the commercial transactions between the author of an original work and the audience as a user of such works assume that such transactions have been negotiated in good faith. But the contractual nature of the transaction also carries strong moral-affective connotations, at least in civil law traditions. They enmesh the author and the audience in relationships of mutual acknowledgment and respect that are simultaneously deontic and consequentialist. For example, the author's interest in his or her work is treasured, but so too is the public's affective labor and attachment to the author.[116] Lastly, fair dealing and fair use exceptions resonate with both republican and individualist ethics by benefiting institutions with a clear ethical mandate, such as schools and libraries, while at the same time they enjoin these institutions to refrain from abusing the exceptions.

Despite all of this, one cannot but notice a certain discrepancy between the potential of virtue ethics for the protection of indigenous cultural expressions and the place of ethics in IP jurisprudence more generally. While ethical concerns about IP have gained new urgency in the wake of the digital revolution and the ever-wider gulf between private rights and the public interest, the debate has largely been framed in terms of natural rights and utilitarian justifications for copyright protection.[117] Alternative approaches are few and far between. But it is precisely nondeontological and nonutilitarian interventions that seem particularly germane to rethinking the relationship between traditional cultural expressions and ethics-based forms of belonging. For example, drawing on Foucault's work on "ethopoietic" self-writing, Victor Tadros argues that the ethics of different legal and practical approaches to writing—which, in my view, comprise any form of cultural reproduction—is concerned with more than justice. It is about the production and reproduction of a certain kind of ethical subject.[118] This subject, however, cannot be that of the sovereign author whose writing, according to Foucault, constitutes a narrative of oneself; nor, in fact, can it be what in an earlier essay on authorship he described as a mere "function" impeding the free circulation and manipulation of ideas.[119] Rather, this subject is one whose ethics are shaped by the cultural text and a notion of cultural reproduction as a technique of the self. In his work on the ethics of file-sharing, David Lametti likewise argues for what he calls an "ethics of aspiration." This is a form of situated ethics that goes beyond mere rule-following by directing individuals to "aspire to the best exemplars of actions or norms." Concretely, in merging copyright teleology with the virtues of sharing that are intrinsically appreciated in cultures around the world, some forms of file-sharing might foster a copyright ethics governed by judgments that are sensitive to the specific contexts in which they occur.[120]

Another variant of this *as-if* ethics is proposed by Reinold Schmücker, who conceives of an ethics of copying as a set of specific rules that fill the void left by current legal norms and might nurture the "intersubjective recognition of moral principles for distinguishing between legitimate and illegitimate forms of copying."[121] However, given that there are no normative foundations for an ethics of copying, it can do no better than other ethical models than to forward a set of normative assumptions and rules assumptions or moral judgments relative to acts of copying that he calls "domain-specific ethics."

Finally, Charles Ess is interested in the correlation among different notions of selfhood, ethics, and property. In contrast to copyright utilitarianism's individualistic concept of selfhood, he reasons, virtue ethics does not only rest on a strong relational sense of self; in the context of the digitization of cultural production, the analogous idea of property as an inclusive right increasingly asserts itself. Thus, copying an important text—as in the Confucian or the humanist tradition of the commonplace book—entails the acquisition and practice of important virtues like respect, care, and patience, contributing to "reflection upon and cultivation of one's own judgment (phronesis) and thereby one's character as a human being."[122]

Mapping these and Bowman's reflections on the indigenous community envisaged by the Intellectual Property Laws Amendment Act, there does not appear to be a neat fit between the forms of citizenship imagined by either the republican-civic or the liberal version of ethics. In fact, there is hardly any avenue through which indigenous communities might legitimately advance claims to a special form of citizenship beyond the narrow, homogenizing parameters set by the liberal-democratic state in the first place. This lacuna is particularly pronounced in contexts where such claims are intimately intertwined with a posture that explicitly flouts the rules of moral conduct expected from the law-abiding citizen while, at the same time, insisting that these claims accord with the virtue ethics of the person it is good to be. A good example of this tension is the aesthetics of Zulu *ngoma* dancing explored by Louise Meintjes in her groundbreaking *Dust of the Zulu: Ngoma Aesthetics after Apartheid*. Men dancing ngoma, Meintjes argues, are engaged in an ethical practice that seeks to simultaneously remember, contain, and transcend the legacy of violent encounters during the colonial and apartheid eras through bodily and sung displays of manly ferocity and competence. One of the high points of this expertly controlled symbolic aggression is *ulaka*, or anger. Whether anger is born from feelings of frustration with one's own performance, inner-team rivalries, or experiences of collective injustice, key to ulaka's potency in preventing its inherent potential for violence from turning into actual violence is that it is an ethical disposition. A socially and historically rooted practice of expression, it is offered as a justification for "unwavering (ethical or moral) action in specific circumstances."[123] In a powerful illustration of the workings of ulaka, Meintjes recounts how decades-long tensions within the ngoma dance community fueled by the brutal assassination of Dudu Ndlovu, a dancer in Johnny Clegg's band Savuka, are reconciled through the ability of aesthetics to turn ulaka into a "fully lived quality of a responsible man." In a "responsible act of manhood," the two teams most affected by the strife engaged in a competitive dance that incorporates memory and reconciliatory work by reactivating rather than repressing anger within the confines of ulaka ethics. However, as Meintjes is careful to point out, this aestheticization of violence does not, and most likely is not meant to, provide final resolution of the conflict. Rather, it is the ambiguity of ngoma aesthetics of constantly hovering between virtual and actual violence that "enables the use of ulaka for social ends."[124] The instrumentalization of the arts for projects of social restoration, then, is not compromised by aesthetic ambiguity; it is made possible by it.

The intersection of aesthetics and ethics also looms large in other expressive forms, such as hip hop and even in what many consider to be its frivolous precursor, *kwaito*. In *Kwaito's Promise: Music and the Aesthetics of Freedom in South Africa*, Gavin Steingo rejects both "struggle" narratives of art as a weapon and denunciations of kwaito as an apolitical aberration. Instead, he wishes to "reinvigorate a politics of aesthetics at a time when aesthetic judgment is often dismissed as mere ideological mystification."[125] In Soweto—the site of Steingo's ethnographic activities—this politics plays out on an uncertain terrain marked by debilitating job insecurity, rampant crime, and, most crucially, the art of "survivalist improvisation."[126] In other words, freedom is experienced not as liberation from an oppressive regime but as freedom from employment, safety, and stability. Or, as Steingo puts it, "If music during apartheid expressed the struggle *for* freedom, then kwaito expresses the struggle *of* freedom."[127] In light of this dire assessment, to speak of aesthetics in Kantian terms as the realm par excellence of disinterested judgment and "purposiveness without purpose" would most likely strike most Sowetans as counterintuitive, if not utterly preposterous. And yet, it is precisely some of this sense of autonomy that Steingo seeks to reclaim as the ground from which to foster the kind of "ethical resources" needed for the elaboration of the "person it is good to be."[128]

Similarly, in Born to Kwaito: Reflections on the Kwaito Generation, anthropologist Esinako Ndabeni and journalist Sihle Mthembu grapple with the "burden of responsibility" imposed on the first generation of black South Africans born into, or coming of age in, the new postapartheid order to be socially and politically conscious and that enjoins artists to harness kwaito's "potential in the socio-economic development" of the country. However, alleviating this burden by asserting the poststruggle generation's "newfound right to unbridled expression" and to free kwaito from its pejorative association with political abstinence and wanton immorality reveals some uncomfortable truths about kwaito's ethical foundations from which this recovery of the freedom of expression might derive its justification.[129] For instance, in one chapter, Ndabeni discusses the hypermasculinity exuded by some kwaito artists and the domestic and sexual violence against women allegedly committed by kwaito luminaries such as "Dr. Mageu" Ntshebele or Arthur Mafokate. These and similar acts, she implies, are part of an epidemic waiting to happen. "Since there is a link between language and action, there is a link between the way kwaito's men, and by extension black men, sing about women and how they will treat them. . . . The warning signs are often in the lyrics we ignore."[130] In another take on male braggadocio and misogynist lyrics—in short, unethical behavior—in gangsta rap, media scholar Adam Haupt discusses the "burden of representation" and the refusal to recycle mainstream media's uplifting images of black lives. Following Eithne Quinn, he reads this burden as finding expression in a "tyranny of authenticity" that interpellates hip-hop artists to provide images of ghetto life as true representations of black culture while simultaneously demanding that they speak on behalf of black communities and their cultural achievements in uplifting terms.[131]

I want to amplify Ndabeni's and Haupt's assertion by tying it back to the notion that artistic practices are centrally concerned with habits and values that serve neo-Aristotelianism's "internal goods."[132] Kwaito is about more than lyrics. It is fundamentally about a whole new type of personhood after apartheid—one that is as much enabled by the new liberties afforded in democratic South Africa as it is constitutive of that very freedom in everyday aesthetic practice. It is in the pragmatics of cultural reproduction as a whole—in the compositional strategies, technologies of studio production, structures of circulation and reception—and not in the products or their semantics that the ethical is bound to reside. And it is precisely in this area that the South African hip-hop industry—and, as the #MeToo debate has shown, cultural industries across the world—has failed miserably. As of this book's writing, the evidence of female artists being sidelined, exploited, harassed, and raped keeps coming in on an almost weekly basis.

Where is the audience in all this, the reader might ask? Among them, the above interventions might be said to suffer from an author-artist-centrism that leaves important questions about the aesthetic agency of audiences and what Jerrold Levinson calls an "ethics of response" unanswered.[133] While the virtuous artist-citizen is idealized as an exceptional figure occupying the moral high ground, the specific ethical qualities that might bestow an equally elevated status on audiences remain somewhat undertheorized. In fact, from Plato to Adorno, audiences have been seen as easily corruptible and in need of either education or outright moral censure. How, then, might we theorize in nonnormative, nonmoral terms the relationship between aesthetic and ethical practices that incorporates both artist and audience? If the connection between sensory perception and aesthetic features is always culturally and socially mediated, how can we grasp this relationship in terms other than those of some pure individual aesthetic experience or, conversely, an "ethical absolutism" dictating conformity with majority morality?[134] How is an aesthetics and ethics of appropriation possible that takes into consideration the rapidly changing circumstances of South African cultural reproduction while at the same time being committed to an ethics grounded in changing human needs and what Mark Banks calls "creative justice?"[135] And lastly, how can such an ethics be enforced?

From a normative perspective, one might argue that what's good for the goose is good for the gander. That is, in a perfect world of shared values, the artist's ethics does not precede that of the audience: both share the same commitments. Reasoning further along this line of thought, one might also postulate that in aesthetic practices like the ngoma ethics described by Meintjes, a collectively held sense of moral duty and its articulation through the affective register of ulaka is made possible when the distinction between artist and audience has not yet reached the salience it has gained in the West. But even where such a distinction might be absent in remote parts of the country, the more likely scenario is that this absence is owed to traditional cultural expressions increasingly becoming absorbed into an emerging culture of "configurability."[136]

In the remaining pages of this chapter, I want to pursue a different tack, however. To the extent that TCE should be considered as texts in the sense that they are webs of unstable semiotic relations that are irreducible to a single author or referent, an ethics of the kind envisaged by Bauman cannot stop at the ethical artist as the sole driving force of alternative ways of protecting TCE. It must also include this intertextual network and the reading practices embroiled in it. In other words, there can be no ethics that is not also attuned to the text itself. In this vein, I will begin with a discussion of Elaine Scarry's concept of "perceptual care."[137] Beautiful things, she argues in her extended essay, *On Beauty and Being Just*, serve as "small wake-up calls to perception, spurring lapsed alertness back to its most acute level."[138] Her position is markedly at odds with the banishing of beauty as a category of academic discourse over the past couple of decades because, as Scarry herself emphasizes, it directly challenges the claim that by preoccupying our attention, beauty prevents us from attending to injustice. Another reason why the expatriation of the beautiful from the humanities must be questioned is that it has placed the act of looking—and by extension, any form of sensory engagement with beauty—under general suspicion as reifying the source of pleasure. Those two arguments against reinstating the beautiful, she writes, are not only questionable in themselves, but they also fundamentally contradict one another. The first assumes that generous attention is justified only if it can be "made to latch onto a specific object," such as an injustice. But according to the second argument, sustained attention—otherwise known as the "gaze"—will always do damage to the object, thus making ethically sensitive attention inconceivable from the outset.[139]

Having refuted the arguments of the opponents of beauty as a self-evident category of aesthetics, Scarry then proceeds to an exquisitely written exploration of how the beautiful "assists us in the work of addressing injustice" and precisely what aspect of beauty it is that "continually recommits us to a rigorous standard of perceptual care" and justice.[140] Scarry lists several attributes of beauty: the symmetry of form or evenness in the site of the beautiful object, including the departure and exceptions from itself that symmetry champions; the "generous sensory availability" of beauty offering itself up to "almost all people at almost all times"; the aliveness that the beautiful thing affirms in the perceiver to protect it and, vice versa, the lifelikeness the perceiver confers on the object; the pressure beauty exerts toward the distribution or extension of our attention from one particular object to all beautiful objects; and, finally, a "radical decentering" inherent in beauty to dislocate us from our imaginary position as the center.[141]

Delving deeper into these attributes would be beyond the scope of this chapter. What matters for my inquiry is Scarry's insistence that each of these attributes can be found at the site of the beautiful object, of the perceiver's beholding of the object, and in the act of creating the object in equal shares. In this way, the perceptual care owed to beauty can never be a solitary affair involving only one site and one attribute, be it the object, creation, perception, aliveness, or pressure toward distribution. All are intertwined in inviting us to move from the beautiful to the just. For instance, symmetry, as a hallmark of aesthetic fairness, assists us in recognizing it as akin to John Rawls's definition of social fairness as the "symmetry of everyone's relations to each other."[142]

Postcolonial theorists, anthropologists, or even ethnomusicologists may wince at the aesthetic essentialism underlying Scarry's advocacy for the politico-moral neutrality of beauty, considering it somewhat passé if not flat Eurocentric.[143] Perhaps they are right. Surely, some of us would emphatically deny the universality of aesthetic norms, such as symmetry of form. Others may even assert our host communities' capacity for aesthetic pleasure independent of any moral imperatives or social function. And many are likely to argue that in parts of the Global South, beautiful things in and of themselves do, in fact, exert the kind of pressure that makes people attend to those things and other people equally affected by them in responsible, just ways. But most of us also insist that there is no contradiction between this defense of beauty as a sui generis domain of human creativity and the attention to its location within or adjacent to other domains of human endeavors, such as the immense effort on numerous fronts and through a vast array of techniques, rules, and beliefs to achieve some kind of lasting balance between a meaningful existence as living, sentient beings and the scarcity of the resources the world has in store for us. A balance that some call "society" or "community," others prefer to render in images of transcendental harmony, and yet others like to couch in terms of ubuntu. The worlds described by Meintjes, Steingo, Ndabeni, and Mthembu are each, in their own way, a case in point.

What might elicit the most spirited objections to Scarry's argument, however, is the rather nonchalant way she glosses over the precise nature of these attentive continuities between beauty and justice. In fact, she readily admits that they are essentially little more than analogies. "In the absence of its counterpart, one term of an analogy actively calls out for its missing fellow.... An analogy is inert and at rest only if both terms are present in the world." Or in more florid terms: "Ongoing work is actively carried out by the continued existence of a locus of aspiration: the evening skies, the dawn chorus of roosters and mourning doves, the wild rose that, with the sweet pea, uses even prison walls to climb on."[144] In other words, where justice is lacking, beauty will demand it. The dilemma, then, for Scarry and perhaps for an alternative intellectual property ethics and the aesthetic citizenship enabling and being enabled by it might be how to simultaneously hold on to beauty and justice as distinct spheres while anchoring the beauty-justice, aesthetic-ethic nexus in more stable configurations. What kind of relationality can be imagined that is neither causal nor analogous? How can the brittle alliance between domains as heterogeneous as the realm of aesthetics (by definition, a perceptual and, according to Scarry, permanent and universal domain) and justice (a more transcendent, incomplete, transient kind) be made into assemblages available to anthropological inquiry? Or is it, rather, this very fragility that constitutes the actual ethnographic object? And instead of uncovering the intrinsic nature of the aesthetic and ethical domain by analogy or comparison as an older brand of anthropology was wont to do, might it, therefore, make more sense to bring into view the relational contingency and in-betweenness that keeps beauty and justice in dialogue with one another?

There are no ready answers to these questions. Much less is the above easily translatable into the idiom espoused by the Intellectual Property Laws Amendment Act. When I discussed my reflections on ethics and aesthetic citizenship as an alternative form of protecting TCE with some well-known legal scholars, one of them echoed the old maxim *ubi jus ibi remedium*, where there is a right, there is a remedy. In other words, a right is a right as long as it can be enforced. But as conventional copyright excludes traditional cultural expressions from the categories of protected works, and the Intellectual Property Laws Amendment Act, in turn, is unlikely to compensate for this lacuna, there is an urgent need for alternatives. Hence, given the more impromptu, noncoercive nature of the alternative form of justice sketched above, I resist offering a clear-cut answer to this question that might be concordant with copyright's means-to-end logic. Instead, I will end with a few preliminary thoughts on how to align this alternative vision more closely with my home disciplines' concerns with the complex material relations binding people, things, and ideas together. The first is obvious enough. We have to look beyond either intellectual property law or some form or other of sui generis legislation by exploring concepts of belonging that transcend both reified notions of community and formal definitions of citizenship underwriting liberal democracies. The second thought may appear somewhat counterintuitive in light of the emphasis above on the intrinsic value of the beautiful: we need more quantitative and qualitative work on the material conditions under which TCE are produced and what intersections if any exist between aesthetic practices and livelihood strategies without reducing either to the instrumentalist logic of copyright law. The scope of such an inquiry may, for instance, encompass the relationship between land and music as expounded, for example, in Grace Koch's work on song and land claims among Aboriginal and Torres Strait Islanders or Dylan Robinson's fascinating work on the compositional and representational practices in the context of indigenous cultural politics in Canada.[145] But it also needs to go beyond those established locations of indigenous aesthetic practice and explore more recent deployments of beauty and ideas of access, attachment, and belonging in the construction, restoration, and reproduction of different forms of TCE not only in nonproprietary settings, such as museums and archives, but also in more commercial contexts, such as tourism and the heritage industries. Finally, it must ask questions about how cooperative structures of material production and expressive practice may become necessary prerequisites of—or to use Scarry's felicitous phrase—"demand" a new ethics and vice versa.

FOUR

Circulating Evidence
The Truth about Piracy

Violent conflict is nothing new in South Africa—the country was founded on violence from the very start. But of late, South Africans are witnessing a different kind of violence. In addition to reruns of battles long staged (and lost) in much larger theaters elsewhere—US President Lyndon Johnson's War on Poverty, Nixon's war on drugs, and George W. Bush's war on terror come to mind—the country now finds itself in the grip of a more permanent state of warfare in which a dizzying array of political, economic, social, and cultural disputes regularly spill over into (increasingly lethal) violence. Specifically, in no particular order: taxi wars between competing minibus operators or (more recently) between old-style cabbies and Uber drivers; deadly assaults on immigrants who are mocked as *izinunu* (monsters) and *amakwerekwere* (those speaking unintelligible languages); a war on rhinoceroses and a counterattack on the crime syndicates killing them by the thousands; violent clashes between rivaling trade unions; gang wars in the country's overcrowded and drug-infested prisons; poo wars that see Cape Town residents dumping buckets of sewage at municipal offices to protest unenclosed cabriolet toilets temporarily set up in the city's informal settlements; and, finally, and grimmest of all, an epidemic of sexual violence and femicides.[1]

And then there are the culture wars. These are the kinds of altercations that regularly pit traditionalists of various stripes against more liberal-minded sections of the populace over the authority to define the country's moral boundaries in matters ranging from a painting of a half-naked president to TV soaps featuring gay men in open embrace.[2] In December 2011, however, an entirely novel type of culture war loomed—a war over the ownership of ideas. At a press conference opening the South African Police Service's festive season operations, then Minister of Police Nathi Mthethwa declared what he called a "people's war" on piracy. Speaking to a group of senior police officials, representatives of various government agencies, entertainment industry associations, and "various artists, most of whom are direct victims of piracy," the minister boasted in true "struggle" lingo, that this war had the "resolve and support of many law-abiding South Africans." And since piracy, he added mingling violence with religion, was "tantamount to daylight robberies" that destroy the country's artistic legacy, "society" should join the police in a "crusade to clean out the streets."[3]

In politics, a few months can be a lifetime. But it is probably no coincidence that just months prior to Mthethwa's belligerent speech, the Business Software Alliance (BSA) released the 2010 edition of its *Global Software Piracy Study*, an annual report on what it describes as "key trends and findings" in cybersecurity. Speaking for the world's leading software producers (i.e., copyright owners), the body claimed that South Africa's "piracy rate" was 35 percent.[4] Although this number compared favorably to much higher rates in the rest of Africa and the Middle East, the document goes on to state, South Africa still ranked much higher than the advanced economies of North America and the EU, giving an idea of just how enormous a drain piracy is on the country's economic growth. Legislative reform—which includes the criminalization of any and all forms of copyright infringement—and "education" on the wider significance of copyright, the report concludes, would be key to "social progress."

Criticism of Mthethwa and the BSA was not long in coming. Andrew Rens of the Creative Commons think tank Shuttleworth Foundation, for instance, argued that the proposed policy would be out of touch with the realities of the country where "there has never been a process in which the development needs of South Africa were taken into account in writing intellectual property legislation."[5] Worse, he cautioned, if the BSA were to succeed in its lobbying efforts to make copyright law more onerous and protectionist, "it wouldn't be long before the country would see extended copyright terms and ACTA-[Anti-Counterfeiting Trade Agreement] like 'three strikes' laws kicking people off the internet for being suspected of infringing copyright." Rather than protect innovation, Rens went on to state, oddly confusing the justification for copyright with patent law, copyright law could "stifle innovation to benefit a broken business model that has better funding." Other commentators took a more cynical view. For instance, blogger Elimentals, had the broader rationale of criminal justice in mind: "So they want our already overburdened Justice system to foot the bill for something that mostly benefits international companies?" Still another blogger, Reelix, parodying a 2004 slogan created by the Motion Picture Association of America that equates piracy with theft, proclaimed: "I might not steal a car . . . but I'd copy/paste one if I could."[6]

Society? Progress? Development? Robbery? Terms such as these abound in South Africans' everyday conversations and are not limited to conversations about piracy. Yet, they are far from being self-evident. They are the discursive currency through which South Africans negotiate much larger visions of statehood, personhood, citizenship, prosperity, property, legality, and morality. And although these visions, in part, reflect core liberal ideals, they also obscure the ambivalent historical relationship between liberalism and South Africa's legacy of settler colonialism and apartheid. Take the term *people*. On the one hand, it seems to imply that piracy forms the backdrop against which the integrity of the nation should be asserted. At the same time, however, the category of the *people* obscures the fact that the aggregation of socially and economically disparate sets of people into a unified national subject is the result of what Chantal Mouffe and Ernesto Laclau call a prior "constitutive exclusion" that washes over the incompatibility of African nationalism and democracy.[7] Someone is always already excluded in order to uphold the idea of the people.

Similarly, the term *society*, tellingly invoked without the qualifying adjective *civil*, might be read less as an effort to expand the opportunities for democratic participation in a broader debate about the role of copyright in the country's cultural fabric than as the desire to shore up the state's legitimacy by portraying it as the incarnation of civic ethos and social cohesiveness. At the same time, the term papers over the profound disparity between the state's complex and strained relationship with the plethora of grassroots organizations (many of whom have deep roots in the infamous civics of the struggle era) and a decidedly cozier rapport with industry associations euphemistically referred to as public-private partnerships. Furthermore, the claim that piracy is tantamount to theft contradicts accepted jurisprudence of copyright whereby works of authorship are nonrivalrous goods or public goods whose use by one person will not diminish another person's opportunity to enjoy them, too. Finally, inherent in Rens's assumption that copyright is meant to serve the development needs of South Africa is the notion that the best way to achieve this goal is through market mechanisms, such as pricing models. As such, this position resonates with the logic of indicators underpinning the BSA piracy rates, whose main function is to gauge the global competitiveness of entire countries.

Unsurprisingly, South Africa's legal fraternity has been hesitant to join the fray, even though some of the country's leading IP experts have long been fervent supporters of more stringent criminal sanctions for copyright infringement on a commercial scale.[8] And although such interventions rarely rise to the clamorous level of publicity enjoyed by policymakers and anti-IP activists alike, legal experts are second to none when it comes to making full-throated claims about the broader social benefits of the criminalization of copyright infringement. Anthropologists, finally, approach the issue of piracy, crime, and law in yet another discursive register. In *The Truth about Crime*, one of the most trenchant analyses of crime in postapartheid South Africa to date, John and Jean Comaroff dissect a wide range of legal, social, and moral imaginaries clustering around criminality and the iridescent hue that debates about crime frequently take on in academic discourse, the media, and popular culture. Referring to Émile Durkheim's famous dictum that crime is a prism through which society knows and maintains itself as a sovereign sphere of life, they suggest that these debates are indicative of a deeper epistemic uncertainty about the very possibility of a moral public gripping late modernist nationhood everywhere. That is why, the Comaroffs argue, the "meaning" of criminality is "not just to patrol normative margins, it is to yield ethnosociological truths about a universe that appears to be growing increasingly inscrutable."[9]

All three responses—the policy-oriented, jurisprudential, and anthropological—to South Africa's piracy crisis share an essentialist line of reasoning. They take for granted the notion that an indissoluble relationship exists between the law and some broader frame of reference, in terms of which the peculiarity of legal understandings of the world might appear as rather less unique and more as another version of such framing. While the precise nature of this overarching entity may vary, students of policy and anthropologists invoking concepts like society or the public, and legal scholars leaning more to words such as the *public interest*, all attribute extraordinary powers to this frame to make up for law's intrinsic lack of reflexivity and precarious grasp of its Other. Taking up the argument I began in chapter 1 and the discussion of race, colonialism, and copyright in chapter 2, in this chapter, I want to resist the functionalism inherent in the notion that by probing the "meaning of crime," anthropology might be better equipped than other disciplines to make sense of the ways that citizens understand, portray, and act upon the "social ecology" of their increasingly complex lives.[10] Equally, though, I do not consider piracy a uniquely moral phenomenon, an economic problem to be addressed by economic means, or a legal challenge or political question requiring distinct legal or political responses—in other words, a phenomenon that can be conceptually controlled by delineating it according to the parameters provided by policy prescriptions, statistics, or legal norms. And, of course, pirates are not the abject Other of the society imagined by Mthethwa—the absolute demarcation line that separates them from us the people. In lieu of deducing piracy from the lived sociality in which it is said to be embedded or, alternatively, externalizing it from that sociality, it is this ecology that requires scrutiny in the first place. Rather than always keep at our disposal, à la Durkheim, a stable third term like the *social* in order to translate a set of idiosyncratic practices and vocabularies into a readily comprehended lingua franca, in the pages that follow, I invite the reader to become part of a journey where all the intersecting and competing imaginaries of social, moral, and legal order and the practices they host or are hosted by multiply to the point that the assumption of an a priori analytic framework is rendered moot and emerges instead as a question rather than as the final answer to a potentially endless series of questions. Concretely, it is by drawing out the valences and entanglements of seemingly disconnected actors and phenomena, such as police raids, forensic technology, urban planning, or statistics, that I hope to paint a richer picture of the concatenation of copyright law, lawlessness, politics, culture, and race in postapartheid South Africa. In so doing, I rely on my participant observation from 2012 to 2013 of the South African Police Service (SAPS) and other agencies and organizations involved in enforcing copyright against vendors of fake CDs and DVDs and entertainment venues where unauthorized copies of sound recordings are played from jukeboxes and DJ equipment. While enforcement strategies in recent years have undergone significant change reflecting the overall shift from physical to digital formats—revenues in the former category from 2014 declined by 31 percent, while income from streaming is projected to increase by 20 percent in 2023—I believe that the essence of the broader argument pursued here remains unaffected by these changes.[11]

War at the Mall and the Club

Initially, Mthethwa's crusade appears to have been able to build on the spectacular successes of the early 2000s, when entire warehouses full of infringing CDs and DVDs shipped in from Singapore and other countries were being raided.[12] Egged on by the Creative Workers Union of South Africa and accompanied by a mix of sympathetic media coverage and apocalyptic forecasts predicting 3.6 million illegal downloads per month and annual monetary losses of $24 million, enforcement agents from SAPS, the South African Armed Forces, and an alliance of industry associations, in the first two months of 2012 alone had seized around twenty-one thousand physical recordings and opened 159 criminal cases, of which forty-four had gone to trial.[13] But almost two years later, when I was invited to witness the purported effect of Mthethwa's "crusade" on "social progress" firsthand, little was left of the fervor of 2012. To be sure, raids continued to bring in the occasional big catch, such as in a Johannesburg restaurant where the waiters were found to have sold more than 190,000 tracks. But the "people's war" had already fizzled out into a series of isolated skirmishes and was widely derided as a publicity stunt glossing over the state's failure to effectively protect life and limb of its citizens. The invitation came from the South African Federation Against Copyright Theft (SAFACT), a South African subsidiary of the UK-based international Federation against Copyright Theft. I was to join SAFACT officials and a cohort of officers from the Boksburg North Police Station in an operation targeting street vendors plying their illicit trade in CDs, DVDs, T-shirts, and steering wheel caps around the East Rand Mall, one of the continent's largest shopping malls, situated somewhere between Johannesburg's international airport and Ekurhuleni Metropolitan Municipality. The "raid," as the operations are commonly referred to, was part of SAFACT's "mission" to create what it called "an anti-counterfeiting climate in which the purchase, sale or possession of counterfeit goods is actively discouraged and intellectual property rights are respected."[14] In addition to SAFACT, such raids also frequently involve other public agencies besides the police, such as the Customs and Excise Division of the South African Revenue Service (SARS), the National Liquor Authority, or local fire marshals in so-called private-public partnerships, designed to, as one of the SAFACT agents put it to me, "hammer them [the pirates] from all sides."

After a short roll call in the courtyard of the police station, we head out to the mall. The mood among the squad of six huddled into the van is upbeat. Everybody is chatting about their favorite type of weapon, about the last raid, or waxing lyrical about the ethnographer's home state of Texas and its notoriously lax gun laws. It is Saturday, a good day, I figure, not only for the throngs of shoppers on the lookout for a flick to watch later that night but also for the police to catch the scores of street vendors peddling their illicit wares. "There isn't actually a specific day," Sergeant de Villiers corrects me. Because of its proximity to the airport, she explains, the area is a major artery for the traffic in counterfeit goods, with the "pirates" operating there "contributing to the general crime in the area." This is why the Boksburg police pictures itself as somewhat of a vanguard in the fight against crime, charged with "a certain number of operations per week" and regularly applauded for its successes by the media. But on this particular Saturday, things appear to run less smoothly. No sooner does our convoy pull into the parking lot in front of a small flea market facing the mall than several pirates, shouting out "*amaphoyisa!*" (police), dash off in all directions, setting in motion a long and arduous process of combing through warehouses and other places surrounding the flea market where street vendors typically hide their stock.

The first stop is a pub that also doubles as a betting office. The bartender watches silently as one of the police officers searches in vain for fake CDs under the counter and in the restrooms. The expression on his face reminds me of the dazed look on black South Africans' faces during the apartheid era when being ordered around by a white person. But outside, on the sidewalk, a woman demands ID from one of the SAFACT agents attempting to search her. "I'll show you now," he retorts while rummaging through her belongings anyway, which only contain secondhand clothes. At a warehouse, de Villiers suspects to be a stash, the security guard, unfazed by the sergeant's assurance that "we are actually trying to do something good for the community," refuses us entry. At last, an hour into the operation, we seem to strike gold. In what looks like a decommissioned transformer station, we find a stack of CDs, but none of them are pirate.

"They never claim the goods," de Villiers says, visibly frustrated with the slow progress of the operation.

"What next?" I ask.

"Time for fun and games," Captain van der Spuy, the commanding officer, replies gleefully.

Fun and games, it turns out, means that we all pile back into the van and, seat belts fastened and abandoned CDs all bagged up, find ourselves cruising at breakneck speed along back roads and across parking lots in hot pursuit of more street vendors desperately trying to escape. Minutes later, the van comes to a screeching halt, and several SAFACT agents jump out, only to reemerge moments later, cheered on by the crew waiting by the van, with three suspects in tow. But one of them is bleeding from his hand and knee after one of the police offers pounced on him from behind and pushed him to the ground as he attempted to flee. The sight of a bleeding black man being patted down by a white police officer does not go over well with several bystanders, some of who pull out their cell phones to take pictures of the scene.

"Is there a problem?" one of the SAFACT agents asks as he walks over to them. "You have a right to complain. We just have a job to do."

I am not sure whether it is because of this episode, but suddenly the commander decides to return to base, bundling the suspects in one of the police's infamous *kwela-kwela* pick-ups used to transport arrestees.

Ekurhuleni means "place of peace" in the Tsonga language, but the patchwork of formerly whites-only mining towns, such as Benoni, Boksburg, Springs, Brakpan, or Germiston, and the black townships surrounding them, like Tembisa, Daveyton, or Kwa-Thema, is anything but peaceful. The site of some of apartheid South Africa's fiercest battles, Ekurhuleni, for the past several decades, has been on a downward spiral of civil unrest, skyrocketing unemployment rates, and rampant crime, turning it into one of the country's most heavily policed areas. With some 1,900 police officers on the beat on any given day, the law is constantly on the minds of Ekurhuleni's 2.5 million inhabitants. No wonder, then, that to the ears of many of its residents, de Villiers's comment about "doing something for the community" has a slightly ironic ring. The conflation of policing and the good of the community resonates with South Africans' yearning for an order in which rights empower them rather than the other way around, where power produces rights—such as the right to search another person's property. In other words, while South Africans do welcome policing, they just don't want *this* police.

A year and several operations later I was invited by another organization to participate in a slightly different kind of raid. The Recording Industry of South Africa (RiSA) is the trade association for the South African recording industry. Prior to my arrival, the focus of RiSA's operations had been street piracy of music CDs. From May 2012, however, after having outsourced these activities to SAFACT as part of its DVD-focused operations, RiSA concentrated its efforts solely on the public performance rights of its members' repertoire by raiding clubs, pubs, and restaurants. In addition, for a while it also ran a series of fake websites and email accounts, such as computerdistributors.co.za or blogdotdadu@blogspot.co.za, to lure vendors into putting jukeboxes loaded with infringing tracks up for sale. The operation I was invited to took place on a cold winter night in Sunnyside, an entertainment district at the heart of the nation's capital city, Tshwane (Pretoria), and involved three police vans and a large contingent of police officers from the Lyttelton station in Centurion, about ten miles south of Sunnyside. (The station had been selected because the Sunnyside station refused to take part in the operation and because one of the commanders at Lyttelton had participated in previous operations in the Gauteng area.) On weekends, Sunnyside's main strip, Robert Sobukwe Street (formerly van Esselen Street), is packed with revelers out on a beer and music-soaked *jol* (jaunt). Though not a hotbed of street piracy, like the East Rand Mall, the Bruma Lake flea market in Johannesburg, or South Africa's many taxi ranks, Robert Sobukwe Street is Pretoria's infringement central. Infringement of the right to the public performance of sound recordings that is, not of the right to distribute such recordings.

The first stop is O Canto Latino, a watering hole that has been reported to play unlicensed music over its makeshift stereo system. The pub had been in RiSA's crosshairs for some time, like other enterprises of its kind having previously been raided for a jukebox loaded with unlicensed MP3 files. This time around, however, it turns out that its Chinese owner not only kept a vast collection of MP3 files on his laptop, he also used his friend's ID to masquerade as an asylum seeker. He is arrested. Next door, at the more upscale Europa Lounge, a DJ is working the crowd from an impressive controller loaded with hundreds of MP3 tracks. Most are his own compositions, he claims, pointing to the handwritten inscriptions on the CD labels. Others are more readily recognizable as compilations of international and South African artists. Here, as during the Boksburg operation, the atmosphere is thick with resentment. Patrons frequently turn to me with my backpack and slightly puzzled look as the presumably more approachable-looking member to vent their feelings.

"Other restaurants play very loud music," one of the O Canto regulars blurts out.

"There are other places selling liquor anytime," another chimes in. "But the police don't want to go to those places. Really, it is totally unfair."

Yet another person who introduces himself as hailing from South Africa's northernmost Limpopo province touts himself and his drinking companions as "law-abiding" and "highly educated" Venda-speaking people who have nothing to hide and just wish to be left alone.

"It is foreigners who cause all the problems," he ventures. "Here there is no crime, there is no violence. No drugs, no dagga [cannabis], no knives, no guns, no nothing, no prostitution. There is no foreigner here, only South Africans. It seems like they are targeting this place and we don't know the reason why."

At the Europa, the revelers voice their displeasure musically, erupting into a rousing rendition of one of pop duo Mafikizolo's classic tunes:

> Niwabizelani amaphoyisa iparty imnandi kangaka?
> Thina siyilaba abangafun' ukuhamba sizawuhamba nxa kuphuma ilanga.
> (Why are you calling the police to stop such a great party?
> We do not want to leave, we only leave at sunrise.)

And at the western end of Sunnyside, at the posh Café del Khuze, a group of students strikes up a heated conversation about the imbalances of the global music industry. RiSA, SAMRO, and their ilk, one of them demands, seemingly oblivious to these organizations' decidedly "American" affiliations, "should go after the big guys, the American companies that rip off our artists."

The specter of violence, too, is frequently in the air. Police often manhandle or threaten suspects with violence. Conversely, while there are few reports of pirates turning violent, bystanders and patrons at nightclubs and beerhalls are not the only ones dismayed at the collaboration between the police and private enforcement agencies, and what they perceive to be unwanted intrusions into their space by these organizations. On occasion, murmurings of discontent even reach the courts. For example, in the summer of 2016, I attended a meeting set up by the state attorney in Pretoria to discuss a case in which the owner of Aandklas (Evening Class), a pub in Hatfield popular with students of the University of Pretoria, sought an interdict against the same police officer from Lyttelton who also conducted the Sunnyside raid. The officer, the complaint stated, had entered the premises in the company of a "large contingency [sic] of police officers fully armed with fire arms and equipment," claiming that the venue was licensed as a restaurant and was only permitted to serve liquor with meals.[15] Worse, the affidavit went on to state, the officer ordered that the music playing in the background be turned off and all patrons leave the premises. What the pub owner referred to here is the fact that, as we have seen, RiSA and SAFACT frequently piggyback on search-and-seizure operations conducted by the SAPS and other public enforcement agencies, such as the Liquor Board. The presence of RiSA staff was not only illegal, the pub owner further opined, as a private, not-for-profit organization, RiSA had no right to require club owners to hold a license because there was "no provision in the Criminal Law which makes it a criminal offense to play and/or reproduce music in a way which is in conflict with the aims and purposes of SAMPRA as a non-profit company."

This was not the pub's first brush with the law, having on previous occasions been sued for illegally selling liquor to minors and making excessive noise. It was, however, the first time that a complaint was brought that, if only indirectly, questioned the authority of the police to search and seize during raids in cooperation with organizations like the South African Music Performance Rights Association (SAMPRA) and RiSA. In the end, the state attorney held that s 27 of the Copyright Act specifically authorizes the criminal enforcement of copyright infringement and that, hence, the complaint—brought by a lawyer notorious for his fanciful interpretations of the law and for frivolously leading his clients to believe they might have cause of action—was "wishy-washy."

As we leave Robert Sobukwe Street to return to Lyttelton, I overhear one of the officers observe gloomily: "Why do they call it Sunnyside? There's very little sun there."

Enlisting: Pirate Networks, Antipiracy Raids, and Their Logic

How does the enforcement of the Copyright Act, I kept wondering after blitzes such as the ones in Ekurhuleni and Sunnyside, further the official vision of society as united in the protection of artists' legacies? To be sure, the people had asserted themselves, against what one of the cops referred to as the Chinaman, among others. But what about the other part of society, including the O Canto Latino patrons and the chanting crowd at the Europa, who felt harassed by the very institution that professes to serve society? A good place to begin unpacking the complex physics and metaphysics of copyright policing is a document that appeared for a while in nearly every issue of RiSA's *Enforcement Bulletin*. Titled *The Investigation Process*, it describes twenty steps that are followed from the initial stage of information gathering to the final destruction of seized goods.[16]

1. Information is established by the Enforcement Officers (EOs) from the RiSA Anti-Piracy Unit (RAPU) or it is reported to them.
2. A file is opened and booked out to an EO.
3. The information is investigated, which includes the verifying of information received, surveillance, direct contact with the suspect, etc.
4. A test purchase is set up and executed, the exhibits are "bagged and tagged."
5. The test purchase is analysed and a formal criminal complaint is drafted, commissioned and filed with the Organised Crime or Commercial Crime Unit of the South African Police Service (SAPS).

ENFORCEMENT Bulletin

HOTSPOTS

IN THIS ISSUE:
- Hotspots 1
- 5000 DVDs seized 1
- Eastern Cape Clean up 2
- Suspects dealt with 3
- Convictions 4
- Internet training 5
- Meeting with ISPA 6
- Investigation Process 7
- Awareness & Education 8

MUSIC PIRACY REPORTING DETAILS:
Music piracy can be reported through the following methods:
Tel: 011 886 1342
Fax: 011 886 8553
Email: piracy@risa.org.za / piracy@stoppiracy.org.za
www.stoppiracy.org.za
Write to: P O Box 367, Randburg, 2125
Hotline: 011-886 1342

GAUTENG
Van der Walt Street
On 25 July 2008 the SAPS and the Film and Publications Board conducted a raid at Van der Walt Street. An estimated 4 000 infringing products were seized by the Police. The products seized included infringing copies of music and movies in DVD-R format. One of the suspects was criminally charged, the suspect appeared in court on 28 July and the matter has been postponed for further investigation.

Chameleon Village
Three hours of surveillance was carried out in the area and three suspects were identified selling music titles. The Police are due to conduct a raid in the area.

Noord & Plein Street
On 11 September 2008 operations were conducted at this well-known piracy hotspot. Five suspects were arrested, charged and detained at Hillbrow Police station as well as at Johannesburg Central Police station. The case concerns a manufacturing plant that was identified in Hillbrow as well as a storeroom identified in Fordsburg. Criminal charges have been laid and the matter is still under investigation.

This hotspot was visited again and with the help of an informant several offenders were identified. On 2 October two more suspects were arrested, charged and detained for possession of 3 500 infringing copies of music and movies.

Germiston Taxi Rank
On 13 August 2008 a raid was conducted at the Germiston Taxi Rank. During the raid, three suspects were arrested and taken to Germiston SAPS where they were charged and detained. A total of 200 infringing copies of music and movies were seized.

Fordsburg
It appears that a link exists between Fordsburg and Bruma Flea Market, particularly in relation to the distribution of infringing copies of music. The information is being investigated.

NORTH WEST
Rustenburg Taxi Rank
A manufacturing plant at a residential premises has been identified. According to reports the plant is supplying the area with infringing copies. The Crime Intelligence Unit of the Police is currently investigating the matter.

EASTERN CAPE
Matatiele
It has been found that shops are once again selling infringing copies in the area. The Umtata Commercial Crime Unit will assist in raids.

Umtata CBD
Raids are being planned with the Umtata Commercial Crime Unit.

Bruma Flea Market
5000 DVDs Seized in Raid

The following article appeared in the Sowetan written by Rathabile Mateka.

Police yesterday confiscated more than 5 000 pirated DVDs after they raided a shop at the Bruma Lake Flea Market in Johannesburg. The shop allegedly owned by a Rojaah Mohammed, contained the latest music videos of gospel singers such as Lundi, Rebecca Malope, Hlengiwe Mhlaba, Joyous Celebration and the Soweto Gospel Choir.

The DVDs, sold for between R120 and R180, included American movies, comedies and porn videos. The police were accompanied by members of the Recording Industry of South Africa (RiSA) when they raided the shop. Oupa Moloi of RiSA, said they had received a tip-off from a buyer. According to Moloi, a pirated DVD is blue on the inside while most originals are silver. He said his association would open a case against the owner of the shop. ■

PAGE 1/8

FIGURE 4.1 RiSA, *Enforcement Bulletin*. Courtesy of RiSA.

6. A criminal case is registered, a criminal administration system (CAS) number is obtained and a planning meeting is scheduled with the Police.
7. An application for a search and seizure warrant as well as a pro forma search and seizure warrant is prepared for the police.
8. The SAPS apply to a Magistrate for the issuing of the search and seizure warrant.
9. On the planned date the police at the premises concerned executes the search and seizure warrant. The SAPS request access to be granted to the EO of RiSA from the owner of the premises.
10. The EO assists the Police with the identification of infringing copies of music and also supplies the bags and seals to the Police. In most instances the EO also assists with the drafting of the inventory and the bagging and tagging of the seized goods.
11. In most instances the suspect is arrested and the seized goods booked into the SAP13 store at the nearest Police station. The goods are then directly booked out again to the EO of RiSA for purposes of analysis.
12. A short report of the case is compiled by the EO of RiSA and submitted to head office in Randburg.
13. The seized and booked out goods are then removed to the offices of RiSA where the analysis will then begin.
14. During the analysis phase, each and every disc is analysed and the results of the analysis recorded in an analysis statement drafted by the EO of the case.
15. Once the manager of RAPU has perused the analysis statement, the analysis statement will be commissioned and furnished to the Police for purposes of the criminal trial.
16. The Police will then obtain and file any outstanding statements where after the criminal docket will be submitted to the prosecutor for a decision on prosecution.
17. If the prosecutor decides that there are reasonable grounds for a successful conviction a charge sheet will be drafted and the suspect subpoenaed for trial.
18. Several consultations are then held between the investigating officer from the SAPS, the EO of RAPU, other witnesses and the prosecutor.
19. Exhibits will then be marked and prepared for trial purposes. If the defence lawyer indicates that his client wants to enter into a plea agreement, a plea agreement would be drafted by the defence lawyer

and submitted to the manager of RAPU where after the prosecutor would also comment regarding the plea agreement. Only once all the parties agree on the plea agreement would it be handed to the court for consideration and if accepted then for an order.
20 The seized goods and equipment are removed to a depot where they are stored until they are destroyed.

Compared to my account of the Ekurhuleni and Sunnyside operations, with their irritations, lapses, and mishaps, *The Investigation Process* reads like an ode to the rule of law and a comforting fantasy of moral order amid ever-present violence and rampant corruption. How, then, might one make sense of the disconnect between this litany and life in the ordinary? What is it that unites SAFACT, RiSA, and the police officers in enacting the litany despite the constant potential for disruption or even failure—the trademark expert who did not show up for the operation; the chanting crowd that might have gotten out of control; the bystanders or the Hatfield pub owner who might have filed charges against the police for injuring a suspect or searching the premises? Is it a tacit recognition that every actor enlisted in the whole enterprise can be both an author of and subject to the investigation process and that only by performing the list, week after week, raid after raid, bulletin after bulletin, and by simultaneously striking a delicate balance between both roles, a broader objective will eventually be realized? And what is this objective? A moral goal? A legal one? Or even a political one? And last but not least, what about the possibility that these operations may be more than just conduits toward the liberal vision of a more equitable society anchored in individual personhood and private ownership—that they may actually yield quite the reverse—namely, the creation of an order patently at odds with the progressive premises of the democratic South Africa in which *people* means not only freedom and national identity but also equity, inclusion, and opportunity?

At the same time, the list affords a glimpse of how policymakers, administrators, and legal scholars justify the criminalization of copyright infringement.[17] At the most general level, for instance, the criminal prosecution of copyright infringement on a commercial scale derives from South Africa's international obligations, most crucially s 61 of the TRIPS agreement. But things get a little murkier when it comes to a definition of *commercial scale* in national legislation. Formulations such as "in the course of trade" (s 2 of the Counterfeit Goods Act 37 of 1997) (hereafter Counterfeit Goods Act) or "by way of trade" (s 27 [1] [b] of the Copyright Act) are most often construed as meaning that anyone who willingly engages in such infringing activities is guilty of a criminal offense. But just as importantly, such language might also be read as signifying the ambiguity surrounding market relations as both the cause and panacea of crime. For if we are to believe law and economics scholarship, the criminal is a rational actor who, like any other market participant, weighs the costs and benefits of their misdeeds. And so too is the state, enforcing copyright law by weighing the pros and cons of criminal penalties versus civil liabilities in terms of transactions costs. At a slightly more sophisticated yet hardly more transparent level, the proponents of harsh penalties for even the most minor infringements invoke loss of investor confidence and foreign investment as potential consequences of piracy. Another strategy to rationalize criminal liability is to suggest a parallel between copyright and other intellectual property doctrines, such as trademark, through the somewhat casual use—in the Counterfeit Goods Act, for instance—of terms like *counterfeit* or by pointing to the growing significance of piracy in opening new channels for drug and arms smugglers.[18] But in an alternative approach, critics with a strong penchant for fair use and access to knowledge theories also appear to espouse free markets as the most effective answer to piracy. In *Media Piracy in Emerging Economies*, Joe Karaganis, for instance, argues that instead of a matter of criminality, piracy is better described as a global pricing problem. The most important question, he writes, "is not whether stronger enforcement can reduce piracy and preserve the existing market structure . . . but whether stable cultural and business models can emerge at the low end of these media markets that are capable of addressing the next several billion media consumers."[19]

Regardless of which justification prevails, however, all appear to take for granted the existence—indeed, necessity—of functioning legal and administrative infrastructures as prerequisites of a vibrant copyright culture. For instance, in a series of articles on the enforcement of copyright in the African music industries, Kenyan copyright expert Marisella Ouma writes: "The enforcement of copyright and related rights in most countries in sub-Saharan Africa is not optimal and this has a negative impact on the development of the copyright industries." To achieve an "optimal" degree of enforcement, she elaborates, there has to be in place a "system that ensures the highest conformity to the law of copyright and related rights." Beyond a solid grounding in national copyright legislation, a key component of this system must be a stable and efficient "infrastructure" that converts the legal rationale into a "positive perception of copyright" and "maximum adherence to the law."[20] Ouma's point is echoed, in various forms, by numerous official publications issued by international bodies, such as WIPO or, in the South African context, the Companies and Intellectual Property Commission (CIPC).[21]

For the anthropologist, however, the "restless quest for effective measures" and its legitimization in neoclassical economics or the instrumentalist means-ends relationship between law and the liberal vision of ownership serving the public interest, provokes a different set of questions.[22] What are the criteria for all these values that allow them to add up to an optimal policy, he wonders? For example, what are the marks of a positive perception? When consumers, in a spontaneous reawakening of their sense of civic duty, flock en masse to nearly deserted retail stores to stock up on their treasured CD collection instead of acquiring MP3 collections from dealers plying their illicit trade right in front?[23] When street pirates remorsefully trade their makeshift existence on the margins of the legal and economic order for a marginally more law-abiding life in South Africa's burgeoning informal sector that is just as improvised and forever threatened by a new city ordinance, a shift in policing tactics, or another plan to convert a decaying town into a "world-class African city," as Johannesburg advertises itself? Or when the economics of sharing, borrowing, stealing, and, yes, looting and witchcraft accusations that entangle South Africans in networks of mutual dependency miraculously transmogrifies into a supposedly higher-order ethics grounded in legally sanctioned sharing and streaming? And when exactly is a system suboptimal? When the rational choice, will power, and self-interestedness said to determine the behavior of *homo oeconomicus* are thwarted by irrational, spontaneous, and altruistic patterns of behavior—by the rule of thumb, impromptu decisions, or random acts of kindness?

Taking the discussion to a level where the notion of efficiency and infrastructural integrity itself becomes the primary object of critical scrutiny, the anthropologist will want to know what theoretical purchase is obtained by investing infrastructures with the same qualities that are also attributed to that which precedes or even maintains them—the pirates' own infrastructures of distribution. In much the same way, she may wonder whether the malfunction and breakdown of the structures and institutions of the public sphere, instead of being extraneous to institutional stability, are, in fact, its a priori and therefore symbiotically intertwined with it through a logic that gauges everything in terms of efficiency. But at the same time, she suspects that all the scouring of the country's clandestine warehouses, makeshift flea markets, dingy shisanyamas, and drinking dens amounts to more than "pissing in the wind," as one music industry observer mocked the police raids. The frantic combing of pubs, bars, and restaurants where DJs may be performing; the endless meetings where disgruntled activists assail the government to take a more proactive stance on piracy; and all the policy papers, memoranda, and impact studies urging for more stringent criminal enforcement measures may seem to be empty and self-reproducing, but they are not about nothing.[24] Likewise, even if the failure of the police to clean out the streets is rooted more in the state's inability to locate the cause of that failure in its own assumptions about what constitutes an infrastructure than in any defects within the infrastructure itself, this failure does create a structure in the end. One might call it an interstructure: a structure that is neither a macrostructure nor a loose assortment of isolated microstructures. It is a structure whose existence is the very result of the things, forces, roles, ideas, and symbols that pass through it. In short, RiSA's *Investigation Process* and the policy, economics, and legal discourses it reflects, recall what has been this book's argument from the outset. The black-boxing of the means-end relationship inherent in this document blinds us to the possibility of envisaging a different form of analysis in which the social output is not assumed to automatically follow from the legal input and in which, consequently, the assumption of a black box to be opened when the institutional framework meant to implement the policy is found to be suboptimal becomes redundant. To better grasp this alternative analytic and its relevance for the study of piracy and the emerging "information societies" of the Global South more broadly, it may be helpful to briefly digress on the current fixation in the humanities on alternative ways of theorizing complexity and systemicity through theories of infrastructures, networks, or "access."[25]

The notion that piracy is creating new, rather than destroying existing, networks of information-sharing and that, consequently, the criminalization of such networks is counterproductive has been a staple of media and communication scholarship in the postcolony for much of the 1990s and 2000s.[26] And the argument is certainly not without merit. Yet, even where this scholarship entails significant ethnographic fieldwork, as in Brian Larkin's pioneering *Signal and Noise*, little consideration is given to how legal and regulatory practices, such as policing or forensics, are intertwined with antipiracy activities. More problematically still, refocusing the discussion of piracy from proprietary considerations to questions of distribution and access has the adverse effect of making legal practice appear to be more monolithic than it actually is. Moreover, the argument that pirate modernity is an imagined social order based on a bottom-up, participatory, and distributive utopia only works if one takes its antithesis—Western modernity—for the real thing rather than a colonial fiction.

The piracy-as-creativity hypothesis might give us pause for another reason as well. Pirate networks, Larkin, for instance, suggests, are "nonideological."[27] For Ravi Sundaram, likewise, the hallmark of piracy is that it is everywhere and nowhere at the same time. "Post-liberal" and "subjectless," it "escapes the boundaries of space, of particular networks, of form, a before and after, a limit."[28] At first sight, it would indeed appear that piracy, by its very parasitical nature, refuses to align itself with a political project critical of capitalism. As the quintessential heir to a now almost moribund industrial world in which "proper jobs" are increasingly replaced by what Ferguson calls "distributive modes of livelihood" that rely on accessing the income streams of others, the merely reproductive, lumpen proletarian pirate is incapable of the revolutionary politics of the wage-earning worker of yesteryear.[29] But this supposed lack of critical agency also calls into question some of the network euphoria underwriting Sundaram's and Larkin's studies and other theorizations of networked cultural production and consumption. For example, in his book *The Age of Access*, self-styled activist and economist Jeremy Rifkin unfolds a grand panorama of two opposed kinds of what he calls the "access economy" of the twenty-first century. In the first type, fundamental ideas about social relations, freedom, and property are recoded through a broader shift from market transactions based on property relations toward a "network approach" in which the exchange of physical goods between sellers and buyers is increasingly replaced by short-lived relationships between suppliers and users of intangible goods and "experiences." But because this type of access is based on commercial, rather than social, contracts, it favors monopolies, dries up cultural resources, and destroys communities. Access, then, in this type of "access economy" is tantamount to "merely inclusion in the commercial sphere." This is where Rifkin's vision of the second, alternative type of access economy comes into play—an economy that is predicated on community and culture, on social relationships embedded in and building social trust. But above all, this is an economy that is rooted in deep feelings of empathy.[30] Unlike markets and the first kind of access economy, whose very existence is dependent on preexisting social communities, an economy steeped in empathy in the first instance builds bonds of civility. (Here, and in subsequent publications, Rifkin draws heavily on the sentimentalism of Adam Smith, John Stuart Mill, and their present-day emulators, moral philosopher Martha Nussbaum and former policy adviser to Tony Blair, Matthew Taylor.) And in contrast to the extractive character of the market and network economies, and unlike the global music industry and its alleged "watering down" of shared values and historical legacies through "world music," the empathetic economy preserves the rich cultural diversity of human experiences around the world. In fact, this is the reason why it is more of an ecology, striking a balance between culture and capitalist economy. While in the access economy of the first, corporate kind culture "withers" away, the "ecology of culture and capitalism" recognizes culture as the realm of "lived experience," the "soil" from which the feeling of empathy is "nurtured."[31]

The social scientist may wince at such bio-essentialism. But it is precisely this "ecology" that casts doubt on the notion of a nonideological network economy as the harbinger of a new era when right-left politics is subsumed under a "new social dynamic" that prizes the "intrinsic value" of culture above its utility value.[32] The belief in an essential, organic value of culture bespeaks the distinctly ideological roots of the concept of access in eighteenth-century liberal constructions of culture as the manifestation par excellence of property, markets, statehood, and identity. And so, once again, the question that must be posed by an ethnographically informed critique of the rhetoric of pirate networks and its antithesis, the construction of criminal enforcement as infrastructure, is not whether these practices produce tangible results but whether they are, in fact, merely reproducing themselves as *network form*. The term stems from Annelise Riles's *The Network Inside Out*, a study of UN-sponsored networks of human rights organizations. According to Riles, rather than models of efficient global governance, such networks are autopoietic systems that "internally generate the effects of their own reality by reflecting on themselves." Hence, networks do not serve as conduits for the flow of information—they *are* the information. And instead of being the cause of action, the "existence of a network is synonymous with Action on its behalf." In short, networks are a "form" of the contemporary global order whose effectiveness subsides in "generating the effect of effectiveness."[33]

Clearly, an analysis based on infrastructures or networks that are already fully formed and operational does not appear to be the subtlest way of thinking about piracy and the criminal enforcement of copyright infringement. This does not mean, however, that by maintaining a critical distance from network and infrastructure instrumentalism, the anthropologist should desist from coming up with empirically grounded, richly layered accounts of how piracy and its criminalization does create a variety of social, cultural, and legal articulations that can be grasped through a methodology and analytical categories transcending the merely singular, culturally contingent, and deterritorialized type of sociality students of piracy, like Sundaram or Larkin, seem to consider the essence of postcolonial modernity. Au contraire. The attention to ethnographic detail, I contend, may offer a corrective to the tendency among policymakers to reduce ethnographic descriptions to a mere tool for unblack-boxing legal policy's means-end mechanism whenever it runs afoul of the reality it is meant to shape. Which brings me to actor-network theory.

As I argued at the beginning of this book, language is critical in anthropological accounts of the lives of others, especially in the anthropology in law I seek to develop. Speaking legally rather than about law is key to the claim that in studying an epistemic world other than one's own, there can be no a priori location from which to speak without inflicting violence on the world of the other. Actor-network theory, I further suggested, offers a rich array of conceptual tools to redirect our accounts from exhausted, reifying forms of representation toward a more reflexive view that situates the anthropological project at the intersection of a multitude of competing discourses, rationalizations, metanarratives, and other material truth-making practices. In what follows, I deploy just two of those tools. The first is Bruno Latour's concept of "infra-language." The role of an infra-language, Latour writes, is to help the analyst to "become attentive to the actors' fully developed meta-language, a reflexive account of what they are saying."[34] However, this attention to the metalanguage of others goes beyond the sensitivity toward what anthropologists have traditionally idealized as what used to be called the native point of view as the foundation of a genuine kind of anthropological ethics and hermeneutic. Nor is infra-language another way of turning said native point of view into the raw material for the anthropologist's abstractions by assuming "that there exists somewhere a dictionary where all the variegated words of the actors can be translated into the words of the social vocabulary."[35] In fact, such infra-language may itself turn out to be yet another metalanguage—the anthropologist's own metalanguage, among others. As such, it will, in turn, necessitate more infra-language in order to be taken seriously as a metalanguage of its own. In other words, the point about the concept of infra-language is not that it is a somehow watered-down or weaker version of more weighty pronouncements about things like social forces, structures of domination, social constructs, or power relations. It is, rather, that an infra-language does not say anything about the essence or substance of what it indexes to begin with. And therein lies its strength. It is precisely because of its weakness that an infra-language becomes a powerful tool for the anthropologist to connect disconnected and contradictory frames of references into traceable and relatively durable configurations and associations without resorting to supposedly strong terms such as *society*, *law*, or *economy*.

The second tool I borrow from actor-network theory is the concept of the actor or, rather, the ANT scholar's first and most important responsibility: to follow the actor. Based on my account of the raids in Boksburg and Sunnyside, the reader might think that following the actor consists of figuring out what protocol, procedure, or structure makes actors like the SAFACT agents act the way they did. Indeed, one prominent feature of the operations is that they always seemed to follow a script and that this script is, in large part, based on a host of rules set out in the Criminal Procedure Act 56 of 1955 (hereafter Criminal Procedure Act), evidentiary principles at the level of substantive and common law, or other directives governing police work. But that is not what is meant by following the actors. The typical ANT actor does not execute an already-existing plan of action; he, she, or it—yes, there are nonhuman actors, as we shall see further below—scripts that plan. Through countless recurring operations across different legalities, spaces, materialities, and forms of inscription, police and other actors coproduce the effect of effectiveness by black-boxing the discontinuities of everyday enforcement practices that make the script necessary in the first place. I call this scripting through practice the circulation of evidence. The collection of evidence and its circulation through a dense tangle of institutions, technologies, rules, and epistemologies constitutes the chief mechanism for moving the enforcement process forward and, concurrently, provides the thread along which the story of this chapter develops. But first, I need to introduce some of the actors involved in the circulation, beginning with RiSA and SAFACT, arguably the most active organizations in the larger criminal enforcement effort of the 2010s.

Follow the Actors

RiSA is the trade association of the South African recording industry, and, as such, it is closely aligned with SAMPRA. Both are housed in the same building, and their boards are virtually identical. SAMPRA serves as the collecting society for RiSA's members, licensing what the collecting society regulations refer to as the "public playing rights" of sound recordings—the right to broadcast a sound recording, the right to cause a sound recording to be transmitted in a diffusion service, and the right to communicate a sound recording to the public.[36] As a member of the International Federation of the Phonographic Industry (IFPI), RiSA is something like the South African equivalent of other IFPI members, such as the British BPI. Yet, with just under a dozen employees, RiSA is not only significantly smaller, but its portfolio of activities is also more narrowly focused on just a handful of objectives. Apart from promoting the "group interests of entities or individuals who carry on the business of producing, manufacturing or distributing records," and running the South African Music Awards, the company takes up the cause of taking "such action as may be necessary by legal or other processes, for the protection of rights including intellectual property rights, of members or group of members."[37] In practice, this means that, in the words of RiSA chairman Keith Lister, the organization works with "the Police, Customs and the Government as well as any other stakeholders that are willing to make a contribution to the fight against music piracy."[38] In addition to these efforts, RiSA also offers workshops for police on copyright issues, runs a crime line to anonymously report copyright infringers, and, for a time, also published the aforementioned *Enforcement Bulletin*. Finally, RiSA has been gathering statistical data for a number of years on the scope and recent trends in street piracy. All these activities are closely intertwined and mostly involve the same set of actors, except for a number of differences in legal procedure. During the early period of my fieldwork up until 2014, most of these tasks were coordinated under the umbrella of RAPU, comprised of a staff of four investigators and an office assistant. But due to a series of budget cuts and a shift in policy, RiSA reduced the number of investigators to one, and from 2012, they outsourced the raids on street vendors to SAFACT—hence, the Boksburg operation.

At the time I participated in its activities, RAPU was led by Angus Rheder. Because Rheder was a central actor in South Africa's antipiracy scene, a few observations on his biography and personal outlook may be helpful in defining RiSA's role in the broader antipiracy scheme. A study in Afrikaner obstinacy, Rheder was a product of the ancien régime. For over fifteen years prior to joining RiSA, he was a member of the old South African police—first the border police and the Internal Tracing Unit, before he signed on to the Selected Organised Crime Investigation Unit and the commercial branch. And then, he explained, "something happened." I didn't have the temerity to ask what exactly happened, but it was clear that this turn of events sheds significant light on the way Rheder organized his activities. Uncomfortably positioned in the interstices of democratically legitimized state power and an industry widely resented for its complicity with the apartheid regime and its cozy relationship with "foreign" interests, he had no time for abetting "criminals," as he called the street vendors. But neither did he nourish particularly warm feelings toward the current political dispensation. "After 1994 I stopped listening," he told me. (At one point when we were discussing the memoirs written by former cops, he went as far as raving about the notorious Koevoet counterinsurgency unit that is alleged to have committed numerous atrocities against civilians during the border war in South West Africa between 1979 and1989.) A man of few words, he wore many hats as complainant, crime scene investigator, RiSA's enforcement officer, who pursued his objectives with a mix of grim determination, respect for the law, and the rapport he had established with predominantly white, Afrikaans-speaking police officers, such as the commander of the Sunnyside and Aandklas raids and other enforcement agencies across South Africa. One of the latter, as we saw in my account of the Boksburg raid, was SAFACT. As a proxy of the Motion Picture Association of America, the organization commanded a much larger budget than RiSA, maintaining two branches in different parts of the country in addition to a head office in Johannesburg with about half a dozen enforcement agents.[39]

Mention must also be made of a partnership of an entirely different kind that, although already discontinued by the time I worked with RiSA and SAFACT, came to be known under the name Operation Dudula (Operation Eradicate) during the early phase of the piracy scare. Dudula was the brainchild of Mzwakhe Mbuli, a man who had taken up a number of colorful identities over the course of a long and checkered career. Starting out as the "people's poet," pounding out bulky verse during the heyday of the anti-apartheid struggle, Mbuli eventually found himself locked up on (allegedly trumped-up) charges of armed robbery, only to reemerge several years later as a preacher and gospel singer—and as the figurehead of Dudula. At first, things appeared to run smoothly. Having secured the blessing of SAFACT and RiSA, the campaign specialized in protest marches featuring Dudula-T-shirt-wearing artists symbolically cleaning out the streets littered with fake CDs, organizing awareness-raising concerts, and lobbying the SAPS for a more aggressive stance on piracy.[40] One can only speculate about the reasons behind RiSA's decision to catch a thief with a (alleged) thief, as it were, other than the fact that Mbuli was tremendously popular.[41] In addition to generous coverage of Dudula's antipiracy activities by the nation's public broadcaster (in one broadcast, he can be seen sifting through a stack of confiscated CDs flanked by uniformed customs officers), Mbuli had been anointed early on by the likes of President Nelson Mandela (at whose inauguration in 1994 he performed), his estranged wife Winnie, and a host of other political luminaries. Soon after the first spectacular protests, however, the relationship soured when mobs of exasperated artists, in a move allegedly orchestrated by Mbuli's organization, began assaulting suspected pirates and destroying their humble stalls. Just as he persistently maintained his innocence in the robbery case, Mbuli feigned ignorance of these attacks as well.[42] Eventually, in the fall of 2006, the RiSA-Dudula romance deteriorated to the point that RiSA severed its ties with Dudula following an attempt by Mbuli and his cohort to crash a SAMPRA board meeting where the self-appointed eradicator accused the board members of diverting RiSA's antipiracy budget into what he called "white salaries."[43]

All of this did little to placate the antipirate, anti-immigrant mood, though. For example, in 2011, award-winning gospel artist Lusanda Mcinga decided to take religious fervor to new heights when she and several of her associates, in what the press described as "faked CD fury," assaulted and abducted a street hawker whom they suspected of selling unauthorized copies of Mcinga's albums.[44] Meanwhile, her adopted son suffered the inverse fate when he, too, tried to confront a suspected vendor of illegal CDs but was instead roughed up by police intervening in his act of vengeance.

Another critical actor, finally, is the police, as we saw in my account of the Boksburg and Sunnyside raids. But this prominence is not rooted in the agency demonstrating any initiative of its own, let alone is it as decisive and flamboyant as Mthethwa's festive-season proclamation suggested. True, in 1999, in the wake of the establishment of the first commercial crime court in the country, the SAPS had begun to create commercial crime branches. But this effort, made possible in large part through the financial backing of Business Against Crime South Africa (later renamed Business Leadership South Africa), was less the result of what the authors of the first major study of piracy in South Africa refer to as a "typical case of a multi-national dominated media market and an exemplary case of government cooperation with those multinationals on enforcement."[45] Rather, it was owed to the government bowing to the latter's agenda of seeking to "build an environment in which globally competitive and national responsible companies can prosper."[46]

Yet while on one level public-private partnerships reflect more private interests than any greater good, in keeping with this book's commitment to tracing even the most inconspicuous, mundane agencies in an ant-like fashion from the ground up rather than from their imagined telos, I want to cast my ethnographic net a little wider. Rather than narrowing the cast of actors to a small nucleus of big business and state power, a full account of the public policing of piracy would need to include a much broader and more complexly interlaced range of actors. Policing, I argue, is as much hosted by those being policed—both pirates *and* consumers—as it is produced by entirely extraneous factors, like the availability of cheap consumer technologies, the excessive cost or even complete absence of broadband service, the equilibrium of high prices and a small market, and, last but not least, the law and the judiciary.

While most of these factors are beyond the scope of this chapter's purview, a word about the latter is in order, beginning with the Copyright Act. Here, s 27 sets out the penalties for infringement of copyright in sound recordings. A person is guilty of an offense, the section reads, when he or she "makes for sale or hire; sells or lets for hire or by way of trade offers or exposes for sale or hire; by way of trade exhibits in public; imports into the Republic otherwise than for his private or domestic use; distributes for purposes of trade; or distributes for any other purposes to such an extent that the owner of the copyright is prejudicially affected, articles which he knows to be infringing copies of the work, shall be guilty of an offense." Things get more complicated at the level of proceedings. Copyright owners can pursue either civil or criminal proceedings, but all acts of criminal copyright infringement also constitute civil copyright infringement. The choice of proceedings has evidentiary consequences with regard to the subsistence of copyright, the onus of proof (balance of probability in civil proceedings, beyond a reasonable doubt at common law criminal liability), or methods of proof (affidavit evidence in civil proceedings, oral evidence plus physical copy of the original recording at common law criminal procedure).[47] Other differences include the need for proof of title in civil proceedings but not in criminal procedure and damages (which may or may not be available in civil proceedings).

As for the actual penalties, s 27 (6) (a) of the Copyright Act provides that "a person convicted under the section shall be liable in the case of a first conviction to a fine not exceeding five thousand rand or to imprisonment for a period not exceeding three years or to both such fine and such imprisonment, for each article to which the offense relates." If a person is convicted more than one time, s 27 (6) (b) stipulates that this person is liable to a fine "not exceeding ten thousand rand or to imprisonment for a period not exceeding five years or to both such fine and such imprisonment, for each article to which the offence relates."

But the Copyright Act is frequently not the only and most efficient way of prosecuting piracy. The Criminal Procedure Act, the Counterfeit Goods

Act, and a host of additional statutes, such as the Customs and Excise Act 91 of 1964 and the Prevention of Organised Crime Act 121 of 1998, may also be considered in seeking a conviction. As for the judiciary, in their 2011 study, Primo and Lloyd diagnosed a "judicial pushback" against the enforcement agenda across the entire court system, including the newly created commercial crime courts. Strikingly, despite the quasi-privatization of the criminal justice system, judges rarely give in to sponsors' demands to mete out harsher punishment. Many prefer to either impose "fines more commensurate with the ability of offenders to pay" or suspend fines and jail sentences after sentencing altogether.[48] But judicial lenience is also a function of a system that, in addition to being understaffed with judges qualified in copyright law, is chronically overburdened with problems, such as prohibitive bail and lengthy pretrial detention, not to mention the avalanche of murder trials that compel "judges to triage a variety of low-level offenses, including most forms of street-level piracy."[49]

Chains of Obviousness: Forensics and the Production of Certainty

Devotees of CSI, the blockbuster TV series about a team of crime scene investigators in Las Vegas, may have become accustomed to the reassuring feeling that evidence speaks for itself; that members of the criminal justice system are united in the heroic pursuit of truth and justice; or that a straight line links the facts to the conviction. The meaning of the term I am invoking in this chapter, *evidence chain*, takes the discussion of forensics in a slightly different direction. My concern is less with what one might call the chain's rewind button—the fact that it enables investigators to reversibly trace any sources of potential contamination. Rather, I am more interested in the chaining itself—the investigative stages, shifts of referentiality, transformations of facticity, and especially the procedural hoops, the affidavit, the presumption, the proof of title, the balance of probability, and mens rea that objects drift through en route, like a ship slowly disappearing behind the horizon, toward that elusive goal of progress, development, or welfare at the heart of how South Africans envisage a socially more responsive copyright system.

But what does it mean to chain something? To get started, we might think of a bicycle chain. At first glance, a bicycle chain is little more than a simple device that enables the cyclist to get from A to B with relative ease by connecting a number of sprocket wheels of different sizes. But as every cyclist knows from painful experience, keeping one's chain well-greased at all times to make the transmission of energy from one wheel to the other as effortless as possible is essential. Something must be prevented from getting lost; something must be kept unchanged—after all, that is the meaning of custody. In the case of our bicycle chain, it is the energy the cyclist generates with their body. In the chain of custody, it is the integrity of the objects that must not be tampered with. The gun and the DNA sample received at the crime lab must be the same gun and the same DNA sample retrieved from the crime scene.

But this is where the analogy begins to reveal some subtle differences between the conventional meaning of the term in criminal procedure and my adaptation of it. At its most basic, and as the etymology of *evidence* suggests, what remains constant in the transfer of evidence, from the moment of its first encounter with the enforcement agents to the court, is what one might call obviousness. Evanescent like *energy* and immaterial like *integrity*, the term *obviousness* indexes a state of indeterminacy where the nature of things is subject to ascriptions of value and meaning rather than to irrefutable empirical proof. As such, obviousness has several unique qualities that lend themselves particularly well to the type of analysis attempted in this chapter. One of these is that the obviousness of a piece of evidence is based on a referential relationship to something else in which obviousness itself does not inhere. Thus, a stack of CDs found on a sidewalk in Twist Street in downtown Johannesburg was obviously placed there by someone, but this referential link does not tell us much about the intention or, indeed, the identity of the person who placed it there before making off from the approaching police van. To again use the bicycle metaphor, the degree of obviousness at this rudimentary stage is contingent on a fairly short chain with few links. Therefore, to keep this low level of obviousness from diminishing even further and for the integrity of the chain to remain intact, the number of links has to be multiplied. Yet unlike the old Aquinian doctrine, *adaequatio intellectus et rei*, it is not the job of circulation to narrow down the number of obvious linkages to one but, on the contrary, to multiply them. The more evidence, the more tightly strung and robust the chain. In other words, as obviousness emerges through circulation, enactment, and activation, it is, by the same token, formative of the chain through which it circulates.

This brings us back to RiSA's "Investigation Process." In contrast to the linearity of the chain envisaged in that document, my reinterpretation of the chain of obviousness foregrounds the uncertain terrain that is traversed as the chain produces and is generated by obviousness. The advantage of this method is that it obliges the analyst to forsake conventional ways of thinking about crime, law, or policing as a matter of epistemology, meaning, or perspective—in other words as discrete, homogenous objects upon which different representations with different claims to truth can be brought to bear and around which competing narratives about development, national identity, democracy, or social cohesion may coalesce. Similar to the referential chains constructed by the pedologists studying the soil of the Brazilian rainforest that Latour writes about, the risky business of circulating obviousness is not made any less precarious by any one representation successfully claiming authority over the object it purports to represent but by recognizing the fact that instead of distinctions among objects, the only thing that exists is circulation.[50] Concretely, then, how might the predominant legal narrative of piracy as a criminal (and/or civil) liability change when looked at from different locations within the cycle? What happens to this narrative when street piracy goes from being referenced in relation to s 27 of the Copyright Act to merely being dealt with as a question of vagrancy under local ordinances? To what extent does the choice of prosecution or legal rules impact the types of actors conscripted to enforce such rules? And vice versa, how do different enforcement agencies shape ideas about the preferred method of enforcement? What is the boundary between piracy understood as copyright infringement and a contravention of the Counterfeit Act, and how are such fluctuating boundaries, if any, redrawn when subject to the rules of criminal procedure?

Back at the Boksburg station, the police officers, SAFACT agents, and two of the suspects (after being stitched up by a paramedic, the bleeding suspect was released because there was no expert qualified to process his counterfeit T-shirts on hand) sit around a large table in a conference room at the back of the station. The walls are lined with notices urging officers to be mindful of their work environment: "Do not forget to wear your bullet resistant jacket. Your family needs you." Or, "Don't become a statistic," a sardonic memento of the hundreds of police killed in the line of duty every year. Darren, like many freeborns whose job prospects are virtually nil, is a young SAFACT recruit who aspires to become a policeman and has spent the past year going out on raids almost daily.

"We believe in helping SAFACT," he says. "Even if we get only one street vendor today, it's one less. We are slowly but surely making it."

Another SAFACT agent, Emile, was with the police force for seven years before he joined SAFACT. He worries about the public's perception (and

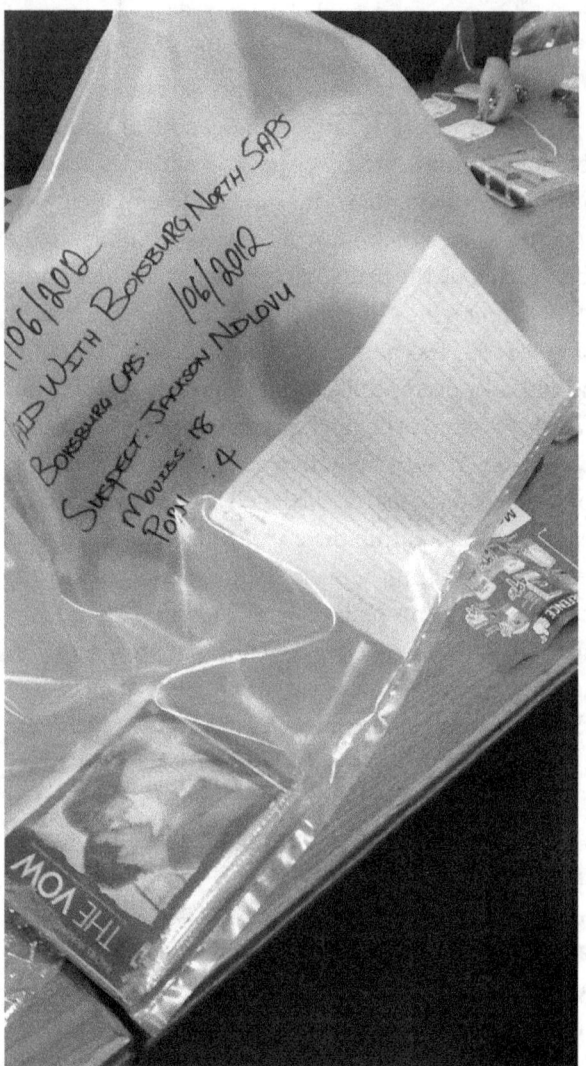

FIGURE 4.2 Exhibit bag at Boksburg North Police Station. Photograph by the author.

my videotaping) of operations, insisting that "piracy" hurts the economy. His sister, he elaborates, was working in the marketing division at SONY SA before she was retrenched due to the effects of piracy. At the other end of the room, the commander lectures the suspects on mens rea: "It is not allowed to sell anything that is name branded. You know it is wrong, you understand?" They nod silently.

By contrast, the mood at the Lyttelton Police Station is much more subdued. After sending the Africa and Khuze Club DJs home to register with SAMRO, Rheder and the shift get to work on the O Canto DJ. "Are you married?" one of the officers asks. "Occupation: asylum seeker, eh? Standard of education? Where were you born? And don't tell me China. What town in China? Fujian? Fujian is a province, not a town." Meanwhile, Rheder searches the suspect's hard drive. "He's got everything," he tells me. "International, local, South African music, even Chinese music, Oliver Mtukudzi." And again, turning to the DJ: "There is more than 70GB of music here—1,336 tracks, to be precise, not 400, as you told us. So you lied to us."

For the next several hours, the suspects and the ethnographer will look on as the officers work their way through a veritable paper maze, filling out a First Information of Crime (FIC) form, labeling exhibit bags, opening a crime docket, informing the suspects of their constitutional rights, or updating the investigation diary. Unlike the fun and games of the wild chase by the Boksburg mall, police loath all the sorting, labeling, and listing—the "paperwork," as they call it. To the ethnographer, however, all these lowly objects—the exhibit bags, forms, investigation diaries, labels, and crime dockets—provide the grist for his mill. For what they, and the actions they host, reveal is not some invisible hand of global capitalism or neoliberal rationality but something far less mysterious and, yet, infinitely richer and meaningful than all the instrumentalist-normative legal reasoning, law, economics, socio-legal, or critical cultural studies of law taken together. It is perhaps the single most underrated, if not denigrated, feature of the law—the ability to define the valences governing the combination of different epistemologies and material practices of truth-making.

Let us take a closer look at this "paperwork," beginning with the seized CDs and DVDs. At first glance, the discs and the exhibit bags where they are kept seem to serve a simple enough purpose—to gather in one place the material evidence needed to determine whether a person is criminally liable for infringement under s 26 of the Copyright Act. Things get more complicated, however, when considering how these objects establish a series of references to a set of as yet disparate points: the name of the suspect on whom the goods were found, the date and place of the operation, the place of the goods in SAFACT's collection of forensic materials, and, most significantly, the Criminal Administration System (CAS). One way to think about these referential links is as what Latour calls "forced attachments" or "attributions," through which a person is bound to an enunciation or act.[51] Yet, the matter is not quite so simple. What is it that is, almost literally, bundled together here? And according to what logic or system? Of course, one might argue that the arrest and the paperwork form the gateway into the criminal justice system with its labyrinthine rules, procedures, and institutions. Now criminal justice systems the world over are notorious for occasional malfunctioning because the output—justice—is frequently out of step with the input—criminal law. Or so it may seem to the instrumentalist. Yet, there is nothing to prevent us from claiming just the opposite, namely, that it is the CDs, labels, bags, and case numbers that create the criminal justice system. We should, therefore, never speak of institutions as frameworks providing more or less stable boundaries to what happens within them but as that which is framed by their content.

How, then, are our CDs chained once they encounter the exhibit bags, the labels, the CAS number, and the crime docket? The first thing to notice is that one and the same bag will host quite different chains. Thus, the bag itself and the inscription on it initiate a relatively simple chain interlinking the suspect and the seized goods: no more, no less. No more, because it is immaterial at this point whether Jackson Ndlovu, to quote from s 23 of the Copyright Act, "by way of trade offering or exposing for sale" these CDs was doing so mens rea, that is, with criminal intent. No less, because Ndlovu, apart from being a Zimbabwean citizen, an illegal immigrant, or a father of four, for the purposes of the chain, is Jackson Ndlovu. By contrast, the number on the red SAFACT label and the CAS number link the contents of the bag to quite another chain that stretches well beyond the individual suspect-seized goods relationship to the larger cluster of suspect-seized goods-relationships-handled-by SAFACT-in-2012 or even to the totality of all criminal offenses prosecuted by the state.

Yet, for all the differences of scale, these different frames of reference also have something in common. As the word *custody* suggests, they keep something stable throughout the journey. But what is this something? Clearly, it is not the materiality of the CDs themselves—their shape, size, or color. Nor is it the suspect, who is the legal subject "Nldovu" as he watches his illicit ware being sorted, labeled, and bagged, and who will be "Ndlovu" as he is locked up in the station's holding cell before his arraignment the following Monday. Least of all, is it any kind of truth, fact, or proof the CDs might point to, such as that they are really infringing someone else's copyright; that Ndlovu is not only "Ndlovu" but also a criminal; that by selling the infringing copies in front of the East Rand Mall, he diminished the number of potential sales of the original; and that he, thereby, increased the cost of making music or supported terrorism. Regardless of their length, beginning, or endpoint, then, and despite the different translations and encodings that allow a pile of plastic to bind into a larger compound, one might say, recuperating the etymology of *evidence*, that our chains transport obviousness.

But it would be misleading to assume that it is pure, ready-made facticity itself that is transported by our chain of obviousness or that such a trajectory might be comparable to the experimental path scientific research takes toward objectivity. Rather, when a plastic bag containing seized DVDs and CDs full of MP3 files is inscribed with the names of the suspect, the police station, the date of the raid, and the CAS number, what all these references establish is little more than the simple claim that the bag, indeed, contains what the inscription says it does. Yet, when the contents of the same bag end up at the RiSA offices for a forensic analysis of each and every individual track burnt onto the discs, it is something else that is being transported and that builds up, as it were, the chainness of the chain. The CD/DVD-suspect linkage has made the trip from Boksburg to Randburg unchanged. So, too, has the seized-goods-exhibit-bag-CAS number connection remained constant. Looked at in terms of the narrower, chain-of-custody meaning, then, this something else is clearly not the referentiality of each and every item traveling along the chain, whether these references point to the raid conducted by the Boksburg North police, the rights holder whose copyright has been infringed, or the recording artists. Nor is the chainness made more real, or the evidence rendered overwhelming and factually more relevant by moving through another relay or filter. What is kept once the evidence ends up in the courtroom is something simpler and more abstract—it is the integrity of the chain as a chain.

Obviousness is, of course, not the same as proof. Even though there is a high degree of obviousness to Ndlovu having "exposed for sale" the CDs, the probative value of the CDs is still relatively low at this stage of the investigation. *Probative value* is a key term in the law of evidence. It denotes the significance of evidence in proving a claim. For instance, a photo of a driver speeding at 100 miles per hour 50 yards before running a red light is of higher probative value than a photo of the same person driving at 100 miles per hour, 500 yards from the traffic light. In other words, probative value is a matter of weight. And this is where another element of the maligned paperwork comes in—the crime docket.

At first glance, a crime docket is little more than another method of collecting the evidence generated during an investigation in one convenient

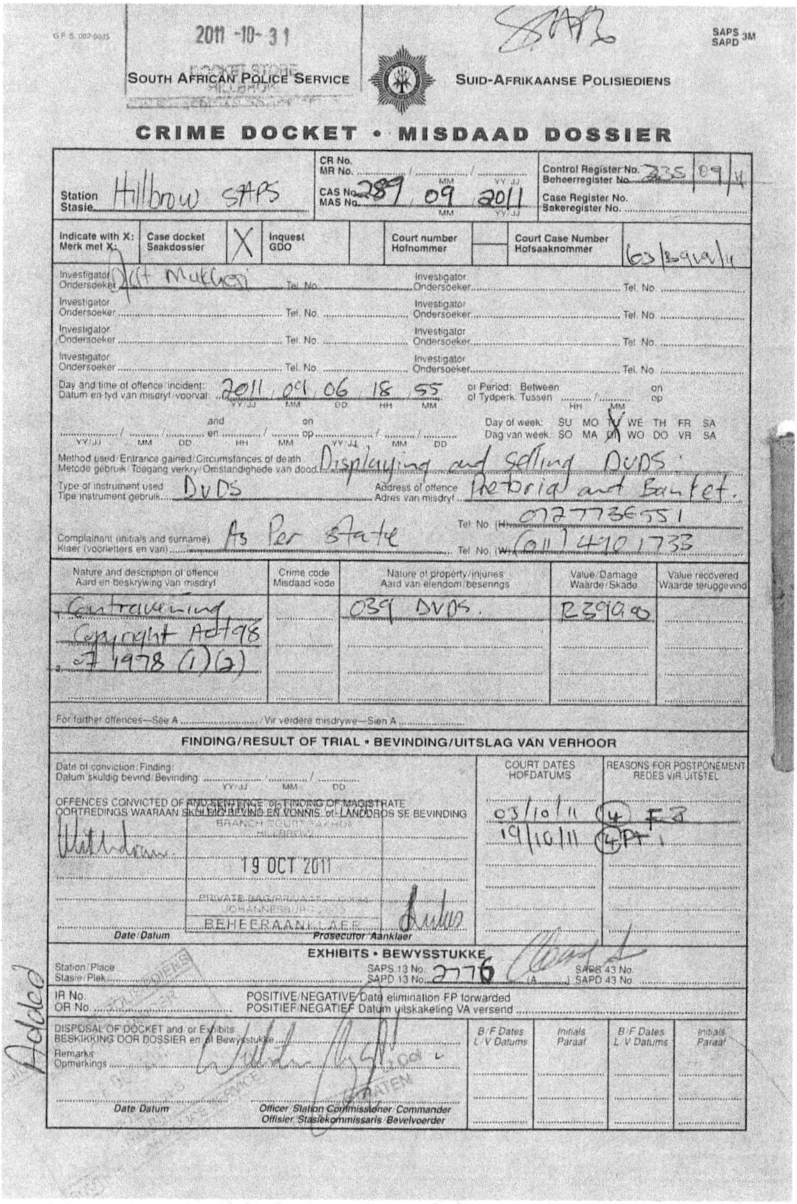

2011 -10- 31

SOUTH AFRICAN POLICE SERVICE · SUID-AFRIKAANSE POLISIEDIENS

SAPS 3M / SAPD

CRIME DOCKET • MISDAAD DOSSIER

Station / Stasie: Hillbrow SAPS

CAS No. / MAS No.: 289 / 09 / 2011

Control Register No. / Beheerregister No.: 335 / 09 / 11

Indicate with X / Merk met X: Case docket / Saakdossier: X · Inquest / GDO

Court Case Number / Hofsaaknommer: 63/Bq1a/11

Investigator / Ondersoeker: ... Mukheri

Day and time of offence/incident / Datum en tyd van misdryf/voorval: 2011 / 09 / 06 18:55

Day of week / Dag van week: TU

Method used/Entrance gained/Circumstances of death / Metode gebruik/Toegang verkry/Omstandighede van dood: Displaying and selling DVDS.

Type of instrument used / Tipe instrument gebruik: DVDS

Address of offence / Adres van misdryf: Pretoria and Banket.

Complainant (initials and surname) / Klaer (voorletters en van): As Per State

Tel. No. (H): 0727736551

Tel. No. (W): (011) 4101733

Nature and description of offence / Aard en beskrywing van misdryf	Crime code / Misdaad kode	Nature of property/injuries / Aard van eiendom/beserings	Value/Damage / Waarde/Skade	Value recovered / Waarde teruggevind
Contravening Copyright Act 98 of 1978 (1)(2)		039 DVDS.	R390.00	

For further offences—See A / Vir verdere misdrywe—Sien A

FINDING/RESULT OF TRIAL • BEVINDING/UITSLAG VAN VERHOOR

Date of conviction/Finding / Datum skuldig bevind/Bevinding

OFFENCES CONVICTED OF AND SENTENCE or FINDING OF MAGISTRATE / OORTREDINGS WAARAAN SKULDIG BEVIND EN VONNIS of LANDDROS SE BEVINDING: Withdrawn.

BRANCH COURT HILLBROW · 19 OCT 2011 · PRIVATE BAG · JOHANNESBURG · BEHEERAANKLAER

Date/Datum · Prosecutor/Aanklaer

COURT DATES / HOFDATUMS	REASONS FOR POSTPONEMENT / REDES VIR UITSTEL
03/10/11	(4) F.B
19/10/11	(4) PT

EXHIBITS • BEWYSSTUKKE

Station/Place / Stasie/Plek · SAPS 13 No. / SAPD 13 No.: 2776 · SAPS 43 No. / SAPD 43 No.

IR No. / OR No. · POSITIVE/NEGATIVE Date elimination FP forwarded / POSITIEF/NEGATIEF Datum uitskakeling VA versend

DISPOSAL OF DOCKET and/or Exhibits / BESKIKKING OOR DOSSIER en/of Bewysstukke · Remarks / Opmerkings: Withdrawn

Date/Datum · Officer/Station Commissioner/Commander / Offisier/Stasiekommissaris/Bevelvoerder

B/F Dates / L/V Datums · Initials / Paraaf

Added

FIGURE 4.3 SAPS crime docket. Photograph by the author.

place. There is, for instance, the FIC form, a printout of the Criminal Record System, the investigation diary, and possibly also a warrant of arrest and a constitutional warning informing the suspect of their constitutional rights. All these documents are neatly arranged in so-called clips labeled A, B, and C. Clip A is the most important part of the docket, containing information about the suspect, the crime scene, statements by officers and witnesses, and, most crucially, forensic reports. Clip B contains material of lesser importance, such as correspondence with other police stations, newspaper clippings, and the like, while the investigation diary is placed in clip C.

All this sorting, formatting, and numbering might appear as purely technical in nature or what one anthropologist of policing refers to as "the documentary-disciplinary interface between state and society."[52] Yet, crime dockets are more than neutral, unchanging intermediaries or criminological archives. As a docket travels across the criminal justice system from the uniformed branch to the detective branch to the prosecutor and eventually the magistrate court, it becomes a moving target, or what Geoffrey Bowker and Susan Star call a "boundary object."[53] It is at once an agent *and* an effect of networked relations whose contours, identity, and coherence can never be taken for granted. From the moment a raid gets underway, to the arrest of a suspected pirate and the opening of a crime docket, all the way to a forensic report and, ultimately, a conviction and victory in the police minister's "people's war," dockets provide an element of stability to the production of proof unlike any other component in the entire enforcement process. But they do so not by being stable entities themselves. Rather than fixed texts, they are more performances or enactments that keep evidence in constant circulation throughout the criminal justice systems and beyond, into the music industry, as we shall see further below. Along this trajectory, dockets thicken materially and metaphorically. The more "arrest statements," "statements regarding interview with suspect," or "affidavits in terms of the Copyright Act" are assembled between its grayish covers, the more weight the docket holds and the higher the probativity of the evidence needed for a criminal conviction. But dockets are also always in danger of losing their hard-won weightiness when the admissibility of their contents is contested in court. That is why they are also sites for reduction and standardization. Dockets entangle police, suspects, lawyers, and judges in ever-changing configurations, sometimes consolidating these fragile relationships through standardized legal language, sometimes undermining them because of sloppy police work, an incomplete affidavit, or an overly cautious judge ordering the investigation to start all over again.

To illustrate, take the case of Borges Balami (not his real name), a street vendor from Mozambique, arrested in Hillbrow, one of Johannesburg's most crime-ridden inner-city districts. His docket shows how a constant feedback loop between the arresting officer and the detective assigned to the case ensured a relatively smooth transition from the arrest to the conviction. The chain begins with A1, the first page in clip A, which contains the report by the warrant officer who arrested Balami for "contravening of the Copyrights Act no. 27" by selling "counterfeit goods to the public." After informing the suspect of his constitutional rights, the crew found thirty-five DVDs "to the value of R350." The statement closes with a standard paragraph where the officer confirms that he understands the contents of his statement, that he is prepared to take the prescribed oath, and that the oath is binding on his conscience. Barring the mislabeling of the Copyright Act—it should have read Copyright Act and s 27—and the confusion of copying and counterfeit, the statement is rather symptomatic of the language common in the several dozens of dockets I was able to review at the Hillbrow station. Two weeks after his arrest, Balami entered a plea agreement and was sentenced to a fine of R3,500 (R100 per DVD) or ten days of imprisonment.

In other cases, matters are less straightforward. The docket may be returned to the police because the investigating officer failed to include the 212 statement (which stands for the affidavit under section 212 of the Criminal Procedure Act that provides for exceptions to hearsay as evidence); because the arrest statement did not specify the number of seized CDs; an accused released on bail gave a false address and did not show up at trial; or simply because the prosecutor decided to nolle prosequi, that is, abandon the case.[54]

The material-semiotic entanglements that characterize the production of dockets as a vital link in the chain of obviousness are also observed in the forensic work conducted at the RiSA offices in Johannesburg, where the investigation is taken to another level or category of obviousness—proof of copying and infringement. Located in a drab business park in Randburg and surrounded by the South African branch offices of the major international media conglomerates, RiSA's suite is a relatively frugal affair. Apart from a reception area, kitchen, conference room, archive, and the offices of the SAMPRA CEO and CFO, it houses Angus Rheder's office cum forensic lab. A small space strewn with exhibit bags, desktop computers and their peripheries, CDs, and DVDs, most of which have been seized during previous raids, there is a lot of coming and going. A coworker next door asks for a pencil sharpener; a person from Namibia calls to inquire about how he might get a license to play recordings in his club; an associate of Easi Eight Amusements, then one of South Africa's largest manufacturers of jukeboxes, stops by to put the finishing touches on a license agreement; a Cameroonian restaurant owner and "his" DJ, caught using unlicensed sound recordings, wonder why music from "other African countries" must also be licensed. The line between office and forensic lab is perilously hazy. On one occasion, Rheder, a SAMPRA staff member, and I were comparing our respective ideas of professional ethos when Rheder mumbled something about his office being a mess, a confession whose significance I downplayed by jokingly referring to the mess as "mere outer appearance." But perhaps I was wrong. The objects that pile up in the lab, like flotsam washed ashore, are more than a peripheral aspect of forensics' real work. Forensics thrives on clutter. As I suggested earlier, forensics is a process that entails a series of knowledge moves designed to keep obviousness as stable as possible as it travels along the discontinuous chain that stretches from the crime scene of the nightclub and the streets all the way to the court. But within this chain, there is one segment that deserves more detailed scrutiny.

Rheder had just received a package of items from the police, seized during a raid in Khayelitsha (a township in Cape Town) the previous week, containing a PC, four CDs, and two USB sticks with some three hundred MP3 tracks. In addition to these carriers, the PC's hard drive was also loaded with an additional 150 tracks, bringing the total copies up to 450. But how does one prove that such a large number of what s 27 of the Copyright Act refers to as "articles" actually infringe on RiSA members' rights? The term *article*, like the act as a whole, is a rather antiquated one, harkening back to an era when an analog sound recording, such as an LP, was generally considered a self-contained unit, infringing copies of which usually comprised the entire master tape. In the digital age, this equation no longer holds. When large quantities of MP3 compilations sourced from many different albums can be cheaply produced on home computers and duplicator towers, not only does the term *article* acquire a whole new meaning, the level of obviousness or the probative value of each article is greatly diminished, destabilizing the entire chain as a result.

What follows is a sequence of steps—painstakingly photographed and recorded in a log—whose nature and order are determined by the specific characteristics of what forensic experts call "digital evidence." Unlike classic forms of physical evidence, like fingerprints or tool marks, digital evidence presents a different sort of challenge because potential contamination is more often a matter of a single mouse click than visible forms of interference.

That is to say, in contrast to more standard forensic procedures where the evidence's physical features are often translated into a digital format, pirated music is already the result of prior shifts from one digital format to another. In fact, as we will see further below, even within the broader category of digital audio data, different sorts of translations or format changes, such as from AAC to MP3, are common, presenting even more challenges along the chain of obviousness. Moreover, in the transition from one carrier to another—internet to hard drive, hard drive to USB stick—it is not just copies of existing files that are produced but also additional metadata. This information about information may enter into yet another type of hosting relationship with the law, producing different levels of probativity where the mere fact that a transition took place can yield evidence of higher probative value than information about what and how much was copied.

Before we delve deeper into this imbroglio of formats, transitions, and translations, a number of cautionary measures must be taken. To initiate the forensic process proper, Rheder must transfer the entire contents of the seized HD to one of RiSA's own drives by creating a bit-by-bit duplicate. (The latter drive will be erased and used for another analysis once the case has been closed.) Although on the face of it, this might seem a straightforward procedure that is easily accomplished by means of basic cloning software like EaseUS Scan-Disk or HDClone, during which no formats are changed and nothing gets erased, it is certainly not risk-free. Existing content on the destination drive may have been left intact, thus opening the entire process to charges of planting evidence. No wonder Rheder takes extra precaution in photographing both the dialogue warning that "all data on the destination will be erased" and the final window indicating that there were zero read and zero write errors.

However, things become much trickier in the next stage of the analysis. During this phase, our HD, CDs, and USB sticks actually begin to give away all the little secrets of the DJ's illicit craft—information that is encoded in a specific language and that must be rendered in another idiom in order to become legally pertinent. Although *legally pertinent* is not a very elegant, let alone legal, term, the word *pertinent* does capture some of the profoundly relational nature (after all, that is where etymologists say *pertinent* comes from) of the process, we will now examine in more detail. Again, it is simple software that is being deployed. Using *Where Is It?* cataloging software, Rheder extracts the metadata from the legitimate CDs on which the infringing copies are based. This process is critical because it allows him to create another set of references necessary to bring proceedings for copyright infringement. Unlike the previous steps that established proof of copying having taken place, this phase of the investigation foregrounds the ownership of the rights in the infringed sound recording. One way to look at this stage is by thinking of the continuity of our chain of obviousness as indebted to more than shifts in its material base from fake CDs or USB sticks to one of RiSA's hard drives. In contrast to the fattening of the docket, what takes place here is a kind of thinning out, a distillation or condensation of the evidence into ever more fine-grained components down to the metadata of each track. And as we shall see a little further below, this shift in analytic technique also carries with it another aspect of the chain of obviousness. Unlike the time-consuming, error-prone steps of the investigative process from its inception all the way to forensic analysis, the chain finally picks up steam just before the evidence is turned over to a prosecutor. Narrowing the evidence down to just two statements—the fact that copying *and* infringement of the rights held by RiSA's members occurred—enables RiSA to produce an affidavit that will serve as prima facie evidence of copyright infringement, which will then speed up the judicial process.

Before we rejoin Rheder for this last step, however, it may be useful to briefly compare the concept of circulation to some of the processes of scientific fact-making that have preoccupied STS scholars and, to a much lesser degree, socio-legal scholars for much of the past half-century. Given its close connections with criminal procedural law, forensics provides a good entry point into this discussion. Recent years have seen a lively debate among forensic scholars, criminologists, and experts of criminal law about the perceived differences between forensic, legal, and scientific "epistemic cultures."[55] Essentially, there are two camps in this debate: the absolutists and the relativists, as one might call them. According to the former, there is a fundamentally unbridgeable gulf between the epistemic cultures of forensic science and research science. For example, Bruno Latour has persistently highlighted what he sees as the fundamental "ontological" difference between scientific and legal forms of fact-making. The former, he argues, is predicated on the idea that the singular can be subsumed under the general or—put another way—that phenomenon A is an instance of category B and that, consequently, anyone who has B in their possession can know A. From the point of law, however, the only true kind of chain is that which subordinates the "A is an instance of B" chain to another chain, the "A is an instance of B as defined by statute C" chain. In other words, the sciences and the law may both establish numerous linkages and pathways between A and B, but the grids enabling these linkages "differ as much as a grid of fiber optic cables differs from an urban gas supply network."[56] Yet, other scholars have stressed the way that the dissimilarities between scientific reference chains and legal chains of obligations are reflected, for instance, in how scientists communicate their findings. Scientists produce research papers, but forensic experts, for the most part, produce reports and affidavits and appear in court as expert witnesses. Likewise, the audience of researchers forms their own peer group, whereas, in forensic science, legal actors do the listening. And lastly, the broader scientific "agenda" of both fields differ, too—driven by paradigms and programs among scientists and the demands of law enforcement and the courts among forensic experts.[57]

Relativists see the matter differently. For them, the question of whether law and science, at least in the context of forensics, are embedded in opposite cultures is moot, largely because forensic science is not a science, to begin with. Forensics, in the words of legal scholar Paul Roberts, is already an "inveterate hybrid" and, as such, intersects with both law and science in significant ways. Thus, contrary to what the absolutists claim, law and science do not operate on the basis of vastly contrasting epistemic standards and protocols of truth-making. Nor are they divided in their relationship to tradition and innovation. And above all, the adversarial procedure of common law jurisdictions (which includes South Africa) is not inimical to science.[58]

However, there is one point that science studies, science and technology studies, and forensic scholars appear to agree on. Neither forensic science nor research science and law are situated in a vacuum. Much like molecular biology and nuclear medicine are more than just products of laboratories—thought to be irrefutable, objective, and uncontaminated by the world outside—so, too, is forensic science intricately connected to its context. As Corinna Kruse writes, forensics, like the criminal justice system as a whole, is a "product of the society both the system and the evidence are part of."[59] However, the application of this statement to the South African context, like so many others of its kind we have encountered in this book, is problematic. The sociocultural factors that STS scholarship tends to invoke with predictable regularity cannot easily be grafted onto a world whose contours, in many ways, defy Western modernist notions of the social as the foremost substance of human interaction and as providing a sense of direction and shared meaning. Nor do such factors determine scientific epistemologies, much less produce specific scientific results. To the contrary, it is these epistemes that embroil a variety of actors in the formation and consolidation of intersecting social, cultural, economic, and legal networks in the first place. This is not to suggest, though, that science simply conjures up communities of judgment out of the thin air of scientific work or that it rallies people around an idea, fact, or truth simply because that fact was arrived at through the application of reason and rigorous experimentation. Science functions on what I call the principle of valence, circulating reference across different—at times even incompatible—epistemic domains.

The second aspect that bears reiterating when talking about the limitations of the relativist stance is that, unlike research science, in general, forensics is not an open-ended process. Integral to the forensic process is the tendency to strive for legal certainty, a condition of stability sociologist Andrew Abbott, in a nonlegal context, calls "jurisdiction."[60] The term is a felicitous one for the subject matter at hand because the series of knowledge moves necessary for an investigation to move forward are goal-directed in ways that scientific truth-making is not. Jurisdiction in the former refers to the fact that someone somewhere—a complainant, prosecutor, or judge—has the authority to dispense with legal action, drop charges because the prosecution is deemed to serve no substantial public interest, or, in fact, sentence the infringer and close the proceedings. No such closure can ever be claimed by research science. Today's finding is tomorrow's question.

Back at Rheder's office/lab, there is one last step he must take before RiSA forwards the assembled forensic evidence to the prosecuting authority. Contrary to the emphasis on criminal enforcement in the "Process of Investigation" document quoted above, civil and criminal liability for copyright infringement may overlap under South African law, giving complainants a choice with regard to issuing summons in lieu of damages or a reasonable royalty or to lay criminal charges. For instance, because SAFACT is funded by the world's major film companies, and the main target of its street operations are vendors whose proceeds from their illicit trade in DVDs are negligible but who may otherwise be willing to disclose the identities of their suppliers in exchange for a reduced fine, the organization has a choice in pursuing civil or criminal proceedings. SAFACT may seek a criminal conviction when the suspected infringer is uncooperative or their revenue too small to claim damages. If, however, the supplier of the infringing copies is a substantial trader, the association may also file a civil claim for damages and, perhaps, an interdict. Operations conducted at RiSA's behest follow a different strategy. As these operations from 2012 tended to be primarily directed at DJs and club and restaurant owners, RiSA officials pressure suspected infringers into signing cease-and-desist agreements obliging them to obtain licenses from SAMPRA for the performance of sound recordings (and, every so often, also from SAMRO, the collecting society for the performing rights of works). In the case of international artists, Rheder forwards a spreadsheet of the infringing tracks with their titles, authors names, and metadata to RiSA's digital forensic expert who then checks everything against illegal download sites, which will then be asked to take down the tracks. Or, if no response from those sites is forthcoming, removal notices will be sent to the internet service provider and, in some cases, to the IFPI, pursuant to the provisions of the US Digital Millennium Copyright Act. Additionally, suspected infringers may also be required to deliver up their laptops and infringing copies for further forensic analysis in the event that RiSA requires court-proof evidence for bringing criminal charges against a suspected infringer who has been caught again.

Regardless of the option pursued, the law grants complainants a fair amount of discretion as to how the evidence collected will be used in court. Physical proof of infringement arrived at by the comparison described above, between duplicated, infringing, and legitimate tracks, need only be adduced if a case goes to trial. In civil proceedings, an affidavit will suffice. The latter, however, is by no means less elaborate than all the labeling, tracing, and counterchecking going on in Rheder's office/lab. A document called "Affidavit in Terms of the Copyright Act, 1978 (Act 98 of 1978)"—the document mentioned above in relation to s 212 of the Criminal Procedure Act—illustrates the extent of the effort investigators must go to in managing the risky transition from the material form of the evidence gathered to a semiotic form encoded in the terms and templates rules usually set out in court-issued "notes of practice."[61] Key to this is a number of workarounds, called rebuttable presumptions of law. There are countless such presumptions—perhaps the most familiar and fundamental is the presumption of innocence. But in copyright law, there are a number of statutory presumptions that have a significant impact on our chain of obviousness as it draws near its endpoint. To initiate the quantum leap from a presumption of law to proof beyond reasonable doubt—the legal standard of proof for a criminal conviction—in section "7. Analysis" of the affidavit, the deponent must provide evidence that the seized goods are infringing copies by drawing on three criteria. First, the CDs are CDR or CDR-W that can be used to burn copies; second, unlike original CDs that are usually silver, such recorded CDs are of a different color; and third, and most important, recorded CDs, unlike factory-made replicated CDs, lack the SID code, an established international industry standard that indicates the plant where the CD was manufactured and is meant to simplify the identification of legitimate copies. But this is not enough. Appended to the affidavit is an inventory of the analyzed exhibits

111213-01 AKR Hillbrow CAS 1388/10/2011 Page 1 of 11

A ____

AFFIDAVIT IN TERMS OF THE COPYRIGHT ACT, 1978 (ACT 98 OF 1978)

I,

ANGUS KENNETH RHEDER

state under oath as follows:

1.

Details of Enforcement Officer

I am an Enforcement officer of the Anti-Piracy Enforcement Unit of the Recording Industry of South Africa (hereafter referred to as "RiSA"). I have received extensive training in the identification of infringing copies of sound recordings and counterfeit goods. I received this training during the period 1 August 2005 to 13 August 2005. I have also passed stringent written and practical examinations on the identification of these goods. Furthermore, during the same period I have been trained by the Regional Anti-Piracy co-coordinator: Africa of the IFPI (International Federation of the Phonographic Industry) in relation to product identification.

Prior to myself becoming an Enforcement officer with RiSA, I was employed by the South African Police Service for 14 years where I worked in the following different Units:

1) Border Police: Internal Tracing Unit: Pretoria

2) Selected Organised Crime Investigation Unit: SAPS Head Office

3) Commercial Branch: Pretoria

While in the Commercial Branch I also dealt with infringing copies and/or counterfeit goods for approximately 3 years. I therefore submit that I am qualified to identify infringing copies of music (sound recordings) on behalf of the Recording Industry of South Africa. The offices of the Recording Industry of South Africa are situated at 150 Bram Fischer Drive, Randburg, Gauteng, South Africa.

Initial: Deponent

Initial: Commissioner

FIGURE 4.4 Affidavit in terms of the Copyright Act. Courtesy of RiSA.

that lists the title of the copy (column A), the artist and title of the original disc (column B), and, most crucially, the name of the rights-holder (column C), as well as the number of copies per disc type (column D) and the number of infringing and noninfringing copies (column E).

But the affidavit is only one of several ways of producing prima facie evidence. Additional presumptions that link the act of copying to subsistence of copyright in the recording are a more complex matter. Here, s 26 (7A) of the Copyright Act provides that an author whose name—preceded by the © sign—appears on a copy or on the inlay of a copy is presumed to be the author of the recording and that any trader who is found in possession of such copy sold such copy. Presumptions, one might conclude, are little more than a series of shortcuts that allow obviousness to pass more quickly.

As a final example of how our RiSA affidavits manage the passage from the production of obviousness, through the stages I described above, to the admissibility of an affidavit as prima facie evidence, I'd like to mention two conditions that must be met for such evidence not to fall under the hearsay verdict. These include the rather broad requirement that the deponent of the affidavit must have "any skills" in a number of fields and must also be "in the service" of certain institutions and has personally examined the evidence. Hence, the language in the analysis section of the affidavit addressed earlier: "my findings," "my analysis," "by me," and so on. It is, of course, no secret that forensics, even at a small, understaffed institution like RiSA, is a highly differentiated and time-consuming process that involves more than one person and, most crucially for CD forensics, draws on an array of technologies for extracting ISRC metadata. Factor in the shifting nature of music piracy from copied CDs to MP3 compilations to file-sharing, and the line that separates statements about the facts of the case from mere opinion, the evidence, like so many other lines we encountered in this chapter, becomes very thin.

But sometimes thin lines may also have practical benefits, as the search-and-seizure operations in Boksburg and Sunnyside show. In the eyes of most South Africans, cops-and-robbers tactics are among the most resented and vigorously contested components of policing, reviving traumatic experiences of the police invading people's privacy with impunity during the apartheid era. Consequently, there are three legal mechanisms antipiracy and anticounterfeit efforts may draw on when conducting search-and-seizure operations in line with the constitutional foundations of the new, democratic South Africa.[62] Two of these are based on statutory provisions as set out in sections 5–7 and 11–12 of the Counterfeit Goods Act. The first provides for a procedure on the basis of a complaint to an inspector and a warrant for a search-and-seizure operation to locate and remove any book, document, article, item, or object relevant to the institution of criminal or civil proceedings in regard to counterfeiting and piracy. The second mechanism provides for a complainant to approach a court for an order to initiate a search-and-seizure operation to locate and remove documents, records, or other materials pending the institution of civil proceedings in cases of counterfeiting. The third mechanism is based on the common law and is usually referred to as an Anton Piller order. Sought by way of an ex parte application, its primary objective is the preservation of evidence *before* a case is instituted. As such, it is subject to stringent rules. For instance, to obtain the order, an applicant must provide prima facie evidence that they have cause of action against the prospective respondent and that the latter has in their possession specific (and specified) documents or objects that constitute vital evidence in substantiation of the applicant's cause of action. Most importantly, the applicant must demonstrate that there is a real and well-founded apprehension that this evidence may be hidden or destroyed before discovery or by the time the case goes to trial.

In a way, then, search-and-seizure operations governed by Anton Piller orders appear to be perfectly suited for copyright, where enforcing efforts are often stymied by the high mobility and ability of pirates to erase their tracks, as well as by the growing sophistication of internet-based forms of copyright infringement in circumventing detection. It is not surprising, then, that the practice has met with near-total approbation from the legal fraternity and the music industry as strengthening the position of copyright owners. And just as unsurprising, after many planned operations had to be called off because a warrant or Anton Piller order was not granted, Rheder has given up on either the Counterfeit Goods Act or Anton Piller orders to provide legal certainty to RiSA's mission. "First there must be a complaint from copyright owner," he says. "Then this must be registered with a court or a police officer who will open a case. That case then goes to the prosecutor who will determine whether there is a case to proceed. Then it goes back to investigating officer, who will then file an application for search and seizure warrant. Any business under Counterfeit Act must be under a search and seizure warrant issued by a magistrate. Once the seizure has occurred there is a period of ten days during which actions of police officer must be confirmed by the court that his actions were correct. Within that period, the copyright owner must confirm his complaint. After that, the court has to issue a prosecution notice during a certain deadline. If any of those deadlines are not met or any of those letters isn't received in time, the whole case is gone. That's why all cops know the Criminal Procedure Act. You do the arrest and the search and take it to the prosecutor who puts it on the court roll and when the court is ready for trial, we go to trial."[63]

What Rheder is referring here to are sections 22, 23, 24, and 26 of the act, all of which provide for certain conditions under which a peace officer may search and seize. As always, there are a number of gray areas where the statute leaves officers a wide margin of discretion in conducting search-and-seizure operations without a warrant, as was the case in all raids I witnessed. For instance, under the provisions of s 22a and 22b, a warrantless search may be conducted when the police official has "reasonable grounds" to believe that a warrant would be issued if they were to apply for one and that the "delay in obtaining such warrant would defeat the purpose of the search." Section 26 also provides that where a "police official in the investigation of an offense or alleged offense reasonably suspects that a person who may furnish information with reference to any such offense is on any premises," such police official "may without warrant enter such premises for the purpose of interrogating such person and obtaining a statement from him: Provided that such police official shall not enter any private dwelling without the consent of the occupier thereof." But what are reasonable grounds, and what does it mean to believe, the SAPS Secretariat for Safety and Security wonders in a report about members' compliance with the requirements governing search warrants.[64] When does the suspicion that someone may be hiding pirated CDs in a garbage bag turn into the belief that these CDs are actually pirate copies and not the person's collection of legitimate CDs borrowed from a friend? Grounds or facts, the report advises members, can only be established by at least one of a person's five senses. But such facts need not necessarily be evidence admissible in a court of law. It may also consist of information gained by hearsay from another person, such as a fellow police official or an informer who previously supplied reliable information.[65]

Another example is s 23, which authorizes a police official making an arrest to search a person without a warrant and seize any article that is "in the possession of or in custody or under control of the arrested person." According to the SAPS legal service department, an article is still considered to be under the control of the arrested person even when it is in the physical possession of someone else, but the arrested person is entitled to it. And lastly, another example of the legal ambiguity surrounding warrants is s 26, which provides that an officer who is investigating an alleged offense does not require a warrant to enter the premises of a person they suspect of being able to provide information on such offense. The conundrum here is not only that the officer cannot enter the premises without the consent of the occupier, but they also cannot search the premises unless they intend to arrest the occupier because they suspect them to be involved in the commission of the offense being investigated. And finally, while premises are defined as a private dwelling, the section is silent about the legality of warrantless searches and seizures in public spaces such as bars, clubs, and restaurants where piracy-related offenses are likely to be committed on a much larger scale than in a private home.

These are just some examples that illustrate the fragility of lawfully obtaining evidence by way of search-and-seizure operations. But the main reason for us to get into the tricky business of defining terms such as *reasonable grounds* is theoretical in nature. It is an error to assume that proof is obtained at the end of a well-oiled chain and that this chain begins with a set of rules that determine a number of basic parameters within which to lawfully generate a body of evidence whose degree of obviousness, like the photo made by the speed radar, increases the closer the offending object gets to the forensic eye. If we were to follow the legal practitioner in taking the provisions of the Criminal Procedure Act as the alpha and omega of the analysis, we would merely end up with the instrumentalist input-output automatism that this book has sought to replace with an emphasis on the contingency of legal and other practices, such as pirates selling fake CDs in front of a mall, police raiding a pub, or a forensic analysis of seized CDs in producing intermittent associations. If, however, we consider the legal framework governing the production and circulation of evidence as not producing but being reproduced by these operations, we might be able to grasp the criminal enforcement of copyright as the kind of network that, recalling Riles's pithy phrase, generates the effects of its own reality by reflecting on itself.[66] The point about such an analytic shift, then, is that the extent to which an enforcement system may be considered optimal appears less as a function of a priori given rules or infrastructures and more as the means by which every operation can be turned into an allegory of the people and those infrastructures forming a harmonious whole. In this sense, the tale RiSA weaves around the consistency of the investigative process is neither descriptive nor prescriptive. It is more what one might call postscriptive. It does not set out the path along which antipiracy operations are meant to progress. Like the operations themselves, it vindicates the integrity and ability of the law to reproduce itself as one of several means in a larger, instrumentalist chain about the optimal solution for combatting piracy.

A War of Numbers

The criminal prosecution of piracy in cooperation with the South African police is not the only form of policing RiSA is involved in. Another is a kind of policing that takes place in an equally attention-commanding, albeit just as debatable, articulation of misleading information policies, moral censure, and surveillance. Prior to outsourcing its operations to SAFACT, RiSA for several years provided its parent body IFPI with extensive databases that detailed every conceivable aspect of its operations in any given year. For example, the master spreadsheet for 2011 contains data for a staggering 890 cases handled that year alone. This mountain of information is organized in no fewer than 115 columns that, in turn, are spread out over six classes of data labeled as follows: the "enforcement agency utilized," "suspects arrested," "seizure address," "hotspots," "exhibits resealed after analysis," and "sentences." Each of these classes is then subdivided into further columns. The "suspects arrested" group, for instance, lists the number of suspects who are South African citizens, legal aliens, or illegal aliens, while "exhibits resealed after analysis" provides a tally of the type of sound carriers and the format of the tracks.

Statistics are hardly standard anthropological fare. To assess their place within an ethnography of copyright law calls for a brief review of the history of numerical data in the discipline. Traditionally, anthropologists have shunned statistics because, as in Evans-Pritchard's canonical formulation, the "raw material" of anthropological inquiry was viewed as constituting "social life itself."[67] Hence, true ethnographic representation of this material would be achieved by presupposing that social life was an integral whole and, as such, was directly accessible through immersion rather than apprehended at a distance through quantification. If numerical data were accepted at all, it would merely serve as a supplement to, rather than a replacement of, description. It is not until the later phases of the colonial era, as once allegedly homogeneous, small-scale social formations developed into more heterogeneous spaces, that the limitations of the emphasis on personal observation, mono-sited fieldwork, and the attendant distrust of numbers became apparent and that scholars, however haltingly, began to admit statistical evidence into anthropological discourse. (Interestingly, some of this change in perspective was couched in the semiotics of networks, such as the efforts by the Manchester School of the 1950s to conceptualize forms of social order cutting across conventional units of analysis like family, class, or occupation.)

This state of affairs persisted until well into the 1990s as the discipline found itself in the throes of what came to be known as the crisis of representation. One of the main causes (or symptoms?) of this crisis, as classics of the era, such as Michael Fischer and George Marcus's *Anthropology as Cultural Critique* or James Clifford and Marcus's *Writing Culture* made clear, was skepticism about the ability of totalizing models of representation to capture an increasingly fragmented social reality.[68] The whole, as envisaged by previous generations of anthropologists, was a construction of the observer, while the synecdochic relationship between the part and the whole that had provided much of the rationale of traditional ethnography had also become questionable. As the disciplinary terrain shifted toward more globally dispersed and unpredictable forms of identity formation, it became increasingly difficult to justify anthropological projects of systematization and typification that readily assimilated the part to the whole. Yet, strikingly, neither of these canonical texts discusses the role of quantification in the new politics of ethnography. Realist ethnography, Marcus roundly declared, "can never gain knowledge of the realities that statistics can."[69] And for all the celebration of political economy as a major source of renewal of anthropology as cultural critique, only scant recognition is given to the fact that ever since Foucault first discovered the intimate relationship between statistics and governmentality, politics and economy have long been recognized as the very products of enumeration. Likewise, as anthropologists came to grasp social and cultural practice as texts that the ethnographer would cowrite rather than merely reproduce from a position *en dehors du texte*, forms of inscription other than field notes or diaries, such as tables or lists, were shunned.[70] Even as anthropologists began realizing that data production was no longer their province alone, and national governments, the private sector, and even local communities increasingly defined themselves and contested one another's claims to explanatory hegemony through the medium of statistics, numerical data continued to occupy the lower ranks of anthropology's empirical hierarchy.

Interestingly, though, there is one area where scholars had already been making significant headway well before, or at least concurrently with, the experimental moment heralded by *Anthropology as Cultural Critique*. Starting in the 1990s, legal anthropologists following in the footsteps of sociologists of law began to incorporate metrics, quantification, and probability calculus into their accounts. Realizing that the most pertinent question to ask about quantification was not whether statistics lie; whether numbers fail to capture the singular, lived experience of those subject to the science of the state; or whether, indeed, the term *raw data* is an oxymoron, these scholars became more attuned to what data do, specifically with regard to the relations between democracy and global markets in contemporary forms of governance. As early as 1994, Talal Asad argued that statistics not only reconstruct the material and cultural conditions of those caught in its calculus, but in the context of developing countries they also convert incommensurable cultures into commensurable social arrangements "without rendering them homogeneous."[71] More recently, Sally Engle Merry has built on earlier developments in science and technology studies in her work on indicators and their effects on regulation and governance.[72] Yet others have explored the role of quantification in anything from practices of accountability-making in the prosecuting authority to settlement projects in South Africa to public health campaigns in Uganda and the impact of global health statistics on clinics in West Africa and Germany.[73] Here, much like in other metric technologies around the globe ostensibly geared toward greater transparency and participation in democratic decision making, the idea is to organize the public, policymakers, and capital to perform in calculable and profitable ways. And finally, closer to the topic at hand, John and Jean Comaroff have written compellingly about postapartheid South Africans' obsession with crime statistics, arguing that these have the capacity to contrive or recode meaningful social relations, both because of how they circulate and their very "semiotics."[74]

There is much value in this critical literature of what one might call metric-power, in a nod to Foucault. For it reminds us that processes of quantification, while encoding cultural understandings of what can be named and counted, are themselves products of prior processes through which commensuration moves, from what Foucault famously called the episteme of resemblance toward an episteme of representation.[75] And yet, I am left wondering about the all-too-facile way that the statistics-as-governance paradigm is invoked for projects of social critique without paying sufficient attention to the underlying instrumentalist logic itself. How do statistical data circulate, and by what routes? In what way do negotiations or "conventions," as Alain Desrosières calls them, about the criteria that generate, weigh, and aggregate statistical data shape the institutions where they occur, and whose mandates do they respond to?[76] In what, exactly, resides the material and symbolic power of quantitative data generated in the shadow of the more or less visible world of public policymaking? And why is it that in South Africa, enumeration has come to almost completely supersede an older repertoire of critical analysis grounded in categories such as class, race, and gender? In the remaining pages of this chapter, I will reposition the issue of statistics from an exclusive concern with the accuracy of representation, the efficacy of implementation, and the social dimension of quantification toward its connective valence. Statistics, I posit, have a normative, stabilizing function, not because of what they say but largely because of how they say it. And so I will examine how various numerical, narrative, and visual strategies intersect, over and above the provisions of the Copyright Act, in performatively framing piracy as a crime that requires a concerted effort on the part of "society" to combat. While this approach may not provide a complete picture of the mix of industry lobbying and international pressure that led to the criminalization of piracy in 1995 (the year South Africa joined the TRIPS agreement), it does offer a glimpse of how such a policy is reproduced and stabilized on a largely invisible, routine basis.[77]

The first aspect is the hotspot, which is one of the columns in the master stats and, as we will see further below, was a staple news item in RiSA's awareness work. Although it is more reminiscent of telecommunication networks, the term *hotspot* has actually become a fixture of South Africa's topography and its rendering in an imaginary of law and order. Traffic signs warning motorists of centers of criminal activity are ubiquitous, demarcating boundaries where there appear to be none and providing an elusive sense of control over an otherwise uncertain social terrain. Beyond traffic signs, the semiotics of hotspots is also locked into a deep symbiosis with a wide range of additional media, genres, and styles of figuring crime. From journalists (and sometimes anthropologists, such as the present writer) riding in police vans, online crime maps such as https://www.crimestatssa.com, YouTube video clips of police car chases, the *Citizen's Guide to Crime Trends in South Africa*, *Municipal IQ*, and a sizeable body of what one might call cop-lit—memoirs and notes from the frontlines written by (ex) police officers—there is always a hotspot waiting to be discursively and visually monitored and made salient as the raw material for fueling projects of fashioning a citizenry forever on the alert for the opportunities and dangers posed by the new "risk society" of postapartheid South Africa.[78]

In contrast to all this frenzy, however, RiSA's list of hotspots seems rather banal. Two main categories can be identified. The first comprises places of public transit, such as bus stations (sometimes called taxi ranks in South Africa) and railway stations. Closely linked to South Africa's history of segregated mass transportation, they tend to cater to the economically least secure sector of the population, as informal surveys conducted in 2010 reveal.[79] The second type of hotspot includes shops, the perimeters of large malls, and open-air markets. In comparison, some of the country's most crime-ridden areas, such as Hillbrow or Diepsloot in Johannesburg, Delphi, or Khayelitsha in Cape Town, are, if not completely absent far and few between. (In fact, a quick sampling of dockets at the SAPS Hillbrow revealed that during 2011 policing piracy in Hillbrow appears to have been left to random street arrests by police on foot patrol, but that only thirty-six organized raids had been conducted over the same period.) When I confronted Rheder with these numbers, he sneered: "Those Hillbrow cops there are too lazy and knock off at 4 PM. That's when the criminals get started." Lackadaisical or not, this kind of mapping is anything but a neutral description of the national territory the postapartheid state imagines as a unified space where social relations, now unshackled from group areas and Bantustans, are solely governed by core liberal values, and high concentrations of crime are merely exceptions to the rule of law. Least of all is the list of hotspots a road map for the way that crime is being handled. For example, one of the most enduring legacies of apartheid geography is the misconception that black urbanization is the root cause of crime and, hence, that crime in rural areas is but a mere after-effect of unfettered urban migration. This is why South Africans' obsession with the question of whether Johannesburg or Cape Town is the murder capital of the country obscures the fact that remote rural areas of the Eastern Cape or Limpopo are not far behind the metropolitan areas. It is also why a Foucauldian understanding of spatialized governmentality is probably not the best way to comprehend efforts at stemming the tide of piracy hitting the country. The spatialization of crime is often uncritically coproduced through a complex assemblage of state power, private security firms, vigilante street patrollers, journalists, and fiction writers. Thus, unwittingly or not, much of this collective effort at comprehending crime through a spatial prism is embedded in an environment in which the "tactics" initially designed to enforce racial segregation are now repackaged as "ostensibly 'modern' means of reducing violent crime."[80]

How did this play out in RiSA statistics? The first thing to note is that hotspots are anything but fixed nodes, points of high density, or places of heightened activity in preestablished networks. And, as such, they are a far cry from the Western modernist imagination of the colonial city as the epitome of rationality exemplified, for instance, by its neat separation of public and private spaces and their concatenation in a carefully thought-out grid of roads, power lines, and channels of communication. In fact, hotspots aren't spaces to begin with. They are the contemporary semiotic manifestation of the enduring legacy of apartheid socio-spatial relations. There is probably no better illustration of this than the column titled "types of location," here especially that of the "street vendor." At first glance, the conflation of "street vendor" and "location" would appear to be somewhat of an oxymoron, given that the first is a person and the second a space that can be occupied by a person. On closer inspection, however, it turns out that, like so much else in the South African vernacular of race and class, the statistical aggregation hosted by these categories is shot through with conflicting meanings. For instance, it conceals colonial and apartheid histories of displacement and dislocation, and, in some instances, it may even obscure the conceptual and practical persistence of these histories in (potentially unconstitutional) vagrancy by-laws or compulsory rehabilitation programs in so-called community villages.[81] Likewise, the term *street vendor* bespeaks a rather dubious ancestry. Conveniently lumping together a set of assumptions about the economic activities of more than 60 percent of the country's population under the rubric "informal economy," it papers over the fact that there is little "informal" about mobile trading, at least when informality is seen as primarily an employment strategy instead of it being fueled by tax evasion.[82] Finally, the term indirectly glosses over the debate about largely unspoken claims embedded in copyright law regarding the nature of the public and how these claims are manipulated by corporate copyright owners attempting to impose ever more restrictive provisions regulating the uses of sound in space or, conversely, to expand the notion of the private when it benefits corporate real estate. Thus, the concern is not entirely unfounded that future legislation vesting the "communicate to the public" right will all but eliminate the space where music can be legitimately shared, for instance, over headphones bleeding sound to persons nearby.

If then, the figure of the street vendor bears the imprint of some of the class and racial divisions of postapartheid South Africa's urban geography, it is not too far-fetched to suggest that strategies of crime management based on the notion of the hotspot endure *because* of that geography rather than in opposition to it. Much like apartheid infrastructure constrained the mobility of black labor by, perversely, facilitating its circulation, RiSA's topography seeks to disrupt the infrastructure of infringement by conceptually replicating it. Or, as James Ferguson phrases it in a different context, like all planned interventions, the outcome of RiSA's antipiracy strategy ends up being "incorporated into anonymous constellations of control."[83]

But the "street vendor" is not the only category of hotspot where this logic seems to be at work; so-called flea markets are another case in point. Contrary to their name, many of these markets are actually housed in permanent structures erected in an effort to curb the massive spread of street trading after the collapse of the apartheid group areas scheme. Often owned by municipalities and located at the interstices of former (in many cases, still) black areas and whites-only middle-class suburbs, markets like the Bruma Lake Market in Johannesburg or the Bangladesh Market in Chatsworth (a suburb of eThekwini) are touted as vibrant alternatives to conventional shopping malls, not to mention inner-city shopping districts. Although the pirates that operate in these spaces, for the most part, either fly under the radar or work with full knowledge of the security forces patrolling them, the bulk of the activity RiSA statistics list under "flea market" actually takes place in the immediate vicinity around them—in back alleys and on sidewalks. In a way, then, these spaces might be thought of as the actual hotspots, which, precisely because of their liminality, work like revolving doors. Feeding on the traffic going through the area, the pirates enter the door as jobless immigrants and sole bread-earners of an entire village, coming out at the other end, in most cases, as criminals. For their part, the middle-class clientele drawn to these markets, who might otherwise feel inhibited approaching an under-the-counter vendor, go in and, tempted by the air of informality, come out on the precarious edge separating modes of unruly consumption from legally unproblematic impulse shoppers in possession of counterfeit goods or MP3 compilations comprised of infringing copies unlawfully generated by format-shifting. Indeed, these flea markets function as miniature replicas of the larger infrastructure of apartheid/postapartheid cities.

The interplay of urban planning and policing is brought into even sharper relief in hotspots located within, or in close proximity to, so-called central business districts, as the face-lifted sections of South Africa's decaying metropolitan centers are called. Sunnyside is one such area. In the dying days of apartheid, Sunnyside was the quintessential South African heterotopia— "the place to be," as Angus Rheder waxed nostalgically. Or at least the kind of place where there was what critical journalist Bongani Madondo calls "a modicum of understanding between the races," despite the fact that "every police officer was Van der-this or Van der-that."[84] But coinciding with the downfall of racial segregation, crime rates in Sunnyside skyrocketed, and the neighborhood's standing plummeted to one of the ten most dangerous places in South Africa, following hard on the heels of Hillbrow, the epitome of postcolonial inner-city blight. Yet, even though Sunnyside's rates for capital and property crimes dropped over the following decade—a fact that earned the Sunnyside police station an impromptu visit by former President Jacob Zuma—its central position at the heart of the nation's capital also turned it into a target of intense policing, scholarly scrutiny, and improvement. With the creation in 1999 of the (now moribund) Esselen Street City Improvement District (CID), Sunnyside has followed a trend, pioneered in Johannesburg, of restructuring the inner city from an epicenter of a racialized economy to a more inclusive and livable place. While this shift was initially embedded in a state-driven, social-equity-oriented policy framework, as the ANC increasingly veered toward more efficiency and a growth-centered concept of development enshrined in its GEAR program, local governments were encouraged to pursue a more corporatist agenda based on the professionalization and consultization of public decision-making processes and cost-benefit calculations.[85] Apart from a broad range of measures, including traffic regulation, landscaping, street lighting, and some token social programs for the homeless, informal trading became a major target of CID's vision for a property owner–friendly environment.

There is no telling whether RiSA's fixation on hotspots is, in fact, part of a broader strategy in which operations interlock with CID-driven agendas of urban governance. Nor is there any evidence to suggest that the organization, apart from its *liaison dangereuse* with Dudula, cooperates with other interests, such as the country's ubiquitous privately run security firms or specific stakeholders within the CID. Quite the contrary, RiSA (and SAMPRA) are quite blunt about serving the interests of their members only. And yet, it might be argued that raids like the ones I described earlier and the data they generate about hotspots are examples of the uncanny convergence of the corporatization and enclaving of inner-city districts as well as the legacy of the apartheid spatialization of crime and its enduring impact on the criminal enforcement of copyright. Some of this convergence may be interpolated by reading RiSA's stats laterally, as it were, in parallel to South Africa's official crime statistics. In the latter, for instance, crimes are generally classified as belonging to one of the following three categories: contact crimes (crimes against the person), contact-related crimes, and property-related crimes. But while these categories are usually subdivided—contact crimes, for instance, comprise murder, rape, or common assault—the subcategories of property-related crimes are limited to offenses like burglary and motor vehicle theft. Piracy, although generally considered to be a property-related crime, is either not reported separately and subsumed under broad categories such as "commercial crime" or is not accounted for at all.

RiSA's stats have not been made publicly available. With good reason. South Africa has been quietly cooperating with the Special 301 process overseen by the Office of the United States Trade Representative (USTR) in the patent domain, ending a prolonged battle over the right of TRIPS members to parallel importation of drugs (in this case, antiretrovirals for the treatment of HIV/AIDS) that raged throughout much of the 1990s, earning South Africa a mention on USTR's Priority Watch list. Not to be outdone, the powerful copyright industry association International Intellectual Property Alliance (IIPA) continued lobbying the USTR well into the 2000s to keep the country on the list, backing up its claims with but the flimsiest of numerical evidence.[86] Although these efforts ultimately proved unsuccessful and South Africa was the only country among the group of emerging economies that was spared USTR censure, the data IIPA generated went on to serve as fodder for the industry's PR machine, feeding the public with "qualitative accounts of enforcement efforts and . . . prescriptions for legislative and administrative reform."[87]

By contrast, what is publicized on a grand scale in IFPI's *Global Music Reports* and *Record Industry in Numbers* are the losses the industry claims to suffer as a result of piracy. But how are these numbers generated? The answer is: through a simple trick or, as Karaganis calls it, a "secret sauce."[88] Toward the bottom of the spreadsheet, and easy to miss, is a rubric titled "Value of: Seized Physical & Digital Copies & Estimated Illegal Downloads." Within this rubric, the street and the industry value appear side by side for the total value of seized physical, digital albums and illegal downloads. However, these figures have not been determined on the basis of street price fluctuations. Nor is the overall industry value a true reflection of the average retail price, calculated on the basis of the published price to dealer (PPD). And finally, it is not clear whether substitution rates are factored into the calculation and where, exactly, the claimed losses fall within the overall range. All it takes, then, is a minute shift from one column to another to tie the whole muddle of public-private partnerships, plastic bags, crime dockets, affidavits, and prison cells to the music industry's claims of huge revenue losses.

Criticism of IFPI statistics and the industry's "historically loose relationship to evidence" has been muted.[89] Apart from the larger point that a pirated CD does not necessarily translate into a lost sale and that the declining revenue of the music industry is not owed to piracy alone, such criticism has focused mainly on the lack of uniformity in the way IFPI aggregates local data and on the failure, more broadly, of taking into account local forms of music making and commercialization.[90] Writing about Tanzania, Alex Perullo adds that privileging statistics as a means to gauge growth presumes that African "forms of cultural relations to music" are analogous to the West. "Western music businesses frequently depend on quantifying music in terms of album sales, concert revenue, and the frequency of radio airplay," whereas in Tanzania, "music depends on networks of personal relations, ideas, and communities that form and reform through constant negotiations of success, popularity, and cultural importance."[91] While this is true on one level, lacking in such critiques of industry statistics is the fact that the critique itself is frequently countered in more complex ways that condense various numerical, legal, and moral levels in order to simultaneously naturalize the authority of statistics and weaken political debate. For instance, countering the vociferous criticism it received in 2011, the BSA reaffirmed the validity of global comparison by pointing out that it "uses a cluster analysis technique to find like characteristics with countries with varying software loads and uses these characteristics to assign loads to countries not surveyed." This is then validated by "looking at correlations between the known software loads from surveyed countries and their scores on an emerging market measure published by the International Telecommunications Union, called the ICT Development Index, and dividing them into cohorts in order to compare them to unsurveyed countries."[92] And so on, and so forth.

The local resonance of the BSA survey, RiSA stats, or, for that matter, counternarratives like the Shuttleworth Foundation's Creative Commons–inspired espousal of innovation is, of course, rather limited. But that is perhaps beside the point. As metric-power, the effect of statistics does not reside in their superior power to patrol the boundaries of legitimate uses of music. It is, rather, that they naturalize specific pricing and marketing models as the only legitimate way to produce and participate in culture. In light of this, it is little wonder that IFPI's attempt to create public buy-in for its narrative of piracy-induced revenue loss dovetails nicely with RiSA's education and awareness programs. A quick review of ten issues of its *Enforcement Bulletin* published between 2008 and 2010 illustrates this tactic. Each issue rehearses a few standard templates also found in similar publicity put out by other copyright industries. The first, "Hotspots," might be read as creating a narrative around the data compiled in the master stats, albeit by adding further details not contained in the statistics, such as specific spectacular arrests, the monitoring activities of RiSA enforcement officers, and so on. Another column, "Provincial Successes," expands on this theme, highlighting the number of arrests or the number of admission of guilt fines in each province. Finally, under the "Awareness & Education," or "Awareness and Public Relations" columns, the bulletin offers accounts of RiSA's efforts to strengthen its relations with public enforcement agencies, such as SAPS, and prosecutors by conducting workshops on the Copyright Act or just by generally sensitizing police to the severity of piracy. Running through all sections are three threads. The first is couched in the idiom and iconography of the law. Bordered by brightly colored images of fingerprints, handcuffs, gavels, or crime scene tape, these texts are noteworthy for the absence of the kind of accusatory, vindictive language often espoused by other industry publications or news coverage. Instead, they draw on the formal language of criminal procedure—terms such as *suspect*, *arraigned*, and *custody* abound. Additionally, every issue also includes a half-page précis of the "Investigation Process." All of this is clearly not only meant to instill respect for the long arm of the law but also to convey a sense of propriety, due process, and even the law's moral commitment to evenhandedness. Plea-bargaining is often cited as one of the outcomes of criminal proceedings instituted by RiSA.

The second thread ties RiSA's antipiracy effort to an overarching sense of professional ethos. Thus, the *Enforcement Bulletin* frequently foregrounds the dedication and hard work of RAPU staff who go out of their way to ensure that hotspots are taken off the watch list by making follow-up visits to these sites or who undergo extensive training at the IFPI offices on how to adapt WebCrawler software to infringing local websites. Conversely, uncooperative police stations or officers caught taking bribes from suspected pirates are singled out for censure, while those that cooperate are praised for their effectiveness and occasionally awarded tokens of appreciation.

The third strand, finally, consists in articulating the notion of professional ethos with South Africans' allegedly newfound love for civic duty and self-control more generally. In several issues, for example, Jet Music, during the mid-2010s, one of South Africa's few remaining music retailers, is applauded for its collaboration with RiSA in monitoring and reporting suspected pirates operating in the vicinity of its outlets. Another example is the destruction of confiscated copies at recycling facilities. RiSA, the *Enforcement Bulletin* proudly informs its readers, has been able to negotiate favorable deals with such facilities, thereby alleviating taxpayers' burden in enforcing copyright. While the effect of such stories is hard to gauge, the angered reactions to RiSA's operations described earlier cast a more ambiguous light on these tales of industry benevolence and fantasies of civil society. Instead, readers may be mildly amused by the uncanny parallels with earlier attempts to fictionalize law and order in two blockbuster movies set in South Africa's urban jungle. *District 9* tells the story of desperate extraterrestrials struggling to find safe haven in postapartheid Johannesburg, while *Tsotsi* recounts the transformation of a tsotsi (thug), who, after noticing a baby in the backseat of the car he just stole, returns both car and baby to its rightful owners. Readers of the *Enforcement Bulletin* might also recall that, in the movies, the aliens and the *tsotsi* are not confronted (at least not initially) by a massive onslaught of state power as in the real world of South African police brutality but are met with compassion and forgiveness instead. In other words, what RiSA's awareness stories seem to suggest is that somewhere some kind of neutral space exists—a Shangri-La of self-policing communities bound by a sense of moral purpose and law-abidance, and a realm of affective bonds and shared cultural meanings typified by the teary-eyed, half-human alien and its newfound, half-alien friend Christopher Johnson in *District 9*, the parents of the abducted baby in *Tsotsi*, and the Jet Music manager.

In closing, allow me to return to my critique of the instrumentalist-constitutive binary and to the suggestion of a postdisciplinary anthropology in law. So far, nobody has told us what the public interest or the good of the community is—not Judge Posner or Sergeant de Villiers of the Boksburg police. South Africans are quickly losing faith in the ability of the post-apartheid order to bring them closer to this elusive goal. All the antipiracy rhetoric, statistics, or spectacular police operations in the world are about as likely to persuade the public of the virtues of the liberal-democratic order as an organogram of the Vatican is to move a disillusioned Catholic to renew their religious commitment. So what insights, if any, does an ANT perspective add to our understanding of piracy? At the very least, I hope that my analysis will put an end to the notion of the law-society nexus—both in its instrumentalist and constitutive version—as a black box. As well, the idea that there is a yawning gap between crime, society, or the people as the polar opposites imagined by the police minister and the legal scholar alike. Instead of bridging this imaginary gap by a rather bloodless and uncertain input-output correspondence, or some rhetoric of interdisciplinarity, the kind of ANT-inflected approach I pursued in this chapter might render visible more sturdy relationships between the legal and the extralegal by multiplying the connections—however heterogeneous and discontinuous—that it finds in and among things. The proper space for finding the truth about piracy is, thus, not a third space or some kind of interdisciplinary realm because any move in such a direction is already prefigured in the structure of the instrumentalist means-end relationship itself. It is, rather, to be looked for in a different kind of chemistry in which a range of statutes, the state's interest in displaying its commitment to the rule of law, the creative industry, and right holders' interest in linking their benefits to South Africans' fear of crime, or musicians' frustration about diminishing royalty streams, form a more or less stable compound, all with their own valences.

FIVE

Which Collective?
The Infrastructure of Royalties

"We are not crooks," André Le Roux, then-general manager of SAMRO Foundation, said. The Southern African Music Rights Organisation (SAMRO) is a not-for-profit collective management organization (CMO) or what in the Copyright Regulations of the Copyright Act is called a collecting society, administering the performance rights in musical works held by its member composers, authors, and publishers.[1] Headquartered at SAMRO Place, a ten-story office building perched on a ridge separating downtown Johannesburg's wild mix of decay, urban renewal, and bohemia from the leafy, affluent, and sedate northern suburbs, SAMRO is the African continent's largest performance rights organization. Representing more than eighteen thousand members and providing work for as many as 230 employees, it collects approximately R400 million each year from some fifteen thousand licensees operating in numerous sectors of the South African economy. In addition to SAMRO, there are three other CMOs working in the South African music business. SAMPRA (South African Music Performance Rights Association) licenses the rights of sound recordings owned by the members of the trade association, Recording Industry of South Africa (RiSA). Most of its revenue derives from needle-time royalties payable by the broadcasting sector. Members of RiSA may also join RiSA Audio Visual Licensing, a body issuing video producer licenses. The mechanical rights of SAMRO members are managed by the Composers, Authors and Publishers Association (CAPASSO). Additionally, the Performers' Organisation of South Africa is a trust established to administer needle-time rights on behalf of recording artists and musicians who have assigned their needle-time rights to SAMRO. Finally, there is the Independent Music Performance Rights Association. Founded in 2014, it casts itself as an alternative to SAMPRA, administering needle-time and video rights for around one thousand indie performers.

At first, I was taken aback by Le Roux's statement. It was thanks to his advocacy that I had been invited to pursue a short internship at SAMRO in June 2014. Having reached the end of my time at the organization, I had come to bid him farewell and to express my appreciation for the courtesy the people I worked with had shown me in indulging my ignorance and never-ending questions. So why this almost preemptive disclaimer, as if he needed to refute an allegation that hadn't even crossed my mind until after I had left SAMRO? I did know that SAMRO, like some of its counterparts elsewhere—PRS (Performance Rights Society) in the United Kingdom, SACEM (Société des auteurs, compositeurs et éditeurs de musique) in France, or GEMA (Gesellschaft für musikalische Aufführungs- und mechanische Vervielfältigungsrechte) in Germany, but unlike the American Society of Composers, Authors, and Publishers (ASCAP) in the United States—is a de facto natural monopoly. Although subject to regulation under the Copyright Act, the Performers' Protection Amendment Act, the Competition Act 89 of 1998 (hereafter Competition Act), and the Companies Act 71 of 2008 (hereafter Companies Act), it enjoys wide latitude in how it uses the performing rights assigned to it by its members by issuing blanket licenses to a broad range of users, from TV and broadcasting stations to retail stores, restaurants, sports stadiums, and taxis. Though costly, these licenses—a kind of all-you-can-eat music buffet granting users access to SAMRO's entire repertoire in return for set tariffs—along with SAMRO's practice of collectively bargaining royalties on behalf of its members, are believed to minimize transaction costs and generate economies of scale. In theory, then, SAMRO's monopoly status and modus operandi might be said to be congruent with copyright's consequentialist justification of serving the public interest by granting authors exclusive rights in their creative work and thereby incentivizing them to produce more works. But there is a catch. Natural monopolies like SAMRO have significant anticompetition potential. Although generally considered a "necessary evil" to be tolerated in light of the special nature of the music licensing market, this potential raises two questions of judicial and normative interest. Should SAMRO be allowed to exist as a monopoly or not? Or, rather, might the exercise of the monopoly have to be regulated to prevent SAMRO from abusing its market dominance to restrain copyright owner's exclusive rights, refuse to accept or discriminate between members or users, charge excessive royalties, or engage in openly fraudulent behavior?[2]

As it happens, the specter of such adversities has been haunting the organization from the beginning, prompting Le Roux to repudiate the dim view many South Africans take of SAMRO—that it is an ineffectual government department, a musicians' union, a corrupt cabal siphoning off musicians' hard-earned royalties, or simply, as one disillusioned musician put it to me, "*abantu bafuna ukudla izimali zethu*" [people who just want to eat up our money]. But this is only one side of the perception South Africans have of SAMRO. Many also look to SAMRO as a cultural powerhouse equipped with an almost magical capacity to deliver the country's musicians from deprivation and disregard and reshape South Africa's musical landscape into an inclusive sphere that redresses past injustice and promotes the economic empowerment of underserved black communities. Hence, the insight an anthropology in law might bring to bear on this state of affairs is not whether a collective management organization such as SAMRO should be regulated. Rather, it asks what cultural work the calls for regulation and almost cargo cult-like expectations actually accomplish. It is then that anthropologists—and perhaps legal scholars as well—might begin to get a better sense of how these reformist aspirations are intertwined with other imaginaries and narratives of creative justice or corporate ethics, and to what extent such entanglements might become motors for a different cultural politics and the creation of more capacious collectives uniting authors and users in novel and yet unknown ways.

Divided Histories

The story begins in 1925. In that year, the British PRS, founded in 1914 by the likes of music publishers William Boosey and Oliver Hawkes, opened an office in South Africa, seeking to cash in on the emergence of broadcasting in the country two years prior. PRS remained the sole performance rights organization until 1961, when South Africa left the Commonwealth after members demanded that the country be expelled from the association due to its apartheid policies. This, however, did not put an end to the cozy relationship the organization had established with its predominantly white South African members. On the contrary, not only did PRS provide startup capital and expertise in setting up the South African Society of Composers, Authors and Music Publishers (SAFCA) in 1961, but the racial bias built into collecting societies in Europe and elsewhere from the start also reached an all-time high in South Africa.³ The key element in this shift to all-out racial discrimination was an unholy alliance between SAFCA, the South African Broadcasting Corporation (SABC), and Gideon Roos, the founder of SAFCA and its first general manager. More than two decades after his death in 1999, Roos's photograph still adorns the gallery of SAMRO notables on the executive floor of SAMRO Place, and the organization's publications to this day routinely wax lyrical about his "visionary commitment" and "formidable and magnetic leadership."⁴ A closer examination of Roos's role in the making of SAMRO, however, paints a more complex picture and provides an opportunity for reflection on the causes of SAMRO's tarnished image sixty years later.

Prior to heading up SAFCA, Roos served as director-general of the SABC from 1948, the year that the Nationalist Party came to power and embarked on its agenda of grand apartheid. Although a staunch supporter of the party himself, he resigned from the post in April 1961, allegedly because the secretive, ultraconservative Broederbond faction of the Nats (shorthand for the National Party) had by then gained total control of the government and the SABC as a major pillar of its propaganda machine. At least that is how Ivor Wilkins and Hans Strydom tell the story in their 1979 bestselling *The Super-Afrikaners*.⁵ But in an alternative reading of events, Roos's departure from the SABC may have been motivated by other, albeit no less nefarious reasons. For just as Roos started up SAFCA and the Broederbond took over the SABC, the broadcaster expanded its African-language services into the largest FM, ethnically and racially divided radio network on the continent. From January 1962, when it first went on air, Radio Bantu (as the services were henceforth referred to) went from some five hundred thousand listeners a day to an average of 2.3 million in 1967, two million of whom owned a radio set.⁶ Traditional, choral, and township music were the cornerstones of Radio Bantu's musical offerings, with the latter two categories comprising a large amount of works protected under the Copyright Acts of 1916 and 1965, respectively.

The advent of Radio Bantu not only led to an exponential increase in airplay of protected musical works and, thus, SAFCA and SAMRO's licensing revenues for the public performance of those works, it also provided an opening for Roos to perfect the existing system of racial discrimination by clouding it behind a facade of race neutrality. From 1962, SAMRO had accepted black composers in its ranks, among them Strike Vilakazi (already a member of PRS), Rubert Bopape, Zacks Nkosi, and Gideon Nxumalo. But while these 1960s stars were admitted as full members, most of their lesser-known colleagues were assigned a new category of membership called "candidate member."[7] The move, first debated by SAFCA's board of directors in October 1963, provided that a candidate member "shall not be entitled to notice of, or vote at, General Meetings." Furthermore, candidate membership should lapse after two years unless the board of directors either elected the candidate to associate or full membership or extended the duration of the candidate status. And finally, the criterion for promotion to associate or full status was that the member produced a "reasonable number of works of such a standard that some of them were performed in public."[8] *Standard* is not so much an aesthetic term as code for the type of social stratification that SABC ideologues from as early as the 1950s had dreamt up in which "traditional Bantu music; modern light Bantu music; choral music by Bantu composers; . . . and European music" neatly mirrored apartheid's class and racial hierarchies.[9] This is not only to say that all standards are not created equal, but also that any attempt at crossing the boundaries of these so-called standards was prevented ab ovo. The role of Radio Bantu was to "heighten the listener's pride in his own culture," or, as the SABC's Bantu/indigenous music organizer Yvonne Huskisson would put it as late as 1969: "It is in their own characteristic expression" that the Bantu "will best become original contributors to world artistic and cultural collections."[10]

It is immediately apparent that these warped perceptions of black creativity and its de facto long-standing diasporic connections greatly disadvantaged the large number of black composers who, for the first time in the history of South African music, were able to reach millions of listeners on a daily basis; contrary to the likes of Eric Gallo, for instance, who, as a music publisher, was not only a full member but also sat on the board of directors. But that is not all. Just two years after the new membership rules came into effect, the South African all-white legislature, under pressure from the Broederbond-led SABC, eliminated needle time—that is, the public performance right for sound recordings, on the books since 1916, in the Copyright Act 63 of 1965 (It would only be reinstated in 2002!). Apart from saving the broadcaster millions in royalties due on Radio Bantu content, the measure not only left thousands of black performers empty-handed, but in combination with the SABC's racialized standards it also in a way made them pay for their own cultural isolation.

Note that in all of this, there was never the slightest hint that these measures might be directed against black South Africans as such. Nor did it affect SAFCA, as it only collected public performance royalties of musical works. Either way, in addition to gaining control over the vastly enlarged performance royalty pool for works built up by Radio Bantu, Roos shrewdly exploited a particularly perverse division of labor whereby SAMRO determined black membership on the basis of the criteria the SABC, as its largest licensee, had itself concocted—the "standard" allegedly determined by the ethnically and racially divided public it had literally created from scratch. It is this form of what one might call double gatekeeping, rather than an explicitly racist agenda, that established a system where the meager royalties generated by SAMRO's black candidate members, as per SAMRO's point system, ended up in the accounts of its predominantly white members.

The membership system remained in place until 1994.

Dark shadows of past wrongdoing, sinister machinations, and all manner of everyday shenanigans—real or rumored—were nothing new, then, by the time I was at SAMRO, and, as such, they were customarily glossed over as minor mishaps blown out of proportion by politicians, labor unions, or the tabloid press. In more recent years, however, a completely new dynamic set in, rekindling old suspicions that would ultimately go on to threaten the very existence of the organization all told. Starting in 2010 the organization found itself on a downward spiral of declining revenue, exploding staff costs (68 percent of total spending), and steeply falling distribution rates (from 81 percent of net profit in 2010 to 63 percent in 2019). And as if that was not enough, it was also increasingly becoming the subject of lawsuits and scandals, ranging from accusations of board members overpaying themselves, to unilaterally altered employment agreements, to the firing of board member and kwaito pioneer Arthur Mafokate following allegations that he had assaulted his fiancée.[11] By 2017, even darker clouds were gathering on the horizon. In October, annual general meeting attendees, still reeling from the commotion of previous years, could hardly believe their ears when CEO Nothando Migogo announced that her organization had withdrawn from a R40 million ($2.8 million) investment partnership with the Arab Emirates Music Rights Organization (AEMRO). But the investment not only failed to yield the financial rewards "it could have produced at another moment in time," as she euphemistically explained, it also reeked of graft. Apart from the fact that AEMRO was not licensed to operate in the UAE, a subsequent audit of the deal—discussed in more detail at the end of this chapter—revealed that former CEO Sipho Dlamini had misled the board about its prospects and paid "exorbitant" monthly salaries of R518,200 ($48,000) to two fixers in Dubai. To add insult to injury, even after the plug had been pulled on AEMRO, SAMRO "concocted" fake contracts for the two in the form of settlements totaling approximately R7 million.[12]

By early 2018, SAMRO was undergoing open-heart surgery. Renowned gospel singer Hlengiwe Mhlaba went on record accusing SAMRO of unlawfully funneling R8.5 million of her royalties to her former producer and manager, fellow gospel artist Sipho Makhabane. On top of this, twenty-four out of ninety of her songs administered by SAMRO—all adaptations of gospel classics in the public domain—were paying out only 16.67 percent instead of the 100 percent due on arrangements. The remaining 83.33 percent was paid to what in collecting society taxonomy is called "domaine publique" or DP, a category of IP (interested party) that is used in CIS-Net, the network of databases administered by CISAC (Confédération internationale des sociétés d'auteurs et compositeurs), the international umbrella organization of 228 collecting societies in 120 countries.[13]

Eventually, in May SAMRO was put on life support. After only two years at the helm, Migogo resigned as CEO, citing the Dubai fiasco, the R100 million in unpaid licenses due by the SABC, the DP imbroglio, and an entrenched culture of ageism and patriarchy, making it difficult for "young, black, female leadership, which is dynamic, honest and hardworking" to change the status quo.[14] What she neglected to mention was that the organization's turnover and growth rate had taken another hit, declining even further from R371 million ($21 million) and an annual rate of 9 percent to R475.6 million ($26.4 million) and only 0.1 percent of growth. Similar dismal figures were reported for losses, staff costs, and distribution revenues.[15] Although eight board members followed Migogo's example in December, before long, even newly elected board members, such as Sipho Sithole, an anthropologist, former director at Gallo, and a founder of the Native Rhythms Productions label, also came under fire for corruption charges brought against them.[16]

Collectives of Worlding

Without a doubt, the Dubai debacle and the Mhlaba incident were wake-up calls—a stinging reminder of the long history of the kind of abuse that seems to follow monopolies like a shadow—and the first major scratch on SAMRO's carefully groomed image as a core cultural institution of the new democratic South Africa, committed to serving the shared interests of its members and those of the public at large. In this chapter, I use my 2014 internship to launch an inquiry into the conditions that make this image possible and the tensions and counterforces that threaten to subvert it while necessitating it in the first place. But in so doing, my primary goal is not to critique this image as a misrepresentation of SAMRO's true nature or to uncover any incriminating information that might expose it as a myth beyond what is already in plain view. Rather, it is to query SAMRO's battered reputation as a "factish," that is, as a construct that takes on a life of its own independent of its creator, in the process transforming it by enmeshing it with other institutions, social settings, and truth-making conventions.[17] However, I would also argue that these entanglements are not arbitrary. Just as the causes of the company's woes are more of a systemic nature than the product of individual misconduct or flawed corporate governance (although these will also come under scrutiny in the final section of this chapter), so too can SAMRO's attempts to refurbish its impaired standing be accounted for by attending to collecting societies' inherent contradiction between private and public interest, individual copyright owners and collective management, and monopoly and competition.[18] At the same time, however, there is something distinctly homegrown, South African about SAMRO's never-ending troubles, which lie in the social, racial, and economic inequities of the apartheid past as well as in the structural continuity and augmentation of those imbalances due to globalization, deregulation, and digitization. And perhaps, unlike the wealthier countries of the Global North, these systemic defects do not solely impact authors. Users and the public at large also stand to be deeply affected by the way the music industry—and SAMRO as a more visible part of that industry—operates.

I initially contacted SAMRO CEO Sipho Dlamini with the intention of learning more about the administration of copyright from a practical point of view. Although I was under no illusion that many aspects of SAMRO's operation would be off-limits for me, I anticipated that much of what I might find would confirm my long-held belief that the music industry—and collective management organizations such as ASCAP, BMI, GEMA, or SAMRO—operate in a field of what anthropologist Anna Tsing calls "global friction," the "awkward, unequal, unstable, and creative qualities of interconnection across difference."[19] I further assumed that people in the South African music industry labor within, and, more often than not, on behalf of, the global music industry. But I also expected that those same people would seek to translate this unpredictable and volatile encounter into a set of stable parameters in order to ferment a sense of locally grounded collective identity while simultaneously leaving the door open to a more equitable participation in that global economy. What turned out to be more difficult to establish was who and exactly what are being collected by and within this hyperspecialized, subtly networked, and somewhat reclusive organization beyond its members and royalties. What do composers and users have in common other than being figured as rational market participants of the neoclassical economic imagination? What infrastructures, databases, work processes, policies, and business models must be present to convince mostly impecunious musicians and a handful of well-to-do publishers that their financial affairs are best served by an institution that still struggles to leave behind the ghosts of the apartheid past? How might the idea of a collective management of copyright run counter to a system that assigns members different levels of membership status with unequal voting rights and different shares of the royalty pool? Widening the scope of the inquiry beyond 2014, were the dramatic developments mentioned above little more than a continuation of the aporia at the heart of SAMRO since its very foundation? And, if so, how might this impact the key assertion of this book that we need a novel analytic to grasp the intricate valences that articulate copyright, authors, and users in continually changing configurations of practice and interest? It is with questions like these in mind that the idea of my internship developed and that I invite the reader to approach this chapter.

Research on the operation of collecting societies in the South African music business is scarce. With the exception of Desmond Oriakhogba's major study on South Africa's three music rights societies, there are no detailed, empirically grounded analyses of the organizations there—or anywhere else in the world for that matter.[20] Rather, what dominates the literature is an assortment of works stretching from textbook, manual-like publications on how to set up and run a society, to studies of the economics of copyright collective management, to straight doctrinal analyses of the intersection of copyright and competition law. Thus, the motivation behind combining my fieldwork in what must be one of anthropology's most improbable field sites with the broader theoretical thrust of this book is to yield insights into the pragmatics of copyright's instrumentalist rationale and its skewed place within the world of postcolonial cultural reproduction. Much like in previous chapters where I have been eager to reposition copyright scholarship away from its ivory tower of normative reasoning and reified social relations and more toward a realistic, embedded type of relationship within the ruptures and discontinuities of the music industry, here, too, I query some of the most ingrained notions about the nature of copyright collective management. More specifically, I hope that this exercise will provide a much-needed corrective to the representation of collecting societies like SAMRO as mere intermediaries whose sole rationale is facilitating market transactions at the lowest marginal cost without considering that this function itself is socially and culturally productive but frequently also a destructive force in its own right.

The bulk of my interactions took place in the Licensing & Sales Department, the revenue-generating core of the organization, located on the third floor of SAMRO Place. But I also had informal conversations with staff in other departments and divisions spread out over the remaining floors, including Rightsholder Services, Legal, Quality Control, and Credit Control. More specifically, at "Sales," as the Licensing & Sales Department was commonly referred to, I was introduced to and participated in a set of operations known in industry jargon as "capture" and "match and link." These are essentially methods for gathering and aggregating data from radio and TV stations, retailers, and a host of other music users, and, to ensure territorial reciprocality between 228 collecting societies in 120 countries, a means for relating these data to the information stored in SAMRO's and other databases controlled by CISAC. In the case of industry giants such as ASCAP, these methods include sophisticated digital monitoring systems, such as Numerator, to track music use in TV commercials, census surveys, or the near real-time intelligence provided by companies like Media Monitors. In the South African music industry of 2014, however, these technologies were still at a more embryonic scale and involved, as I will detail further below, a great deal of manual labor, personal contact, paperwork, and error-prone data processing. However, I foreground these technical-structural differences not to rehash modernist narratives of lag and lack in the Global South or in order to gauge SAMRO's performance against some international standard but because they allow us to better grasp the harmful impact that run-of-the-mill, sometimes dysfunctional work processes can have on the livelihoods of authors *and* users. In contrast to the author/owner-centrism of performance rights organization scholarship, I am more interested in the mechanisms that entangle authors and users, along with a range of material objects, with one another in what I call collectives of worlding.

Worlding is a malleable term that has animated a wide range of projects from Heideggerian ontology, to science and technology studies, to anthropology. In the latter context, especially, worlding has come to denote ways of knowledge-making and their intersection with everyday socialities that cannot be accounted for in conventional narratives that emphasize structural cohesion or posit the prior existence of clearly demarcated domains of knowledge and belonging. *Collectives of worlding* should therefore not be confused with *communities of practice*, a term coined by anthropologist Jean Lave and educational theorist Étienne Wenger and subsequently popularized by Susan Leigh Star. In the postcolonial context of this chapter, the term *collectives of worlding* is preferable because, unlike communities of practice, defined by a shared domain of interests and commitment to that domain, collectives of worlding are more transient formations. Rather than the assumption of an initial commitment to the interests of the collective, collectives of worlding are a form of social poetics, inducing the colonized to view their own world in terms suggested by the colonizer without altering the power imbalance between the two. In this sense, then, collectives of worlding, such as the members and licensees of SAMRO, are not conceptually and spatially distinctive springboards for world-making as much as makeshift outcomes of routine processes and technologies of standardization, classification, and aggregation. By the same token, these technologies and processes are more than mere extensions of a collective that has already been fully formed and armed by other forces, such as copyright law, regulatory state power, or large corporations like the music majors. Rather, it is through their interaction that capturing and matching and linking become potent social technologies, drafting dispersed and socially and economically heterogeneous groups of people to a common cause and naturalizing their imbrication with these technologies as a meaningful and equitable way of serving this cause. In keeping with the thrust of previous chapters, here again, the point to emphasize is the relational, formal aspects of everyday licensing operations, technologies of data processing, and distribution procedures and how these may reproduce the inequities of the past and potentially generate future disparities.

But these operations, technologies, and workflows are not limited to objects or material practices. Affect-laden attachments—or what Kathleen Stewart calls "ordinary affects"—political mythologies, rhetorical strategies, and scientific theories are also powerful factors that constitute collectives of worlding.[21] Among the latter, neoclassical economic theory plays an especially central discursive role in naturalizing collective entanglements around and with information technologies. Key concepts such as externalities, transaction-cost efficiency, and economies of scale are more than neutral descriptors of already existing relationships. In the context of postcolonial states seeking to alter the terms of their integration into the global economy, such universalizing constructs become major factors in facilitating and naturalizing this integration on the Global North's terms. By offering the frictionless translation of idiosyncratic local conditions into the Esperanto of economics—thereby obscuring the difference between local meanings and universal norms—they become as material an object of ethnographic inquiry as the reality they profess to grasp.

Infrastructures are another potent form of worlding. Beyond articulating commonplace materialities, from water pipes to global computer networks with a wide spectrum of institutions, legal systems, and knowledge practices, infrastructures have emerged in recent anthropological scholarship as key locations to critically examine narratives in which nation-building, development, modernization, or democratization are cast as contingent on the seamless flow of capital, labor, goods, and ideas.[22] The chapter concludes with a discussion of SAMRO's ongoing efforts to reinvent itself in the wake of the backlash it experienced after the Dubai debacle and the central role a 2018 audit played in bringing the organization and the collectives of worlding that cluster within and around it in line with the changing face of the music industry and the twenty-first-century politics of transparency.

Capturing: Selling Compliance

I am sitting in John Anderson's office in Sales, a department comprising six divisions: Regional Markets, Key Accounts, International, Credit Control, Licencing Administration, and Community Radio/TV. Anderson is the regional manager of the inland division—one of two regional markets—inland and coastal—into which SAMRO has divided the country.[23] We are talking about some of the issues that have come up over the last couple of days with a range of uncooperative licensees. In his earlier life, Anderson was a sales representative in his hometown of Durban, and this is exactly what his entire persona exudes. Bossy, fast-talking, and relentlessly pushing his coworkers to rake in as many new licenses as possible while simultaneously resenting his superiors, he seems to have internalized the bait-and-hook tactics that has become the mantra of the brave neo-world of the post-Mandela, postreconstruction era, and the very raison d'être of SAMRO.

Anderson is upset about Top Gear South Africa, a company that puts on wildly popular shows promoting upscale vehicles—and plays matching music to boot. "Our tariff for 30–40 percent of music is 2 percent," he says, describing a field trip to one such event held the previous week. "I matched the ticket price to the number of seats that had been allocated to that ticket price and then worked out the Rand value. Over the four stadium shows, they made R370,050 ($34,320). I then played my recordings and told them that from 10 AM to 1 PM the doors were open, music was playing, and everybody was walking to their seats. I started to physically record at 1:23 PM, and the total time of the show was two hours and forty minutes out of which music played for one hour and thirty-nine minutes or 58 percent of the total time. And I actually broke it down to what music was being played."

"They were worried about having to pay the 2 percent SAMRO charges in licensing fees," he continues. "But for 58 percent of music, the rate is 4 percent. So I said, "Suit yourself; if you don't wanna pay 2 percent, I can make it for 4 percent. I've got the physical recordings and we just have to identify the actual songs and find one song that's been assigned to us, which I actually did for 2014, 2013, and 2012. So, if they want to do infringement for 2 percent, we can sue at 2 percent for all three years or we can go straight for 4 percent as per-music usage for those years. You don't want to pay me a measly R370,050? We can take you out at R4 mill." And with a triumphant air, he turns to me: "You see, this is how far we go."[24]

At this point, Agreement Molapo, one of Anderson's field agents or "licensing consultants," as SAMRO prefers to call them, walks in. He wants to go over some of the irregularities in a license application the owner of a restaurant in the Moyo franchise had submitted earlier. There are more than fifty types of licenses for anything from hairdressers and salons, to hotels and skating rinks, to radio and television broadcasting services, to coffee shops and restaurants. The information licensees must provide differs from form to form, but apart from the type and ownership of the venue, for venues like theaters and restaurants, parameters such as floor size, seating capacity, days and hours of operation, and gross annual income are paramount. In the case of the Moyo restaurant, Anderson suspects that its owner falsely claimed an inside seating capacity of just 270 instead of the total seating capacity of 900 by arguing that the outside seats are only used for private functions and events. And of these 270 seats, only 250 are booked on average per day. When Anderson then demanded a list of such outside events, the owner amended his earlier calculation to indicate that in 2013 there were 712 bookings per day for both the inside and outside areas. Of course, as Molapo is quick to point out, having monitored countless franchises like Moyo, the gastronomy industry relies heavily on walk-ins for their revenue. To be fair to the owner, Anderson wraps up the conversation; SAMRO will not insist on 900 seats. We will, he says, drawing out his words, "ki-in-dly a-ll-ow him to take out a license for 712 seats at an annual fee of R13,670 ($1,270)."

Later in the afternoon, several Sales colleagues and I are relaxing in the third-floor kitchenette when Molapo returns from Luthuli House, the national headquarters of the governing party ANC, where he has spent part of the morning trying to convince the party bosses to honor the license they had signed for using SAMRO repertoire at ANC rallies. Anderson doesn't like to go there himself, he says, visibly shaken by the experience because they always mix business with politics. So he sends Molapo. "I'm done with the other political parties, but the ANC always want to know my standing, wants to know which organization I'm with. They are like, 'You are from the Eastern Cape, you must be with us, comrade.' Everything is like an interview with them. They want to know how I'm feeling about them." "I no longer know what to do," he gasps. "All this comrade this, comrade that, blah blah blah. Even when I tell them it's the law, *their* law, they think that SAMRO is a company that is white. But I'm telling them that the majority of artists in South Africa are black, and as our leaders, they must support our people."

"Ja boet" [yes mate], another colleague chimes in, "but even if you want to sue them [the ANC], you'll lose. They'll go straight to the magistrate and tell them to throw out the case."

"They can do that?" another asks.

"Yeah, they have the power, these people," Molapo responds. "They are the power, *yabona* [you see]."

The following day Anderson sends us on a grueling tour of restaurants on the outskirts of Johannesburg that Molapo previously reconnoitered, filling out report forms and handing out license application forms. We start with a Mugg & Bean coffee shop in Fourways, one of a dozen nondescript suburbs that have sprung up north of the city after the end of apartheid. Molapo isn't sure they have a license, so he calls the back office to ask whether they're in the system. They are not. We explain the application form to the owner (Molapo has a folder of them he always carries with him). The next stop is a mall in Linden. But the restaurant that is on Molapo's list of potential new licensees isn't open yet. From there, we head out to Morningside, where the owner is not present. "Those retailers know what is expected, but they also know how to dodge," Molapo says. Further west, in Krugersdorp, we have more luck. In a burger and steak franchise, the owner recognizes Molapo from a previous visit. "SAMRO is a thorn in my flesh," she says, but she wants to finalize the application anyway. Another owner next door asks for a grace period of one to two months to pay the fee. "Of course," Molapo says, "we are not there to destroy their business."

Back on the road, someone from Luthuli House calls to cancel a meeting Molapo had squeezed out of one of the ANC lawyers the day before. We keep plodding along, to another mall, another Mugg & Bean, another white-owned restaurant where the owner is, ironically and metaphorically

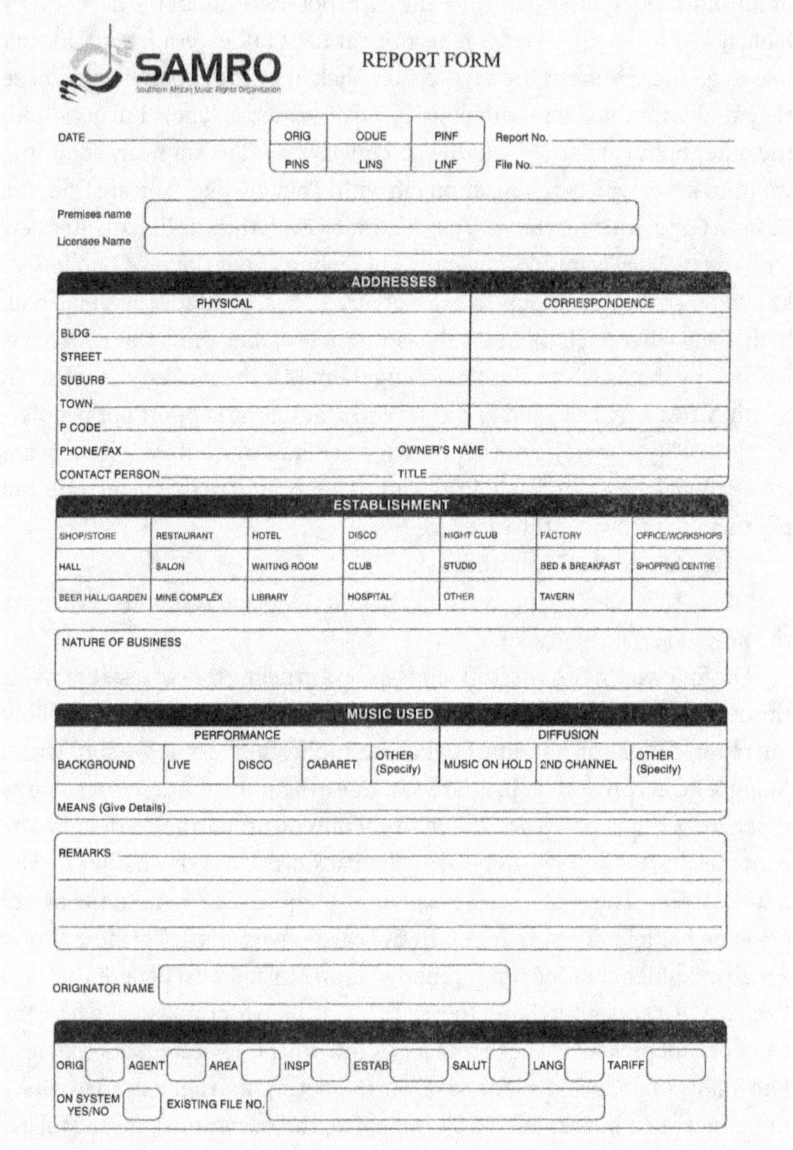

SAMRO
Southern African Music Rights Organisation

REPORT FORM

DATE

ORIG	ODUE	PINF
PINS	LINS	LINF

Report No.

File No.

Premises name

Licensee Name

ADDRESSES	
PHYSICAL	CORRESPONDENCE
BLDG	
STREET	
SUBURB	
TOWN	
P CODE	
PHONE/FAX	OWNER'S NAME
CONTACT PERSON	TITLE

ESTABLISHMENT						
SHOP/STORE	RESTAURANT	HOTEL	DISCO	NIGHT CLUB	FACTORY	OFFICE/WORKSHOPS
HALL	SALON	WAITING ROOM	CLUB	STUDIO	BED & BREAKFAST	SHOPPING CENTRE
BEER HALL/GARDEN	MINE COMPLEX	LIBRARY	HOSPITAL	OTHER	TAVERN	

NATURE OF BUSINESS

MUSIC USED							
PERFORMANCE					DIFFUSION		
BACKGROUND	LIVE	DISCO	CABARET	OTHER (Specify)	MUSIC ON HOLD	2ND CHANNEL	OTHER (Specify)

MEANS (Give Details)

REMARKS

ORIGINATOR NAME

ORIG AGENT AREA INSP ESTAB SALUT LANG TARIFF

ON SYSTEM YES/NO EXISTING FILE NO.

FIGURE 5.1 SAMRO report form. Courtesy of SAMRO.

speaking, out to lunch. "But it's worse in the townships," Molapo ventures. "In the township they use jukeboxes. There is no law that prohibits jukeboxes, but the jukebox guys are worse than criminals." I'm reminded of the stacks of jukeboxes loaded with infringing MP3s that RiSA seized and stored away in a warehouse while cases against their owners were pending. "The law gives you loopholes," Molapo demurs. "That's what I like about law." I'm not sure whether he is applying this to himself, to the alleged criminals, to SAMRO's customers, or all three. By noon, I calculate, our door-to-door salesman tour had netted a mere handful of applications and had coaxed about the same number of restaurant owners into a grudge purchase. But we had also missed half a dozen or so who were not around, spent several hours on the road, and burned through four gallons of gas. Is this what SAMRO calls efficiency?

"Ducking and diving," as everybody calls these evasive tactics, is not the specialty of restaurants alone. State institutions can also get creative, as Glory Kekana knows all too well. Kekana is the senior manager of the Key Accounts division. A graduate of the University of South Africa (UNISA) with a degree in market finance, Kekana is primarily responsible for broadcast licenses that comprise 80 percent of SAMRO's revenues, but she also deals with general licenses worth over R100,000. The twenty-five or so private broadcasters that operate in the country are easy to deal with, she says. They are charged on a monthly basis per advertising and other revenue, such as subsidies or grants. The state-owned SABC, however, is a different animal altogether. For years, SAMRO has been in a running battle with the public broadcaster, which refuses to pay its bills. Add to that some large retail stores unable or unwilling to grasp the nature of licensing, and Kekana has her hands full, keeping the organization's revenue streams flowing and engaging in what she calls "educational marketing." "These corporations have legal departments that know copyright law," she explains, "but they don't understand the business of collecting fees. They don't see us as a supplier, like a dairy factory delivering milk or something, but as double-dipping on something they have already paid for, like the CDs they play to attract customers. To them our tariffs are more like a tax. But really, what we are selling is not licenses; it's compliance." What Kekana is referring to is blanket licenses, the core of CMO operations and the legal mechanism by which, to quote Article 13 (1) of the Berne Convention, countries may impose "reservations and conditions on the exclusive right granted to the author of a music work." That is, SAMRO is permitted to set tariffs for the usage of music without obtaining the copyright owner's permission. As a result, she says, she feels "stuck" like a "bridge" between the statutory rights and livelihood strategies of SAMRO's members on the one hand and the "excuses" of users wanting to keep fees low on the other hand. Judging by some of the posts on SAMRO's Facebook account, that bridge must stretch across a wide chasm indeed, as this post by one Mugwanti Gp Ronny demonstrates: "Licensing consultants? . . . we called this other licensing consultant last year he promised 2 attend us . . . We r yet 2 c him . . . so how sure r u tht those so-called licensing consultants r really working? . . . What is their reporting strategy tht u assess 2 c if they r working?"[25]

To learn more about the nuts and bolts of educational marketing, I join Fikile Mokoena, another worker in Sales, whose job it is to follow up on licensees that field agents like Molapo have met while scouring the country in search of new grudge purchases. She just received an email from someone who wants to know why he needs another license in addition to the one he obtained from SAMPRA, the PRO for needle-time rights. She gets a lot of inquiries like this, Mokoena says, and she uses a standard template to respond. Minutes later, the owner of two garages in Empangeni-Richards Bay calls to complain about an application form he received. "There is no music being played in our garages," he protests. "One of our people came to inspect the premises and there was music playing," Mokoena insists. "I'll send you the registration form so you can fill in the details about the size of the garages, the opening hours, and the number of people visiting every day." "We don't play here," she tells me after hanging up. "Everybody that uses our music must pay, even if you play music from your iPhone in public or use music on hold." But because there are so many tariffs that she doesn't always remember, she simply downloads the tariff sheets to licensees. At this point, the chatter around the room strays into slightly different territory. Mokoena has a cold but can't afford to stay at home. "See that board?" she says, gesturing to a large blackboard on the wall. "See that guy at the top? He's the number one who's reached the highest target." What she is referring to is a scoreboard that shows the number of licenses each employee has sold in a month. When I venture to say that it is best to take a day or two off, she reminds me of the difference between being a privileged white male professor in a first-world country and a black woman in South Africa. "Eishhh, I have a target waiting for me. And it's almost end of the month. Plus, we have incentives we have to fight for." Her colleagues in the adjacent cubicles who have been listening in on our conversation concur. Then, again, strange things happen. "I was given a voucher for a spa in Rosebank, *helele* [hurray]. It's valid for two years." "In return for what?" I ask. "The lady called me again to apologize," Mokoena hesitates. "It was not for anything. But I'll keep it anyway."

And then we are back to phone calls, emails, and forms. Mokoena brings "Tiny" Shabangu, the agent in Empangeni, up to speed about her phone call with the garage owner; writes a letter to a KFC, reminding them to sign and return the letter of acceptance; emails a license confirmation to the Richards Bay Civic Center; talks to someone at the University of Stellenbosch requesting a license; and explains to a DJ that he needs to fill out form MD (Mobile Disc Jockeys), supply a playlist, and pay an initial fee of R900. (The DJ would show up hours later at the SAMRO House front desk, armed with the form, playlist, and fee.)

After endless hours of listening in on phone calls with disgruntled shop owners and municipality clerks, and loading mountains of cue sheets into a database, I'm no longer quite sure what exactly is being collected here. Where is the collective in this merry-go-round of miscommunication, missed opportunities, cumbersome licensing practices, and blatant evasion? Buried under a thick layer of paper and data, the public interest that is supposedly at the heart of copyright never seemed more elusive. And why is all this educational marketing called *capturing* anyway? In its broadest sense, one might say, the term suggests a unilateral exercise of power: the ability to define and win control over a territory, domain, person, or practice, and to represent, correlate, or even harmonize these with the terms, images, forms, and interests of those doing the capturing. But such takeovers hardly ever take place without some intermediary. A state needs an army to conquer another country; to catch a thief, you need handcuffs; and, closer to the topic at hand, to control a market, there has to be some knowledge of the key players, the demand for certain goods, the channels of communication, the supply chains, the legal frameworks governing transactions, and so on. But this is only one side of the story. If there is one feature that defines the iron cage of modernity that all of us supposedly live in, it is the daily experience of intermediaries taking on a life of their own. Paperwork, complicated protocols, inscrutable terminology, rigid bureaucracies staffed with faceless apparatchiks—intermediaries such as these seem to be in charge rather than those who actually put them in place. Intermediaries, then, become forces in their own right. Indeed, they are mediators.

In SAMRO's case, forms are the quintessential mediators. They perform the data they encapsulate. There are around sixty types of forms: from membership application, notification of work, and deed of assignment forms to over fifty user license forms. In all of these, the claim to represent reality cannot be taken at face value. Rather than giving unmediated access to an already existing object, this avalanche of paper constitutes that reality in the first place. But at the same time, forms are not entirely divorced from the reality they purport to render legible. Rather, they constitute a hybrid dynamic or a politics of immediation by which the contingencies intrinsic to representational practices are obscured in the name of efficiency and transparency.[26] Contrary to the widely held belief that forms and other formats of information management demarcate a boundary between the rationality and structural consistency of the state or some other organization and the messy heterogeneity of society, it is precisely this ambiguity that is critical to the smooth functioning and reproduction of organizations. It is by constantly making the mediated seem unmediated and declaring the contingent to be definitive that forms are useful for organizations seeking to consolidate their power. The grip that forms have on our lives does not reside in their accurate reflection of the truth as seen through the eyes of an all-knowing apparatus that then lords over or, in Althusserian terms, interpellates those represented by the forms. Quite the contrary, these effects arise from maintaining an interstitial realm of "epistemic murk."[27] Situated somewhere between reality and technologies of inscription, this gray zone offers an infinite range of possibilities of accounting for and ordering what are shapeless, highly fluctuating social and cultural relations into a relatively stable yet provisional grid of spatiotemporal and sociocultural coordinates. But at the same time, this indeterminacy is not absolute. In order for it to guarantee a certain degree of accuracy and to ensure a modicum of practicability and predictability, the grid cannot be easily modified. In other words, unlike the aggregation of digital data, reviewed further below, that allows for an unprecedented level of precision and individual surveillance, or what Marie Andrée Jacob calls the production of "form-made persons," the grid that emerges from and is constantly reproduced by capturing is marked by inertia.[28]

A closer look at those user license forms reveals that classification is the main mechanism. Like its sister organizations in the United States and Europe, SAMRO has spent decades designing and fine-tuning an elaborate system that subsumes users under a panoply of categories referring to the type and size of location, the way music is used (live or background), the number of persons consuming the music, or the hours music is audible. But this system also does more than sort out people, spaces, and things. The acronyms, categories, taxonomies, and parameters that populate its report forms, license applications, and tariff cards perform what Geoffrey

Bowker and Susan Leigh Star call a "juncture of social organization, moral order, and layers of technical organization." In their work on information systems, Bowker and Star have outlined some of the key features of systems of classification, some of which I want to review here in more detail.[29] For instance, while one may easily isolate a classification scheme for analytical purposes (as I will indeed do further below), the fact is that such schemes are rarely stand-alone. Not only are they ubiquitous, but by their very nature as information, they are also layered vertically or arranged horizontally in ecologies of classification, thus facilitating the movement from one context to another. Another feature is the materiality and texture of classification systems—the fact that they are more than products of the mind but a kind of second nature by dint of being embedded in the built environment. Yet another aspect of these systems is what Bowker and Star call the "indeterminacy of the past" or the multivocality of classification. For example, there were many public and private narratives, categories, standard forms, and labels jostling for ascendancy during the early phase of the HIV/AIDS crisis in San Francisco, variously impacting the lives of those afflicted with the disease. The practical politics of classification systems are also a major theme, which impacts what will be visible in the system and to whose benefit it works. In some contexts, this visibility may only materialize as a result of public scrutiny brought to bear on what are often opaque decision-making processes and negotiations. In others, such as colonial and apartheid racial classifications, such visibility has been their very raison d'être.

However, by far the most interesting aspect of classification systems, insofar as it relates to the argument pursued here, is their affinity to the concept of "boundary objects" coined by Star in the 1980s and the kinds of membership and participation in collectives of worlding such objects afford. Cutting across diverse organizations, institutions, and social worlds with conflicting viewpoints and interests—the white owner of an upscale eatery in Camps Bay, say, and a relatively unknown, yet talented, black singer-songwriter whose music is being played from the restaurant's speakers—these collectives require a certain degree of familiarity or a naturalized relationship with the objects routinely encountered while aspiring to become members. But because collectives of worlding differ in their abilities to cohere internally and members' relationships to objects are in constant flux, boundary objects "resolve anomalies of naturalization without imposing a naturalization of categories from one community or from an outside source of standardization." And if we were to follow the liberal-reformist thrust of Star's argument to the end, boundary objects may even gradually lead to a tradition of "reflective de-naturalization," to the sort of introspection enjoining the modern liberal subject to do the right thing.[30]

Given the wider context of postapartheid South Africa, the odds of the song in the Camps Bay restaurant—and the different rights and obligations attached to it—contributing to unified and fully naturalized collectives anytime soon are slim. At a micro level, there are many reasons for the absence of such collectives. One of them is Conway's law (named after US programmer Melwin E. Conway), whereby the structure of an organization in part mirrors that of its product—in SAMRO's case, the tariff system and its underlying classifications are structured like the organization that designed them. Or as Bowker and Star phrase it: "Each subsystem inherits, increasingly as it scales up, the inertia of the installed base of systems that have come before."[31] Another factor impeding the formation of collectives of worlding aspiring toward a condition of reflective denaturalization is, ironically, the free market ideology inscribed in the regulations—or, rather, the weakness or near-total absence of regulation—that govern collecting societies, and is reflected in SAMRO's projected self-image as a stalwart of markets as arbitrators of cultural value. While SAMRO's licensing practices, as mentioned above, do not fall under the provisions of the Copyright Regulations, 1978, they are subject to the supervision of the Copyright Tribunal under chapter 3 of the Copyright Act and, most significantly, to s 22 of the Copyright Act, which provides for the transfer of copyright, either wholly or in part, through assignment, exclusive license, or nonexclusive license. It is no surprise, then, that the act envisages assignors and assignees as individual agents freely entering into market transactions. Small wonder, too, that when describing its relationships to those very users, SAMRO resorts to such staples of South African contract law as *good faith* and *fairness*. Comforting as they may seem, on closer inspection, these words cannot hide the fact that postcolonial reality militates against the perception of SAMRO licensing strategies as fully equipped with built-in safeguards against unequal bargaining and other pitfalls of contract negotiations. But how does this manifest in everyday licensing practice? How does the contractual requirement of fairness square with the grudge-purchase negotiation tactics employed by John Anderson in the episode above? Capturing, I argue, takes users down a slippery path ab initio, to a point where there is little agency left to contest the terms of the license agreement they are compelled to sign. To understand this—and before I revert to the discussion of the inscriptive dimension of licensing—the coercive nature of capturing must be placed in the wider context of copyright maximalism encroaching ever-more forcefully both on the rights of users and the proposed alternatives to increase users' leverage through exceptions and other forms of justice as well as that of authors in wresting control from publishers and crafting new forms of protections tailored for specific local needs.[32]

Beginning with the authors, SAMRO's entire licensing strategy hinges on authors assigning the public performance right of their works to the organization and not on a license (exclusive or nonexclusive) that it merely administers. In common law systems, such an assignment basically amounts to the divestment of ownership from the author to others. The consequences of this mechanism in South Africa and elsewhere on the African continent are apparent. Assigning one's work rather than licensing it traps the vast majority of authors who lack the wherewithal to market—and in many cases also produce—their own works in an endless cycle of limited capacity and meager earnings. In other words, because these authors do not have the financial and technical resources necessary to enter the market as independent, free agents, they are compelled to part with their copyright in exchange for an uncertain future. It is this state of affairs that has stimulated a debate among a small but industry-savvy group of legal scholars about alternatives to the commercial bias of copyright in common law countries. For instance, Joel Baloyi, a UNISA law professor, composer, and former counsel at SAMRO, explores the potential of merging elements of common law, civil law *droit d'auteur*, and human rights into a sui generis African copyright regime.[33] Although the first two have gradually converged in protecting the moral rights of authors, subtle differences still persist between the French and German versions of *droit d'auteur*. While in France, there is a complete separation between inalienable moral and freely assignable economic rights, in the German *Urheberrecht*, moral rights and economic rights form an insoluble unity, granting the author the right to sue and to terminate a license for both moral and commercial reasons. In comparison, a human rights framework is much less conducive to Baloyi's blueprint for the "orchestration" or, if you will, Africanization, of the copyright system—at least in South Africa.[34] In two highly controversial cases—generally referred to as the "Laugh It Off" cases—the Constitutional Court first ruled that intellectual property rights do not qualify as "universally-accepted" human rights, only to subsequently reverse its decision by according trademarks the same status as a fundamental right like freedom of expression, essentially equating the right to hold intellectual property with a universally-accepted human right.[35] Although *Laugh It Off* leaves open other questions pertaining to the evidentiary basis of infringement claims, it was welcomed by some copyright lawyers as pointing the way toward the recognition of the author as an inalienable owner of copyright along the lines of European civil law and, at a later stage, as the cornerstone of a copyright system reflective of Africa's "development" needs.[36]

Given the subject matter and broader gist of Baloyi's reasoning, it is, of course, little wonder that the resulting recommendations that a decolonial copyright regime replaces the transfer of ownership with a licensing system or that the use of legislated material terms of contracts become mandatory are heavily centered on the author-entrepreneur.[37] Yet, here and elsewhere, users' interests are either entirely ignored or tacitly assumed to be coterminous with the welfare of aggregated individual interests measured on the basis of the ability and willingness of users to pay for access to works. And even where there is an effort in the Global South to more thoroughly engage users' interests, it is primarily on the basis of normative and doctrinal reasoning. Apart from limitations (blanket and compulsory licenses), fair use/fair dealing exceptions, and obsolete dichotomies, such as between authors and users as independently constituted domains, the most prominent theme in this scholarship appears to be the notion that a carefully maintained equilibrium between the interests of authors and users will ensure copyright's core instrumentalist objective of the public interest almost by default. The critical examination in previous chapters of copyright scholarship's reticence toward a more substantive definition, especially of the public interest, illustrates the difficulty of translating this literature into the terms of an anthropology concerned with the way SAMRO organizes its relationship with users.[38]

Circling back, then, from normative reasoning to an ethnographic mode of inquiry, it might be more fruitful to foreground a slightly different set of questions. By focusing on some of the more hidden aspects and mythologies of capturing, grudge purchases, and educational marketing, I hope to shed light on a somewhat underrepresented part of CMO operations. Additionally, I would like to query the triad of assignment, blanket licenses, and the case-by-case strategy of tariff negotiation more broadly as potentially detrimental to the interests of economically disadvantaged users, such as small business owners, and the postapartheid project of distributive justice more generally. To substantiate this hypothesis with concrete evidence, a close reading of the forms used by SAMRO to structure the capturing component of its licensing practices is necessary.[39] But rather than focus solely on the content of these documents, I will prioritize their place and function in a chain of inscriptions interlinking a wide array of actors, classificatory systems, and standards. Thus, it is not inscription per se that I am after;

rather, it is the work they do—the mechanics that support the politics of immediation referred to above. Inscriptions, I suggest, cascade from one form to the next until they reach a point at which a mess of more or less guesstimated data can be turned into an incontrovertible statement of fact that then becomes legible in light of the Copyright Act.[40]

Picture, then, four users in the townships of Gauteng: an elderly shebeen-keeper in Soweto named Bongani Mabuza; a bicycle repair shop in Katlehong owned by a young sports fanatic called Kabelo Lekota; a female mobile DJ who goes by the stage name Womanx and lives in Tembisa; and Taifa Hussein, a Somali immigrant who runs a spaza shop in Diepsloot. All use SAMRO repertoire for their own listening pleasure while working and for the entertainment of their customers. And in all four scenarios, the Copyright Act defines such use as a public performance that must be authorized by the owner of the performance right in the work performed. How, then, would SAMRO grudge-sell a license to establishments like these? What role do forms and other written documents play in this process, and how do they enact different forms of agency? As we have seen above, the process is set in motion when field agents such as Agreement Molapo or "Tiny" Shabangu inspect the shebeen, the bicycle shop or, some of the venues where the DJ regularly performs. In many cases, the agent would then assist the licensees in filling out one of the fifty-some types of licenses SAMRO offers. Each license agreement is divided into seven sections, from A to G. While all licenses use identical language on things like payment of the license fee, granting of a license (blanket license), duration and commencement of the license, or basic information such as the licensee's address, VAT registration number, and type of business ([Pty] Ltd, NGO, or sole proprietor), subtle differences in sections C and E may be observed.

Using the example of our four fictional users above, shebeen-keeper Mabuza would have to take out a license for tariff HT, which covers "the performance of background music in taverns, shebeens, pubs, tuck shops and spaza shops where seating is provided for the consumption of liquor and/or other refreshments." Aside from the information required in sections A and B, he would also need to specify the number of premises and total seating capacity. The bicycle shop, in turn, would have to apply for tariff S, applicable to shops, stores, showrooms, offices, banking halls, and similar premises. But in contrast to the shebeen owner, Mr. Lekota must also detail the number of employees, hours per day the music is audible to them, and the number of days his shop is open. As for the DJ, she is a bit of a Cinderella figure in the world of SAMRO application forms. A prime

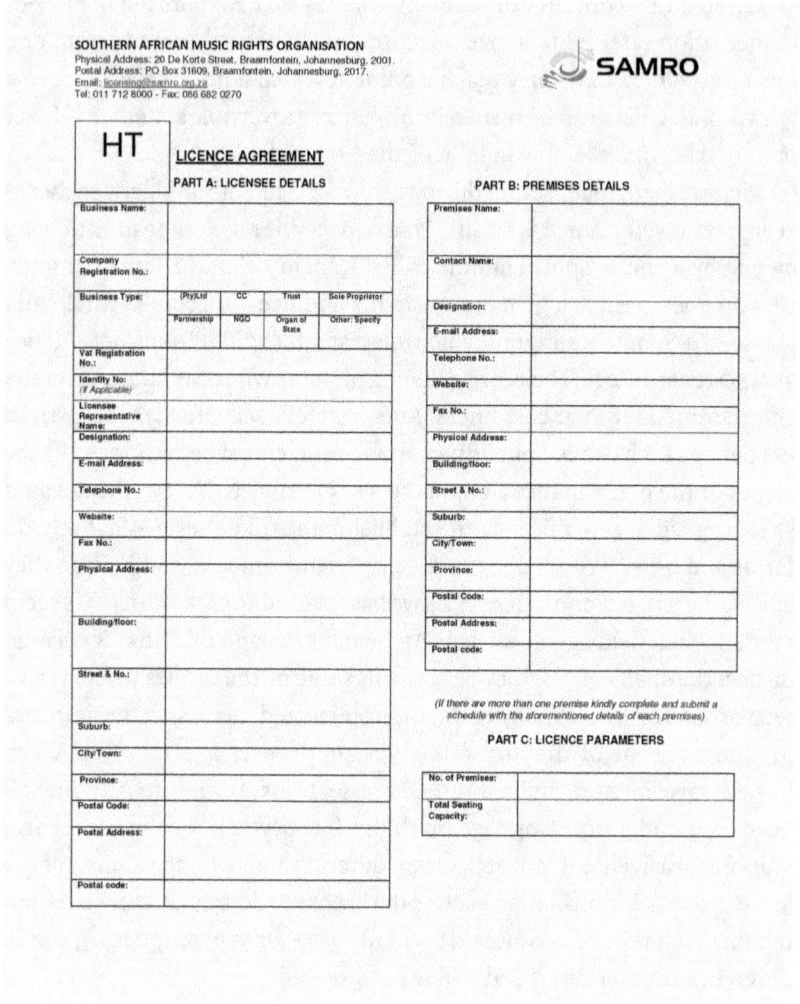

SOUTHERN AFRICAN MUSIC RIGHTS ORGANISATION
Physical Address: 20 De Korte Street, Braamfontein, Johannesburg, 2001.
Postal Address: PO Box 31609, Braamfontein, Johannesburg, 2017.
Email: licensing@samro.org.za
Tel: 011 712 8000 - Fax: 086 682 0270

SAMRO

HT

LICENCE AGREEMENT

PART A: LICENSEE DETAILS

Business Name:				
Company Registration No.:				
Business Type:	(Pty)Ltd	CC	Trust	Sole Proprietor
	Partnership	NGO	Organ of State	Other: Specify
Vat Registration No.:				
Identity No: (If Applicable)				
Licensee Representative Name:				
Designation:				
E-mail Address:				
Telephone No.:				
Website:				
Fax No.:				
Physical Address:				
Building/floor:				
Street & No.:				
Suburb:				
City/Town:				
Province:				
Postal Code:				
Postal Address:				
Postal code:				

PART B: PREMISES DETAILS

Premises Name:	
Contact Name:	
Designation:	
E-mail Address:	
Telephone No.:	
Website:	
Fax No.:	
Physical Address:	
Building/floor:	
Street & No.:	
Suburb:	
City/Town:	
Province:	
Postal Code:	
Postal Address:	
Postal code:	

(If there are more than one premise kindly complete and submit a schedule with the aforementioned details of each premises)

PART C: LICENCE PARAMETERS

No. of Premises:	
Total Seating Capacity:	

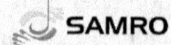

FIGURE 5.2 SAMRO HT license agreement. Courtesy of SAMRO.

example of the blurred contours of contemporary cultural reproduction, Womanx is a prosumer or, in SAMRO-speak, "music creator" and "music user" all in one. She will therefore—in addition to not being employed by any of the establishments she performs at—not only have to take out a license and become a member of SAMRO, but she must also contact SAMRO, as the requisite user license MD is not available on the company's website, and the existing tariff structure does not appear to even remotely reflect the highly unpredictable, improvisatory nature of DJing.[41]

To recapitulate, on the face of it, the capturing of licensees has so far proceeded according to a fairly simple playbook, from an inspection to a report form to a license agreement. Hidden beneath this seemingly smooth flow of data, however, is a whole social and spatio-cultural matrix upon which categories like "shebeen," "open-air events," or "pub" are grafted. Along with a tariff structure that either obscures or reinforces older social imaginaries and, from time to time, even recognizes the emergence of new forms of sociality, the ensuing datafication and monetization of intricately interwoven socio-auditory relationships may end up achieving the very opposite of a vibrant democratic culture. Take the category "shebeen": In the South African context, a shebeen is more than merely the equivalent of a traditional English pub that happens to be located in a black township. It is a space of commiseration that is saturated with the memory of the repression of black communities and the contemporary experience of continued marginalization. But shebeens are also sites of regeneration and vitality nurtured by collective drinking rituals, media consumption, and music-making. How then is this specific context accounted for in the capturing process? Going back to our imaginary shebeen-keeper in Soweto, the report form would have noted the location of the shebeen and possibly classified it as a tavern or "other" establishment with further details being given in the "Nature of Business" box beneath. As for the music used, the inspector may have checked "Background" in the case of a smaller shebeen or, less likely, "Disco" for a larger venue. "Remarks" may have also been added about, for example, the total seating capacity required in form HT.

All this information then migrates, in heavily filtered form, into HT, reassuring the licensees that their business is categorized correctly. Less transparent, however, is how the seating capacity takes on completely different and unspoken valences during this transition. While the frame of reference preset by the report form sets Mabuza's shebeen apart from other shebeens further down the street, in section E (SAMRO tariff), the parameter "total seating capacity" becomes part of a scale of tariffs in which the amount of the annual fee decreases in relation to the total seating capacity by increments of twenty-five and one hundred seats as follows:

7.3.1 An annual fee of R12.66 for every customer seating capacity up to the first 50; thereafter

7.3.2 An annual fee of R10.08 for every additional customer seating capacity from 51 to 75; thereafter

7.3.3 An annual fee of R7.59 for every additional customer seating capacity from 76 to 100; thereafter

7.3.4 An annual fee of R6.30 for every additional customer seating capacity from 101 to 200; thereafter

7.3.5 An annual fee of R4.73 for every customer seating capacity over 200.

While this system of rebates is common in other PROs and might simply be read as an example of the economies of scale inherent in capitalist rationality, what may not be immediately apparent to the uninitiated would-be user is the fact that the scale potentially diminishes the capacity of small businesses to compete. The owners of larger venues are rewarded due to the fact that the average fee per customer is lower than that of the smaller venue. To wit, while the seventy-five seats in Mabuza's shebeen would cost him an average of R7.58 per seat, the competition down the road whose total seating capacity is two hundred would only be paying R7.07 per customer. Assuming that a smaller seating capacity in the *kasi* does not necessarily translate into a high-class establishment with higher revenue as the same capacity might in the white suburbs, the net effect here is that small, township-based businesses are disadvantaged in comparison to larger ones—and not just any larger business in Soweto or other townships. Assuming that the category "pubs" comprises a proportionally higher percentage of businesses owned by whites, located in formerly whites-only areas, and seating more customers than the average township shebeen, the difference between Mabuza's cramped den and a spacious Irish pub in Rosebank becomes even more glaring.

Unsurprisingly, the ratio is similar, if not worse, when comparing Kabelo Lekota's 50-square-meter Katlehong bicycle shop to a similar shop of 450 square meters in Sandton, a suburb replete with plush amenities, glitzy corporate headquarters, and well-heeled customers. Here, the corresponding S license provides for the following licenses:

7.6.1 An amount of R115.30 for every unit of 25 sq. Metres of Shop space or part thereof up to 200 sq. Metres, per annum; and

7.6.2 An amount of R57.64 for every unit of 25 sq. Metres of Shop space or part thereof from 200 sq. to 400 sq. Metres per annum: and

7.6.3 An amount of R57.64 for every unit of 25 sq. Metres of Shop space or part thereof above 400 sq. Metres per annum, and

7.6.4 An amount equal to 57.64 cents for each hour per day (or part thereof) that the establishment is open, for each capacity unit of 25 Employees (or part thereof).

Thus Lekota pays R4.61 per square meter, while the corporate owner of the Sandton shop pays only R2.30. This imbalance might, however, be offset by the fact that an additional R0.57 is payable for each hour the shop is open and, more puzzlingly, for each employee "to whom the music is audible; and the hours in a day that the music is audible."

But let us compare the tariffs for a shop and for a spaza such as the 25-square-meter one that is owned and operated by the Somali immigrant to see whether spazas are better off than white-owned shops in the suburbs. *Spaza* is the South African term for a small-scale, most often unregistered grocery retailer in townships and informal settlements that sells small household, food, and refreshment items and in some cases also features a modest seating area where patrons may linger on a Coke or Lipton ice tea. Much like shebeens, spazas are cultural institutions that provide avenues for communication and solidarity, often in the face of violent xenophobic attacks. Even more critically, spazas also fulfill a key infrastructural function in ensuring food security in sprawling settlements with limited public transport. In other words, they deserve some form of support. Strangely enough, though, neither its classification as a shebeen-like entertainment whose tariff is determined on the basis of seating capacity nor the alternative-yet-unrecognized role as a shop where the tariff is based on floor space would provide any relief to the roughly 33 percent of 1,100 spazas in the country run by what a 2020 survey calls "'survivalist' owner-operators."[42] In the first scenario, one of these survivalists—Taifa Hussein, our Somali immigrant—would easily find himself in a similar situation as Mabuza in his shebeen. With a seating capacity of just five or less, he would be far more vulnerable than a larger shebeen. This situation would be vastly exacerbated if the spaza were licensed as a shop under tariff S. With its 25 square meters, sole owner-employee, and year-round twelve-plus daily hours of operation, it would end up paying R5.53 per square meter as opposed to the R4.29 paid by a grocery store with 300 square meters, five employees, and eight hours of daily operation on weekdays only. Worse, the disparate treatment of spazas might also drive their owners, already mired in misery and questionable labor practices, even deeper into poverty and illegality.[43]

Although the barrage of monitoring techniques, application forms, and countless telephone calls appears to be a neutral way of getting the job done, they are not meaningless or without effect. They have the power to define the terms under which a composer or publisher is interpellated as a "member" or a restaurant owner as a "user" and how these individuals, rendered readily classifiable and predictable, are emplaced as isolated "market agents" first and foremost and only secondly as citizens and members of collectives of worlding. But perhaps, even more significant, these techniques present South Africans with stark choices as to the deeply entrenched social poetics that must be sacrificed in the pursuit of success or, alternatively, how new valences between being "kind"—to use Anderson's term—and the legal and economic demands of the global market might be possible. Do South Africans really have to choose between economic logic and moral priorities? Or should we instead ask what sorts of relationships are forged by opposites such as compliance and excuses? Is the person who imagines themself a bridge and another who defaults on a grudge purchase really living on opposite sides of the fence? Or do they become entangled with one another as mutually enabling conditions of a fragile, ever-shrinking commons?

Obviously, SAMRO's capturing strategy raises more problems than it solves. A highly unstable, costly process, it calls into question the strange blend of self-assured rhetoric and routine, yet often half-hearted, attempts at rationalizing that strategy that permeated my conversations across all levels of the organization's hierarchy as truthful representations of the contingencies and heterogeneous encounters that constitute SAMRO's core business. The cost-to-income ratio; the upcoming financial audit; the ambition to become the continent's leading licensing body; the market penetration; the efficiency gains that are expected to flow from the introduction of a new computer system all rehearse one or the other standard argument of CMO economic discourse. But at the same time, the narratives that are woven around these themes—and that fill the pages of SAMRO's glossy annual integrated reports—are more than mere generalizations or opinions with claims to universal validity. Universals can be taken at face value. But they can also be localized by reducing them to mere folk beliefs, as recent anthropological scholarship in the wake of Dipesh Chakrabarty's trailblazing *Provincializing Europe* shows. Either way, both will erase the making of global connections like those that shape every move and fiber of SAMRO's being.[44] In others words, universals and local epistemologies must be seen as coproducing each other. Rather than outright rejecting neoclassical economics as alien to emancipatory agendas in the Global South, and thus opposed to the anthropological commitment to relativism, it is by attending to this coproduction in the interstices of neoclassical economic theory and its tenuous application to the South African context that the economics of CMO is constituted as an ethnographic object in its own right.

Externalities, Economies of Scale, and Other Myths

Creative industries economist Ruth Towse may be correct in saying that, while copyright gives rights, ensuring the rewards of those rights is a "complex interaction of the law, market forces and institutional arrangements."[45] But working one's way through the relevant scholarship feels like being in a forest with no trees. Beholden to a level of abstraction that makes legal writing appear almost poetic by comparison, economists of copyright collectives have thus far failed to verify their theoretical premises against solid empirical evidence, let alone ground such findings in granular, from-the-ground-up accounts of the inner workings of any specific CMO.[46] Granted, the obstacles to such an endeavor are formidable, as CMOs tend to hold their cards close to their chests, frequently citing privacy concerns and releasing but the barest information required by law. For example, SAMRO's distribution policy is governed by the follow-the-dollar principle adopted by PROs around the world, and it publishes its financial statements in its annual reports. Yet, the finer points of its royalty calculations, such as the algorithms through which a point value is attributed to each second of music used in a pool of music and in which the total revenue is then spread across the total points of that pool, remain inaccessible to outside examination. Adding the fact that SAMRO resists disclosing different revenue levels according to key demographic indicators such as race, gender, or age, one appreciates the difficulty in making any evidence-based economic analysis as well as the widespread image of SAMRO as a rather evidence-resistant organization.

Neoclassical economics, then, has little to offer to the ethnographer of cultural industries in the Global South. Yet, even as heirs to a venerable tradition of economic analysis that reaches all the way back to the anthropologist Bronislaw Malinowski and sociologists like Émile Durkheim and Marcel Mauss, present-day anthropologists have long struggled to carve out a space of their own within which to counter universalist constructs such as the rational, wealth-maximizing *homo oeconomicus* with a version of economic theory that is more reflective of the distinctive forms of economic integration they encountered in tribal economies of the colonial world and other elsewheres. It is only now that the unprecedented incursion of neoliberalism into the hitherto untouched—and as such genuinely anthropological—regions of the world can no longer be ignored that these anthropologists have begun to engage other scales and other disciplines in making sense of the challenge the conjuncture of globalization, climate change, and global health crises poses to marginalized populations everywhere. Still, little of this appears to have inspired the kind of sustained ethnographic inquiry attempted in this chapter. Barring some notable exceptions, the cultural industries of the Global South remain the exclusive preserve of neoclassical economics.[47]

How, then, might one conceive of this interstitial space between neoclassical economics and alternative theorizations, such as "moral economy," "domestic mode of production," "platform economy," or "people's economy," popular with anthropologists?[48] What aspects of an economic system can either of these theories occlude or delegitimize? And which ones are yet to emerge from their convergences and divergences revealed in the ethnographic process? Before homing in on the novel configurations that might arise from this process, I would like to flesh out two key concepts at the heart of CMO economics.[49] The first is the notion of efficiency and, related to it, the concept of externalities. The argument goes something like this: Because in the era of digital music works can be reproduced and disseminated at very low marginal cost, the absence of proper legal policies, sturdy institutional structures, and sound business practices may lead to significant negative effects and, ultimately, an inefficient scenario where authors are discouraged from creating new works, and the market fails. In economics, such effects are called externalities because of the potential impact a market participant's decision has on those who are not part of the market interaction. Contrary to negative externalities caused by decisions that do not factor in the effect on nonparticipants, externalities that arise from a consideration of their outside effect are known as positive externalities. The textbook example of the former is when a factory emitting pollutants that harm nearby crops fails to account for the costs it imposes on the farmer—who is external to the transactions between the factory and its customers—to clean up the mess afterward. An example of positive externalities, by contrast, might be a gardening enthusiast whose magnificent Japanese garden draws visitors from miles around. If the garden were not on a public road, its owner could easily make a living by charging admission instead of working as a salesperson at a florist for $30,000 per year. If, however, in another town, there is a similar garden in a secluded area that people pay to enter, the owner might bring in $40,000. In the first example, the negative externalities (i.e., those of the farmer) may be internalized (by the chemical company), thereby increasing the latter's costs. In the second example, our gardener, unable to internalize the positive externalities of their effort, is obliged to spend more time working at the florist than devoting themself to the more socially beneficial activity of tending to the

Japanese garden. In both scenarios, the market as the key mechanism for obtaining optimal social welfare is imperfect: in the first, private market participants are incentivized to overproduce by disregarding the actual costs implied in negative externalities; in the second, they are discouraged from making an investment.

Collecting societies like SAMRO—and of course the copyright framework hosting them—are supposed to correct such inefficient outcomes. But as we have seen above, negative externalities are not due only to more prominent ills like abuse of market dominance, excessive remuneration for business executives, discrimination among members, or lack of transparency. Seemingly innocuous, low-key operations such as the search for licensees and the bargaining of licensing terms are infused with inefficiencies and externalities through and through. Yet, rather than viewing these as containing a potential risk of market failure, their relative obscurity might present the anthropologist with an opportunity to reverse conventional economic wisdom according to which contractual relations bind market agents in morally neutral bubbles and externalities take on socially charged, either harmful or beneficial, meanings. As ANT scholar Michel Callon argues, the theory of externalities only works when there is the prior assumption that contractual relations are self-sufficient arrangements empowering agents to allocate resources or transfer property by erecting temporary impenetrable barriers between themselves and the rest of the world.[50] These barriers or "frames," as Callon calls them, define the effectiveness of the market by allowing each agent to anticipate the actions of another agent in making a decision. On this view, then, externalities are simply imperfections of the process of framing and, as such, might be better thought of as overflows. If this argument is correct—as I think it is—it follows that the entire majestic edifice of neoclassical economics rests on the simple notion that framing is the norm and that the success of market economies depends on their ability to identify leaks and to develop suitable devices—which might include legal interventions—to contain potential overflows.

Given the constructivist essence of Callon's argument, it is no surprise that, in his view, things work the other way around: overflowing is the rule and framing the exception. A "fragile, artificial result," framing is "always incomplete and . . . without this incompleteness would in fact be wholly ineffectual."[51] For example, exceeding the will of the signatories, an agreement obviously predisposes the enrollment of an entire system of forms, legal texts, and technologies of data collection to be fulfilled. Paradoxically, while solidifying the frame, these components also provide openings for overflow and opportunities to access networks beyond the contractual frame. If not for the economist, for the ethnographer and anthropologist overflows thus provide the grist for their anti-anti-instrumentalist mill. To meaningfully talk about overflows as a market agent, economist, or anthropologist, there has to be an accounting—some kind of quantification or other empirical proof of that which overflows. Thus, where the agent and the economist will want to see invoices, tax records, and the like, the anthropologist might want to learn more about the routes and mechanisms by which networks outside the frame are formed and how these spaces afford decisions and actions that then become legible and calculable for a multitude of diverging interests. But that is where the similarities end. While for the economist, this accounting is an efficient means toward securing the frame, the anthropologist will be more interested in what technical, infrastructural conditions of possibility must exist to even speak of market relations as frames in the first place. Even more urgently, she will want to know how such conditions may either enable ideas of moral order, such as the sanctity of markets to take root in everyday social poetics, or replace them with competing ideas.

Perhaps a simpler way to express this coproduction of frames and overflows—indeed the absolute necessity of the latter for the very existence and stability of the former—is by viewing the interplay of positive and negative externalities as a delicate trade-off: one person's negative externality can be another person's positive externality. For example, by refusing to bargain or failing to capture significant sections of the market, SAMRO may produce negative externalities for the entire community of users who sooner or later will have to pay higher royalties to offset its losses. But it may also produce positive externalities for the patrons of unlicensed restaurants who will not have to pay more for their latte macchiato because the owners' costs, at least for the time being, remain unchanged.

Another example of how frames and overflows mutually constitute each other is the concept of blanket licenses, the fact that, like most music industry PROs, SAMRO does not split up its repertoire in order to offer a greater variety of licenses for specific works or categories of works. Whether it is a Tae Kwon Do studio or a funeral parlor, all users get equal access to Britten's "War Requiem," Rolling Stones's "I Can't Get No Satisfaction," or Black Sabbath's "Never Say Die." In terms of cost efficiency, there are pros and cons to this form of licensing. As stated earlier, the standard view espoused by mainstream CMO economics is that blanket licensing keeps transaction costs well below what a PRO might incur by engaging in price discrimination. But here, too, neoclassical economists are stuck in the same dichotomy as in the previous example. On the one hand, they are likely to argue that price discrimination may generate competition among users, thus strengthening the bargaining position of the PRO. Or that it restrains a monopolistic supplier from excluding users whose willingness to pay falls somewhere between the monopoly price and the marginal cost by charging prices higher than marginal costs. Furthermore, they might add, with price discrimination, the socially negative externalities of monopolies would be turned into positive ones because the surplus appropriated from high-value users is shifted to all rights holders, theoretically leaving social welfare unaffected. But on the other hand, beyond deeming such product differentiation as ineffective in maximizing revenues, these economists will also point to the negative effect it has on the ability of newcomers or rights holders of less sought-after repertoires to compete with more prominent repertoire.[52] Ultimately, however, what remains unaffected by this pro and con of blanket licenses is the frame as the normative space for defining market relations as efficient.

In an alternative interpretation of the alleged efficiency of blanket licenses and CMO economic dogma, one may also consider what Ivan Reidel calls the "Taylor Swift Paradox."[53] This refers to the phenomenon—common in US broadcasting—in which large portions of airtime and leisure time are taken up by commercials so that the ratio of advertising to content negatively impacts the livelihoods of the vast majority of less played singer-songwriters, who derive a substantial part of their income from the public performance of their works in broadcasts. Conventional CMO economics, Reidel argues, has viewed broadcasting as a two-sided platform that delivers content to audiences and then delivers audiences to advertisers. What such scholarship has been largely oblivious to, however, is the existence of a third party—the authors and the PROs that issue blanket licenses for the performance of their works. This fact calls for a different analysis, one where broadcasting, advertising, and music licensing form an ecology—or a vicious circle. Because superstar airplay and highly lucrative advertising work go hand in glove—in any given time span, Taylor Swift fans are likely to be exposed to more commercials than the devotees of a local garage band—and because blanket licenses by their very nature do not discriminate between famous and obscure composers, there arises something of a catch-22. Broadcasters who are saddled with high blanket tariffs will seek to make up for that cost by allocating more time to profitable advertising made possible by the synergy with the pull of the Taylor Swifts of the world—which in turn diminishes airtime for lesser-known artists. Add to this the fact that blanket licenses already eliminate price competition among songwriters so that broadcasters are encouraged to play "You Belong with Me" more often for the same cost than less popular songs, and it follows that royalties disproportionally flow to the superstars. On balance then, the negative externalities, or overflows, generated by the combination of high tariffs and reduced airtime for less successful authors, while being internalized by the broadcaster via increased advertising revenue, may ultimately do more to secure the system of collective management—the frame—than to increase the social welfare of local composers.[54]

Membership rules are another highly contentious area where the tension between the framing, cost-saving side of collective administration and leaky reality on the ground is in full view. Like most CMOs, SAMRO is seeking to tread a fine line between openness and exclusivity of membership. As part of the shakeup after the Dubai and DP crisis, in 2019, SAMRO simplified its post-1994 byzantine membership system by reducing it to just two categories: voting members and nonvoting members. These categories are further broken down into associate and full members, with another subdivision differentiating among authors, author's heirs, and publishers in each of the two membership levels. To warrant performing rights administration by SAMRO, an author's musical works should have achieved what its membership rules call "significant performances." While the threshold for an author to become an associate member is relatively low (R100 in royalties within three years prior to application), the rules up the ante considerably for members desiring to advance to full member status through a convoluted point system.[55] For instance, authors are awarded points for the years of membership, number of documented works, and minimum average earnings for three preceding years. Thus, an author who has been an active member for a minimum of five years qualifies for ten points. If that author, within that or any time period longer than five years, has documented sixty works with SAMRO, they qualify for another ten points, and if any of those works have earned a minimum of R10,000 over three previous years, they will receive yet another ten points. Another form of gatekeeping inherent in the point system is the principle of national treatment. Applying this principle—enshrined in TRIPS and the Berne Convention and with few exceptions observed the world over—to royalty collection, each member of CISAC must apply the same system used by its sister societies, such as reflecting the length of a work in the number of points awarded. But as Mihály Ficsor shows, aesthetic criteria may also prejudice the allocation of points. Thus, more points may be awarded to those categories of works (for example, works in "serious" music) where the number of such works exceeds that of similar works created in another country.[56]

It does not take a math genius to realize that in the South African environment, the selection of members on the basis of the point system and their potential contribution to the collective's finances greatly disadvantages a wide range of authors. For instance, the benefits young black composers with scarce technical and infrastructural resources, such as recording equipment or high-speed internet access, or authors who may be predominantly producing works in folklore-based genres such as *maskandi* Zulu guitar music derive from the collective management of royalties may be well below that of their colleagues in other countries even though their market share in terms of significance (i.e., airtime) in South Africa is greater. And consequently, many such authors barely ever enter the frame to begin with.

As a final example of how CMO economists theorize transaction cost-effectiveness, and as a segue into a critique of such theorizing, it might be helpful to probe what some experts refer to as the solidarity function of CMO. Much of the discussion around this topic is framed against the backdrop of the formidable challenges to the existence and very idea of collective copyright management posed by the deregulation of the tech, media, and creative industries, the rapidly evolving vertical and horizontal integration between different sectors of these industries, and the sway of digital technology over virtually all spheres of life. In its most rudimentary form, the concept of solidarity entails the internal coherence of collectives and the cross-subsidization between successful and less fortunate members. As for the former, CMO scholarship thus far appears to have offered little insight beyond platitudes, such as the claim that coherence can be explained by the rational, self-interested behavior of disaffected members who have no incentive to seek alternative forms of management as long as the net benefits of membership are greater than those expected from such alternatives.[57]

More serious challenges to the solidarity principle still arise from external pressures, especially the potential of digital rights management technologies enabling large corporations to withdraw from the CMO system altogether and replace it with their own system or negotiate lower administrative deductions, thus ultimately shifting the burden to independent publishers and the members they sign. But the foreclosure of solidarity does not stop there. Because there is an intrinsic bias toward global superstars and American content, artists who seek to strike a balance between "making it in America" and a commitment to local cultural values may find that their already fragile position is further impaired by higher administrative levies as well as dwindling public support for their craft.[58] This last concern gives an idea of the corrosive effect the reshaping of CMO in the digital era will have on the livelihoods of marginalized musicians in the Global South and of the corresponding lack of awareness of those consequences in mainstream economic thought more generally.

However, by far the most problematic aspect of neoclassical economics of performance rights organizations is the blindness with which supposedly universal standards, prescriptions, and formulae are applied to the developing world. The second pillar of CMO economics, the theory of economies of scale, is a case in point. Scalability refers to the ability of a business to increase its efficiency and profitability by expanding its capacity without reprograming the business model or making additional investments or significant adjustments to the fixed costs. The economies of scale that ensue are said to be especially beneficial for sectors that are either natural monopolies, part of the internet economy, or both. And indeed, the potential for scalability is at the heart of the tale of infinite expansion that SAMRO likes to tell its members and the larger world around it. Bigger is always better. The more members, the lower transaction costs. The more standardized the parameters of music usage, the more user data can be captured. And so on. To become workable, scalability must, then, be based on a model in which fixed, self-contained elements are designed similar to the pixels of an image that one may zoom into or out of. In other words, stable expansion is only guaranteed when new elements—or to stay with the analogy, pixels—can be added without changing the underlying design.

On a clear day, the saying goes, theory can see forever. But in real life, things don't always play along as desired. The scalability of some things may grate against other things resisting or complicating expansion; scaling up from the small to the large may be upset at any point in time; and some resources, such as raw materials, may disappear during some stages of production only to become scalable at a later point in the supply chain. In other words, scalability is not the only story that can be told about SAMRO. In fact, when placed in the broader context of the South African creative industries, the rhetoric of scalability has all the markings of a fairy tale along the lines of "Little Red Riding Hood" (with or without the happy ending).

The emergence on a global scale of a new type of cultural industry in the mid-1990s, and its meteoric rise as the second-largest sector in the advanced economies of the US, EU, and Japan (and to a lesser extent China and the so-called tiger nations of Southeast Asia) at the beginning of the new century, has become the subject of a vast body of academic writing, trade books, and journalism. A cultural force in its own right, and like its subject matter global in scope, much of this work, at least initially, was wrapped in the most enchanted, techno-optimistic rhetoric. In contrast to the legacy industries of the previous century with their Fordist mode of production, Keynesian economic policies, and analog aesthetics, the new cultural economy would be one of innovation and experimentation, ushering in an era of boundless communicative possibilities and prosperity. And instead of dystopian industrial zones and monotonous suburbs encircling the decaying inner cities, these inner-city spaces themselves would experience a new dawn. Populated by a novel category of denizens known as the "creative class," the "urban" space would be home to a highly specialized workforce along with a wide range of complementary services and high-class cultural amenities providing a sense of local identity and a unique environment for the generation of cultural and symbolic capital.[59]

It fell to a small but influential group of theorists—many of whom trace their intellectual origin to the Frankfurt School and the neo-Marxists of the 1970s—to subject this Shangri-La to more nuanced scrutiny, one that is attuned both to the continuities of older forms of cultural reproduction as sites of domination and the discontinuities enabling the emergence of new, counterhegemonic cultural formations. The move in David Hesmondhalgh's classic study *The Cultural Industries* from a rather monolithic analytical stance in the first edition (2002) to a view of the cultural industries as multifaceted and ambivalent in the fourth edition (2019) is symptomatic of this shift.[60] In the first edition of his book, Hesmondhalgh still adhered to a Marxist dogma that artistic work was no different from other types of labor so that the cultural industries are essentially concerned with the management of creative labor. But in the fourth edition, this labor takes on a more indeterminate role as a "particular type of creativity" and a "manipulation of symbols."[61] In a similar vein, while the cultural industries of the twentieth century were seen as reflective of the broader inequalities inherent in the capitalist mode of production and the broad-based acquiescence to it made possible by the fetishization of the cultural commodity, the fourth edition of *Cultural Industries* softens this stance by foregrounding the "human experience" of culture.[62]

What does this mean for the theory of scalability? Although Hesmondhalgh largely refrains from a critical discussion of neoclassical economics and often employs flowery, universalizing language, his analysis and other similar work make it clear that neoclassical economic theory's mantra of scalability as the motor of cultural industry development misses a crucial point—namely, that the scalability of a project is never a homogenous process.⁶³ Nonscalability, to use Anna Tsing's term, not only has the potential to disrupt expansion, but it can also be the condition of possibility for scalability. And instead of being an obstacle, it can also be a consequence of scalability. The reason for this double-sidedness is that nonscalable forms differ from scalable ones in that they do not demand fixed parameters and uniformity as much as they are contingent on ever-changing relationships among their constituent parts, most notably the human factor. In other words, rather than the antithesis of scalability, nonscalability signifies the way scalability depends on "articulations with nonscalable forms even as it denies or erases them."⁶⁴

Consider, for instance, the independent contractor, work-for-hire practices that are the US music industry's signature form of managing musical labor and the ownership of the works originating from it. Such labor is low-cost because it is based on nonscalable forms of cultural production. An ethos of self-searching and self-fulfillment in combination with a high degree of mobility, semientrepreneurial habitus, or extended personal support networks mitigating the adverse effect of nonexistent social benefits combine in resisting the scalability of such production.⁶⁵ But on the other hand, the boundary-breaking scalability of cultural production in the twenty-first century can also produce niches of nonscalability that are not necessarily, or at least not immediately, absorbed into scalable business models. With their one-man operation and boutique flair, indie labels—which in South Africa account for a remarkable 60 percent of market share—are a case in point. Another is the meteoric rise of the Nigerian film industry, otherwise known as Nollywood, as a global player. This was made possible in part by a form of nonscalable labor better known as piracy. Instead of seeking to control this labor by suppressing it or otherwise destroying the pirate inventory, the industry simply took over the highly localized, personalized trading networks pirates had created. Similarly, live events are the product of the downscaling of the traditional cultural industries that has occurred in much of the contemporary postcolonial world in the wake of 1990s deregulation. What in a bygone era had been high points of national awakening, with stars such as Umm Kulthum or Youssou N'Dour officiating as masters of ceremonies, live events have become a bare necessity for artists' survival, involving the cultivation of nonscalable associations premised, inter alia, on highly flexible networks of personal relationships, a strong sense of place, and an aura of the here and now.⁶⁶

Strangely enough, little if any of the above appears to have found its way into South African scholarship. Available work tends to get caught up in a number of inconsistencies, ambiguities, and lacunae. For instance, the suite of five empirical studies commissioned by the South African Cultural Observatory (SACO), a research project launched by the Department of Arts and Culture, paints a picture of an economic sector on a path of recovery and transformation from the exclusionist cultural policies of the apartheid era to an inclusive sphere committed to the goals of the 2011 National Development Plan 2030 (NDP). These studies' primary focus, however, is not on microeconomics but on macroeconomic data pertaining to the South African trade of cultural goods and services, the size and diversity of employment in the cultural industries, the fiscal impact of these industries, and their implications for the NDP, and so on. Yet, when read more closely against the broader rationale of the NDP, these studies also give an idea as to how mainstream economic theory envisages the industries' future development and what conclusions, if any, government, entrepreneurs, and cultural workers might draw from their findings. Simply put, the SACO studies reflect the mix of inflated and misguided conjectures and policy prescriptions put forward in the NDP and thereby, perhaps inadvertently, weaken some of their own critical thrust. Again, labor is the fault line here.

In essence, the NDP is based on the notion that the goal of adding 11 million new jobs in a first phase (2013–2018) will entail the deregulation of the labor market, the development of small and medium-sized enterprises and "expanding firms" in the service sector, and "mass entrepreneurship" as the main engines of job creation and growth. In a third phase, beginning in 2024, this strategy will ultimately lead to a full-grown knowledge economy in 2030. This vision—which, if not delusional from the outset, already fell behind schedule shortly after its proclamation—conflicts with a more traditional, though no less questionable, view espoused by the country's leading labor unions such as the Congress of South African Trade Unions (COSATU) and their political allies in academia and the progressive movements that prioritize the reindustrialization of the economy by expanding the manufacturing industry and transforming the traditional minerals sector.[67] More troublingly, though, underlying this strategy is the tacit assumption that the bulk of these 11 million jobs will not only be low-quality, low-paid work but will also suppress entry-level wages for young workers.

Comparing this unsettling agenda with the findings of the SACO reports makes it apparent that, apart from domestic service and other low-paying jobs in the service sector, workers in the cultural industries stand to bear the brunt of the NDP strategy. Thus, one study found that as recently as 2017, just under 50 percent of cultural occupations in the cultural industries (which comprise not only core sectors such as film, music, and performing arts but also cultural heritage) were formally employed, while a little over 40 percent were informal.[68] Of the latter, the vast majority were black small business owners who had lower levels of education and chose self-employment because they were unable to secure employment in the formal sector.[69] These disparities intensify when set in relation to income levels. Although cultural occupation workers on average earn more than noncultural, support workers, little more than 22 percent and roughly a third of the former still fall into the bottom two income brackets of R2500 or less and R2501–R6000, respectively.[70] In view of these facts, the difference between the SACO studies and the National Development Plan boils down to a series of simple questions: If the former allows us to zoom in on some of the darker aspects of the state of the cultural industries, will the NDP perpetuate these trouble areas as the new normal going into the future?[71] With the South African cultural industries continuing to be sharply divided over key issues such as security of employment and levels of income, how will SAMRO, as a prominent player within those industries, square its fixation on scalability with its commitment to equity and diversity without reconsidering its business model? Bearing in mind Tsing's reminder that the difference between scalable and nonscalable designs cannot be placed a priori on a normative scale of good or bad, is an anthropology in law forever doomed to choose between plague and cholera, deregulation and regulation, monopoly and competition?[72] Or, again paraphrasing Tsing, if Marxist political economy looked to the scalability of labor as a means to destabilize capitalism (the largest scalable project of the last several hundred years), and conversely, neoclassical economics conceives of the scalability of labor as the exact opposite of destabilizing capitalism, what alternative forms of transformative agency might be imagined? And to what extent will un-scaled, diverse, and yet economically and socially viable forms of cultural reproduction be part of such interventions?

As it turns out, *les jeux sont faits*.

Match and Link: Interstructures of Information

"Let's start with Cula Sibone," Sibongile Gwangwa says and places the first of some twenty so-called cue sheets we must process in front of me. Gwangwa is part of a team of seven workers in another part of the organization called Documentation. As a section of the Operations Department, Documentation staff are tasked with researching and documenting the use of SAMRO

Cue Sheet Sibongile 6/26/2014

PROGRAM TITLE:	CULA SIBONE
INSERT:	
EPISODE No.	44
TAPE BARCODE NUMBER:	170694P
BROADCAST DATE:	22 July 2013
REBROADCAST DATE:	
REBROADCAST DATE:	
REBROADCAST DATE:	
REBROADCAST DATE:	
PRODUCTION COMPANY:	CONNECT TV
CONTACT PERSON	ANET WEGMAN
CONTACT TELEPHONE NUMBERS	011 446 7000/072 742 6931

DUR MIN / SEC	DESCRIPTION OF MUSIC (instrumental, background, vocal or signature tune)	TITLE OF COMPOSITION AND ARRANGEMENT	NAME OF COMPOSER AND ARRANGEMENT	LIVE / RE-PRODUCTION CD NUMBER	NAME OF PUBLISHER	RECORD/CD NUMBER
16"		Logo	Sipho Mphulanyane, Morena Sefatsa			
15"	Backing Track	Lighters up	Lil Kim	3	Universal Music	The Naked Truth

FIGURE 5.3 Mzansi Magic cue sheet. Courtesy of SAMRO.

repertoire on South African television by entering the data from the cue sheets into a database on SAMRO's platform Zeus. Named after the supreme God of ancient Greece on account of its "overarching and powerful nature," the software was developed by Accenture and only became operational in 2013 after SAMRO's own mainframe-based system, in place since 1994, had become out of date.[73] In contrast to Greek mythology, however, the world of information platforms knows no hierarchies. Zeus is part of roughly two dozen nodes within a platform called CIS-Net.[74] Each node is identified as belonging to one of three categories of societies: individual or local societies (such as SAMRO); regional collecting societies spanning several societies in several countries (such as LatinNet, the partner network of the Spanish Sociedad General de Autores y Editores); or CISAC's Works Information Database (WID) documenting international works. Within CIS-Net, the databases for musical works information (MWI), audio-visual information (AVI), interested party information (IPI), and agreements repository (AGM) (2007) are the most widely used, combining data for over 150 million musical works provided by 122 societies for performance rights as part of their daily internal operations.

Cula Sibone (Let's See You Sing) is a game show on the satellite entertainment channel Mzansi Magic, where aspiring singers are challenged to show off their vocal skills and knowledge of music (or lack thereof). For some reason, bits and pieces of the program's basic information, such as its name, episode number, and broadcast date, had been previously loaded into the database, and we only have to update these with the current episode's number and other details like the station's ID and South Africa's CISAC country code before continuing with the more arduous task of transferring the title of the composition, names of the composer/authors and publishers, and the duration of the clip being used. There are, however, numerous blanks on the sheet that I wonder about. The name of the composer or publisher is missing, or, in some cases, the same clip may have different track numbers. Issues like these do not carry the same weight. Gwangwa reassures me, "They are picked up later by the Query & Resolution Department."

At times, I catch myself peering over at Carol Louw's desk. One of sixteen staff in the Music Usage division of the Operations Department, her job is to match and link work title and author on every work that has been played on South African radio. To this effect, she receives what is called a journal—a playlist returned each day by every station in the country. I assume that it's easy work, but after working with her, I realize that it is not. The problem, Louw explains, is that for every song played, there may be different authors, rights owners, or even IP numbers. To match the right information to the right title, she accesses Zeus and sometimes also goes on the internet to search for the name of a composer. To give an example of the steps that must be followed, let us take a look at the January 13, 2014, journal for Jacaranda FM, South Africa's largest independent station. The song we need to match and link is "How Come You Don't Call Me," written by Prince. The search involves more than what a Mac user might do by hitting the ⌘ and F keys. It entails a long succession of menus and submenus that I have to navigate before I arrive at the menu for "How Come You Don't Call Me." The first port of call is "Usage Journals," a page listing all radio stations licensed to SAMRO. I select Jacaranda FM and then proceed to the submenu "Overview," which gives me the option to refine my search further under the next submenus "Lines," "Journal Type," and "Import Date." The one I am interested in is "Lines," because it allows me to sift through the more than two thousand plays Prince's tune had received on that January day by opening the next set of submenus called "All Songs" and "Check Everything." Here, under the parameter R 60 for "Recording," the search brings up the names of Alicia Keys and saxophonist Joshua Redman, two of the better-known artists who have covered the song. But the search for the exact title under the "Work" parameter W 60 yields different entries with different IP and ISWC numbers—an international code for the identification of musical works administered by CISAC—for different recordings of the same title. To be really sure, I check the internet, where I find Universal as the publisher and rights holder. A similar case is "Hit'em Up Style (Oops!)," an R&B title recorded by Blu Cantrell and written by Dallas Austin. Here, too, the search not only produces numerous similar-sounding titles for different covers but also different role codes such as composer/arranger (CA) and publisher (E) assigned to these titles. But another search on the internet and Zeus confirms that the copyright is owned by Arista Records, a subpublisher of Sony Music.

The journey of our two songs is not quite over, though. Having traversed a fragile web of intersecting pathways, from the restaurant to the report sheet and the license agreement to Zeus and its quasi-magical capacity for matching it to every conceivable type of reference point from the name of the composer to a collecting society at the other end of the globe, the most important part is yet to come: the distribution of royalties and very raison d'être of SAMRO. As SAMRO will invoice Jacaranda FM for every second played of "How Come" and "Hit'em Up," the question is: Who will get how much from the revenue pool building up over each cycle of quarterly payments? This is where another round of matching begins, handled by two further divisions within the Operations Department—Copyright and Quality Control. Although the time I spent in each of these divisions was relatively short, the workflow in the first two follows the same match-and-link logic described above, except that in Copyright the works identified by Carol, Thobile, Fikile, and their colleagues in Documentation are matched to the correct copyright owners. For instance, Elwin Ngubane, one of five workers in Copyright, is tasked with what in SAMRO-speak is called "activation"—matching the composer-title pair to the composer and publisher and the portion or "share" of the royalty revenue generated for the performance of the work they own. As an example, take the R&B song "Priceless." It has four composers: Harvey Mason, Eric Dawkins, Antonio Dixon, and Damon Thomas. But all four are simultaneously listed as publishers and record producers. As such, the quartet can theoretically not only be co-owners of the work, but they can also have signed an agreement where only one is the owner and the others figure as publishers or producers. In addition, these different roles, and depending on the agreements that have been concluded between them or other publishers and record producers, have a significant bearing on the distribution of the royalty revenue. Is the contract a standard copublishing agreement where the composer(s) and the publisher are co-owners and have agreed on a certain split of the royalties? Or is it an agreement whereby the publisher is the sole owner and the royalties are split 50/50? Pursuant to this normal split, may our four composers' collective share of 50 percent have to be divided equally among them? And further complicating Elwin's job, what about the fact that copyright is divisible, that is, that different exclusive rights such as the radio broadcast right, the right of public performance, the mechanical right, and so on, may be transferred or assigned to different owners? The question is an important one not only because these rights are administered by different collecting societies in different countries but also as a result of the method by which the royalties due on these rights may be paid out: either directly by the relevant collecting society—a method called "at source"—or on a receipts basis, for instance, by the publisher or any subpublisher(s), as the case may be. (The latter scenario inevitably results in additional administration fees and, ultimately, reduced composer royalties.) And thus, even though SAMRO only administers the public performance right and pays the applicable shares directly to the composer and the publisher, matching the right copyright owner to the exact right, for instance, the performance right, is of the essence. Clearly, coordinating all these data across countless menus, submenus, and mouse clicks to form an almost irreversible concatenation determining the exact amount of royalties to be distributed puts a formidable strain on Elwin as he tries to fill his daily quota (or "stats," to use another industry term for data sets such as the day's cue sheets or list of work titles like "Priceless") of a minimum of thirty-five "activations."

At Quality Control or QC, as Brigitta Hauser and her team call the division, it's all about double-checking that the right people are being paid during distribution by identifying any suspicious-looking operations or actions having taken place anywhere in the system. To do so, they reverse the match-link chain, as it were, by backtracing the course each and every song took across all the other departments prior to showing up on Hauser's computer screen. There are essentially two pathways along which this process evolves. One departs from the demand side, that is, from the capturing process in Licensing and Sales to the cue sheets, usage reports, and so on processed by Documentation. The second pathway from what one might call the supply side consists of the lines mentioned above, that is, the linkages workers like Elwin establish between copyright owners and their registered works, IP numbers, royalty shares, and so on. In an ideal world, both pathways would merge seamlessly where each second or other unit of measuring performance, such as the seating capacity of the Moyo restaurant or the car show, translates into a perfect 1:1 match between the owner(s) and user(s) of the work performed. But in the real world of performance rights administration at SAMRO and other PROs, this convergence of data frequently does not end in a perfect match. Typical questions, or what QC staff refer to as "challenges" that arise on the supply side, for instance, are: Do the royalties for "Bad" have to be paid out to U2 instead of to the rights holder of Michael Jackson's song of the same title? Is Jackson's publisher receiving 100 percent of the publisher's share, or is someone also claiming a part? Has the publisher provided a deed of assignment to support his claims on the author? Are the IPI numbers correct? Or on the demand side: Has the client been visited and the application form forwarded to Sales and captured in the system? Has the client been invoiced, and, if so, did they pay? Where there was no payment, have the client's premises been reinspected? Did the owner change and the old owner canceled the license without paying any outstanding fees? In which case, has the matter been handed over to Legal for further action? To identify any points of potential ruptures and glitches that may have occurred along these pathways and to determine what corrections have to be made and by what department or division, QC staff draw on two techniques: an elaborate, eight-page flow chart that visualizes the steps that must be followed to trace the mismatch back to its source, and a QC report that lists the specific lines where an error was detected.

The word *flow*, I realize after having examined some of the QC reports, is a bit of an euphemism. It is more an endless zigzagging between QC, Documentation, and other divisions. Of the nineteen lines that need to be checked per each work each day, only a small percentage ever passes muster. "We can QC 100 percent on almost everything," Hauser explains pulling up the QC report for June 2, 2014, "except on copyright and cue sheets," she adds, referring to two of the admittedly more important items determining usage and copyright ownership. "There we can only check 20 percent of the work that's been done in terms of matching and linking. The volumes are so enormous, it is absolutely impossible." The consequences of unresolved errors, apart from a steady stream of complaints by members about unpaid royalties flooding her email account, can be severe. "If I can't clear up the errors, it affects my bonus." And then there is the problem of performance management for the rest of the staff. "We can see exactly who is not performing as they should, and our COO looks at our spreadsheets on a weekly basis." "That's pretty tight," I remark. "Yes, it has to be," Hauser responds.

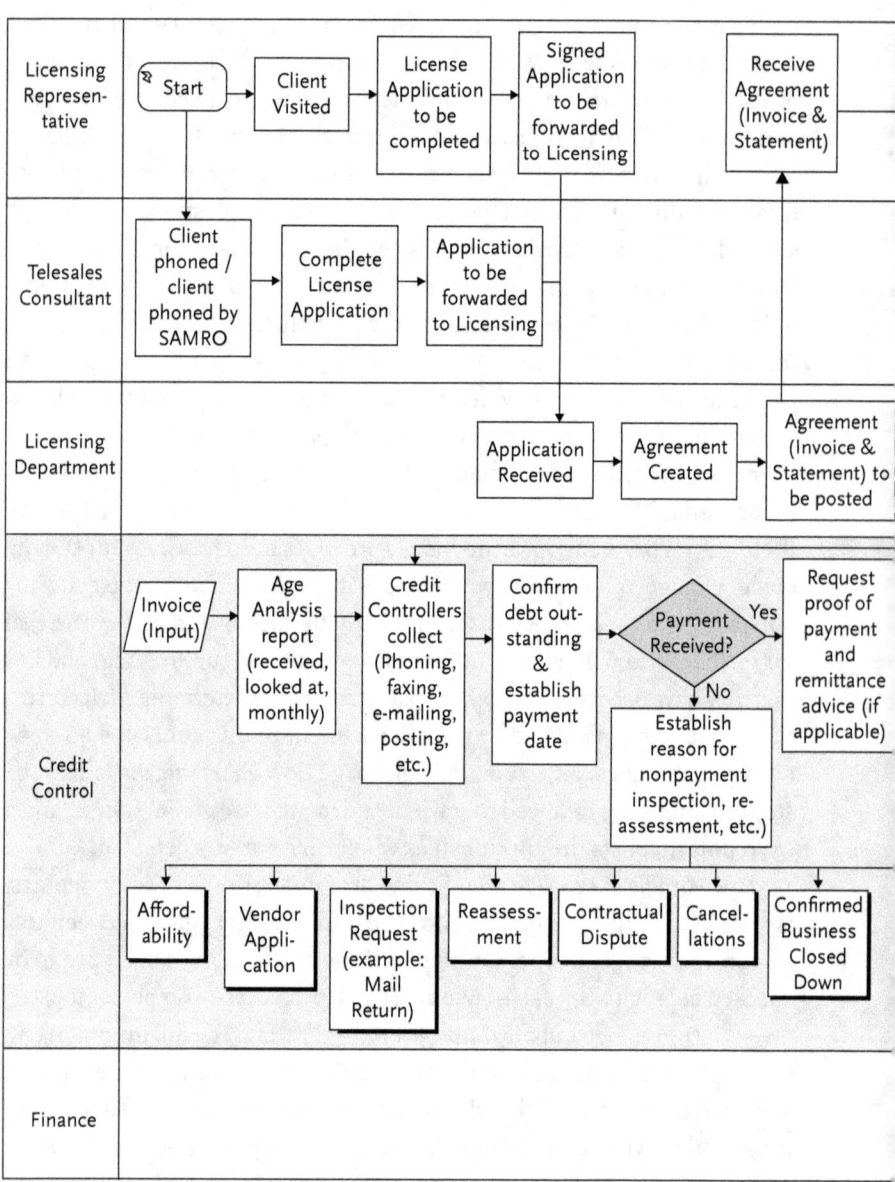

FIGURE 5.4 Credit control flow chart. Courtesy of SAMRO.

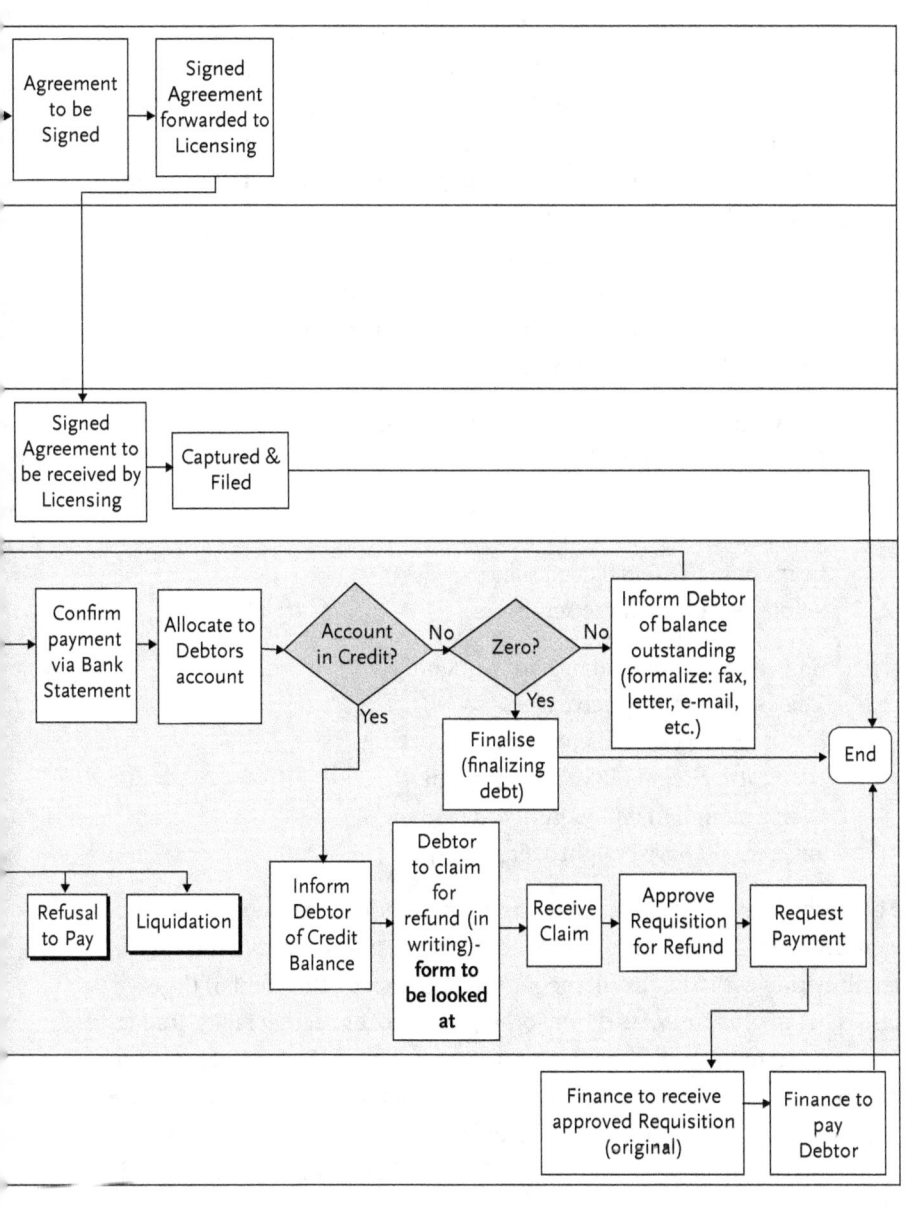

"That's why QC sits on a different floor. You can imagine the intimidation that might take place. We had instances where staff threatened other staff because performance bonuses are based on these figures. Hopefully we get a better culture because we want to get it right, we want to avoid all the rework. It is the mindset, you know. We don't want people to think that they are only earning money. It is also about other people's money; like a composer who doesn't earn a monthly salary as they do."

On my way back to Music Usage, I can't help thinking of *difela* poet Tsokolo Lecheko's verse about a miner who complains about "people" saying that poverty is eliminated by hard work.

> Ha e le bona bo ntsoa ke ho sebetsa feela.
> Ke leshano; ba ea re thetsa.
> Le hoja ho ea ka ho sebetsa boa ka,
> Le li khomo, nka be ke li rekile,
> Le mohoma ke lema ka o lesiba-
> Sefofane, ke kalama se sefubelu!

> (Poverty is eliminated by hard work only.
> This is a lie, they deceive us.
> If this went in accordance with my working,
> Even cattle, I could have bought them,
> Even a plough that ploughs like a feather.
> Yes, I would have bought a jet plane!)[75]

My readers may well find much of the above, if not plain tedious, a distraction from the larger picture of SAMRO's mixed track record of efficiency in combination with a history of inequity. But, to repeat, the point of the exercise is not to censure SAMRO from on-high for those apparent faults. Rather, I ask by what register of ethnographic inquiry one might best account for and question the way routine work processes such as the ones described above may naturalize such deficiencies. By looking for the "work involved in making it easy," as Bowker and Star suggest?[76] The tack that I adopt in this chapter is ambiguously poised between the ethnographic appetite for depth, meaning, practice, and the singular, or what Bowker famously called "infrastructural inversion," on the one hand, and the kind of reduction, abstraction, or "distant reading" that Franco Moretti once shockingly recommended as an alternative model of literary analysis, on the other.[77] In other words, I consider narratives such as those above—heavily condensed though they on one level are—as an approximation of how one might keep track of the manner by which the migration of data across different processes, technologies of inscription, and systems of classification, standardization, delegation, and certification is more than just descriptive of already existing identities and relations of cultural reproduction and ownership. The thicket of pages, menus, sub-menus, sub-sub menus, and fields constituting Zeus and its intersection with CISAC databases also has a performative, operative function in that it at one and the same time reaffirms the integrity of the system and defines the range of available options for future modification. It is through this inherently ambiguous "articulation work" that it generates both inclusion and exclusion and affords the formation of collectives that encompass both techno-informatic and socio-moral ways of ordering the world around us.[78]

This becomes perhaps clearer when viewing the matching and linking in the context of current debates about infrastructure in anthropology and the humanities more broadly.[79] Infrastructures have long been an integral part of the modern imagination. More than just pipes, wires, or roads, infrastructure from the early eighteenth century has become a cornerstone of modern state formation and its attendant ideologies of progress, national identity, and economic growth. In more recent times, infrastructure has resurfaced as part of the attempt to query these narratives, using it as a location from which to explore the articulation of technological domains with a variety of institutional and political actors, modalities of governance, knowledge practices, and legal systems. Infrastructure, then, is a profoundly relational category. Not quite an underneath of other things, as the term's etymology implies, but more an intermediate space where those things are sedimented or suspended like a road on a suspension bridge, infrastructure might more properly be referred to as a kind of in-betweenness or interstructure. Its chief utility for the ethnographic method is that it defamiliarizes standard notions of efficiency and seamlessness and forces a slightly different analytic from both modernist myths and Marxist-structuralist views of the base that determines the ideological, cultural, and politico-legal superstructure. Such an analytic is at once cultural, material, and political. It highlights the frictions and convergences between micro and macro worlds, and it explores the intersection between the discontinuous, transitory phases of capitalist development and its long-standing continuities. Before anything else, though, the study of interstructures allows the ethnographer to focus on the performative functions of an information system such as SAMRO's Zeus. Interstructures offer a vantage point from which to comprehend the subtle translations and discursive moves that must constantly be rehearsed when a technological domain encounters another domain, and the ensuing valences participate in the formation of techno-political, techno-scientific, and techno-administrative ensembles.[80]

Additionally, in South Africa the concept of interstructure has taken on a rather more moral ring, namely in the form of what became known as service delivery protests. Starting in the early 2000s as large-scale, violent attacks on council offices and other public infrastructures in the informal settlements and townships of Gauteng, these protests were the first major expression of discontent with the government's apparent inability to make good on its promise of change in key areas of basic infrastructure development, such as housing, sanitation, and electricity. Over time, the protests spread to include the withholding payment of utilities, bypassing and hacking water and electricity meters, and setting up *izinyoka* (literally, snakes), and illegal electricity connections that wind around people's *jondolo* (shacks) like cobwebs. At the same time, service delivery protests have come to stand in for a much broader agenda through which, as Antina von Schnitzler explains in her *Democracy's Infrastructure*, "conventional and normative accounts of the political as existing in a separate domain, marked by 'free' circulation, rules and norms of 'civil' engagement" are unsettled.[81]

Setting these larger conflicts in relation to SAMRO's Zeus may seem far-fetched. After all, what is at stake here is not, at least not primarily, the circulation of life's basic necessities. And yet, the aggregation and classification of data can have serious material repercussions and provoke vociferous objection, as we have seen at the start of this chapter in the context of the Mhlaba/DP fracas. Similar to the larger service delivery protests spilling over into other terrains of contestation, it elicits questions beyond nonpayment of royalties, such as creative justice, legal protection for adaptations of works in the public domain, the economic rationale of business models, flaws of corporate governance, and so on. At the same time, however, Zeus is situated within its own microcosm, one in which the pragmatic, social "doubles" said to underpin ethnographies of interstructures do not seem to apply. Thus, there is no disconnect between Zeus and the practical realization of its objectives that may even remotely resemble the proliferation of ineffectual bureaucracies or bridges that go nowhere, usually observed throughout the postcolonial world. Nor does the argument that interstructures are largely invisible and only noticed in moments of malfunction or total breakdown seem to hold entirely. For functional or dysfunctional, Zeus is remarkably good at what it does either way. Or rather, it is good at being Zeus, namely, to keep invisibility and visibility in precarious balance. Like all information systems, its invisibility is predicated on the ability to enable judgments of equivalence and comparability by interlinking data dispersed across time and space.[82] Data may migrate holus-bolus to other data sets and networks. But they also may contract or agglutinate into clusters of similar or mutually informing data, thus constituting independent subnetworks. And they live or—to play on Walter Pater's famous dictum about art aspiring to the condition of music—they aspire to the condition of seamlessness; where a composer's name is matched to song titles that link to a cue sheet that connects to a radio station's playlist that mirrors the week's Top 20 that feeds into the amount of the publisher's royalties that loops back to the composer's membership tier and distribution rate that meets up with their bank account number, and so on ad infinitum. Consequently, sets of interlinked data resemble music insofar as they have a tendency to erase the distinction between form and content. And unlike older forms of data aggregation, where form and content could easily get in each other's way, data systems from Excel to the gargantuan datasets of Big Data thrive on the convergence of form and content, technically achieved through so-called relational variables or tables that allow the addition of new data, as well as the reorganization of existing data, without changing the underlying structure.

But Zeus can also become visible because data, contrary to conventional wisdom, are never raw; they take on some of the heterogeneity of the temporal and spatial contexts they traverse even when they retain their ability to afford comparison. And contrary to the notion that heterogeneity impedes comparability, it actually affords it. It is this interchangeability in immutability that imbues interstructures and databases such as Zeus with their otherworldly power of actio ad distans and, even more uncannily, the ability to reproduce and stabilize themselves as durable, virtually incontrovertible representations of a complex, rapidly evolving reality.

Notes on a Scandal: Auditing SAMRO

> Although the Board was misled by Mr Dlamini as outlined above, we find that the Board did not exercise adequate stewardship over this investment in that the Board seemed to be too trusting of the representations made to them without adequate Board intervention and decisive action when the investment seemed not to make sense afterwards.

The above paragraph is from the conclusion of the *Forensic Investigation Report into the United Arab Emirates Investment* submitted to SAMRO in August 2018 by the South African consulting and auditing firm SekelaXabiso.[83] The report is the second of two documents (the first one was found to be unsatisfactory for reasons explained further below) commissioned by the SAMRO executive as part of its attempt to deal with the fallout of the above-mentioned, ill-fated investment three years prior in the United Arab Emirates—easily the biggest scandal in the history of the organization. I begin this last section of the chapter by narrating the sequence of events as seen through the eyes of the report. Reflecting further on its lacunae, silences, and consequences for SAMRO's future, I will then end by contextualizing these "notes on a scandal" in the implementation of some of the report's recommendations and the reinvention of the collective through a makeover of its image as a responsible business.

The tragedy or, better perhaps, farce takes place in four acts. The first begins on June 26, 2014, a day after my departure from SAMRO. At a meeting of the board of directors, CEO Dlamini was given the go-ahead to set up a collecting society in Dubai with the UAE government as a partner and shareholder. Dlamini said that SAMRO "would receive a negotiated administration fee on all collections which would help to grow the organisation's revenue and also ensure that the members in South Africa would start to receive money for the usage of their music in that region."[84] The only wrinkle in the plan, as board member and singer-songwriter (and arranger of yet another adaptation of "The Lion Sleeps Tonight") John Edmond was quick to point out, was that the UAE did not have a copyright act, a point confirmed in a subsequent meeting with a UAE-based law firm. As with any drama, this meeting provides the audience with a sense of the main dramatis personae and conflict lines along which the action over the next three acts would unfold, to wit: CEO Sipho Dlamini; Chairman of the Board Rev. Sibiya, a gospel star and composer of classics such as "God is a Rock," director of the mechanical rights organization CAPASSO, and CEO of such companies as One Gospel TV and audio and postproduction studios Urban Rhythm Factory and Mtommbo Audio Solution; board member Edmond, representing a minority of skeptics; and a coterie of largely offstage supporting acts in the UAE.

Act 2 begins with another board meeting in February 2015, where two of those supporting acts made their first entrance: Yaser AlJabal and Hamzeh Khalaf. Touted as well-traveled, experienced IP and antipiracy experts, they presented the board with a summary of their two-month research of the "strong legal framework" in the IP environment, "zero tolerance of corruption," and the growing market of music usage platforms in the UAE. They would also go on to function as crucial go-betweens and owners of

IPR (Intellectual Property Management), a UAE company that would later acquire a 51 percent holding in the future Arab Emirates Musical Rights Organization. As in earlier board meetings, questions about whether AlJabal and Khalaf had "the required authority, when representing and liaising with Government on behalf of a Private entity," were swiftly brushed aside with assurances that they had "access to the top guys." The cast of actors complete with no resolution taken, Dlamini announced that management had engaged AlJabal and Khalaf's services to "assist with the organization's entry into the UAE."[85]

Act 3: In a meeting on June 25, 2015, Dlamini briefed the board on the permissions he had obtained from ASACP, BMI, SACEM, and PRS to collect royalties on their behalf. In reality, however, the almost identical sounding requests he sent to these organizations either went unanswered or were declined pending further clarification of the legal framework. As in previous board meetings, no resolution was taken on this briefing either. These irregularities notwithstanding, in October 2015, Yaser AlJabal, acting on behalf of IPR, and Hamzeh Khalaf, acting on behalf of SAMRO and pursuant to a power of attorney issued by SAMRO, signed a memorandum and articles of association stating that they agreed to form a civil works company called AEMRO Intellectual Property Rights Organization, with Dlamini serving as CEO and chairman of the board, and SAMRO COO Bronwen Harty and CFO Gregory Zoghby doubling as AEMRO COO and CFO, respectively. Khalaf would serve as managing director and vice-chairman of the board, while AlJabal would have to settle for the position of chief compliance officer. And to round it all off, an office was set up in the posh Aurora Tower in the Dubai Media City.

What emerges clearly during this act is Dlamini's pivotal role as the main force driving the plot by relying on what in ancient Greek theater was known as the messenger report. Yet, while in that tradition, the role of the messenger reporting on past events that have taken place offstage is to maintain the unity of time, place, and action demanded of classical playwrights, in this context, it was to create more of a sense of immediacy and dynamic leadership. Perhaps it is only logical that after having pulled off this stage-effect, Dlamini, along with Harty and Zoghby, exited the stage in March 2016 to work for Universal, Rev. Sibiya stepped in as acting CEO, and following a short intermission, the curtain rises again in May of 2017 on the fourth and final act: the denouement. However, departing from theater tradition, the action this time does not begin in Johannesburg but in Paris at the CISAC headquarters.

Since its incorporation in the fall of 2015, AEMRO had not only been unsuccessful in obtaining a license from the Ministry of Economy to operate in the UAE, but its efforts to be admitted as a member of CISAC also ran aground in large part due to Dlamini having failed to involve CISAC before committing to the investment—a fact allegedly unknown to Sibiya and revealed only at the eleventh hour after SekelaXabiso submitted an interim report ahead of the AGM in 2018.[86] In any case, when contact was eventually established in 2017, CISAC reiterated what SAMRO and AEMRO officials should have known all along had they done their homework and consulted with UAE authorities or, for that matter, had taken a quick look at the article "Collective Licensing of Music in the UAE" in the *Licensing Journal*, the leading periodical on licensing practice in intellectual property, computer technology, and entertainment law.[87] Provisional CISAC membership, the CISAC secretariat informed Sibiya, could only be granted if AEMRO produced documentation showing that "they have initiated the administrative procedures towards obtaining the license."[88] In the end, AEMRO's claim that there is no documented application procedure for that type of license in the UAE and that UAE authorities, in a last-minute meeting, had admitted as much, failed to avert the impending disaster. On June 19, 2017, Sibiya informed the board of CISAC's negative decision, but not without adding in characteristic struggle lingo that British, French, Canadian, and American societies had been "colluding because they want the territory [UAE] and . . . were trying to delay SAMRO for as long as possible, or until SAMRO withdraws its application."[89]

With ASCAP and the other major PROs having cold-shouldered Dlamini & Co., and CISAC's decision not to admit AEMRO, it should have dawned on all but the most fervent proponents of the Dubai adventure that a major overhaul of the company's corporate structure was the order of the day. Instead, what followed was a poorly orchestrated game of musical chairs in combination with a tepid effort at damage control. After a SWOT (strengths, weaknesses, opportunities, and threats) analysis was conducted on June 26, Nothando Migogo took over as CEO on July 1, 2017, while Rev. Sibiya resumed his role as chairman of the board. Finally, on September 8, 2017, the board resolved that "AEMRO be shut down in Dubai . . . and that the partners in Dubai be given notice of termination of their employment contracts immediately."[90]

Lest the readers think that this put an end to the whole drama and the curtain would fall on an audience rubbing their eyes in utter disbelief of what they had just witnessed, we should remember that, much like in ancient theater, what begins with flawed decisions tends to end in catastrophe—for there is an epilogue on the proscenium, as it were. Shortly after Migogo informed the Dubai partners that she would terminate their contracts, AlJabal and Khalaf reminded her of the contracts Dlamini had signed with them. Unsurprisingly, not only did neither the board nor the Risk Committee have any knowledge of those contracts, but there also turned out to be two different types of contracts with different notice periods—an indefinite contract with thirty days' notice and a five-year fixed-term contract. In the end, a settlement was agreed upon to the tune of $560,000 payable to AlJabal and Khalaf. And to fill the cup to the brim, Khalaf also presented Migogo with no fewer than two lease agreements for AEMRO's office space in Dubai Media City without any indication of these rental fees actually ever having been paid. All in all, the adventure cost SAMRO R47,136 364 ($2.8 million), more than 65 percent going to salaries and consulting fees.

Two years after the settlement, after-shocks of the Dubai quake continue to ripple through SAMRO and, indeed, across the entire South African PRO-sphere, foreshadowing a long, drawn-out era of soul-searching, shake-ups, certification, and appeasement. In the interim, the only thing certain at the time of writing is that Dlamini and the old board continue denying any wrongdoing and the fact that SAMRO, in the fall of 2019, announced that due to "cash flow challenges" caused by the SABC defaulting on its licensing fees, workers' bonuses would not be paid for the financial year ending in June 2019.[91] So we are left with this question: What exactly did the Sekela-Xabiso audit accomplish? The report concludes its findings with a summary of thirty-six points. Among other things, these include the assertion that Dlamini and his UAE sidekicks failed to adequately research the UAE rights environment and that the salaries paid to AlJabal and Khalaf were improperly inflated. To complete the string of accusations, Dlamini not only failed to ensure that rights with other collecting societies were secured, but he also concealed the fact that the five-year contract with AlJabal and Khalaf did not exist from the beginning but only emerged a posteriori "for the purposes of extorting a huge and unjustified settlement." But the board did not escape unscathed either. It failed miserably by not properly exercising its oversight responsibility under the terms of South Africa's King IV Code on Good Corporate Governance and s 76 of the Companies Act. Likewise, instead of urging board members to take that responsibility seriously, Sibiya was content to act "on the very direct instructions of the Board."[92]

Predictably, Dlamini was singled out in subsequent meetings and press releases as the sole culprit, while Sibiya and the board's acquiescence was passed over in silence. Even more troubling, no comments were made at all on the eleven recommendations concluding the report. Apart from rather utopian proposals, such as the recovery of wasted funds from Dlamini or an inquiry into the potential of unjustified enrichment and false representation by the UAE government, there are three recommendations that are salient for this chapter's main argument about the formation of collectives of worlding. Under 9.2, for instance, the report recommends establishing a threshold of financial commitments subject to review and approval by the board. And in 9.8, the auditor suggests the formulation of an investment policy in order to regulate future investments decisions. Finally, 9.10 recommends regular board training on corporate governance. As we shall see further below, neither of these proposals resurfaced in the "Three Pillar 2020 SAMRO Strategic Plan" that was announced with much fanfare, beyond boilerplate such as the "optimization of SAMRO's current business to ensure efficiencies in all areas of the business."

How, then, might an anthropology of auditing go about disentangling the complex web of valences interconnecting all these actors? At its most basic, it would need to examine how techniques of accounting and financial management, traditionally held to be the turf of accounting firms or Taylorist scientific management and its contemporary reincarnation in managerialism, may be better conceptualized as part of a broader culture of corporate governance that emerged in the aftermath of post–Cold War deregulation and the downsizing of the welfare state in the advanced economies of the Global North—and, indeed, of what little of such welfare may have previously existed in the Global South soon thereafter. Other than describing some of these "audit cultures" in rather broad strokes, anthropologists, along with a handful of critical accounting scholars, have been slow to tackle the pervasiveness of auditing in the present moment of global uncertainty by tracking its workings in specific ethnographic settings.[93] Nonetheless, there are at least three general themes that can be filtered from the literature that has emerged so far and that resonate with the findings of this chapter. The first and possibly most uncontroversial of these is that audits manage uncertainty by making idiosyncratic and potentially questionable management practices legible within a universal framework of governance. Intimately tied to this is a shift in the way capitalism reproduces itself after the end of the bipolar world order. Instead of the managerial posture adopted by a benevolent welfare state in place since the end of World War II, governing has turned into full-blown governmentality. Henceforth, images of hyperactive public and private organizations in a state of perpetual self-awareness would become the measure of the responsible citizen; permanent self-calibration and internalization of external performance standards replace the Weberian protestant work ethic calling the individual to a life of productivity and virtue. And keywords such as *efficiency, opportunity,* and *liability* would sustain the fractured narratives that people use to represent themselves to one another.[94] In the issue at hand, this stabilizing role is plainly visible in the way SekelaXabiso highlighted the rejection of SAMRO's overtures by CISAC and the major PROs as being out of sync with that framework.

The second theme highlighted by critical studies of auditing could be called the production of compliance. Viewing auditing as an active process of achieving compliance instead of simply working toward compliance as something that is already fully articulated, it becomes possible to focus on the contradictions, interstices, and hidden parts of a practice that tends to be cast as a smooth translation from the findings of the forensic investigation into a set of solutions that are aligned with the new orthodoxy of corporate governance, such as transparency or due diligence. Stated differently, audits do not operate in a given field of knowledge; they enact and legitimate it.[95] That is why an anthropology of audit cultures will need to query the assumption that compliance with codes of conduct, policies, regulatory frameworks, or legislation will quasi-automatically result in compliant outcomes and replace it with a robust examination of what Michael Power calls auditing's "essentially obscure" epistemic foundation.[96] Instead of positioning audits as an alternative to state interference or relying on markets as offering the most effective restraints on managerial power, it is the input-output black box that should be at the center of that effort.

There are several ways one might go about this reorientation of audit studies toward an analytic of what Emma Crewe and Chris Mowles term the "audit function."[97] One of these—the third theme shared by most observers—is by attending to what I call the circularity of auditing. Audits are the cause and effect of themselves. They reproduce themselves as they create a need for further rounds of investigation or "second-order" audits.[98] In some cases, auditors may even become auditees themselves. For instance, Boyce Mkhize, the lead forensic investigator and author of the report on the Dubai investment, found himself in hot water in 2015 after an audit of the embattled parastatal Mpumalanga Economic Growth Agency alleged that during his tenure as CEO of the body, it was rife with corruption and that Mkhize himself was personally implicated in a slew of irregularities—from hiring service providers without tax clearances to signing off on contracts with business partners who had registered more than one company to benefit multiple times on tenders.[99]

In SAMRO's case, the circular flow is rooted in several factors. On the one hand, auditors and auditees are embroiled in webs of mutual dependence because their career paths frequently intersect. The current CEO, Mark Rosin, for instance, is a lawyer and music industry veteran who also trained at international auditing firm PricewaterhouseCoopers, which for many years was responsible for SAMRO's financial audits. But on the other hand, while these relationships may help to maintain a level of mutual honesty and trust required for things such as the procurement of forensic evidence, the absence of such trust is also the prerequisite of the audit in the first place. Furthermore, these tightly knit networks partially mirror the intricately interwoven patron-client relationships typical of the very industry they are supposed to investigate. For instance, Dlamini and Khalaf were old acquaintances from the time Dlamini was vice president at Creative Kingdom Records, a subsidiary of international design and architecture firm Creative Kingdom, responsible for landmark buildings in the Sun City Resort, among other things.[100] As for AlJabal, the ink hadn't even dried on SAMRO's announcement about ending the AEMRO partnership when he and Khalaf were at it again. On November 17, 2017, the duo incorporated a PRO named IPR Africa together with Mzwakhe Reginald Nkabinde, then treasurer of the ANC Youth League, founder of the hip-hop label Mabala Noise, and an alleged "tenderpreneur" of ambiguous ambition and reputation.[101]

Another way to reorient audit studies is to highlight the performative dimension of producing compliance. Some authors have tried to equate the evaluation of performance with ritual practices, using terms such as *verification ritual* or *purification exercise* to refer to what are, in fact, processes whose only difference from other technocratic forms of control is being premised on a more horizontal, introspective form of monitoring.[102] Although I couched my account of the Dubai scandal in theatrical metaphors, I wanted to refrain from using these terms for the discussion of the audit to avoid the impression that auditing practices can be othered as antiquated or exotic. More importantly, I posit that my approach allows for a more multiplex analytic where auditing is not fetishized by reducing it to key sites and actors such as board meetings, documents, and company executives; it also brings to the fore a wider range of settings, materialities, and forms of resistant agency, such as the guerilla auditors examined in Kregg Hetherington's spectacular *Guerilla Auditors* or the walkouts staged by SAMRO workers facing salary cuts.

This brings me to the third and final point—ethnography. There appear to be two contrasting concepts of what the ethnographic method might contribute to the study of audit. The first, mostly familiar to students of accounting or business ethics, is premised on an understanding of ethnography as producing a higher order and supposedly thicker degree of forensic evidence than more conventional methods privileging documents or interviews with key players. In a sense, then, this notion of ethnographic work might be said to achieve little more than doubling the pursuit of transparency that is constitutive of the rationale of audit already. Or if auditing, according to the etymology of *forensic*, is (or ought to be) a fundamentally public affair, then the transparency imagined by this kind of scholarship and the organizations that it tends to be in dialogue with, such as Transparency International, is coterminous with the virtues espoused by the ideal citizen of liberal democracy. In contrast, the kind of ethnography embraced by anthropologists conceives of the ethnographic study of auditing as pursuing the exact opposite. Instead of assuming that transparency is a self-evident prerequisite of development and a vibrant public sphere, anthropologists are more interested in transparency as a construct that legitimizes historically and locally produced socioeconomic relationships as naturally given—or democracy as the political analog to the marketplace. Hence, rather than providing a veneer of interpretative flexibility to the study of a practice shrouded in an aura of secrecy and unassailable objectivity almost by default, they are wont to foreground the social and cultural implications of auditing and, subsequently, to critically relate the resulting insights to other systems, techniques, and idioms of self-making.[103] The most unstable—and therefore antithetical to the interests of both auditors and auditees—of such referrals are those that seek to translate the audit's claims into what Marilyn Strathern, fittingly writing about the overkill of benchmarks, ratings, and reviews in the academy, calls "embedded knowledge."[104] This is the kind of knowledge we encountered in previous chapters—a knowledge that resists being subsumed under the theories, templates, and terminology of the brave, new, postreconstruction era of South African politics, be it smart policy, neoclassical economics, crime statistics, or newfangled legal categories, such as "derivative indigenous work."

To ground my argument about ethnography in the specifics of the SekelaXabiso report, we need to scrutinize its effects in the intervening years from 2019 to 2020, when this book was written. In the remainder of this chapter, I will therefore offer a close reading of SAMRO's annual integrated reports for those years, changing the analytic register from a more distant-skeptical stance toward a cautiously optimistic view of the ability of the politics of auditing to remake collectives of worlding along the lines of the pragmatist prudence theorized at the end of chapter 1. Part of the inspiration for this interpretation comes from Hetherington's argument that what audits accomplish is to turn transparency into a gift. In this book, the Canadian anthropologist shows how the struggles of impoverished Paraguayan campesinos—the guerilla auditors of the title—seek to recuperate vast tracts of land that were stolen from them during the colonial era and under dictator Alfredo Stroessner's decades-long rule by means of convoluted auditing strategies and how in this process they and their allies in the new democratic, post-Stroessner government become embroiled in a politics of mediation that, although imperfect, has the potential to open new forms of democratic participation. Concretely, the gift, in this case, is a binder of documents and maps retrieved from the national land registry office by a high-ranking populist politician and handed to the farmers at the end of their long battle for recognition of their claims. Hetherington suggests that this binder is more than just an ordinary gift, which, as every anthropology student in their first year in graduate school learns, binds the giver and the receiver together in more or less obligatory bonds of reciprocity and displays of superiority. Contrary to what the contents of the binder might make us believe, this is not a free exchange of information subject to contractually agreed-upon terms of transaction. Rather, in the presentation of the binder, it is transparency itself that is given as the ground on which citizens are to simultaneously "make informed choices free of political influence" and commit to an "obligatory relationship with the giver."[105]

Transparency a gift? After all the critical attention the audit function has received, how can the SekelaXabiso report and its aftermath possibly be portrayed in a positive light? Even more counterintuitive, what do we make of Hetherington's bold assertion that in situations of transitional justice, the "gift of transparency" is not an aberration or an example of duplicitous rhetoric but a necessity? In Hetherington's analysis, the campesinos' "guerilla" tactics are to be thought of as part of a new kind of populist politics where projects of transparency and accountability are subtly beholden to the technocratic rationale espoused by the country's new democratic elites. But at the same time, this politics derives its mobilizing effects from attaching itself to the "embedded knowledge" of the very local constituencies it purports to represent and that are "suspicious of documents and expert knowledge."[106] In other words, unlike official politics that grounds itself in the opposition between reality and delusion or ignorance, the mass appeal of this dual politics resides in its ability to provide different points of reference, shuttling between two "realities, manufacturing points of contact and recognition of mutual interest." As such, the politics of transparency may produce as yet unknown inclusive effects.[107]

In the remaining paragraphs, I want to expand on Hetherington's assessment that transparency as populist is critical to an anthropology of post–Cold War development in Latin America by extending it to the South African context where populist movements or—if "populist" comes across as too distasteful a designation for projects of meaningful change—progressive politics are reaching deep even into seemingly more detached spheres of practice, such as SAMRO. On a superficial reading, the events between the demise of the Dubai project in 2017 and the publication of the *Annual Integrated Report 2020* in December 2020 give the impression that the politics of transparency, accountability, and ethics went into overdrive. Over the document's sixty-one pages, the terms appear no fewer than forty-three times. But what might easily be dismissed as rather predictable incantations is, in fact, an expression of only one side of the post-Dubai politics of renewal, the other side being less readily discernable. To understand these dual politics, we need to backtrack to the events that unfolded from 2018. In the fall of that year, recall, the SAMRO executive and directors found themselves between a rock and a hard place. To get out of the dilemma they had maneuvered themselves into, a revamped board of directors, a new executive team, and CEO Migogo—who had returned for two years pending the search for a new CEO—sought to maintain a semblance of cohesion and regeneration by redefining its "strategic themes" from "revenue growth," "focus on members and users," and "operational excellence" in 2017 to "optimisation of the business model," "diversification," and "innovation" in 2018.[108] These pillars are then further broken down into the following goals: increase revenue, improve systems and processing, improve reputation, cost management, and consolidation of the music industry. Upon first glance, these objectives seem eerily similar to the company's goals of prior years, but on closer inspection, they signal a radical departure from a more traditional, embedded preoccupation with member welfare satisfied by growing revenue toward a more abstract, managerial emphasis on the technical, infrastructural aspects and their implementation over the next couple of years. By 2020, eventually, another overhaul was in the offing. This time, however, under Mark Rosin, it was not about the optimization-diversification-innovation triad. Rather, for the first time in the company's history, an unvarnished and unequivocal admission of utter failure greeted readers of the *Annual Integrated Report 2020*. "A malfunctioning organization," Chairperson Nicholas Maweni writes there, "can often be traced back to a malfunctioning board, where corporate governance has been allowed to slide." And if anyone was ever in doubt about this malfunction being unique to the corporate sector, in what can only be read as a thinly veiled reference to Guptagate, one of South Africa's biggest corruption scandals of all time, which implicated former President Jacob Zuma, he cautions: "When personal interests take precedence over the greater good of an organisation, the rot can infiltrate its entire culture. We have seen it countless times in South Africa, with state capture or simple personal greed tainting numerous public and private entities."[109] After this moment of contrition, Maweni closes his remarks with a line from *Die Stem*, the Afrikaans part of the South African national anthem: *Vaderland! ons sal die adel van jou naam met ere dra* (Fatherland! We will wear the honor of your name with dignity). The national spirit thus rekindled, the remainder of the report strikes a decidedly more high-minded if not euphoric note, prognosticating an era of fundamental change brought about by transparency, accountability, and ethical behavior. A year later, Rosin would add a practical view. As there was not enough evidence in the audit report to bring suit against Dlamini and the former board members, he reasoned, chasing "after something without knowing the results would have been too substantial to warrant the expenditure of more millions. . . . There are people who want to see people thrown in jail. . . . So until there is an effective way of trying to get that money back, I am afraid it's going to be just an investment that went badly wrong."[110]

As always, the road to hell is paved with good intentions. How does one enroll all parties—a minority of well-to-do publishers and a majority of struggling authors—into such a massive reorganization? How does one restore trust not just in individual leaders but in the governance structures as well? And what does a practical view have to do with the greater good? This is where the other side—the local, idiosyncratic, populist side or the social poetics of the politics of renewal—comes into play. Much like the programmatic pronouncements of the annual reports, the pragmatics of this poetics is marked by the duality inherent in the blend of techno-audit rationality and embedded knowledge. Since 2019, SAMRO has identified several key issues it hopes to address in improving operational efficiency. Most of these concern the organization's poor record of capturing and monitoring, as demonstrated by my descriptions above. As 350 of its roughly fifteen thousand licensees account for 75 percent of SAMRO's revenue, and within this segment, key broadcasters are the biggest licensees, the cost-saving measures are envisaged in three areas: the outsourcing of the distribution of digital licensing, the consolidation of the PRO industry, and a ramping up of monitoring of key broadcasters. While the first is geared toward streamlining the licensing process for the multiterritorial online usage of works through companies like Mint Services, the second aims at creating a single-license regime across the entire CMO landscape, whereby users would need only one license for the performance of works and recordings administered by SAMRO and SAMPRA respectively. Usually, these sorts of improvements tend to escape the attention of most musicians, as they primarily affect publishers. The third area, however, has enormous significance and potential for critical member intervention. As we saw above in my description of the documentation of music usage in the television sector, the use of written cue sheets was not only a cumbersome, labor-intensive affair, but it was also a source of grave concern to composers and authors, many of who rely on what in industry phraseology is referred to as "written back" for extra income.

Allow me to elaborate. Generally speaking, the term *written back* refers to a type of operating loss that appears as "undistributable income written back" in the financial reports appended to every annual report. "Undistributable income" refers to royalty due to composers and publishers that cannot be distributed for a variety of reasons. For instance, a composer may have failed to register with SAMRO or has changed address; or a radio station submits a cue sheet with incomplete information about the composer. Other sources of written-back distributions include royalty payable to nonaffiliated rights holders (labeled NS for non-society) or royalty for uses of what in industry jargon is called UNDOC, that is, undocumented works that cannot be matched to their authors or publishers and usually remain unclaimed. And finally, undistributable income is also sourced from the 88.3 percent that is notoriously withheld from a known author of an arrangement of a work in the public domain under the DP scheme mentioned at the beginning of this chapter.

SAMRO never discloses the specific amount of written-back royalty extracted from each of these categories. Nor does it provide verifiable evidence about the recipients of this jackpot. The only metric it does publish is the amount of royalty written back each year. As a recently conducted review of the financial statements from 2009 to 2018 revealed, a staggering R390,770 million has been rechanneled in this way. The review also found that an estimated 85 percent of that amount has been disbursed to the top ten publishers ranked by *Billboard* in 2017 on the basis of market share: SONY/ATV, Warner Chappell Music (represented in South Africa by Gallo), Universal Music Publishing, Kobalt, BMG (Bertelsmann Music Group), and

Downtown (which also owns South Africa's formerly largest indie publisher Sheer Music). It can be reasonably assumed that the remaining 15 percent has been paid to SAMRO's composers/authors.[111]

The phrase *market share* is critical here. As the only criterion for determining the distribution of DP, UNDOC, or NS, market share not only disproportionally benefits those multinational publishers, but it is also likely to discriminate against South African publisher and composer/author members who are black. The reason for this disparity is not simply that a single multinational publisher may sign as much as half of SAMRO's composer/author membership. Market share and the share of music used are, in fact, two different calculations. In the former, income is paid on the basis of the total royalties collected by the publisher in any given year, irrespective of the specific works and their actual use. To take a hypothetical example, if international publisher X has signed a South African composer Y whose works have rarely or never been played, it will reap its share of the written-back royalties according to the *global* percentage of works it owns in comparison to that of its competitors regardless. Composer Y will receive nothing.

Only the most seasoned insiders, such as publishers or music industry critics, will be aware of the secretive manner in which SAMRO handles undistributable income. The arcana of written-back distribution offers few points of reference to, say, black singer-songwriters or the free-styling hip-hop MC struggling to put food on the table. What the majority of members and especially the executive are acutely aware of, however, is what one might call the atmospherics of collective rights management. Little wonder, then, that SAMRO's turn-around strategy also attaches great importance to reputation-enhancing initiatives. One of the more hidden of these initiatives, by now familiar to readers because it straddles the business/politics divide that has defined SAMRO from inception, is the company's support for the Copyright Alliance, a collective comprising CAPASSO, DALRO (Dramatic, Artistic and Literary Organization), RiSA, SAMPRA, MASA (Musicians Association of South Africa), and MPASA (Music Publishers Association of South Africa), whose sole purpose is to pressure the government into withdrawing the controversial Copyright Amendment Bill. Another more visible initiative is a series of workshops and roundtable meetings held between April 2018 and November 2019 in all nine provinces. Accompanied by a great deal of PR, the tempestuous—and even violent, in at least one instance—meetings covered a broad range of topics, including the simplification of membership categories, the introduction of more independent directors on the board, SAMRO's commitment to racial diversity or transformation (as it is called in

South Africa), and the local content quotas on broadcasters. The most significant point of discussion, however, was the DP policy mentioned above.

Remember that earlier in 2018, gospel star Hlengiwe Mhlaba had accused SAMRO of unlawfully holding back 83.33 percent of royalties on arrangements of gospel songs in the public domain. Reacting to the allegation, SAMRO argued that DP, the category of IP those 83.33 percent were allocated to, was not a natural person. What it neglected to tell members is that the elusive entity is always linked to a named and deceased composer/author variously labeled "C," "A," or "CA" in CIS-Net databases. Even more striking, contrary to Migogo's assertion that the IP number of said DP is assigned by CISAC, that number is manipulated by SAMRO internally. And it is also the same for all DP administered by it. But the inconsistencies do not end there. Under SAMRO's distribution rules, 100 percent in the "music only" type of work is allocated to the composer, while for a "music arrangement," the composer's share is listed as 83.33 percent, and that of the "arranger" amounts to 16.67 percent.[112] But, absent terms such as *arrangement*, *public domain*, or *orphan work* in the Copyright Act, and irrespective of the questionable attempt of the Intellectual Property Laws Amendment Act (discussed in chapter 3), to vest ownership of "indigenous derivate works" in indigenous communities, the official classification of Mhlaba as an arranger of a work in the public domain is out of step with basic copyright logic. Since works in the public domain are free for the taking, a better term for the person adapting them would be as the author of the arrangement.[113] In short, there is a high degree of credibility not only to Mhlaba's assertion that SAMRO paid only 16.7 percent of her royalties, but also that the remaining 83.3 percent disappeared into what is, according to gonzo journalist and *Rolling Stone* author Hunter S. Thompson's memorable phrase, a "money trench, a long plastic hallway where thieves and pimps run free."[114] Indeed, as lawyer and Mhlaba's counsel Graeme Gilfillan points out in a sharply worded rejoinder to SAMRO's handling of the singer's grievances, Mhlaba was not the only victim of the DP scheme. In 2017 alone, other artists suffered losses of at least R750,000 ($70,000), with many more likely enduring the same fate throughout the organization's history.[115]

After lengthy debate, a formula brought forward by the executive was accepted whereby the traditional 16.7–83.3 percent split would be replaced by a 50–50 split. Yet, the deal is less the result of members having "engaged favourably" with the executive's proposal, as Migogo declared in a letter to members, and more that of a carefully thought out "populist" strategy that keeps technocratic and affective responses in precarious balance.[116] The first is evident in the way the executive excluded virtually the entire spectrum of written-back tricks other than the DP and UNDOC issues from discussion. Complementing this tactic to delimit the range of what can be said is a strategy familiar from attempts elsewhere at manufacturing political legitimacy by erecting a barrier between the inside and the outside against which to define oneself. Continuing her letter in this vein, Migogo argued that the uproar about the DP fiasco was not a reaction to SAMRO's shortcomings but the work of the media spreading an "inflammatory and misinformed SAMRO-narrative." The reporting, she went on to suggest, led to a group of rowdy nonmembers gate-crashing one of the workshops while also illustrating a "lack of understanding of the role SAMRO plays in the music industry" among the public at large who wrongly view it as the central body responsible for policy and socioeconomic issues in the music industry. And then there is the tried and tested method of legal finesse. Knowingly or not, ever since the Mhlaba story broke, SAMRO has been peddling a fictitious category of work previously unrecognized by copyright law, which it calls "original public domain work." This is based on a mistaken reading of the originality requirement under South African—and, in fact, Anglo-American copyright law in general—whereby protection is only available for works that have been "independently created." In the case of eighteenth-century hymns or, indeed, the overwhelming amount of traditional South African music serving as material for adaptations, such independent creation is difficult to ascertain.

What is, however, possible in the music industry and, perhaps, in the make-believe world of the cultural industries more generally, is to pass off fiction as fact. Much of the same us-versus-them logic that informs Migogo's letter also underpinned SAMRO's affective reaction to the crisis as a whole, which involves a battery of measures aimed at creating a sense of inclusivity and connection to a wider sphere of worlding beyond the SAMRO membership. The debate about legally mandated local content quota on broadcasters, for instance, is one such attempt at channeling South African musicians' discontent with the dominance of US and Western music on the country's airwaves into a cozy fairyland of locally bred music. The matter had been brewing since 1997, but the debate only reached fever pitch in 2016 after (subsequently disgraced) SABC CEO Hlaudi Motsoeneng implemented a 90–10 percent quota in favor of local music, and the Independent Communications Authority of South Africa, a regulatory body for the telecommunications and broadcasting sectors, followed suit by mandating a 60–40 percent split (to increase annually by 10 percent, eventually reaching an 80–20 percent split by 2018) soon thereafter. Although by 2020, African language broadcasters have already met or even exceeded the content requirements of the policy directive, larger stations still haven't managed to fill their quota, prompting vociferous protest from mostly young, struggling black composers who simultaneously aspire to global fame while, on some level, yearning for a simpler life and the sounds of *ikasi*, the township.[117] But even if the measure were to become fully operational at some point in the future, there is, so far, no evidence to suggest that it will appreciably alter the underlying dynamic of income inequality.

And then there is the rhetoric of sustainability. Historically intertwined—under different names—with colonial and apartheid fantasies of cultural purity, in the SAMRO imaginary, the idea becomes part of a different semantic field in which cultural heritage and sustainable development form an insoluble whole of growth and employment. Echoing the Intellectual Property Laws Amendment Act and what I have called the assemblage of indigeneity, this strategy envisages increased support for "indigenous African works" through a network involving the SAMRO Foundation and local NGOs funded by foreign aid organizations such as Concerts SA. And in case readers of the *Annual Integrated Report 2020* doubted SAMRO's resolve in bringing these ideas to bear fruit, in contrast to earlier years, its pages are striking for the number of photographs depicting musicians resplendent with brightly colored, African attires and instruments, such as musical bows.

Another topic that occupies a prominent place in the turn-around strategy is the way in which the affective key is modulated to an ethical key. What in philosophy would require some serious fudging of cardinal principles is here accomplished by turning a questionable practice into yet another stratagem with populist appeal. Born from the desire to improve the dismal performance of the company's risk and ethics committees during the Dubai debacle, this part is particularly noteworthy for its deft combination of governance argot, procedural technicality, and legal sanction with a moral codex redolent of tradition. "Parties who will be found to have been involved in any unethical behavior," the report threatens, "will be named and shamed publicly. Two staff members were investigated for fraud in the organization and they elected to resign to avoid the consequences if found guilty. Two members were also suspended after an investigation found them to have had committed fraud."[118] Has such language, the writer wonders, been consciously inserted to play into widespread forms of street justice that walk a razor-thin line between the isolation of suspected delinquents and the patently unlawful "digilantism" whereby women shame their alleged sexual abusers on social media on the one hand, and witch-hunt accusations and the killing of suspected criminals on the other?

And so, everything comes full circle. From the SekelaXabiso forensic report, to the workshops, to the *Annual Integrated Report 2020*, what is confirmed has been implicit in the entire process from the very start: namely, the recognition that compliance with the applicable legal framework and good governance would not alone lead to social and cultural development. During SAMRO's sixty years of existence, the trust in the power of markets to even things out by reducing transaction costs and exploiting economies of scale was never without its nemesis—the ugly legacy of racial capitalism. But neither were the diverse collectives of worlding and the rich panoply of forms of resistance they persistently engender ever absent. After countless cycles of economic downturn followed by solemn promises of change and grudgingly instituted reforms, one has the sinking feeling that the purpose of strengthening its commitment to corporate ethics is not to put SAMRO on a path of serious distributive justice but to consolidate its power and that of the interests it represents. At the same time, it bears remembering that, much like the effort to reform South African copyright, decades in the making, has thus far failed to yield definitive answers to the music industry's most pressing concerns, it is in the nature of collectives of worlding that they never reach a point of conclusion but are always in the making themselves. After all, it is the resilience of musicians like Strike Vilakazi and Hlengiwe Mhlaba or the perseverance of the countless members, users, journalists, activists, and legal scholars who are quietly—and sometimes quite vociferously—querying the organization's modus operandi that brought SAMRO to contemplate, however hesitantly, meaningful change.

Conclusion
How To Speak the Same Language, or at Least Try To

"We do not speak the same language."
 Now that you, dear reader, have followed me in my journey through South Africa's fragmented copyright terrain, examining, through a combination of unlikely locations, evanescent events, and snippets of stories, how the law is made and remade, assembled and reassembled, and how this moment reflects a critical juncture in South African history, politics, and culture, you may have gotten a sense of the difficulty of speaking across disciplinary chasms—as well as the urgent need for a relational language to further such a dialogue. In closing, and reflecting a little further on Coenraad Visser's moment of desperation at the 2019 conference mentioned at the start of this book, I wonder what it means when the country's leading legal experts and lawmakers appear to be talking past one another and what might be involved in finding common ground. Surely, it is not just the shoddy draftsmanship in the controversial Copyright Amendment Bill that upsets the experts. There must be more to the disconnect than amateurish language, such as "copyright protection subsists in expressions" [2 A, 1]). Or might all the misunderstandings and misinterpretations be the result of a lack of consultation? As chapter 3 showed, lawmakers did routinely seek expert advice on several occasions, both from outside and from parliamentary advisors. Or is it because of a culture of cronyism and opportunism that prominent lawyers allow themselves to be drawn into a project whose fundamental flaws were all but apparent to even the most uninitiated observer?

None of these answers are particularly satisfactory. They do not explain the deeper roots of the incomprehension lamented by Visser because they suggest that the source of this fiasco is located solely within one domain—in this instance, lawmaking. An alternative approach is the anthropology in law that I have proposed in this book. Rather than look for single causes and simple teleologies, we should acknowledge that the mess is a consequence of the inability of the system law and the system parliamentary politics to reproduce themselves due to a breakdown of what in systems theory is referred to as connectedness (*Anschlussfähigkeit*). But if decades of poststructuralist critique have taught us anything about language, it is that people do not speak or act out of their own volition, but that *langue* always speaks itself, and that, hence, we speak always through someone else's words and in speech contexts and genres that are not of our own making. Partisan politics, legal indifference, the shadows of the colonial and apartheid past, indigenous claims for belonging, distrust of expert systems, or even professional codes are no more isolated actors than climate change is caused by one country. What lawmakers and legal experts fail to understand, then, is not the language of the Other per se as much as the divergent assumptions about what and for whom these languages might be speaking and what violence they might be inflicting on the Other's speech.

What, then, does it take for lawmakers and academics to speak the same language? How can what appear to be fundamentally different idioms become mutually intelligible? Turning to the humanities, how can we, as anthropologists, translate the concerns of others into our grammar and vocabulary without denying their integrity? This is the question that has been at the heart of this book. In closing, then, I would like to offer some preliminary thoughts on what might be entailed in the effort to craft a common language among law, politics, and the humanities. In this, I am inspired by the boundary-crossing work of Geoffrey Bowker and Susan Leigh Star on classification and boundary objects discussed in chapter 5.

Scholars of information systems, Bowker's and Star's work was based in scientific communities that were distributed over different institutional and experiential settings, lacked good models of each other's work, and had to satisfy different goals, time horizons, and audiences.[1] Despite such disconnects, these communities were successfully able to work together by creating boundary objects that function across any number of divides in terms of epistemology, method, or purpose. There are, however, two conditions for boundary objects to reconcile heterogeneity: they must be "plastic enough to adapt to local needs and constraints of the several parties employing them, yet robust enough to maintain a common identity across sites." Contrary, then, to conventional wisdom that heterogeneity is best reduced by striving for homogeneity or speaking the "same language," the ability of boundary objects to facilitate cross-site translation does not require that they be fully consistent or even logical. Quite the opposite, their strength lies in being "weakly structured in common use, and . . . strongly structured in individual-site use."[2] The second condition for boundary objects to work is that they must be created. They are not objets trouvés that one may simply lift from another context or borrow from another discipline, discourse, or practice and use as one's own. They are constructs that emerge in practice—through discourse or some other collaborative form of communication.

There are several ways Star's concept might resonate with the idea of an anthropology in law. Consider, for instance, the time horizons or period of time that elapses between the identification of a concrete issue and its solution, in which both fields operate. Law, whether as legal practice or theory, is case-based and moves from instance to instance, evidence to evidence with legal norms, statutory provisions, or precedent serving to certify these as legally pertinent. The vantage point of the legal practitioner might be summed up in a sequitur such as "this is what happened and why it is of legal concern." Anthropologists, too, by way of the ethnographic method, depart from the singular as the basis of defining the specificity and facticity of an event. And similar to the lawyer, judge, or law professor, they will argue that naming this fact constitutes it as worthy of anthropological interest. Where they differ from one another is in the specific method of resolving differences and the expectation of what lies behind the horizon, so to speak. In law, what matters is the resolution of the issue at hand through a court order arrived at by bringing "questions of fact" in accordance with "questions of law" coupled with the hope to *change* future behavior. Social scientists, in contrast, have traditionally been more invested in constructing models that organize myriad practices within a general pattern in order to either *critique* or *predict* behavior. More recent modes of inquiry are less preoccupied with predictability and have shifted toward what a particular issue might represent in a wider, more fluid context of cultural relations and how this instability undermines social control and opens up venues for unanticipated opposition. In short, these methods have little in common other than the distance that separates them.

But there are also commonalities. As I have shown in the first two chapters, one of the hallmarks of legal procedure is the incremental, piecemeal fashion by which cases move through various stages before reaching resolution. More than this stop-and-go type of motion, though, what may yet contain the seeds for a more productive, crossdisciplinary communication is the fact that it affords ample space for revision, interpretation, and the integration of new actors and information. Likewise, for anthropologists, the need to go slow is imperative and offers the possibility of demarcating the space of ethnographic jurisdiction at every step while providing opportunities for others to redraw the boundaries of that space.

The type of boundary objects, however, that may be the most mutually translatable and simultaneously respectful of the specificities of law and anthropology are those that, despite having different contents, share what Star terms a "terrain with coincident boundaries."[3] For example, one such terrain that has been common to both law and social scientists for decades is some form or other of collectivity. Furthermore, law and society scholars and social scientists might also agree on this terrain, offering within its boundaries some kind of solution to the issues they are confronting as part of their respective disciplinary rationale. While copyright law scholars may invoke the public as a justification for granting authors exclusive property rights, for decades, policymakers, sociologists, early anthropologists, and other agents of social engineering used it as a device to absorb a multitude of seemingly disconnected phenomena into an overarching entity equipped with quasi-magical power to bestow some sense of logic or cohesiveness on a set of unequivocally inconsistent, even chaotic practices. But at the same time, there is significant potential for disagreement and for turning a weakly structured boundary object such as society into a strongly structured one, not unlike the public interest and wealth maximization in utilitarian and law and economics theories of copyright or the public sphere in the social sciences and political philosophy. As I have argued throughout this book, if the capacity of the social and its various South African postapartheid inflections—social cohesion, *ubuntu*, national identity, or economic integration—for hosting alternative visions of copyright seem all but exhausted, one may perhaps appreciate the need for both a new code and a new *phronesis*—a novel way of speaking prudently across heterogeneous fields of knowledge and practice.

What then might be the concrete elements of this conversation? Boundary objects, as I have said, are not found—they must be created. And they must be recognized and continually reaffirmed as boundary objects by the members of the respective communities in much the same way that society has long been perceived as a shared object of inquiry by both legal scholars and anthropologists. For example, one of the boundary objects that I created in the second chapter is "Mbube." That is, not the song as such but the work as it becomes a subject of rights that intersects, via a whole chain of valences, with a host of material objects: the 1939 recording, various deeds of assignment, license agreements, expert testimony ascertaining originality and substantial similarity, or royalty statements. For the anthropologist, musicologist, and cultural critic, "Mbube" represents something completely different yet entirely adaptable to the constraints of legal process: namely, a groundbreaking example of a tradition that is claimed, recognized, and revered as a moral anchor and genuine emblem of black South African identity.

Another example is the expert featured in the legislative process examined in chapter 3. For the member of Parliament, the expert—or his or her opinion—may serve as a prism through which to zero in on a common denominator that considers the divergent viewpoints and local interests of their constituents and thus renders them judicially legible. The experts, for their part, start from the same premise as the MPs in that they, too, dis-embed the issues under consideration from the local site, where they may carry a multitude of divergent meanings. But unlike the parliamentarian, the expert is not bound to re-embed their expertise in those locales of meaning-making, thus shielding them from having to justify their positions in any idiom other than their own. Anthropologists, finally, may be taking something of an intermediary position between the MP and the expert. On the one hand, they may be playing a role similar to the MP by constantly tacking back and forth between the singular and the general, the local and the universal. But on the other hand, they may also be committed to a view of the local as fundamentally at odds with the boundary-crossing imperative of "speaking the same language," thus potentially missing out on the opportunity to translate it into a more widely understood ecological register.

In this book, I have also gone to great lengths to demonstrate the effects of the absence of boundary objects. In the most general sense, South Africa's decades-long effort to remake its copyright regime may be read as the story of boundary objects that have never been created or as a tale of what Star, drawing on pragmatist philosophers like Dewey, likes to call "interruptions." These are complications and anomalies that arise in the "tension between the ambiguous (outsider, naïve, strange) and the naturalized (at home, taken-for-granted) properties of objects," or when a person or object disrupts the flow of expectations.[4] The hearings of the portfolio committee that deliberated the Intellectual Property Laws Amendment Bill, for instance, were a veritable interruption fest. So, too, are the desperate attempts to combat piracy, discussed in chapter 4. Another one is the Copyright Amendment Bill. But while these interruptions pose a significant risk to the integrity of the country's copyright system, they have provided me with an opportunity to reflect on a moment in the life of copyright as a critical juncture in South African history, politics, and culture more broadly. And in parallel with this renunciation of linear narratives of progress and instrumentalist thought, where legal input and social output are always already assembled, these interruptions prompted a method of inquiry in which various actors—from exhibit bags and crime statistics to members of Parliament and licensing fees—first had to be taken on their own, frequently irreducible, idiosyncratic terms before being collected into a stable social, political, or cultural order. In short, interruptions are the default zero point of ethnography—a productive force not only exposing fissures, techniques of exclusion, sites of abjection but also opening up new possibilities and avenues for change.

But now, in the summer of 2022, as the book entered the final stages of production, some of that optimism has waned. I worry even more about the future of South Africa's copyright system than I did at the start of my journey in 2010. Old interruptions resurfaced, sometimes in much the same configurations as before, sometimes in modified form. Again, the Copyright Amendment Bill is the perfect example. After several revisions and a new version, it is still awaiting presidential signature, and opinions about it are as divided as they were in 2015 when it was first introduced. Another example is the key players. New actors have appeared on the scene, at SAMRO, RiSA, and the Portfolio Committee on Trade and Industry, for example. But the positions and interests they represent have hardly changed with them. Above all, however, from the early months of 2020, a completely novel type of actor has shaken the country to its foundations. The COVID-19 virus has brought misery and despair to millions of South Africans, including and perhaps especially artists. According to a survey conducted by the South African Cultural Observatory in May 2020, almost half of the roughly seven hundred respondents were contemplating quitting live music for good. Among employers in the cultural industries more generally, 33 percent said that they could not continue with their normal business activities, while 53 percent of freelancers said they could not continue at all.[5] Whatever the long-term consequences of all of this, and no matter what the general state of paralysis the country has been in for at least the past ten years might mean for the copyright reform process and how, conversely, that process may still turn out for the better, the future is impossible to predict. And so I am left to ask: Was it all in vain? Was Solomon Linda's fate, the bitter lessons his daughters had to learn about music industry intransigence, and the energy their flawed claims injected into the debate about creative autonomy and termination rights, for naught? And even though the indigenous community the Intellectual Property Laws Amendment Act dreams of will never be more than a chimera, will the flawed act at least kindle a new ethics, a new citizenry bound by the perceptual care owed to vulnerable beauty? Likewise, will the Dubai scandal at SAMRO and the half-hearted measures to create a modicum of equity and some sense of common purpose following in its wake last? Or will things return to business-as-usual, perpetuating old divides and creating new ones?

In the introduction, I referred to the eight years of remaking South African copyright covered in this book as a period of limbo, of crisis even, comparable to or symptomatic of the larger moment of emergency that the country now finds itself in. But, as Janet Roitman has rightly pointed out, through the term *crisis*, the "singularity of events is abstracted by a generic logic, making *crisis* a term that seems self-explanatory." At the same time, the term "implies a certain telos because it is inevitably, though most often implicitly, directed toward a norm." And, finally, crisis narratives tend to "evoke a moral demand for a difference between the past and the future." That is, crisis "occasions critique."[6]

To be sure, a commitment to legal ethnography—such as the one I have sought to renew in this book—must be mindful of Roitman's caveats. Although *Lion's Share* ends on a skeptical, even disillusioned note, where the past sometimes is the present, the kind of intervention I described in chapter 1 as a "performative critique" does have a place in the ethnography of events as sweeping as the ones I have written about here, provided that such a critique is "attuned to the processes through which actors and practices bind to each other in constantly shifting configurations." Therefore, the fact that I chose to query legal instrumentalism's linearity of thought and the mythologies of development and social progress it enables does not preclude other terms, questions, narratives, methodologies, or even entirely new languages in which to talk about copyright law, cultural industries, and authors across disciplinary divides. It simply means that terms such as *development*, *mess*, or *crisis* can be seen as blind spots that allow certain discourses and practices to become dominant while foreclosing other concepts or questions. It would then be possible, for instance, to stop insisting on legal functionality by asking what *went* wrong, and instead foreground a legal ethics that asks what *is* wrong? It is also then that the failures and disjunctures, no less than the well-intentioned strategies and discourses meant to overcome them, that my antinormative, ethnographic approach brought forward, in themselves may become productive as boundary-objects fostering a shared language in which to talk about South African copyright.

APPENDIX

South African Copyright Law: The Basics

The basis of the South African law of copyright is Copyright Act 98 of 1978.

In its current form, the act is the result of a combination of previous British legislation, the Berne Convention and the TRIPS agreement. There have been several amendments, the most notable being the inclusion of software programs as a distinct class of protected works in 1992.

Although only a small number of provisions in the act concern the subject matter of this book directly, a brief survey of the most important ones may be useful.

What Is Protected?

Section 2 (1) of the act lists nine specific types of works that are eligible for copyright protection:

- literary works, including novels, poems, plays, film scripts, textbooks, articles, encyclopedias, reports, speeches, etc.
- musical works, excluding words sung with the music
- artistic works, including paintings, sculptures, drawings, photographs, architectural works, works of craftsmanship, etc.
- cinematograph films
- sound recordings in any medium, but excluding film soundtracks
- broadcast signals transmitted by radio waves and intended for public reception

- program-carrying signals representing audio and/or video and transmitted via satellite
- published editions of literary or musical works
- computer programs

What Are the Requirements for Protection?

For a work in any of these categories to be eligible for protection, the act rather broadly provides that they must be "original." [Copyright Act, s 2 (1)] The meaning of *original* in South Africa differs from the US, however. Whereas in US copyright law (17 U.S.C. § 102), originality is usually defined as requiring "at least a modicum of creativity" and "independent creation," (Feist Publications, Inc. v Rural Telephone Service, 499 U.S. 340, 111 S.Ct. 1282, 113 L.Ed. 2d 358 [1991]) South African courts tend to require that a certain amount of skill or labor was expended in creating the work. This is sometimes referred to as the sweat-of-the-brow doctrine.

Another criterion of eligibility for protection is that a work in any of the above categories (with the exception of broadcasts and program-carrying signals) must be "reduced to material form"—that is, it must be written down or otherwise recorded [s 2 (2)]. Facts or ideas are not protected.

A third requirement is that the author of a work is a South African citizen, domiciled in South Africa, or in the case of juristic person, a body incorporated under the laws of South Africa [s 3 (1)].

Who Owns the Copyright in a Work?

No formalities, such as registration of the work, are required for copyright to subsist. The author of a work is usually the first owner of the copyright in the work. However, because the term *author* as defined by the act [s 1 (1)] is a technical term, there are some exceptions where the author of a work is not necessarily the person who first created it. In a sound recording, for instance, the author is the person who arranged for making of the sound recording. The act also provides for joint authorship of a work.

Is Copyright the Same for All Types of Work?

No. The act distinguishes between specific exclusive rights for each category of work listed above [s 6]. Thus, for a musical or literary work the rights are as follows:

- reproducing the work in any manner or form
- publishing the work
- performing the work in public
- broadcasting the work
- causing the work to be transmitted in a diffusion service
- making an adaptation of the work
- doing, in relation to an adaptation of the work, any of the acts specified above

A word must also be added here about some specifics of the rights embedded in a sound recording. There are three such rights: the rights in the work (otherwise known as the "performance" right); the rights in the recording as such; and the right to the master recording (often referred to as "mechanical" right). The fact that each sound recording contains this bundle of rights is one of the main reasons for the complexity of the music industry.

How Long Does Copyright in a Work Subsist?

The duration or term of copyright protection depends on the type of work. In relation to musical and literary works, the term is the lifetime of the author and fifty years from the end of the year of the author's passing [s 3 (2) (a)]. In a sound recording, the term is fifty years from the end of the year in which the recording is first published [s 3 (2) (c)].

Can Ownership of Copyright in a Work Be Transferred
or Licensed to Someone Else?

According to s 22 (1) of the act, copyright is transmissible by assignment, testamentary disposition, or operation of law. Copyright is divisible, allowing an owner to assign copyright for a specific period of time, assign only a part of the rights such as the performance right, or assign the copyright for specific countries. A license, by contrast, does not transfer the ownership of the copyright but authorizes the licensee to perform specific or all acts falling within the exclusive rights of the owner. The first is called a nonexclusive license, the second an exclusive license. In the case of sound recordings, sections 9 (d) and (e) of the act authorize the owner to control the use of a recording in broadcasts and in public performances. These rights are commonly referred to as needletime rights. Section 9A (1) (a) and (b) further stipulates that a licensee using these rights must pay a royalty to the owner of the recording, which is to be mutually agreed upon by the owner and user. Section 9A (2) further provides that the owner is required to share royalties received with performers whose performance is featured on the recording pursuant to section 5 of the Performers' Protection Act 11 of 1967. Needletime and public performance licenses are obtained from the collecting society administering these rights.

Can I Use Someone's Work without Their Permission?

Yes and no. The mere use of a work, such as listening to a CD or streamed work at home, does not constitute infringement of copyright. But in section 23 (1) the act specifies that infringement takes place when anyone who is not the owner of the copyright without the license of such owner does or causes another person to do any act that falls under the exclusive rights of the owner, such as the right to reproduce or adapt all or substantial parts of the work. This form of infringement is called direct infringement. Indirect infringement, by contrast, occurs when a person trades a reproduction of a work made by another person or when a public place of entertainment permits the performance of a work that infringes on a protected work. Finally, prior infringement is also assumed where a person may invoke a fair dealing exception. Contrary to popular perception, fair dealing exceptions (sometimes also incorrectly referred to as fair use) are not rights but statutory defenses. As such, they are work-specific and in general comprise three circumstances under which a person may rely on a fair dealing exception: for the purposes of private study, criticism or review, and the reporting of current events.

What Remedies Are Available to the Copyright Owner?

Infringements of copyright are actionable at the suit of the owner of the copyright or the exclusive licensee [s 24 (1) and s 25 (1)]. Available remedies can be obtained in the forms of damages for (actual or future) loss sustained by the plaintiff, an interdict commanding the defendant to refrain from further infringement, and/or an order for delivery up of any remaining infringing copies. The onus of proof in such proceedings is on the copyright owner. The act, in section 27 (1) (a) to (f), not only provides for criminal proceedings for types of copyright infringement that are essentially similar to those in civil proceedings for indirect infringement, but also requires that the infringer has a "guilty mind" and knows he is dealing with infringing copies.

For a more detailed discussion of these and other basic features of South African copyright law, see Dean & Dyer *Introduction to Intellectual Property Law*, edited by Owen Dean and Alison Dyer, Oxford: Oxford University Press, 2014, 1–76.

NOTES

Introduction

1 The event in question was the Third Annual Conference of the South African Association of IP Law and IT Law Teachers and Researchers (AIPLITL) held at the University of Cape Town in 2019.
2 For a useful compilation of documents, internet links, and other material relating to the Copyright Amendment Bill see: https://libguides.wits.ac.za/Copyright_and_Related_Issues/SA_Copyright_Amendment_Bill_2017.
3 Among the first and most influential of these pioneering scholars are David Coplan, an anthropologist who later became a professor at the University of the Witwatersrand, and Christopher Ballantine, a musicologist and head of the music department of what was then known as the University of Natal.
4 Lucia, *World of South African Music*, xxii. Apart from an astute introduction, Lucia's anthology gathers in one convenient place some of the most important writing, both past and more recent.
5 See especially Erlmann, *African Stars*; *Nightsong*; and *Music and the Global Imagination*. Also see Meintjes, *Sound of Africa*; Muller, *Rituals of Fertility*.
6 Reckwitz, *Society of Singularities*, 17, 63.
7 In fact, as Stephen Best argues, the two developed in tandem. Best, *The Fugitive's Properties*. Note here, too, that this close relationship between copyright and personhood stands in marked contrast with the labor justification of copyright prevalent in South African copyright jurisprudence.
8 Reckwitz, *Society of Singularities*, 84. On the "pragmatics of citizenship" see Comaroff and Comaroff, "Reflections on Liberalism."

9   Robins, *From Revolution to Rights*, 2, 7; Comaroff and Comaroff, *Law and Disorder*, 27.
10 Here I am in dialogue with one of the foundational texts of fugitivity: Stefano Harvey and Fred Moten's *The Undercommons*.
11 As some legal scholars have argued, the fact that the socioeconomic rights in the Bill of Rights are interspersed with other rights rather than grouped under their own rubric shows that they are indivisible from these rights.
12 Coetzer, "Johnny Clegg," 42–48.
13 Comaroff and Comaroff, *Law and Disorder*, 32.
14 Weheliye, *Habeas Viscus*, 77.
15 Allingham, "From 'Noma Kumnyama'"; Ballantine, "Song, Memory, Power." Examples elsewhere are Röschenthaler and Diawara, *Copyright Africa*; Eckstein and Schwarz, *Postcolonial Piracy*; Feld, "Sweet Lullaby"; Seeger, "Traditional Music"; Perlman, "From 'Folklore'"; Skinner, *Bamako Sounds*; Stobart, "Rampant Reproduction."
16 Some of the key music industry institutions, such as the collecting societies SAMRO and SAMPRA, are led by lawyers.
17 Notable exceptions are Gani, *Creative Autonomy*; and Okorie, *Multi-Sided Music Platforms*.
18 Sindane, *Call to Decolonise*; CHE, *State*, 54; Modiri, "Transformation."
19 To name just a few prominent examples of the past decade, I am thinking of Perzanowski and Schultz, *End of Ownership*; Patry, *How to Fix Copyright*; Sunder, *Goods to a Good Life*. In the South African context, de Beer et al., *Innovation & Intellectual Property*.
20 Comaroff and Comaroff, *Law and Disorder*, 5.
21 For more on this, see Law, *After Method*.
22 Law, *After Method*, 9.
23 Maine, *Ancient Law*.
24 Neely, *Reimagining Social Medicine*; Meintjes, *Dust of the Zulu*; Pollock, *Synthesizing Hope*.

Chapter One. Aspirations and Apprehensions

1 Coombe, *Cultural Life*, 18.
2 Sunder, *Goods to a Good Life*, 91.
3 Halbert, *State of Copyright*, 4.
4 Sunder, *Goods to a Good Life*, 91.
5 Coombe, *Cultural Life*, 18.
6 Halbert, *State of Copyright*, 4.
7 Boyle, "Second Enclosure Movement."
8 Mbembe and Nuttall, "Writing the World," 351.

9 Herzfeld, *Cultural Intimacy*.
10 South African Government, *Copyright Review Commission Report* (2011).
11 SABC NEWS, "ANC Legal Research Group Discusses SA Copyright Amendment Bill," October 14, 2017, YouTube video, 2:00:09, https://www.youtube.com/watch?v=MBoehw1pspY. Other major symposia and conferences on the cultural industries that regularly feature talks and panels on copyright, and several of which I attended, include the Arts and National Development Imbizo, "Rethinking the Positioning of the Arts in South Africa" (Johannesburg, April 10–11, 2019), https://mistra.org.za/mistra-strategics/arts-and-national-development-imbizo/; an Arts & Culture Trust (ACT) conference on the cultural industries held at the University of Johannesburg, August 6–9, 2013; the annual Moshito Music Conference and Exhibition (https://www.moshito.co.za/); and the "Hip Hop Summit," held at the annual "Back to the City International Hip Hop Festival" (https://www.backtothecityfestival.com/).
12 SABC NEWS, "ANC Legal Research," 00:52:33–40.
13 SABC NEWS, "ANC Legal Research," 00:53:41–56.
14 SABC NEWS, "ANC Legal Research," 00:54:56; 00:55:20.
15 SABC NEWS, "ANC Legal Research," 01:31:20.
16 SABC NEWS, "ANC Legal Research," 01:47:14–46. Significantly, the panel failed to broach hot-button topics, such as metadata as the main income source for streaming platforms or the relationships between multisided music platforms. On the latter see Okorie, *Multi-Sided Music Platforms*.
17 Skinner, *Bamako Sounds*, 134.
18 Clifford, *Predicament of Culture*, 22, 26.
19 Tsing, *Friction*, 5
20 Bentham, *Fragment on Government*, 3.
21 For a fascinating collection of essays on this, see Cowan and Wincott, *Exploring the "Legal."*
22 Chanock, *Making of South African Legal Culture*; Chanock, "South Africa, 1841–1924"; Sachs, *We, the People*, 9.
23 Dean and Dyer, *Dean & Dyer*; Ramsden, *Guide to Intellectual Property Law*.
24 Dean, *Handbook of South African Copyright Law*, 1987.
25 Coombe, *Cultural Life*, 19–20. See also Coombes, *Reinventing Africa*; Richards, *Commodity Culture*; Comaroff and Comaroff, *Revelation and Revolution*, vol. 1; Comaroff and Comaroff, *Revelation and Revolution*, vol. 2; Burke, *Lifebuoy Men*.
26 Comaroff and Comaroff, *Revelation and Revolution*, vol. 2, 321, 361.
27 Erlmann, *Music, Modernity and the Global Imagination*, 69.
28 Quoted in Rich, *White Power*, 67–68.
29 Hoernlé, *South African Native Policy*, 150.

30 Rich, White Power, 129.
31 Native Teachers' Journal October 1919, quoted in Erlmann, "Apartheid, African Nationalism and Culture," 137.
32 Kirby, "Indigenous Music," 621.
33 Umteteli wa Bantu, January 9, 1932, quoted in Erlmann, "Apartheid, African Nationalism and Culture," 142.
34 Umteteli wa Bantu, December 19, 1931, quoted in Erlmann, "Apartheid, African Nationalism and Culture," 143.
35 Seeger, Pete Seeger, 281.
36 In her Disrupting Africa, Olufunmilayo Arewa, drawing on hitherto unknown archival material, details how the British Colonial Office not only forced Ghana and other African colonies to clone British copyright law by imposing the Imperial Copyright Act of 1911, they also actively intervened in the administration of copyright, for instance, by preventing the establishment of a system of copyright registration. Similar research on South Africa would be helpful. Arewa, Disrupting Africa, 265–70.
37 Sunder, Goods to a Good Life, 91.
38 Along similar lines, see Alcock, Kasinomics.
39 Terreblanche, History of Inequality; Du Toit and Neves, "In Search."
40 Du Toit and Neves, "In Search," 7.
41 SACO, Employment, 15, 21.
42 SACO, Mapping, 20–21.
43 Ferguson, Give a Man a Fish, 93.
44 Guyer, Legacies, Logics, Logistics, 110–27.
45 Ferguson and Li, Beyond the "Proper Job."
46 See also Stahl, Unfree Masters, 11–15.
47 DTI, Protection of Indigenous Knowledge, 9.
48 Ferguson, Anti-Politics Machine, xiii. See also Coleman, Coombe, and MacAlrault, "Broken Record."
49 Foucault, "What Is an Author."
50 Callon, Lascoumes, and Barthe, Acting in an Uncertain World, 192.
51 Miyazaki and Riles, "Failure as an Endpoint."
52 Li, Will to Improve, 4.
53 Sarat and Kearns, "Beyond the Great Divide."
54 Coombe, Cultural Life, 28. Special Issue Editors, "Law and Ideology," 633.
55 Pound, "Mechanical Jurisprudence," 605.
56 Holmes, Collected Legal Papers, 418, 420.
57 Cardozo, Nature of the Judicial Process, 55–66. For a brilliant discussion of the fixation in US law on "objectivity" and its manifestation in legal and sociological positivism, see Hackney, Under Cover of Science.

58 Latour, "When Things Strike Back," 118.
59 Fisher, "Theories of Intellectual Property."
60 Landes and Posner, "Economic Analysis," 326.
61 Fisher, "Theories of Intellectual Property," 24.
62 Karjiker, "Justifications for Copyright."
63 Tamanaha, *Law as a Means*, 225.
64 Tamanaha, *Law as a Means*, 224.
65 Quoted in Dyzenhaus, *Judging the Judges*, 61.
66 Abel, *Politics by Other Means*; Dugard, *Confronting Apartheid*; Cameron, *Justice*.
67 Klare, "Legal Culture," 150, 152. See also Modiri, "Conquest, Constitutionalism and Democratic Contestations."
68 Jeffery, "New Constitution."
69 Comaroff and Comaroff, *Law and Disorder*, 26; Dugard, *Confronting Apartheid*.
70 Tamanaha, "Lessons of Law-and-Development Studies."
71 Trubek and Galanter, "Scholars in Self-Estrangement." I examine the discourse of transparency in more detail in chapter 5.
72 Tamanaha, "Lessons of Law-and-Development Studies," 484.
73 Trebilcock, "Universalism and Relativism," 340–41.
74 Karjiker, "Justifications for Copyright."
75 De Beer et al., *Innovation and Intellectual Property*, 6; also Ncube, *Intellectual Property Policy*. For an economic correlate of this stance, see Pouris and Inglesi-Lotz, *Economic Contribution*, the first major empirical study on the economic impact of the South African cultural industries.
76 De Beer et al., *Innovation and Intellectual Property*, 5.
77 De Beer et al., *Innovation and Intellectual Property*, 6.
78 Ncube, "Harnessing Intellectual Property."
79 Neves, *Reconsidering Rural Development*, 6.
80 For more details see Neves, *Reconsidering Rural Development*. The above paragraph is heavily indebted to Neves's study.
81 Ncube, *Intellectual Property Policy*.
82 Ncube, "Three Centuries," 3–4.
83 Tsing, *Friction*, 58.
84 Ferguson, *Global Shadows*, 14–15.
85 For more on these, see Comaroff and Comaroff, *Civil Society*.
86 Minister of Home Affairs and Another v Fourie and Another; Lesbian and Gay Equality Project and Others v Minister of Home Affairs and Others, (2005) ZACC 19; S v Makwanyane and Another [CCT 3/94])
87 Mbembe, "Banality of Power," 5.
88 Sen, *Development as Freedom*.
89 Sunder, *Goods to Good Life*, 89.

90   Lessig, *Free Culture*.
91   Sunder, *Goods to Good Life*, 85.
92   Ncube, "Decolonising Intellectual Property Law," 5.
93   For an extended critique, see Kirman, "Whom or What."
94   Port Elizabeth Municipality v Various Occupants 2004 (12)] BCLR 1268 (CC).
95   Bennett, "Ubuntu," 48; Honneth, *Freedom's Right*.
96   Cornell, *Law and Revolution*; Himonga, Taylor, and Pope, "Reflections on Judicial Views."
97   Mauss, *The Gift*; also Hesmondhalgh, "Capitalism and the Media," 352–53.
98   Hayden, "Taking as Giving."
99   Kraft, *Genesis*.
100 Ncube, "Calibrating Copyright," 263.
101 Hutchison, "Decolonising South African Contract Law," 179. For a decolonial theory of copyright that combines ideas of ubuntuism with the moral rights of authors, see Sindane, *Call to Decolonize*. I am indebted to Professor Ncube for pointing out this reference.
102 Nelken, "'Gap Problem.'"
103 Gluckman, *Ideas in Barotse Jurisprudence*, 6.
104 Geertz, *Local Knowledge*, 170.
105 Conley and O'Barr, *Rules versus Relationships*, 1.
106 Riles, "Representing In-Between," 597, 642–43.
107 Darian-Smith, "Ethnographies of Law"; Bens and Vetters, "Ethnographic Legal Studies." For an overview of ethnographies of intellectual property law in particular, see Chapman and Coombe, "Ethnographic Explorations."
108 Darian-Smith, "Ethnographies of Law," 553, 555.
109 Riles, "Property," 776.
110 Verdery, *Property in Question*, 161.
111 Riles, "Property," 776.
112 Riles, "Property," 783, 787.
113 Maurer, *Mutual Life, Limited*.
114 Riles, *Network Inside Out*; *Financial Citizenship*.
115 Latour, *Making of Law*.
116 Latour, *Making of Law*, viii.
117 Stengers, *Cosmopolitics* 1, 106.
118 Stengers, *Cosmopolitics* 1, 168.
119 Riles, "[Deadlines] Removing the Brackets," 62–64.
120 Pickering, *Mangle of Practice*, 26. For a good discussion of these dilemmas in Pickering's work and elsewhere in coproductionism scholarship, see Jasanoff, "Ordering Knowledge," 24, and Law, *After Method*.
121 Helmreich, "Anthropologist Underwater," 632.

122 Helmreich, *Sounding the Limits of Life*.
123 Luhmann, *Kontingenz und Recht*.
124 Serres, *Parasite*.
125 Gluckman, *Ideas in Barotse Jurisprudence*, 6; Geertz, *Local Knowledge*, 170.
126 Latour, *Reassembling the Social*, 36.
127 Latour, *Inquiry into Modes of Existence*, 144.
128 Hariman, *Prudence*, 27.
129 Callon, "What Does It Mean," 8.

Chapter Two. The Past in the Present

1 The findings of this research appeared in 1991 as chapter 6 of my book *African Stars*. In 1987, I also released an album of vintage isicathamiya music that includes the 1939 recording of "Mbube." Erlmann, *Mbube Roots*.
2 Walt Disney Company, "The Walt Disney Company," accessed April 10, 2022, https://thewaltdisneycompany.com/.
3 Walt Disney Company. *Annual Report 2006*, 57.
4 https://www.imdb.com/video/vi3764362265?playlistId=tt0110357&ref_=tt_ov_vi.
5 In reality, Abilene Music, a somewhat obscure US publisher owned by George Weiss, one of the authors of the "Lion Sleeps Tonight," was the true defendant in the case. But since it was not possible to subject the company to the jurisdiction of the South African court, Disney, as the main licensee of Abilene that not only held trademarks in South Africa but was also more vulnerable to negative publicity, was chosen as a surrogate defendant. It is for the same reason that in addition to Disney, three other South African companies were included in the list of defendants: Nu-Metro Cinemas that was licensed to screen *The Lion King* in South Africa; David Gresham Entertainment—a subpublisher of Memory Lane, itself a licensee of Abilene—as the South African publishers of the sound track of the movie; and David Gresham Records. For a compilation of some two hundred of "Mbube" covers and adaptations see: https://www.youtube.com/user/FLORENCOM/videos. Also see https://en.wikipedia.org/wiki/The_Lion_Sleeps_Tonight. For recordings of "Wimoweh" see https://archive.org/search.php?query=Wimoweh.
6 Spoor and Fisher, "After Seven Decades, Justice at Last for Solomon Linda," Press Statement.
7 "In the Jungle, the Unjust Jungle, a Small Victory," *New York Times*, March 22, 2006.
8 Sunder, *Goods to a Good Life*; Wirtén, *Terms of Use*.
9 "Minister of Arts and Culture P Jordan's Speech for Budget Vote 2006/07," *Polity*, February 6, 2002, https://www.polity.org.za/print-version/jordan-arts-and-culture-dept-budget-vote-200607-02062006-2006-06-02.

10 For another non-celebratory critique see Haupt and Ovesen, "Vindicating Capital."
11 Riles, "New Agenda."
12 There was, however, a regrettably short-lived attempt to establish a South African edition of the magazine.
13 Malan, "In the Jungle." Unless otherwise cited, all quotes in the next few paragraphs are from this source.
14 Malan, *My Traitor's Heart*.
15 For the sake of convenience in what follows, I shall be using "Gallo" as shorthand for some of the names that the company and its divisions have taken on during its almost one-hundred-year-long history, such as Gallo Africa, Gallo Record Company, Gallo Records South Africa, and Gallo Music Publishing. On the history of Gallo, see Pietilä, *Contracts*, 19–25.
16 Interview with Thembinkosi Phewa, Durban, November 11, 1985. Erlmann, *African Stars*, 159.
17 Malan, "In the Jungle." Unless otherwise cited, all quotes in the next few paragraphs are from this source.
18 Feldstein, *How It Feels*, 51, 62.
19 Said, *Orientalism*, 10, 13.
20 While orientalist discourse on Africa focused mainly on ancient Egypt, it is perhaps no coincidence that orientalist tropes suffuse colonial and present-day constructions of Zulu history and culture. See, in this regard, Carolyn Hamilton's aptly titled *Terrific Majesty* on the construction of Shaka Zulu and Louise Meintjes's work on Zulu *ngoma* dancing, masculinity, and violence. Hamilton, *Terrific Majesty*; Meintjes, *Dust of the Zulu*.
21 In "Anoku Gonda," recorded in 1940, the nexus between rapid social change and the personal experience of dislocation is projected back to a fictitious period when the nation was at one with itself. For a reissue of the recording, see Erlmann, *Mbube Roots*.
22 Malan, "In the Jungle." For a detailed history of the South African recording industry, see Pietilä, *Contracts*. On Gallo especially see 19–25.
23 3rd Ear Music Forum, "Mbube—Letters, Links & Feedback: Part II," accessed April 25, 2008, http://www.3rdearmusic.com/forum/forumjul05/mbubefeedback2.html.
24 Howard Richmond, Letter to the editor, *Rolling Stone*, May 23, 2000.
25 Pete Seeger, Letter to Rian Malan, May 15, 2000. None of these responses was published by *Rolling Stone*.
26 Bently, "Extraordinary Multiplicity." On the impact of the Imperial Copyright Act on South Africa see Pistorius, "Imperial Copyright Act."
27 Moss, *Charles Dickens' Quarrel*.
28 Dickens v. Eastern Province Herald (1861) 4 Searle 33. For a detailed discussion of the case, see Glover, "Maybe the Courts."

29 Tarantino, "Long Time Coming." For the impact of the Imperial Copyright Act in India, see Reddy and Chandrashekaran, *Create, Copy, Disrupt*; and for Palestine, see Birnheck, *Colonial Copyright*.

30 François Verster's documentary *A Lion's Trail*, released in 2002, nicely captures that phase in the lives of the daughters.

31 Interview with Rob Allingham, July 5, 2019.

32 Dean, "Stalking the Sleeping Lion," 17.

33 Dean, *Application of the Copyright Act*.

34 Dean, *Application of the Copyright Act*, 445.

35 Mechanical rights refers to the right to reproduce a sound recording from a so-called master. The format of the masters varied historically from acetate discs (used during Linda's time), analog tapes, to digital session files.

36 All three assignments were signed by Ralph Trewhela, a singer-songwriter who went on to become a director at Gallo. In his book *Song Safari*, Trewhela discusses the making of "Mbube," incorrectly and possibly even disingenuously claiming that it had been recorded in 1952. Trewhela, *Song Safari*, 138–39.

37 Interestingly, the legality of the 1952 assignment was never challenged—for good reason. For, as Dean pointed out, the entire strategy relied on that "agreement to trigger the operation of the reversionary interest. The last thing that we wanted to do was to set it aside and deprive ourselves of the whole basis of the cause of action that had been developed." Owen Dean, "Awakening the Lion in the Jungle," Spoor and Fisher (website), May 31, 2019, https://spoor.com/awakening-the-lion-in-the-jungle-the-story-of-the-lion-sleeps-tonight-case/.

38 Dean, *Ownership*, 13.

39 Seeger had already renewed his rights in "Wimoweh" in 1977 and Weiss et al. would follow suit, renewing their rights to "The Lion" in 1989.

40 Davis and le Roux, *Precedent & Possibility*.

41 Dugard, "Raymond Tucker (1932–2004)," 509.

42 Letter, Solomon Linda to Seeger, January 17, 1962. For the foundation of the USAA, see Tucker, *Just the Ticket*, 127; and Kruger, *Drama of South Africa*, 84.

43 One wonders whether the Linda in a three-piece suit and two-tone shoes visible on the photograph everybody knows and the person Bloom claims to have handed the check to and whom he describes as "illiterate and simple, with snuff boxes stuck in his pierced ear-lobes, and rough shoes cut out of an old tyre," are one and the same person. Bloom, *King Kong*, 10.

44 Williams, *King Kong*; interview with Pat Williams, April 26, 1983. Also Coplan, *In Township Tonight*, 268; Fleming, *Opposing Apartheid*, 51–56.

45 The record of those royalty transfers from the early 1970s to the early 1980s is spotty, at best. But according to available royalty statements for the years between 1985 and 2004, the daughters received $25,854.38 or 12.5 percent, of

the earnings on "Wimoweh" from Folkways and another ca. $4,000 on "The Lion Sleeps Tonight" from George Weiss for the period from 1997 to 2000.

46 Raymond Tucker, Letter to the Law Society of the Northern Provinces, August 20, 2001. The society declined my request for a copy of the complaint, citing attorney-client privilege. Of course, the person who had "put them up to it" was Hanro Friedrich, who had succeeded Tucker as the daughters' counsel. For more on the Tucker affair, see Cavalier, "More Lessons."

47 Curiously, in his numerous publications and statements about the case, Dean never mentions those royalty payments. It might thus be reasonably inferred that disclosure of these facts would have put a dent into the anti-American strategy, ultimately forcing him to accept the settlement terms imposed by Disney.

48 Owen Dean, Letter to Hanro Friedrich Attorneys, October 4, 2002.

49 The assignment of March 30, 1983, did not transfer the reversionary right to "Mbube" to Folkways. At that time, the only conceivable copyright owned by Regina Linda would have been the right to renew the second term of the United States copyright in "Mbube."

50 Sonnekus, "Reversionary Interest," 465. The article served as the basis for the opinion. I am grateful to Professor Sonnekus for pointing this out to me and providing me with a copy of the original opinion. For ease of reference, I base my discussion on the "Reversionary Interest" article. See also Sonnekus, "Matrimonial Property Law."

51 Sonnekus, "Reversionary Interest," 472.

52 Sonnekus, "Reversionary Interest," 480.

53 "Music Industry Hits False Note," news 24, November 24, 2002, https://www.news24.com/news24/music-industry-hits-false-note-20021124. Earlier, in May and June of 2002, Lloyd Coutts, a journalist writing for Business Report had uncovered irregularities in Johnnic's tax reporting. In a heated email exchange with Coutts, Paul Jenkins denied any wrongdoing. Unfortunately, of the article Coutts eventually published only a draft contained in a letter to Graeme Gilfillan survived. Lloyd Coutts, email to Graeme Gilfillan, June 28, 2002. Lloyd Coutts, email to the author, July 15, 2015.

54 Bhe and Others v Khayelitsha Magistrate and Others (CCT 49/03) [2004].

55 Comaroff and Comaroff, "Reflections on Liberalism," 44.

56 CCT 49/03, 17. For the "traditionalist" view see, for instance, Himonga, "African Customary Law."

57 Disney Enterprises, Inc v Griesel NO and Others (12003/04) [2004].

58 Tugendhaft et al., Letter to Owen Dean, July 20, 2005. The arbitration case is Folkways Music Publishers, Inc v Weiss, 989 F.2d 108.

59 Owen Dean, Letter to Tugendhaft et al., August 11, 2005.

60 Owen Dean, "Awakening the Lion in the Jungle," May 31, 2019, https://blogs.sun.ac.za/iplaw/2019/05/31/awakening-the-lion-in-the-jungle/.

61 In actual fact, this was more wishful thinking on Dean's part; it took a fair amount of correspondence and prodding for the government to deliver on its promise.
62 Owen Dean, Letter to Adams & Adams, November 9, 2004.
63 Tugendhaft et al., Letter to Owen Dean, July 20, 2005.
64 The "eminent musicologist" was the composer Khaba Mkhize.
65 Radano and Bohlman, *Music and the Racial Imagination*, 17.
66 Miller, *Segregating Sound*.
67 Meierhenrich, *Legacies of Law*.
68 See Allingham, "From 'Noma Kumnyama';" Pietilä, *Contracts, Patronage and Mediation*.
69 Chanock, *Making of South African Legal Culture*, 169. Also see Chanock, "South Africa, 1841–1924."
70 Ochiltree, "Just and Self-Respecting System."
71 Geoff Paynter, email to Owen Dean, February 17, 2006.
72 *De Zuid Afrikaan*, December 21, 1838. Quoted from Watson, *Slave Emancipation*, 23.
73 Arewa, "Writing Rights"; Greene, "Copyright, Culture & Black Music." See the latest example of this visual bias in the so-called Blurred Lines case, Pharrell Williams et al. v Bridgeport Music et al., No. 15-56880 (9th Cir. July 11, 2018). Also Lester, "Blurred Lines."
74 Greene, "Copyright, Culture & Black Music," 353–54, 372.
75 Arewa, "Blues Lives," 600.
76 Brackett, *Categorizing Sound*, 13.
77 Greene, "Copyright, Culture & Black Music," 373–74.
78 Vats, *Color of Creatorship*, 33. Other writings on copyright within critical race theory are Aoki, "(Intellectual) Property and Sovereignty"; Best, *Fugitive's Properties*; and Kraut, *Choreographing Copyright*.
79 Vats, *Color of Creatorship*, 16, 21.
80 Vats, *Color of Creatorship*, 39. Williams v. Bridgeport Music, Inc. Dist. Court, CD California 2015.
81 Vats, *Color of Creatorship*, 267.
82 Vats, *Color of Creatorship*, 268.
83 Holmes, "Codes," 1.
84 Dean, *Awakening the Lion*, 35.
85 Owen Dean, "Awakening the Lion in the Jungle," Spoor and Fisher (website), May 31, 2019, https://www.spoor.com/en/News/awakening-the-lion-in-the-jungle/, 14–15.
86 Owen Dean, Letter to Hanro Friedrich, August 11, 2005. Gallo Africa Limited t/a Gallo Music Publishers and the Solomon Linda Trust, *Administration Agreement*. The terms of the agreement are as follows: 12.5 percent

publishing royalties, 12.5 percent reproduction, 85 percent mechanical, 80 percent synchronization, 70 percent mechanical reproduction aka covers. The fact that these points are a far cry from decades of nonpayment and either conform to or slightly exceed industry standards does not invalidate my argument about the broader disconnect between legal reason and moral norms. Nor can they dispel all doubt about the possibility of Johnnic/Gallo's bait-and-switch strategy being a deliberate attempt at retaining control of the Southern African rights in "Mbube" without having to run the risk of taking on Disney. At least, this is the view of Graeme Gilfillan, who as a music industry veteran was not only part of the initial deliberations between Rian Malan, Paul Jenkins, and Geoff Paynter but was also feared for his critical views of the abuses of that industry. Interview with Hanro Friedrich, March 1, 2012. Gilfillan, communication to the author, May 29, 2021.

87 Among those who advanced claims to coauthorship of "The Lion Sleeps Tonight" and "Mbube," respectively, are Tokens band member Jay Siegel and the children of Evening Birds member Gilbert Madondo.

88 Geertz, *Interpretation of Cultures*, 17.

89 Latour, "Plea for Earthly Sciences."

90 Geertz, *Interpretation of Cultures*, 18.

91 Latour, "Plea for Earthly Sciences," 76.

92 Deed of Trust, 2006, sections 7.1 and 7.2.

93 *First and Final Distribution Account in the Estate Late Solomon Masazeni Ntsele*. Pretoria: Executor's Certificate, 2008; *First and Final Distribution Account in the Estate Late Tobi Reginah Ntsele*. Pretoria: Executor's Certificate, 2008.

94 According to Owen Dean, the fees were slightly above $345,000. Letter to Zwelakhe Mbiba, Director General, Department of Arts and Culture, May 9, 2006.

95 Oliphant, "Lion King's Heirs," 5. Some of the subsequent uses include $5,000 for the unforgettable "The Husband Sleeps Tonight" in *Menopause. The Musical*; $15,000 for the 2005 HBO "Classical Baby" series of animated films; $10,000 for the *Empty Nest* sitcom; and unknown amounts for Johnny Walker, Australian Weetbix, and South African fast food chain Hungry Lion commercials. For Abilene's offer of an additional five years of royalties see Browne, "The Lion Sleeps Tonight."

96 Dean, "Return of the Lion," 10.

97 Interview with Hanro Friedrich, March 1, 2012. Oliphant, "Lion King's Heirs," 5.

98 Interview with Hanro Friedrich, March 1, 2012.

99 In this vein, see Gani, *Creative Autonomy*, 10, 274.

100 *ReMastered: The Lion's Share*, directed by Sam Cullman (Los Angeles: All Rise Films, 2018). While its director, Sam Cullman, was still working on his film, I told him that the title of my book was going to be *Lion's Share*. Coincidence?

Chapter Three. Assembling Tradition, Representing Indigeneity

1. Drayton, *Nature's Government*, 121, 183.
2. Many committee meetings are open to the public. But documents that are handed out during the meetings, and the minutes and sound recordings of meetings can also be accessed at the website of the Parliamentary Monitoring Group at https://pmg.org.za/bill/276/. All quotations from the meetings of the Portfolio Committee on Trade and Industry are from this source.
3. Adas, *Machines as the Measure*; Scott, "Modernity's Machine Metaphor." For a historical overview, see Agar, *Government Machine*, 15–44.
4. Barry, *Political Machines*, 2–3.
5. Abélès, *Quiet Days*; Crewe, *Lords of Parliament*; *House of Commons*.
6. Crewe, "Ethnography of Parliament," 158.
7. Latour, *Making of Law*, 244.
8. Marx and Engels, *Manifesto*, 44.
9. Reckwitz, *End of Illusions*.
10. Rosa, *Resonance*.
11. Reckwitz, *Society of Singularities*; Agamben, *Homo Sacer*; Mbembe, *Necropolitics*.
12. On the liberals versus neo-Marxists debate see Lipton, *Liberals*.
13. Comaroff and Comaroff, "Reflections on Liberalism"; Himonga and Bosch, "Application of African Customary Law."
14. By implication, the equation of the author with the individual as envisaged during the Enlightenment seems just as ill-suited in capturing the "singularization" of cultural production everywhere. See Reckwitz, *Society of Singularities*.
15. The theory of social capital is a vast interdisciplinary field of social thought that stretches from the focus on domination and a relatively undifferentiated use of the term *capital* in concepts such as "cultural capital" or "economic capital" in the work of Pierre Bourdieu to more recent interventions, only tangentially related to Bourdieu, by James Coleman, Robert Putman, and others. For a critical overview see Baron et al., *Social Capital*. On patron-client relationships in the South African music industry see Pietilä, *Contracts*.
16. Putnam, "Tuning In," 664–65.
17. Du Toit and Neves, *Vulnerability and Social Protection*, 125–34.
18. For instance, Hornby, *Social and Cultural Aspects*.
19. Bayart, *State in Africa*, 271.
20. DST, *Indigenous Knowledge Systems*. The policy was the result of five year-long interdepartmental consultations that lead to the formulation by the Department of Trade and Industry of another policy document on *The Protection of Indigenous Knowledge through the Intellectual Property System*. DTI, *Protection*.
21. DTI, *Presentation*.

22 Johnny Clegg was one of South Africa's most celebrated musicians of all time whose rise to global stardom as the "white Zulu" was allegedly made possible because of his adaptations of Zulu *maskandi* street music. On maskanda, see Olsen, *Music and Social Change*. On Clegg, see Conrath, *Johnny Clegg*; and on his postapartheid career Meintjes, *Dust of the Zulu*, 151–81.
23 Scott, *Seeing Like a State*, 3–5.
24 Callon, "Some Elements."
25 Clarke et al., *Making Policy Move*; Shore, Wright, and Però, *Policy Worlds*.
26 For TK policies in other African countries see Kongolo, *African Contributions*; Ncube, *Intellectual Property Policy*.
27 Anderson, *Law, Knowledge, Culture*, 114.
28 On the recognition of indigenous people, see, however, the *Report of the African Commission's Working Group on Indigenous Populations/Communities* by the African Commission on Human and Peoples' Rights: https://www.achpr.org/presspublic/publication?id=51.
29 Antons, "Intellectual Property Rights."
30 "Tunis Model Law on Copyright," WIPO, February 23–March 7, 1976, https://www.wipo.int/publications/en/details.jsp?id=3177&plang=FR.
31 UNESCO-WIPO, *Model Provisions*.
32 Boyle, *Shamans, Software, and Spleens*.
33 Sunder, *Goods to Good Life*, 129–30.
34 Quoted in Perlman, "From 'Folklore' to 'Knowledge,'" 125.
35 Perlman, "From 'Folklore' to 'Knowledge,'" 127.
36 Lee, "Subjects of Circulation"; Comaroff and Comaroff, *Politics of Custom*; Hardt and Negri, *Empire*, 238.
37 DTI, *Presentation*.
38 Guyer, *Legacies, Logics, Logistics*, 125.
39 Drahos, *Intellectual Property*, 4, 12, 31, 40.
40 Many performing artists of the older generation still see themselves has healer-diviners of the *sangoma* kind.
41 Hardt and Negri, *Empire*; Impey, *Song Walking*; Janzen, *Ngoma*; James, *Songs of the Women*.
42 Guyer, *Legacies, Logics, Logistics*, 125.
43 Latour, *Politics of Nature*.
44 Latour, *Politics of Nature*, 10.
45 Beinart, Brown, and Gilfoyle, "Experts and Expertise," 414–15.
46 Priestley, *Letters*, 150.
47 Dubow, *Commonwealth of Knowledge*, 14.
48 Tilley, *Africa as a Living Laboratory*, 10.
49 Green, "Beyond South Africa's," 4.

50 Green, "Beyond South Africa's"; Foster, *Reinventing Hoodia*; Green, *Rock, Water, Life*; Ives, *Steeped in Heritage*; Osseo-Asare, *Bitter Roots*; Pollock, *Synthesizing Hope*.
51 Anderson, *Law, Knowledge, Culture*, 9.
52 Anderson, *Law, Knowledge, Culture*, 10–11.
53 Coombe, "Properties of Culture," 85. Boatema Boateng similarly argues that nationalist claims over culture "have to do with the power to make such claims 'stick' long enough that their association with specific locations appears naturalized." Boateng, *Copyright Thing*, 120.
54 Niezen, *Origins of Indigenism*, 215.
55 Engle, *Elusive Promise*. Elizabeth Povinelli likewise suggests that in Australia "indigenous subjects are called upon to perform an authentic difference in exchange for the good feelings of the nation and the reparative legislation of the state." Povinelli, *Cunning of Recognition*, 6. Along similar lines, see Coombe, "Properties of Culture."
56 DTI, *Presentation*.
57 Comaroff and Comaroff, *Ethnicity, Inc.*, 29.
58 UNESCO, *Framework*, 20.
59 SBP, *Regulatory Impact Analysis*, 4.
60 Du Toit, "Social Exclusion," 1003.
61 Du Toit and Neves, "In Search of South Africa's Second Economy," 14.
62 DST, *Indigenous Knowledge Systems*, 12.
63 De Beukelaar, *Developing Cultural Industries*; Yúdice, "Cultural Diversity," 110.
64 Yúdice, *Expediency of Culture*; Miller and Yúdice, *Cultural Policy*, 66.
65 Chipkin, "Set up for Failure."
66 Bauman, *Retrotopia*.
67 Comaroff and Comaroff, *Ethnicity, Inc.*; Oomen, *Chiefs*.
68 Giddens, *Consequences of Modernity*, 79–80, 21–22.
69 Giddens, *Consequences of Modernity*, 34.
70 Giddens, *Consequences of Modernity*, 80.
71 Gupta, *Postcolonial Developments*.
72 Here I follow Wynberg and Chennells, "Green Diamonds."
73 Barnett, "In Africa."
74 Pratt, *Imperial Eyes*.
75 Wynberg and Chennells, "Green Diamonds," 107.
76 Wynberg and Laird, "Bioprospecting," 77, 69.
77 Robins, *Revolution to Rights*, 36.
78 Foster, *Reinventing Hoodia*, 130.
79 Maton, *Knowledge and Knowers*.
80 Riles, "[Deadlines]"; Gardey, "Turning Public Discourse."

81 In South African law, these are respectively designated as s, followed by subsections in Arabic numerals, followed by lowercase Roman letters in alphabetical order, followed by lowercase Arabic numerals.

82 See also Hull, *Government of Paper*, 14.

83 The term *intertextuality* should be taken with a grain of salt. While it has little in common with the narrow range of connotations it has in law, where it may refer to cross-references between sections of an act, and as such often rests on prepositions such as *subject to*, it does not incorporate the entire range of meanings *intertextuality* has in literary theory and deconstruction either. The sense in which I use it here is thus meant to convey more of a sense of the self-reproducing circularity of lawmaking.

84 WIPO, *Protection*, Annex, 1, note 16.

85 Blavin, "Folklore in Africa."

86 Quoted in Collins, "Traditional Knowledge," 218.

87 Chatterjee, *Nationalist Thought*, 169.

88 Chatterjee, *Nationalist Thought*, 38, 50.

89 Nwauche, *Protection of Traditional*, 97; Beharie and Shabangu, "Traditional Knowledge," 359.

90 Gallo Africa Ltd and Others v Sting Music (Pty) Ltd and Others (40/2010) [2010], http://www.saflii.org/za/cases/ZASCA/2010/96.html.

91 Various, *Sanscapes One*, Electric M.E.L.T.—ELM 8037, CD, Europe, 2001; Chennells, "Putting Intellectual Property Rights," 221–22.

92 Interview with Pops Mohamed, February 21, 2012.

93 For a compelling discussion of Baartman's performances and the repatriation of her body, see Young, *Illegible Will*.

94 Various, *Sanscapes One*, Electric M.E.L.T.—ELM 8037, CD, Europe, 2001.

95 YoYo Ma & the Kalahari Bushmen, "CH4 Distant Echoes," Edutainment, July 24, 2019, YouTube video, 50.09, https://www.youtube.com/watch?v=9Qji1kRZ5uo.

96 Various, *Sanscapes One*.

97 For an overview of these alternatives see Posey, *Traditional Resource Rights*; Posey and Dutfield, *Beyond Intellectual Property*.

98 Rose and Novas, "Biological Citizenship"; Delanty, "Citizenship"; Foster, *Reinventing Hoodia*, 15; Clammer, *Cultural Rights*, 57.

99 Taylor, "Politics of Recognition"; Kymlicka, *Multicultural Citizenship*.

100 Scott, "Culture in Political Theory," 111. For another influential critique of the "politics of recognition," see Fraser and Honneth, *Redistribution or Recognition?*

101 Habib and Bentley, *Racial Redress* provides a good idea of the debate.

102 Habib and Bentley, *Racial Redress*, 6.

103 Mbembe and Nuttall, "Writing the World."
104 Bhandar, "Cultural Politics"; Delanty, "Citizenship."
105 Attali, *Noise*.
106 Schmidt Campbell and Martin, *Artistic Citizenship*; Elliott, Silverman, and Bowman, *Artistic Citizenship*.
107 Kant, *Critique of Judgment*, 160, 232.
108 Martin, "Artistic Citizenship," 14.
109 Bowman, "Artistry, Ethics, and Citizenship," 61.
110 Bowman, "Artistry, Ethics, and Citizenship," 64, 65, 68.
111 Bowman, "Artistry, Ethics, and Citizenship," 68, 70.
112 Bowman, "Artistry, Ethics, and Citizenship," 70–72, 75, 76.
113 Kant, *Critique of Judgment*, 48.
114 Bowman, "Artistry, Ethics, and Citizenship," 76, 77.
115 For more on copyright law's "default ethical vision," see Grimmelmann, "Ethical Visions," 2015–16.
116 Hardt, "Affective Labor"; Morris, "Artists as Entrepreneurs."
117 Bently and Maniatis, *Intellectual Property and Ethics*; Lever, *New Frontiers*.
118 Foucault, "Self Writing"; Tadros, "Few Thoughts," 129.
119 Foucault, "Self Writing," 210; "What Is an Author," 221.
120 Lametti, "Virtuous P(eer)," 288, 298. See also Demuijnck, "P2P Sharing."
121 Schmücker, "Normative Resources," 361–62.
122 Ess, "Ethical Approaches," 298. See also Lever, *New Frontiers*.
123 Meintjes, *Dust of the Zulu*, 65.
124 Meintjes, *Dust of the Zulu*, 119.
125 Steingo, *Kwaito's Promise*, viii.
126 Ferguson, *Give a Man a Fish*, 93.
127 Steingo, *Kwaito's Promise*, 2.
128 For a slightly different take elsewhere on the African continent see Skinner, *Bamako Sounds*.
129 Ndabeni and Mthembu, *Born to Kwaito*, 1, 12.
130 Ndabeni and Mthembu, *Born to Kwaito*, 1, 43–44.
131 Haupt, *Stealing Empire*, 149.
132 MacIntyre, *After Virtue*, 12–13.
133 Levinson, *Aesthetics and Ethics*, 2.
134 Brown, "Can Culture Be Copyrighted?," 200.
135 Banks, *Creative Justice*.
136 Sinnreich, "Ethics, Evolved."
137 Scarry, *Beauty and Being Just*, 81. Space does not allow a more extended discussion of some of the new ways of thinking about the ethical and aesthetic ramifications of copyright in the creative industries and in the arts and

culture more broadly. For instance, in *Music and Ethics*, Marcel Cobussen and Nanette Nielsen explore the potential of what they call an "aural ethics" (10). As an aural art form, they argue, music is not limited to *depicting* certain ethical values, such as hospitality, solidarity, or respect for the other, the irreducible, irreconcilable, and irrational. In and through music "ethics sets itself to work" (23). But this ethical work must not be thought of as merely directed at a nameable, already identified object or situation that may call for an ethical response. It is, rather, a highly performative, tentative, aesthetically interactive way of performing good in unknown spaces and moments of uncertainty without lapsing into the normativity of morals. Other works that are centrally concerned with an ethics of the cultural text as a question of aesthetics is Marcus Boon's elegant *In Praise of Copying*, Darren Hick's and Reinold Schmücker's edited volume *The Aesthetics and Ethics of Copying*, or James O. Young's and Conrad Brunk's excellent collection of essays on *The Ethics of Cultural Appropriation*. The list would be incomplete without two works by musicologist Will Cheng—*Just Vibrations* and *Loving Music*.

138 Scarry, *Beauty and Being Just*, 81.
139 Scarry, *Beauty and Being Just*, 58–59.
140 Scarry, *Beauty and Being Just*, 60, 79.
141 Scarry, *Beauty and Being Just*, 108, 111.
142 Scarry, *Beauty and Being Just*, 11.
143 But Banks, despite his defense of an "aesthetically realist" perspective on the intrinsic value of cultural objects, still holds on to the possibility of a sociologically informed attempt to value such objects in a nonreductive manner (Banks, *Creative Justice*, 15). Similarly, Georgina Born follows Janet Woff in calling for a "non-idealist, non-essentialist theory of aesthetic experience" that refuses to let go of the prospect of a "sociological aesthetics" and what she terms the "analytics of mediation." Born, "Social and the Aesthetic," 175; 171.
144 Scarry, *Beauty and Being Just*, 99–100.
145 Koch, *We Have the Song*; Robinson, *Hungry Listening*.

Chapter Four. Circulating Evidence

1 Tristen Taylor, "Police Brutality Is Government Policy," *Mail & Guardian*, July 12, 2020, https://mg.co.za/opinion/2020-07-12-police-brutality-is-government-policy/.
2 Dubin, *Spearheading Debate*.
3 "SAPS declare war on piracy," MyBroadband, December 2, 2011, https://mybroadband.co.za/news/technology/39263-saps-declare-war-on-piracy.html.
4 BSA, 2011 *Global Software*, 3. That figure did not change significantly in more recent years and was reported to be 32 percent in 2017.

5   Paul Furber, "Lies, Damn Lies and the BSA," *Brainstorm Magazine*, July 1, 2011, http://www.brainstormmag.co.za/cover-story/36-cover-story/9288-lies-damn-lies-and-the-bsa.

6   Both of these posts and others like them are available at: https://mybroadband.co.za/forum/threads/criminal-record-for-piracy-in-south-africa.328542/.

7   Mouffe and Laclau, *Hegemony*; Chipkin, *Do South Africans Exist?*

8   Dean, *Application of the Copyright Act*; Harms, *Role of the Judiciary*.

9   Comaroff and Comaroff, *Truth about Crime*, xiii–xiv.

10 Comaroff and Comaroff, *Truth about Crime*, xiv.

11 PricewaterhouseCoopers, *Insights from the Entertainment & Media Outlook: 2019–2023. An African Perspective*, 155–56.

12 In 2004 alone 1.9 million CDs were impounded. RiSA, *Annual General Meeting*, 5.

13 "'All-Out War' on CD and DVD Piracy," *The Citizen*, December 13, 2011; RiSA Digital Statistics, February 25, 2012; Interviews with Angus Rheder, February 2, 2012, and June 6, 2012; RiSA, *Master Statistics 2013*.

14 SAFACT (@SAFACT), "PiracySucks" (profile description), joined February 2011, https://twitter.com/safact?lang=en.

15 Freefall Trading 217 (Pty) Ltd and the Minister of Police, Sergeant Macnish, April 25, 2016.

16 RiSA, "Investigation Process," 6–7.

17 The criminalization of copyright—and intellectual property in general—prior to the early 2000s has received only scant attention. For more recent scholarship, however, see the contributions to Geiger, *Criminal Enforcement*.

18 CIPC, *South African Training Manual*, 11.

19 Karaganis, *Media Piracy*, i.

20 Ouma, "Optimal Enforcement," 617, 607, 618.

21 See Harms, *Role of the Judiciary*; CIPC, *South African Training Manual*.

22 Hilty, "Economic, Legal and Social Impacts," 10.

23 At the start of 2021, Musica, the country's last remaining music retail brand closed its doors for good. Reuters, "UPDATE 1-South Africa's Clicks Drug Chain to Close Musica after 29 Years," January 28, 2021, https://www.reuters.com/article/clicks-group-outlook/update-1-south-africas-clicks-drug-chain-to-close-musica-after-29-years-idUKL8N2K31BX.

24 For instance, in 2013, I attended a meeting of the Creative Industries Forum of Tshwane (CIFT) where members—mostly performing artists—after intense debate, threatened to occupy the offices of the city's Sports and Recreational Services in protest of its alleged lack of support for local artists.

25 Anand, Gupta, and Appel, *Promise of Infrastructure*; Elyachar, "Next Practices"; Fredericks, *Garbage Citizenship*. In the South African context, Simone, "People as Infrastructure." Finally, infrastructure has also become a powerful tool

for organizing emergent scholarship in music: Devine and Boudreault-Fournier, *Audible Infrastructures*; Magaudda, "Popular Music."

26 Prominent examples are Larkin, *Signal and Noise*; Sundaram, *Pirate Modernity*; and Eckstein and Schwarz, *Postcolonial Piracy*.
27 Larkin, *Signal and Noise*, 226.
28 Sundaram, *Pirate Modernity*, 112.
29 Ferguson, *Give a Man a Fish*, 23.
30 Rifkin, *Age of Access*, 4, 243, 245.
31 Rifkin, *Age of Access*, 248, 246.
32 Rifkin, *Age of Access*, 257.
33 Riles, *Network Inside Out*, 3, 172.
34 Latour, *Reassembling the Social*, 49.
35 Latour, *Reassembling the Social*, 34.
36 Collecting Society Regulations 2006, s 1 (ii) (a); Copyright Act 1978, s 9 (c), (d), and (e).
37 RiSA, "About Us," accessed February 6, 2022, https://www.risa.org.za/website/about.
38 RiSA, *Annual General Meeting*, 21.
39 SAFACT shut down in 2018 following allegations of corruption and sexual harassment by its office staff.
40 Primo and Lloyd, "Chapter 3," 130–31.
41 Primo and Lloyd, "Chapter 3," 130. Interview with Angus Rheder, June 6, 2012.
42 Interview with Mzwakhe Mbuli, June 18, 2012.
43 Diane Coetzer, "Anti-Piracy Dispute Disrupts Board Meeting," *Billboard*, August 17, 2006, https://www.billboard.com/articles/business/1351335/anti-piracy-dispute-disrupts-board-meeting.
44 Andile April, "Lusanda Accused of Assault," December 11, 2011, https://www.pressreader.com/south-africa/sunday-world-8839/20111211/281711201480339.
45 Primo and Lloyd, "Chapter 3," 143.
46 "Our Vision & Mission," Business Leadership South Africa, https://www.blsa.org.za/about-us/vision-mission/.
47 To satisfy the physical copy requirement, Rheder keeps a collection of over four thousand CDs at his home!
48 Primo and Lloyd, "Chapter 3," 127. According to Rheder, of the 879 investigations made by RiSA in 2011, only 312 resulted in the opening of criminal cases of which a mere 44 went to trial. Interview with Angus Rheder, June 6, 2012.
49 Primo and Lloyd, "Chapter 3," 129. Perhaps it is as a result of these findings that I relied more on informal conversation with RiSA staff or visits to police stations than in attempting to attend piracy-oriented trials. Although I was

present at several nonpiracy trials at the Johannesburg Commercial Crime Court, another factor that impeded a more sustained effort at court ethnography is the fact that in criminal proceedings South African court rolls are only publicized on the day of the trial.

50 Latour, *Pandora's Hope*, 24–79. In a similar vein, Lam, "Making Crime Messy."
51 Latour, "Plea for Earthly Sciences," 272.
52 Hornberger, *Policing and Human Rights*, 113.
53 Bowker and Star, *Sorting Things Out*, 297.
54 For a discussion of dockets along similar lines see Arend, "Taming Tensions."
55 Knorr Cetina, *Epistemic Cultures*.
56 Latour, "Plea for Earthly Sciences," 232.
57 Cole, "Forensic Culture," 43.
58 Roberts, "Renegotiating Forensic Cultures," 48–49.
59 Kruse, *Social Life*, 1.
60 Abbott, *System of Professions*.
61 Kruse, *Social Life*, 70.
62 At the time of my fieldwork on piracy, early signs that the days of RiSA's heavy-handed approach were numbered were hard to overlook. In fact, RiSA had already hired a tech expert specializing in tracking and tracing upload activities on the internet. Interview with Pierre Rautenbach, February 20, 2012.
63 Interview with Angus Rheder, August 21, 2013.
64 SAPS, Secretariat for Safety and Security, "Report," accessed April 13, 2022, http://www.policesecretariat.gov.za/publications/reports.php.
65 SAPS, Secretariat for Safety and Security, "Report," 2.2.2.
66 Riles, *Network Inside Out*, 3.
67 Evans-Pritchard, *Social Anthropology*, 74.
68 Fischer and Marcus, *Anthropology as Cultural Critique*; Clifford and Marcus, *Writing Culture*.
69 Marcus, "Contemporary Problems," 190.
70 However, the second edition of *Anthropology as Cultural Critique* includes some gestures of recognition toward statistics as enriching the discipline's methodological warehouse.
71 Asad, "Ethnographic Representation," 78.
72 Merry, *Seductions of Quantification*.
73 See the essays in Rottenburg et al., *World of Indicators*; and Erikson, "Global Health Business." For the anthropology of data more generally, see Douglas-Jones, Walford, and Seaver, "Anthropology of Data."
74 Comaroff and Comaroff, *Truth about Crime*, 143–80.
75 Foucault, *Archaeology of Knowledge*.
76 Desrosières, *Politics of Large Numbers*.

77 For more on this, see Karaganis, *Media Piracy*. For the music industry specifically, Osborne and Laing, *Music by Numbers*.

78 Altbeker, *Dirty Work*; Brown, *Street Blues*; Kriegler and Shaw, *Citizen's Guide*. Contrasting with these narratives is anthropologist Julia Hornberger's self-reflexive account of an antipiracy raid in Hornberger, "Complicity." The term *risk society* stems from Ulrich Beck's acclaimed book *Risk Society*, and although it is primarily concerned with the West in my view its core argument is applicable to South Africa as well. Beck, *Risk Society*.

79 Primo and Lloyd, "Chapter 3."

80 Vigneswaran, "Contours of Disorder," 92.

81 For instance, in 2014, the Cape Town City Council was reported to moot a plan to rid the city center of people eking out an existence on the streets. "Reports of CPT Homeless 'Work Camps' Alarming," *Mail & Guardian*, April 11, 2014.

82 See, inter alia, Alcock, *Kasinomics*.

83 Von Schnitzler, *Democracy's Infrastructure*, 13; Ferguson, *Anti-Politics Machine*, 20.

84 Madondo, *Sigh, the Beloved Country*, 309.

85 Peyroux, "City Improvement Districts," 154.

86 Primo and Lloyd, "Chapter 3," 102. According to Primo and Lloyd, the absence of South Africa from the USTR watch list can be attributed to the US being "weary of further conflict" after a compromise had been reached in which South Africa backed off threats of parallel importation in return for more favorable agreements with the pharmaceuticals and an end to US trade pressure.

87 Karaganis, *Media Piracy*, 8.

88 Karaganis, *Media Piracy*, 6.

89 Karaganis, *Media Piracy*, 4.

90 While the organization aggregates surveys from local affiliates, such as RiSA, "each affiliate makes its own choices about how to conduct its research." Karaganis, *Media Piracy*, 6. See also Pietilä, *Contracts*, 46; Marshall, "Recording Industry," 54; Harker, "Wonderful World of IFPI."

91 Perullo, *Live from Dar es Salam*, xvii.

92 BSA, *Global Software Survey*, 11.

Chapter Five. Which Collective?

1 Another term is *performing rights organization* (PRO). Depending on the context in which they occur, I will be using all three terms interchangeably.

2 Oriakhogba, *Copyright*.

3 The name was changed in 1966 to South African Music Rights Organization (SAMRO) and again in 1975 to its current name Southern African Music Rights Organization.

4 "SAMRO celebrates legacy with Builders' Awards," SAMRO, accessed February 8, 2022, https://www.samro.org.za/news/articles/samro-celebrates-legacy-builders'-awards. And as late as the mid-1990s, when the University of the Witwatersrand awarded Roos a doctor honoris causa in law, it extolled his "great percipience" in building SAMRO into a "non-racial" national institution. University of the Witwatersrand, Honorary Graduate. Gideon Gabriel Roos, https://www.wits.ac.za/alumni/distinguished-graduates/honorary-degrees/.

5 Wilkins and Strydom, Super-Afrikaners, 127–29.

6 Hamm, "Constant Companion," 159.

7 In her acclaimed Soweto Blues, music journalist Gwen Ansell claims that "until the 1990s, SAMRO paid royalties at two different rates. The black rate was lower." Ansell, Soweto Blues, 131. Not only has no evidence of such an overtly racialized distribution scheme come to light, the statement is also confusing because it comes at the end of a paragraph in which she discusses the fact that Copyright Act 63 of 1965 did away with so-called needle-time rights—i.e., protections for sound recordings. But these rights differ, of course, from the performance rights of works that, from 1925, have been administered by PRS and its successors SAFCA and SAMRO, respectively.

8 SAFCA, Special/Ordinary Resolution. December 17, 1963. SAFCA, Minutes: Eighth Meeting of the Board of Directors, October 26, 1963. I am indebted to Graeme Gilfillan for providing me with copies of these documents.

9 SABC, Annual Report 1952, 36; quoted in Hamm, "Constant Companion," 150.

10 SABC, Annual Report 1953, 32; quoted in Hamm, "Constant Companion," 150; Huskisson, Bantu Composers, xxii.

11 Patience Bambalele and Julia Madibogo, "Arthur Mafokate Kicked Out of Samro," Sowetan Live, July 11, 2018, https://www.sowetanlive.co.za/entertainment/2018-07-11-arthur-mafokate-kicked-out-of-samro/.

12 "Samro's Rocky Place," City Press, September 23, 2018, https://www.news24.com/fin24/economy/samros-rocky-place-20180923-2.

13 For a detailed account of the matter see Gilfillan, Auditing.

14 Ano Shumba, "Nothando Migogo: Why I'm leaving SAMRO," Music Africa, March 22, 2019, https://www.musicinafrica.net/magazine/nothando-migogo-why-im-leaving-samro.

15 Struan Douglas, "Africa's Largest Collecting Society Appoints Mark Rosin as Turnaround Strategist," Billboard, April 15, 2020, https://www.billboard.com/articles/news/international/9358736/mark-rosin-samro-turnaround-south-african-collecting-society/

16 Charl Blignaut, Ntombizodwa Makhoba, and Dewald Van Rensburg, "'Rigged Board, Dodgy Dubai Deal': Musos up in Arms over Samro Shambles," City Press, December 12, 2018, https://www.news24.com/citypress/news/rigged-board-dodgy-dubai-deal-musos-up-in-arms-over-samro-shambles-20181218.

17 Latour, *On the Modern Cult*, 21–24.
18 For more on some of these CMO scandals elsewhere, see Band and Butler "Some Cautionary Tales."
19 Tsing, *Friction*, 3.
20 Oriakhogba, *Copyright*. But there is a growing number of articles and book chapters on the policies of music rights management in countries such as Nigeria, Kenya, Ethiopia, or Rwanda and, of course, countless *How to Make It in the Music Business* guidebooks.
21 Stewart, *Ordinary Affects*.
22 Anand, Gupta, and Appel, *Promise of Infrastructure*.
23 With the exception of SAMRO executive and board members in this chapter, all names of my coworkers have been anonymized.
24 The tariff, "MS" (Municipal Facilities and Stadiums), Anderson is referring to here was changed in 2016 to an annual fee calculated according to total seating capacity.
25 https://www.facebook.com/1265794826846735/posts/are-we-being-legally-scammed-by-our-south-african-music-organizations-are-you-ge/1825299097562969/.
26 Mazzarella, "Internet X-Ray."
27 Taussig, *Shamanism, Colonialism*.
28 Jacob, "Form-Made Persons."
29 Bowker and Star, *Sorting Things Out*, 33, 37–50.
30 Bowker and Star, *Sorting Things Out*, 297, 308.
31 Bowker and Star, *Sorting Things Out*, 33.
32 Chapdelaine, "Copyright User Rights and Remedies."
33 Baloyi, "Demystifying the Role of Copyright." Another lawyer who has extensive practical experience in the music industry is Nick Matzukis, who specializes in recording contracts. Matzukis, *South African Music Law*.
34 Baloyi, "Demystifying the Role of Copyright," 16. For a parallel argument in Nigeria, see Gani, *Creative Autonomy*.
35 Ex Parte Chairperson of the Constitutional Assembly: In re Certification of the Constitution of the Republic of South Africa, 1996 1996 4 SA 744 (CC); Laugh it Off Promotions CC v SAB International (Finance) BV t/a Sabmark International and Another (CCT 42/04) [2005] ZACC 7. For additional comment on these cases, see Dean, "Case for Recognition."
36 Baloyi, "Demystifying the Role of Copyright," 121. Helfer, "Collective Management."
37 Baloyi, "Demystifying the Role of Copyright," 127, 134.
38 See, however, Hudson, *Drafting Copyright Exceptions* for an empirical, law-in-action study of exceptions.
39 Although some of the forms I was working with in 2014 have since been updated, for ease of reference I will be referring to the ones available at the

40 Latour, "Drawing Things Together," 40.
41 "Seven Misconceptions about DJ Licences," SAMRO, accessed February 9, 2022, https://samro.org.za/news/articles/seven-misconceptions-about-dj-licences.
42 Petersen et al., *What Price Cheap Goods?*
43 As if SAMRO had anticipated the critique of its tariff structure, it updated tariffs in 2020 by substantially lowering the annual fee for a seating capacity below twenty, while leaving those for a capacity over twenty either intact or slightly reducing them.
44 Chakrabarty, *Provincializing Europe*; Tsing, *Friction*, 6.
45 Towse, "Managing Copyrights," 5.
46 For a modest attempt at more empirical research, see Watt, *Collective Management*.
47 For ethnographies of the economics of the music industry in India and Tanzania, see Beaster-Jones, *Music Commodities*, and Perullo, *Live from Dar es Salam*, respectively. A pioneering, still-inspiring work is Wallis and Malm, *Big Sounds*.
48 Guyer, *Legacies, Logics, Logistics*.
49 For classic introductions to collective management organizations in the copyright industries, see Ficsor, *Collective Management*; Gervais, *Collective Management*; and Uchtenhagen, *Copyright Collective Management*. Among more specialized publications on the economics of copyright CMO are Towse, *Copyright in the Cultural Industries*, and Handke, "Collective Administration."
50 Callon, "Essay on Framing."
51 Callon, "Essay on Framing," 252.
52 For a representative example of these and similar arguments, see Handke, "Collective Administration."
53 Reidel, "Taylor Swift Paradox."
54 South Africa is home to a plethora of broadcast research bodies, such as the Broadcast Research Council of South Africa (BRC): https://brcsa.org.za/. A thorough analysis of the rich data generated by these institutions with respect to the issue being examined here is beyond the scope of this book.
55 For an example of the point system used by SAMRO's sister organization—and predecessor—PRS, see Performing Right Society Limited, *Distribution Rules*.
56 Ficsor, *Collective Management*, 48.
57 Handke, "Collective Administration."
58 Wallis et al., "Contested Collective Administration," 25.
59 Florida, *Rise of the Creative Class*; and Scott, *Cultural Economy of Cities*.

[Note: page begins mid-sentence: "time of writing on the SAMRO website at https://www.samro.org.za/forms. Differences in the scope and wording of these documents are minimal enough to be of no consequence to the argument presented here."]

60 Hesmondhalgh, *Cultural Industries*, 4th edition; Hesmondhalgh, *Cultural Industries*, 1st edition.
61 Hesmondhalgh, *Cultural Industries*, 4th edition, 9.
62 Hesmondhalgh, *Cultural Industries*, 4th edition, 11.
63 See, however, Hesmondhalgh, *Cultural Industries*, 4th edition, 49–52, where he proposes the concept of "moral economy" as an alternative to the tendency to equate the well-being of people with the ability to meet their consumer preferences. See also Hesmondhalgh, "Capitalism and the Media."
64 Tsing, "On Nonscalability," 506.
65 Stahl, *Unfree Masters*.
66 White, *Rumba Rules*.
67 COSATU, *Summary of Critique*. According to the National Development Commission, the agency tasked with development planning, in a 2020 report found that "progress towards achieving the NDP's main goals has been slow." For instance, unemployment between 2010 and 2019 grew from 24 to 29 percent. NDC, *A Review of the National Development Plan 2030*, Pretoria: National Planning Commission of South Africa, 2020, https://www.nationalplanningcommission.org.za/assets/Documents/NDP%20REVIEW.pdf. See also Matiba Sibanyoni, "NDP 2030 Targets: SA's Targets vs Reality," February 8, 2021, https://www.sabcnews.com/sabcnews/ndp-2030-targets-sas-targets-vs-reality/. For a more sophisticated approach advocating "labour-intensive growth and a rising employment elasticity of growth" as being "essential for inclusive development," see Nattrass and Seekings, *Inclusive Dualism*, 2. Delusional or sophisticated, neither of these positions bodes well for the future of cultural workers however.
68 SACO, *Employment*, 18. The term *cultural occupation* and its counterpart *non-cultural occupation* are part of the so-called creative trident. While the first includes workers with a cultural profession working in a cultural sector (such as an opera singer) but not workers who have a cultural profession outside the cultural industries, such as a designer in the automobile industry, non-cultural occupations refer to workers without a cultural profession who work in the cultural sector (such as a truck driver in a film production company).
69 SACO, *Employment*, 18.
70 SACO, "Mapping," 34.
71 See also COSATU, *Summary of Critique*, March 2013, https://www.polity.org.za/article/summary-of-critique-of-the-national-development-plan-march-2013-2013-04-19.
72 Tsing, "On Nonscalability," 514.
73 SAMRO, *Annual Report 2015*, 36.
74 The platform is owned by thirteen CMOs that are shareholders of FastTrack (FT the Digital Copyright Network) and members of CISAC, the International Confederation of Societies of Authors and Composers, FastTrack's only licensee.

75 Coplan, *Time of Cannibals*, 135.
76 Bowker and Star, *Sorting Things Out*, 39.
77 Bowker, *Science on the Run*; Moretti, *Graphs, Maps, Trees*.
78 Bowker and Star, *Sorting Things Out*, 308.
79 Anand, Gupta, and Appel, *Promise of Infrastructure*; Harvey et al., *Infrastructures and Social Complexity*.
80 To this list I would also add techno-aesthetic ensembles. These would include more than, say, just infrastructures *of* music but interstructures in which music itself becomes part of large-scale networks of surveillance that "close the gap separating our data doubles from our selves" and reveal "who we really are." Drott, "Music as a Technology," 262. Also Magaudda, "Popular Music."
81 von Schnitzler, *Democracy's Infrastructure*, 8–9.
82 Bowker and Star, *Sorting Things Out*, 290–91. In addition to Bowker's and Star's work, I am inspired by the rich literature of the past twenty or so years on data and information systems, notably Gitelman, *"Raw Data" is an Oxymoron*. For South African contributions to the debate, see Breckenridge, *Biometric State*; and Simone, "People as Infrastructure."
83 SekelaXabiso, *Southern African Music Rights*.
84 SekelaXabiso, *Southern African Music Rights*, exhibit 1.
85 SekelaXabiso, *Southern African Music Rights*, 7.3.13.2; 7.3.11.
86 "SAMRO Members Demand Answers over Lost Money," *Music in Africa*, August 13, 2018, https://www.musicinafrica.net/magazine/samro-members-demand-answers-over-lost-money.
87 Balloch and Deans, "Collective Licensing of Music in the UAE."
88 SekelaXabiso, *Southern African Music Rights*, 7.9.5.4.
89 SekelaXabiso, *Southern African Music Rights*, 7.11.1.3.
90 SekelaXabiso, *Southern African Music Rights*, 7.11.9
91 CWU Media Statement, SAMRO Threatens Security of South African Music Industry, October 31, 2019.
92 SekelaXabiso, *Southern African Music Rights*, 8.22; 8.28.
93 Power, *Audit Society*; Shore and Wright, "Governing by Numbers"; Strathern, "From Improvement to Enhancement"; Strathern, *Audit Cultures*.
94 Giri, "Audited Accountability," 178.
95 Power, *Audit Society*, 9.
96 Power, *Audit Society*, 11.
97 Crewe and Mowles, "Audit as Political Struggle," 2.
98 Douglas-Jones, "'Good' Ethical Review," 54.
99 "Parastatal Boss Exposed after Bagging R4.4m Golden Handshake," *City Press*, April 5, 2015, https://www.news24.com/Fin24/parastatal-boss-exposed-after-bagging-r44m-golden-handshake-20150405.

100 "Samro's Dubai Scandal Deepens," *City Press*, September 2, 2018, https://www.news24.com/fin24/companies/ict/samros-dubai-scandal-deepens-20180902-2.

101 Mabala Noise Entertainment, "About Us," Linkedin, accessed April 13, 2022, https://www.linkedin.com/company/mabala-noise-enter/?originalSubdomain=za.

102 Hetherington, *Guerilla Auditors*, 96, 151; Spira, *Audit Committee*; Strathern, *Audit Cultures*.

103 Crewe and Mowles, "Audit as Political Struggle"; Hetherington, *Guerilla Auditors*; Strathern, *Audit Cultures*.

104 Strathern, "Improvement to Enhancement," 19.

105 Hetherington, *Guerilla Auditors*, 209.

106 Hetherington, *Guerilla Auditors*, 221.

107 Hetherington, *Guerilla Auditors*, 220, 209.

108 SAMRO, *Annual Integrated Reports*, 2017 and 2018.

109 SAMRO, *Annual Integrated Report*, 2020, 6.

110 Ano, Shumba, "Interview: SAMRO CEO Mark Rosin," *Music in Africa*, October 11, 2021, https://www.musicinafrica.net/magazine/interview-samro-ceo-mark-rosin.

111 Gilfillan, *Investigation*.

112 SAMRO, "Performing Rights Royalty Distribution Rules," SAMRO, 9–10, https://samro.org.za/files/legal/performing-rights-royalty-distribution-rules.

113 But see also Okorie, "Exploiting Arrangements of Traditional (Gospel or Folk) Music in South Africa," IPKat, https://ipkitten.blogspot.com/2019/02/exploiting-arrangements-of-traditional.html.

114 Thompson, *Generation of Swine*, 43.

115 "SAMRO CEO Response to Media Reports," April 1, 2018, https://www.samro.org.za/news/articles/samro-ceo-response-media-reports; Gilfillan, "Review."

116 Migogo, c. May 2018, "Member Letter," SAMRO, *Annual Integrated Report 2020*, 9.

117 Ntombizodwa Makhoba and Phumlani S. Langa, "'It's an American Circus!' Artists up in Arms over Local Content Quota on Radio," *City Press*, May 3 2020, https://www.news24.com/citypress/trending/artists-up-in-arms-over-local-content-quota-on-radio-20200503. See also Dlamini, *Native Nostalgia*.

118 SAMRO, *Annual Integrated Report 2020*, 39.

Conclusion

1 Star, "Structure of Ill-Structured Solutions," 251.

2 Star, "Structure of Ill-Structured Solutions," 251.

3   Star, "Structure of Ill-Structured Solutions," 254.
4   Star, "Structure of Ill-Structured Solutions," 295.
5   SACO, "Measuring the Impact."
6   Roitman, *Anti-Crisis*, 3, 4, 8.

BIBLIOGRAPHY

Primary Sources

Constitution of the Republic of South Africa
https://www.gov.za/documents/constitution-republic-south-africa-1996

Statutes
Black Administration Act 38 of 1927, https://www.gov.za/documents/black
 -administration-act-5-jul-1927-0000
British Copyright Act 1911, https://www.legislation.gov.uk/ukpga/Geo5/1-2/46
 /contents/enacted
Companies Act 71 of 2008, https://www.gov.za/documents/companies-act
Competition Act 89 of 1998, https://www.gov.za/documents/competition-act
Copyright Act 98 of 1978, https://wipolex.wipo.int/en/legislation/details/4067
Copyright Amendment Act 63 of 1965
Counterfeit Goods Act 37, 1997, https://www.gov.za/documents/counterfeit-goods-act
Criminal Procedure Act 56 of 1955, https://www.gov.za/documents/criminal
 -procedure-act-19-may-2015-1252
Customs and Excise Act 91 of 1964, https://www.gov.za/documents/customs-and
 -excise-act-31-jul-1964-0000
Intellectual Property Laws Amendment Act 28 of 2013, https://www.gov.za
 /documents/intellectual-property-laws-amendment-act-0#
Native Lands Act 27 of 1913
Patents, Designs, Trade Marks and Copyright Act 9 of 1916
Performers' Protection Amendment Act 8 of 2002
Prevention of Organised Crime Act 121 of 1998, https://www.gov.za/documents
 /prevention-organised-crime-act
Restitution of Land Rights Act 22 of 1994, http://www.saflii.org/za/legis/num_act
 /rolra1994301/

Case Law

Bhe and Others v Khayelitsha Magistrate and Others (CCT 49/03) [2004], http://www.saflii.org/za/cases/ZACC/2004/17.html

Dickens v Eastern Province Herald (1861) 4 Searle 33

Disney Enterprises, Inc v Griesel NO and Others (12003/04) [2004], http://www.saflii.org/za/cases/ZAGPJHC/2004/1.html

Ex Parte Chairperson of the Constitutional Assembly: In re Certification of the Constitution of the Republic of South Africa, 1996 1996 4 SA 744 (CC), http://www.saflii.org/za/cases/ZACC/1996/26.html

Folkways Music Publishers, Inc v Weiss, 989 F.2d 108, https://law.resource.org/pub/us/case/reporter/F2/989/989.F2d.108.92-9061.929.html

Gallo Africa Ltd and Others v Sting Music (Pty) Ltd and Others (40/2010) [2010], http://www.saflii.org/za/cases/ZASCA/2010/96.html

Laugh it Off Promotions CC v SAB International (Finance) BV t/a Sabmark International and Another (CCT 42/04) [2005] ZACC 7, http://www.saflii.org/za/cases/ZACC/2005/7.html

Minister of Home Affairs and Another v Fourie and Another; Lesbian and Gay Equality Project and Others v Minister of Home Affairs and Others, (2005) ZACC 19, http://www.saflii.org.za/za/cases/ZACC/2005/19.html

Port Elizabeth Municipality v Various Occupants 2004 (12)] BCLR 1268 (CC), https://collections.concourt.org.za/handle/20.500.12144/2209

S v Makwanyane and Another [CCT 3/94)], https://lawlibrary.org.za/za/judgment/constitutional-court-south-africa/1995/3

Official Documents

CIPC (Companies and Intellectual Property Commission). *South African Training Manual on Investigation and Prosecuting IP Crime for Senior Law Enforcement Officials.* Pretoria: CIPC, 2017.

Council on Higher Education, CHE. *The State of the Provision of the Bachelor of Laws (LLB) Qualification in South Africa.* Cape Town: CHE, 2018.

DST (Department of Science and Technology). *Indigenous Knowledge Systems.* 2004.

DTI (Department of Trade and Industry). *The Protection of Indigenous Knowledge through the Intellectual Property System: A Policy Framework.* South Africa: Department of Trade and Industry, 2004. https://pmg.org.za/policy-document/167/.

DTI (Department of Trade and Industry). *Presentation by Department of Trade and Industry to Portfolio Committee on Trade and Industry and Select Committee on Trade and International Affairs.* February 16, 2010.

National Development Plan 2030. 2011.

SAPS. Secretariat for Safety and Security. *Report on Meeting the Legal Requirements for Search Warrants.* No date.

SBP. *Regulatory Impact Analysis: The Intellectual Property Laws Amendment Bill.* 2009.

South African Government. *Copyright Review Commission Report (2011).* South Africa: Department of Trade and Industry, 2011. https://www.gov.za/documents/copyright-review-commission-report-2011.

UNESCO-WIPO. *Model Provisions for National Laws on the Protection of Expressions of Folklore against Illicit Exploitation and Other Prejudicial Actions.* Paris-Geneva: UNESCO-WIPO, 1985.

WIPO. *The Protection of Traditional Cultural Expressions/Expressions of Folklore: Revised Objects and Principles.* Geneva, 2005. https://www.wipo.int/meetings/en/doc_details.jsp?doc_id=144441.

Reports and Surveys

Performing Right Society Limited. *Distribution Rules.* London: no date.

PricewaterhouseCoopers. *Insights from the Entertainment & Media Outlook: 2019–2023. An African Perspective.* 2019.

RiSA. *Annual General Meeting*, June 5, 2007.

SABC. *Annual Report.* 1952.

SABC. *Annual Report.* 1953.

SAMRO. *SAMRO Annual Integrated Report.* 2015.

SAMRO. *SAMRO Annual Integrated Report.* 2017.

SAMRO. *SAMRO Annual Integrated Report.* 2018.

SAMRO. *SAMRO Annual Integrated Report.* 2020. https://www.samro.org.za/pdfs/annual-reports-pdf

Walt Disney Company. *Annual Report.* 2006.

Interviews

Rob Allingham, July 5, 2019

Hanro Friedrich, March 1, 2012

Mzwakhe Mbuli, June 18, 2012

Pops Mohamed, February 21, 2012

Elizabeth Ntsele, August 10, 2013

Thembinkosi Phewa, November 11, 1985

Pierre Rautenbach, February 20, 2012

Angus Rheder, February 2, 2012

Angus Rheder, June 6, 2012

Angus Rheder, August 21, 2013

Pat Williams, April 26, 1983

Secondary Sources

Abbott, Andrew. *The System of Professions: An Essay on the Division of Expert Labor.* Chicago: University of Chicago Press, 1988.

Abel, Richard. *Politics by Other Means: Law in the Struggle against Apartheid, 1980–1994.* New York: Routledge, 1995.

Abélès, Marc. *Quiet Days in Burgundy: A Study of Local Politics.* Cambridge: Cambridge University Press, 1991.

Adas, Michael. *Machines as the Measure of Men: Science, Technology, and Ideologies of Western Dominance.* Ithaca, NY: Cornell University Press, 1989.

Agamben, Giorgio. *Homo Sacer: Sovereign Power and Bare Life.* Palo Alto, CA: Stanford University Press, 1998.

Agar, Jon. *The Government Machine: A Revolutionary History of the Computer*. Cambridge, MA: MIT Press, 2003.

Alcock, G. G. Marc. *Kasinomics: African Informal Economies and the People Who Inhabit Them*. Johannesburg: Tracey McDonald Publishers, 2015.

Allingham, Rob. "From 'Noma Kumnyama' to 'Pata Pata': A History." *African Music* 8, no. 3 (2009): 117–31.

Altbeker, Antony. *The Dirty Work of Democracy: A Year on the Streets with the SAPS*. Johannesburg and Cape Town: Jonathan Ball, 2005.

Anand, Nikhil, Akhil Gupta, and Hannah Appel. *The Promise of Infrastructure*. Durham, NC: Duke University Press, 2018.

Anderson, Jane E. *Law, Knowledge, Culture: The Production of Indigenous Knowledge in Intellectual Property Law*. Cheltenham, UK: Edward Elgar, 2009.

Ansell, Gwen. *Soweto Blues: Jazz, Popular Music, and Politics in South Africa*. London: Continuum, 2004.

Antons, Christoph. "Intellectual Property Rights in Indigenous Cultural Heritage: Basic Concepts and Continuing Controversies." In *International Trade in Indigenous Cultural Heritage: Legal and Policy Issues*, edited by C. B. Graber et al., 144–74. Cheltenham, UK: Edward Elgar, 2012.

Aoki, Keith. "(Intellectual) Property and Sovereignty: Notes toward a Cultural Geography of Authorship." *Stanford Law Review* 48, no. 5 (1996): 1293–1356.

Arend, Moeain. "Taming Tensions: Police Docket Production and the Creation of Trans-contextual Stability in South Africa's Criminal Justice System." *Social Semiotics* 25, no. 4 (2015): 501–16.

Arewa, Olufunmilayo. "Blues Lives: Promise and Perils of Musical Copyright." *Cardozo Arts & Entertainment Law Journal* 27 (2010): 573–619.

Arewa, Olufunmilayo. "Writing Rights. Copyright's Visual Bias and African American Music." *Legal Studies Research Paper Series No. 2012-9* (2012): 3–63.

Arewa, Olufunmilayo. *Disrupting Africa: Technology, Law, and Development*. Cambridge: Cambridge University Press, 2021.

Asad, Talal. "Ethnographic Representation, Statistics and Modern Power." *Social Research* 61, no. 1 (1994): 55–88.

Attali, Jacques. *Noise: The Political Economy of Music*. Minneapolis: University of Minnesota Press, 1986.

Ballantine, Christopher. "Song, Memory, Power, and the South African Archive." *Musical Quarterly* 99, no. 1 (2016): 60–80.

Balloch, Harriet, and Rob Deans. "Collective Licensing of Music in the UAE." *Licensing Journal* June/July (2015): 26–27.

Baloyi, Joel J. "Demystifying the Role of Copyright as a Tool for Economic Development in Africa: Tackling the Harsh Effects of the Transferability Principle in Copyright Law." *Potchefstroom Electronic Law Journal* 17, no. 1 (2014): 89–167.

Band, Jonathan, and Brandon Butler. "Some Cautionary Tales about Collective Licensing." *Michigan State International Law Review* 21, no. 3 (2013): 689–728.

Banks, Mark. *Creative Justice: Cultural Industries, Work and Inequality*. Cambridge, MA: MIT Press, 1977.

Barnett, Antony. "In Africa the Hoodia Cactus Keeps Men Alive: Now Its Secret is 'Stolen' to Make Us Thin." *The Guardian*, June 17, 2001.

Baron, Stephen, John Field, and Tom Schuller, eds. *Social Capital: Critical Perspectives*. Oxford: Oxford University Press, 2001

Barry, Andrew. *Political Machines: Governing a Technological Society*. London: Athlone Press, 2001.

Bauman, Zygmunt. *Retrotopia*. London: Polity Press, 2017.

Bayart, Jean-François. *The State in Africa: The Politics of the Belly*. 2nd ed. London: Polity Press, 2009.

Beaster-Jones, Jayson. *Music Commodities, Markets, and Values: Music as Merchandise*. New York: Routledge, 2016.

Beck, Ulrich. *Risk Society: Towards a New Modernity*. Los Angeles: SAGE Publications, 1992.

Beharie, Tertia, and Tshepo Shabangu. "Traditional Knowledge, Traditional Cultural Expressions and Folklore." In *Dean & Dyer Introduction to Intellectual Property Law*, edited by Owen Dean et al., 331–59. Oxford: Oxford University Press, 2014.

Beinart, William, Karen Brown, and Daniel Gilfoyle. "Experts and Expertise in Colonial Africa Reconsidered: Science and the Interpretation of Knowledge." *African Affairs* 108, no. 342 (2009): 413–33.

Bennett, Tom W. "Ubuntu—An African Equity." *Potchefstroom Electronic Law Journal* 14, no. 4 (2011): 30–61.

Bens, Jonas, and Larissa Vetters. "Ethnographic Legal Studies: Reconnecting Anthropological and Sociological Traditions." *Journal of Legal Pluralism and Unofficial Law* 50, no. 3 (2018): 239–54.

Bentham, Jeremy. [1776] *A Fragment on Government*. Cambridge: Cambridge University Press, 1988.

Bently, Lionel. "The 'Extraordinary Multiplicity' of Intellectual Property Laws in the British Colonies in the Nineteenth Century." *Theoretical Inquiries in Law* 12, no. 1 (2011): 161–200.

Bently, Lionel, and Spyros Maniatis, eds. *Intellectual Property and Ethics*. London: Sweet & Maxwell, 1998.

Best, Stephen. *The Fugitive's Properties: Law and the Poetics of Possession*. Chicago: University of Chicago Press, 2004.

Bhandar, Davina. "Cultural Politics: Disciplining Citizenship." In *Cultural Citizenship in Political Theory*, edited by Judith Vega and Pieter Boele van Hensbroek, 87–100. Milton Park: Routledge, 2012.

Birnheck, Michael. *Colonial Copyright: Intellectual Property in Mandate Palestine*. Oxford: Oxford University Press, 2012.

Blavin, Jonathan. "Folklore in Africa: Memorandum." Open Knowledge Network, January 8, 2003. https://cyber.harvard.edu/openeconomies/okn/folklore.html.

Bloom, Harry. *King Kong: The African Jazz Opera*. London: Collins, 1961.

Boateng, Boatema. *The Copyright Thing Doesn't Work Here: Adinkra and Kente Cloth and Intellectual Property in Ghana*. Minneapolis: University of Minnesota Press, 2011.

Boon, Marcus. *In Praise of Copying*. Cambridge, MA: Harvard University Press, 2010.

Born, Georgina. "The Social and the Aesthetic: For a Post-Bourdieuian Theory of Cultural Production." *Cultural Sociology* 4, no. 2 (2010): 171–208.

Bowker, Geoffrey C. *Science on the Run: Information Management and Industrial Geophysics at Schlumberger, 1920–1940*. Cambridge, MA: MIT Press, 1994.

Bowker, Geoffrey C., and Susan Leigh Star. *Sorting Things Out: Classification and Its Consequences*. Cambridge, MA: MIT Press, 1999.

Bowman, Wayne D. "Artistry, Ethics, and Citizenship." In *Artistic Citizenship: Artistry, Social Responsibility, and Ethical Praxis*, edited by David J. Elliott, Marissa Silverman, and Wayne D. Bowman, 59–80. New York: Oxford University Press, 2016.

Boyle, James. *Shamans, Software, and Spleens: Law and the Construction of the Information Society; Law and the Construction of the Information Science*. Cambridge, MA: Harvard University Press, 1996.

Boyle, James. "The Second Enclosure Movement and the Construction of the Public Domain." *Law and Contemporary Problems* 33 (2003): 66–74.

Brackett, David. *Categorizing Sound: Genre and Twentieth-Century Popular Music*. Berkeley: University of California Press, 2016.

Breckenridge, Keith. *Biometric State: The Global Politics of Identification and Surveillance in South Africa, 1850 to the Present*. Cambridge: Cambridge University Press, 2014.

Brown, Andrew. *Street Blues: The Experiences of a Reluctant Policeman*. Cape Town: Zebra Press, 2008.

Brown, Michael. "Can Culture Be Copyrighted?" *Current Anthropology* 39, no. 2 (1998): 193–222.

Browne, David. "'The Lion Sleeps Tonight': The Ongoing Saga of Pop's Most Contentious Song." *Rolling Stone*, November 7, 2019.

BSA (Business Software Alliance). *2011 Global Software Piracy Study*. Washington, DC: BSA, 2011.

Burke, Timothy. *Lifebuoy Men, Lux Women: Commodification, Consumption, and Cleanliness in Modern Zimbabwe*. Durham, NC: Duke University Press, 1996.

Callon, Michel. "Some Elements of a Sociology of Translation: Domestication of the Scallops and the Fishermen of St Brieuc Bay." In *Power, Action and Belief: A New Sociology of Knowledge?* edited by John Law, 196–223. London: Routledge, 1986.

Callon, Michel. "An Essay on Framing and Overflowing: Economic Externalities Revisited by Sociology." *Sociological Review* 46, no. 1 (1998): 244–69.

Callon, Michel. "What Does It Mean to Say That Economics Is Performative?" CSI Working Papers Series 005. Paris: Centre de Sociologie de l'Innovation (CSI), 2006.

Callon, Michel, Pierre Lascoumes, and Yannick Barthe. *Acting in an Uncertain World: An Essay on Technical Democracy*. Cambridge, MA: MIT Press, 2001.

Cameron, Edwin. *Justice: A Personal Account*. Cape Town: Tafelberg, 2014.

Cardozo, Benjamin. *The Nature of the Judicial Process*. New Haven, CT: Yale University Press, 1921.

Cavalier, Ken. "More Lessons about Professional Responsibility from the Lion Sleeps Tonight Case." *Journal of the Copyright Society of the U.S.A.* 53, nos. 3–4 (2006): 529–44.

Chakrabarty, Dipesh. *Provincializing Europe: Postcolonial Thought and Historical Difference.* Princeton, NJ: Princeton University Press, 2000.

Chanock, Martin. *The Making of South African Legal Culture 1902–1936: Fear, Favour and Prejudice.* Cambridge: Cambridge University Press, 2001.

Chanock, Martin. "South Africa, 1841–1924: Race, Contract, and Coercion." In *Masters, Servants, and Magistrates in Britain and the Empire, 1562–1955,* edited by Douglas Hay and Paul Craven, 338–64. Chapel Hill: University of North Carolina Press, 2004.

Chapdelaine, Pascale. "Copyright User Rights and Remedies: An Access to Justice Perspective." *Laws* 7 (2018): 1–26.

Chapman, Susannah, and Rosemary J. Coombe. "Ethnographic Explorations of Intellectual Property." In *Oxford Research Encyclopedia of Anthropology.* Oxford: Oxford University Press, 2020: 1–41.

Chatterjee, Partha. *Nationalist Thought and the Colonial World: A Derivative Discourse?* Minneapolis: University of Minnesota Press, 1986.

Cheng, Will. *Just Vibrations: The Purpose of Sounding Good.* Ann Arbor: University of Michigan Press, 2016.

Cheng, Will. *Loving Music till It Hurts.* Oxford: Oxford University Press, 2019.

Chennells, Roger. "Putting Intellectual Property Rights to Practice: Experiences from the San." In *Indigenous Peoples, Consent and Benefit Sharing: Lessons from the San-Hoodia Case,* edited by Rachel Wynberg, Doris Schroeder, Roger Chennells, 211–309. Dordrecht: Springer, 2009.

Chipkin, Ivor. *Do South Africans Exist? Nationalism, Democracy and the Identity of "the People."* Johannesburg: Wits University Press, 2007.

Chipkin, Ivor. "Set up for Failure: Racial Redress in the Department of Public Service and Administration." In *Racial Redress and Citizenship in South Africa,* edited by Adam Habib and Kristina Bentley, 129–52. Cape Town: HSRC Press, 2008.

Clammer, John. *Cultural Rights and Justice: Sustainable Development, the Arts and the Body.* Singapore: Palgrave Macmillan, 2019.

Clarke, John, Dave Bainton, Noémi Lendvai, and Paul Stubbs, eds. *Making Policy Move: Toward a Politics of Translation and Assemblage.* Bristol, UK: Polity Press, 2015.

Clifford, James. *The Predicament of Culture: Twentieth-Century Ethnography, Literature, and Art.* Cambridge, MA: Harvard University Press, 1988.

Clifford, James, and George E. Marcus, eds. *Writing Culture: The Poetics and Politics of Ethnography.* Berkeley: University of California Press, 1986.

Cobussen, Marcel, and Nanette Nielsen. *Music and Ethics.* Burlington, VT: Ashgate, 2012.

Coetzer, Diane. "Johnny Clegg: The Rolling Stone Interview." *Rolling Stone,* no. 22, September (2013): 42–48.

Cole, Simon A. "Forensic Culture as Epistemic Culture: The Sociology of Forensic Science." *Studies in History and Philosophy of Biological and Biomedical Science* 44 (2013): 36–47.

Coleman, Elizabeth, Rosemary Coombe, and Fiona MacAlrault. "A Broken Record: Subjecting 'Music' to Cultural Rights." In *Ethics of Cultural Appropriation,* edited by James O. Young and Conrad Brunck, 179–210. London: Blackwell, 2009.

Collins, Stephen. "Traditional Knowledge: Protecting the Intangible and Tracing the Development of International Protection of Folklore." In *Research Handbook on Intellectual Property and Creative Industries*, edited by Abbe E. L. Brown and Charlotte Waelde, 216–29. Cheltenham, UK: Edward Elgar, 2018.

Comaroff, John L., and Jean Comaroff. *Of Revelation and Revolution*. Vol. 1, *Christianity, Colonialism and Consciousness in South Africa*. Chicago: University of Chicago Press, 1991.

Comaroff, John L., and Jean Comaroff. *Of Revelation and Revolution*. Vol. 2, *The Dialectics of Modernity on a South African Frontier*. Chicago: University of Chicago Press, 1997.

Comaroff, John L., and Jean Comaroff. *Civil Society and the Political Imagination in Africa*. Chicago: University of Chicago Press, 1999.

Comaroff, John L., and Jean Comaroff. "Reflections on Liberalism, Policulturalism, and ID-ology: Citizenship and Difference in South Africa." *Social Identities* 9, no. 4 (2003): 445–73.

Comaroff, John L., and Jean Comaroff. *Law and Disorder in the Postcolony*. Chicago: University of Chicago Press, 2006.

Comaroff, John L., and Jean Comaroff. *Ethnicity, Inc*. Chicago: University of Chicago Press, 2009.

Comaroff, John L., and Jean Comaroff. *The Truth about Crime: Sovereignty, Knowledge, Social Order*. Chicago: University of Chicago Press, 2016.

Comaroff, John L., and Jean Comaroff. *The Politics of Custom: Chiefship, Capital, and the State in Contemporary Africa*. Chicago: University of Chicago Press, 2018.

Conley, John, and William O'Barr. *Rules versus Relationships: The Ethnography of Legal Discourse*. Chicago: University of Chicago Press, 1990.

Conrath, Philippe. *Johnny Clegg: la passion zoulou*. Paris: Edition Seghers, 1988.

Coombe, Rosemary. "The Properties of Culture and the Possession of Identity: Postcolonial Struggle and the Legal imagination." In *Borrowed Power: Essays on Cultural Appropriation*, edited by Bruce Ziff and Pratima V. Rao, 74–96. New Brunswick, NJ: Rutgers University Press, 1997.

Coombe, Rosemary. *The Cultural Life of Intellectual Properties: Authorship, Appropriation and the Law*. Durham, NC: Duke University Press, 1998.

Coombes, Annie E. *Reinventing Africa: Museums, Material Culture, and Popular Imagination in Late Victorian and Edwardian England*. New Haven, CT: Yale University Press, 1994.

Coplan, David. *In the Time of Cannibals: The Word Music of South Africa's Basotho Migrants*. Chicago: University of Chicago Press, 1994.

Coplan, David. *In Township Tonight! South Africa's Black City Music and Theatre*. 2nd ed. Chicago: University of Chicago Press, 2008.

Cornell, Drucilla. *Law and Revolution in South Africa: Ubuntu, Dignity, and the Struggle for Constitutional Transformation*. New York: Fordham University Press, 2014.

COSATU, Summary of Critique of the National Development Plan, Polity, March 2013. https://www.polity.org.za/article/summary-of-critique-of-the-national-development-plan-march-2013-2013-04-19.

Cowan, David, and Daniel Wincott, eds. *Exploring the "Legal" in Socio-Legal Studies*. New York: Palgrave-Macmillan, 2016.

Crewe, Emma. *Lords of Parliament: Manners, Rituals and Politics*. Manchester, UK: Manchester University Press, 2005.
Crewe, Emma. *The House of Commons: An Anthropology of MPs at Work*. London: Bloomsbury Academic, 2015.
Crewe, Emma. "Ethnography of Parliament: Finding Culture and Politics Entangled in the Commons and the Lords." *Parliamentary Affairs* 70 (2017): 155–72.
Crewe, Emma, and Chris Mowles. "Audit as Political Struggle: The Doxa of Managerialism Clashing with the Uncertainty of Real Life." *Development in Practice* 30, no. 7 (2020): 1–12.
Darian-Smith, Eve. "Ethnographies of Law." In *Blackwell Companion to Law and Society*, edited by Austin Sarat, 545–68. Chichester: Wiley-Blackwell, 2004.
Davis, Dennis, and Michelle le Roux. *Precedent & Possibility: The (Ab)use of Law in South Africa*. Cape Town: Double Storey, 2009.
Dean, Owen. *Handbook of South African Copyright Law*. Claremont, South Africa: Juta, 1987.
Dean, Owen. *The Application of the Copyright Act, 1978, to Works made Prior to 1979*. JD diss., University of Stellenbosch, 1988.
Dean, Owen. "Sound Recordings in South Africa: The Cinderella of the Copyright Family." *De rebus*, October (1993): 913–17.
Dean, Owen. "The Case for the Recognition of Intellectual Property in the Bill of Rights." *Journal of Contemporary Roman-Dutch Law* 60 (1997): 105–19.
Dean, Owen. *Ownership of Copyright in a Musical Work entitled MBUBE: Opinion*. Unpublished typescript, 2000.
Dean, Owen. "The Return of the Lion." *WIPO Magazine*, April 2006.
Dean, Owen. "Stalking the Sleeping Lion." *De rebus*, July (2006): 16–21.
Dean, Owen. *Awakening the Lion: The Case of The Lion Sleeps Tonight*. Cape Town: Tafelberg, 2013.
Dean, Owen, and Alison Dyer, eds. *Dean & Dyer Introduction to Intellectual Property Law*. Oxford: Oxford University Press, 2014.
De Beer, Jeremy, Chris Armstrong, Chidi Oguamanam, and Tobias Schonwetter, eds. *Innovation & Intellectual Property: Collaborative Dynamics in Africa*. Cape Town: University of Cape Town Press, 2014.
De Beukelaar, Christiaan. *Developing Cultural Industries: Learning from the Palimpsest of Practice*. Amsterdam: European Cultural Foundation, 2015.
Demuijnck, Geert. "Is P2P Sharing of MP3 Files an Objectionable Form of Free Riding?" In *Intellectual Property and Theories of Justice*, edited by Axel Gosseries, Alain Marciano, Alain Strowel, 141–59. New York: Palgrave Macmillan, 2008.
Desrosières, Alain. *The Politics of Large Numbers: A History of Statistical Reasoning*. Cambridge, MA: Harvard University Press, 1998.
Devine, Kyle, and Alexandrine Boudreault-Fournier, eds. *Audible Infrastructures: Music, Sound, Media*. Oxford: Oxford University Press, 2021.
Dlamini, Jacob. *Native Nostalgia*. Johannesburg: Jacana Media, 2010.
Douglas-Jones, Rachel. "A 'Good' Ethical Review: Audit and Professionalism in Research Ethics." *Social Anthropology* 23, no. 1 (2015): 53–67.

Douglas-Jones, Rachel, Antonia Walford and Nick Seaver. "Towards an Anthropology of Data." *Journal of the Royal Anthropological Institute* 27, S1 (2021).

Drahos, Peter. *Intellectual Property, Indigenous People and Their Knowledge*. Cambridge: Cambridge University Press, 2014.

Drayton, Richard. *Nature's Government: Science, Imperial Britain, and the "Improvement" of the World*. New Haven, CT: Yale University Press, 2000.

Drott, Eric. "Music as a Technology of Surveillance." *Journal of the Society for American Music* 12, no. 3 (2018): 233–67.

Dubin, Steven C. *Spearheading Debate: Culture Wars and Uneasy Truces*. Johannesburg: Jacana Media, 2012.

Dubow, Saul. *A Commonwealth of Knowledge: Science, Sensibility, and White South Africa 1820–2000*. Oxford: Oxford University Press, 2006.

Dugard, John. "Raymond Tucker (1932–2004)." *South African Journal on Human Rights* 20 (2004): 507–10.

Dugard, John. *Confronting Apartheid: A Personal History of South Africa, Namibia and Palestine*. Johannesburg: Jacana Media, 2018.

Du Toit, Andries. "'Social Exclusion' Discourse and Chronic Poverty: A South African Case Study." *Development and Change* 35, no. 5 (2004): 987–1010.

Du Toit, Andries, and David Neves. *Vulnerability and Social Protection at the Margins of the Formal Economy: Case Studies from Khayelitsha and the Eastern Cape*. Cape Town: PLAAS, University of the Western Cape, 2006.

Du Toit, Andries, and David Neves. "In Search of South Africa's Second Economy: Chronic Poverty, Vulnerability and Adverse Incorporation in Mt. Frere and Khayelitsha." Paper prepared for the Living on the Margins Conference, Stellenbosch, 2007. https://www.plaas.org.za/sites/default/files/publications-pdf/lotm_duToit.pdf.

Dyzenhaus, David. *Judging the Judges, Judging Ourselves: Truth, Reconciliation and the Apartheid Legal Order*. Oxford: Hart Publishing, 2003.

Eckstein, Lars, and Anja Schwarz, eds. *Postcolonial Piracy: Media Distribution and Cultural Production in the Global South*. London: Bloomsbury Academic, 2014.

Elliott, David J., Marissa Silverman, and Wayne D. Bowman, eds. *Artistic Citizenship: Artistry, Social Responsibility, and Ethical Praxis*. New York: Oxford University Press, 2016.

Elyachar, Julia. "Next Practices: Knowledge, Infrastructure, and Public Goods at the Bottom of the Pyramid." *Public Culture* 24, no. 2 (2012): 109–29.

Engle, Karen. *The Elusive Promise of Indigenous Development: Rights, Culture, Strategy*. Durham, NC: Duke University Press, 2010.

Erikson, Susan. "Global Health Business: The Production and Performativity of Statistics in Sierra Leone and Germany." *Medical Anthropology* 31, no. 4 (2012): 367–84.

Erlmann, Veit. "Apartheid, African Nationalism and Culture—The Case of Traditional African Music in Black Education in South Africa." *Perspectives in Education* 7, no. 3 (1983): 131–54.

Erlmann, Veit. *Mbube Roots: Zulu Choral Music from South Africa, 1930s–1960s*. Compact Disc. Rounder 5025. Cambridge, MA, 1987.

Erlmann, Veit. *African Stars: Studies in Black South African Performance*. Chicago: University of Chicago Press, 1991.
Erlmann, Veit. *Nightsong: Power, Performance and Practice in South Africa*. Chicago: University of Chicago Press, 1996.
Erlmann, Veit. *Music, Modernity and the Global Imagination*. New York: Oxford University Press, 1999.
Ess, Charles Melvin. "Ethical Approaches for Copying Digital Artifacts: What Would the Exemplary Person [junzi]/ a Good Person [phronimos] Say?" In *The Aesthetics and Ethics of Copying*, edited by Darren Hick and Reinold Schmücker, 295–314. London: Bloomsbury, 2016.
Evans-Pritchard, Edmund E. *Social Anthropology*. Abingdon, UK: Routledge, 2004 [1951].
Feld, Steven. "A Sweet Lullaby for World Music." *Public Culture* 12, no. 1 (2000): 145–71.
Feldstein, Ruth. *How It Feels to Be Free: Black Women Entertainers and the Civil Rights Movement*. Oxford: Oxford University Press, 2013.
Ferguson, James. *The Anti-Politics Machine: "Development," Depoliticization, and Bureaucratic Power in Lesotho*. Cambridge: Cambridge University Press, 1990.
Ferguson, James. *Global Shadows: Africa in the Neoliberal World Order*. Durham, NC: Duke University Press, 2006.
Ferguson, James. *Give a Man a Fish: Reflections on the New Politics of Distribution*. Durham, NC: Duke University Press, 2015.
Ferguson, James, and Tanya Murray Li. *Beyond the "Proper Job:" Political-Economic Analysis after the Century of Labouring Man*. Working Paper 51. Cape Town: PLAAS, University of the Western Cape, 2018.
Ficsor, Mihály. *Collective Management of Copyright and Related Rights*. Geneva: WIPO, 2002.
Fischer, Michael, and George Marcus. *Anthropology as Cultural Critique: An Experimental Moment in the Human Sciences*. Chicago: University of Chicago Press, 1986.
Fisher, William W. "Theories of Intellectual Property." In *New Essays in the Legal and Political Theory of Property*, edited by Stephen Munzer, 168–200. Cambridge: Cambridge University Press, 2001.
Fleming, Tyler. *Opposing Apartheid on Stage: King Kong the Musical*. Rochester, NY: University of Rochester Press, 2020.
Florida, Richard. *The Rise of the Creative Class, and How It's Transforming Work, Leisure, Community and Everyday Life*. New York: Basic Books, 2002.
Foster, Laura A. *Reinventing Hoodia: Peoples, Plants, and Patents in South Africa*. Seattle: University of Washington Press, 2017.
Foucault, Michel. *The Archaeology of Knowledge: And the Discourse on Language*. New York: Vintage, 1982 [1972].
Foucault, Michel. "Self Writing." In *Ethics: Subjectivity and Truth*. Vol. 1, *Essential Works of Foucault, 1954–1984*, 207–22. New York: New Press, 1997.
Foucault, Michel. "What Is an Author." In *Aesthetics, Method, and Epistemology: Essential Works of Foucault, 1954–1984*, vol. 2, 205–22. New York: New Press, 1999.
Fraser, Nancy, and Axel Honneth. *Redistribution or Recognition? A Political-Philosophical Exchange*. London: Verso, 2003.

Fredericks, Rosalind. *Garbage Citizenship: Vital Infrastructures of Labor in Dakar, Senegal.* Durham, NC: Duke University Press, 2018.

Gani, Mary W. *Creative Autonomy, Copyright and Popular Music in Nigeria.* Cham, Switzerland: Palgrave Macmillan, 2020.

Gardey, Delphine. "Turning Public Discourse into an Authentic Artifact. Shorthand Transcription in the French National Assembly." In *Making Things Public: Atmospheres of Democracy,* edited by Bruno Latour and Peter Weibel, 836–43. Cambridge, MA: MIT Press, 2005.

Geertz, Clifford. *The Interpretation of Cultures.* New York: Basic Books, 1973.

Geertz, Clifford. *Local Knowledge: Further Essays in Interpretive Anthropology.* New York: Basic Books, 1983.

Geiger, Christophe, ed. *Criminal Enforcement of Intellectual Property: A Handbook of Contemporary Research.* Cheltenham: Edward Elgar Publishing, 2012.

Gervais, Daniel J., ed. *Collective Management of Copyright and Related Rights.* 2nd ed. Alphen aan den Rijn: Wolters Kluwer, 2010.

Giddens, Anthony. *The Consequences of Modernity.* Cambridge: Polity Press, 1990.

Gilfillan, Graeme. "A Review of and Response to 'SAMRO CEO Response to Media Reports,'" 2018. http://www.samro.org.za/news/articles/samro-ceo-response-media-reports.

Gilfillan, Graeme. *An Investigation into the Southern African Music Rights Organization (SAMRO) Redistribution Policy "Royalty Distributions Written Back." Its Methodology, Logic and Outcomes.* Unpublished typescript, 2019.

Gilfillan, Graeme. *Auditing Collecting Society Member Royalties: Developing a New Copyright Audit Method for Global Use.* PhD dissertation. Potchefstroom: North-West University, 2021.

Giri, Ananta. "Audited Accountability and the Imperative of Responsibility: Beyond the Primacy of the Political." In *Audit Cultures: Anthropological Studies in Accountability, Ethics and the Academy,* edited by Marilyn Strathern. London: Routledge, 2002, 173–95.

Gitelman, Lisa, ed. *"Raw Data" is an Oxymoron.* Cambridge, MA: MIT Press, 2013.

Glover, Graham. "Maybe the Courts Are Not Such a 'Bleak House' after All? Or, 'Please Sir, I Want Some More Copyright,'" *South African Law Journal* 119 (2002): 63–70.

Gluckman, Max. *The Ideas in Barotse Jurisprudence.* 2nd ed. Manchester, UK: Manchester University Press, [1965] 1972.

Green, Lesley. "Beyond South Africa's 'Indigenous Knowledge-Science' Wars." *South African Journal of Science* 108, nos. 7–8 (2012): 1–10.

Green, Lesley. *Rock, Water, Life: Ecology & Humanities for a Decolonial South Africa.* Durham, NC: Duke University Press, 2020.

Greene, Kevin J. "Copyright, Culture & Black Music: A Legacy of Unequal Protection." *Hastings Communications and Entertainment Law Journal* 21 (1998): 339–92.

Grimmelmann, James. "The Ethical Visions of Copyright." *Fordham Law Review* 77 (2009): 2005–37.

Gupta, Akhil. *Postcolonial Developments: Agriculture in the Making of Modern India.* Durham, NC: Duke University Press, 1998.

Guyer, Jane. *Legacies, Logics, Logistics: Essays in the Anthropology of the Platform Economy.* Chicago: University of Chicago Press, 2016.

Habib, Adam, and Kristina Bentley, eds. *Racial Redress and Citizenship in South Africa.* Cape Town: HSRC Press, 2008.

Hackney, James R., Jr. *Under Cover of Science: American Legal-Economic Theory and the Quest for Objectivity.* Durham, NC: Duke University Press, 2006.

Halbert, Deborah J. *The State of Copyright: The Complex Relationship of Cultural Creation in a Globalized World.* Abingdon: Routledge, 2014.

Hamilton, Carolyn. *Terrific Majesty: The Power of Shaka Zulu and the Limits of Historical Invention.* Cambridge, MA: Harvard University Press, 1998.

Hamm, Charles. "'The Constant Companion of Man': Separate Development, Radio Bantu and Music." *Popular Music* 10, no. 2 (1991): 147–73.

Handke, Christian. "Collective Administration." In *Handbook on the Economics of Copyright: A Guide for Students and Teachers,* edited by Richard Watt, 179–204. Cheltenham: Edward Elgar Publishing, 2014.

Hardt, Michael. "Affective Labor." *Boundary 2* 26, no. 2 (1999): 89–100.

Hardt, Michael, and Antonio Negri. *Empire.* Cambridge, MA: Harvard University Press, 2000.

Hariman, Robert, ed. *Prudence: Classical Virtue, Postmodern Practice.* Philadelphia: Penn State University Press, 2003.

Harker, Dave. "The Wonderful World of IFPI: Music Industry Rhetoric, the Critics and the Classical Marxist Critique." *Popular Music* 16, no. 1 (1997): 45–79.

Harms, Louis. *The Role of the Judiciary in Enforcement of Intellectual Property; Intellectual Property Litigation under Common Law System with Special Emphasis on the Experience in South Africa.* Geneva: WIPO, 2004.

Harvey, Penelope, Casper Jensen, Atsuro Morita, eds. *Infrastructures and Social Complexity: A Companion.* Abingdon: Routledge, 2016.

Harvey, Stefano, and Fred Moten. *The Undercommons: Fugitive Planning and Black Study.* London: Minor Compositions, 2016.

Haupt, Adam. *Stealing Empire: P2P, Intellectual Property and Hip-Hop Subversion.* Cape Town: HSRC Press, 2008.

Haupt, Adam, and Håvard Ovesen. "Vindicating Capital: Heroes and Villains in A Lion's Trail." *Ilha do Desterro: A Journal of English Language Literatures in English and Cultural Studies* 61 (2011): 73–107.

Hayden, Cori. "Taking as Giving: Bioscience, Exchange, and the Politics of Benefit-Sharing." *Social Studies of Science* 37, no. 5 (2007): 729–58.

Helfer, Laurence R. "Collective Management of Copyrights and Human Rights: An Uneasy Alliance Revisited." In *Collective Management of Copyright and Related Rights.* 2nd ed. Edited by Daniel Gervais, 75–104. Austin: Wolters Kluwer, 2010.

Helmreich, Stefan. "An Anthropologist Underwater: Immersive Soundscapes, Submarine Cyborgs, and Transductive Ethnography." *American Ethnologist* 34, no. 4 (2007): 621–41.

Helmreich, Stefan. *Sounding the Limits of Life: Essays in the Anthropology of Biology and Beyond.* Princeton, NJ: Princeton University Press, 2016.

Herzfeld, Michael. *Cultural Intimacy: Social Poetics and the Real Life of States, Societies, and Institutions*. 3rd ed. Abingdon: Routledge, 2016.

Hesmondhalgh, David. "Capitalism and the Media: Moral Economy, Well-Being and Capabilities." *Media, Culture & Society* 39, no. 2 (2017): 202–18.

Hesmondhalgh, David. *The Cultural Industries*. 1st edition. Los Angeles: SAGE, 2002.

Hesmondhalgh, David. *The Cultural Industries*. 4th edition. Los Angeles: SAGE, 2019.

Hetherington, Kregg. *Guerilla Auditors: The Politics of Transparency in Neoliberal Paraguay*. Durham, NC: Duke University Press, 2011.

Hick, Darren, and Reinold Schmücker, eds. *The Aesthetics and Ethics of Copying*. London: Bloomsbury, 2016.

Hilty, Reto. "Economic, Legal and Social Impacts of Counterfeiting." In *Criminal Enforcement of Intellectual Property: A Handbook of Contemporary Research*, edited by Christophe Geiger, 9–23. Cheltenham, UK: Edward Elgar, 2012.

Himonga, Chuma. "African Customary Law in South Africa: The Many Faces of Bhe v. Magistrate Khayelitsha." In *Ubuntu and the Law: African Ideals and Postapartheid Jurisprudence*, edited by Drucilla Cornell and Nyoko Muvangua, 388–404. New York: Fordham University Press, 2012.

Himonga, Chuma, and Craig Bosch. "The Application of African Customary Law under the Constitution of South Africa: Problem Solved or Just Beginning?" *South African Law Journal* 117 (2000): 306–41.

Himonga, Chuma, Max Taylor, and Anne Pope. "Reflections on Judicial Views of Ubuntu." *Potchefstroom Electronic Law Journal* 16, no. 5 (2013): 372–429.

Hoernlé, Alfred R. F. *South African Native Policy and the Liberal Spirit*. Lovedale, South Africa: Lovedale Press, 1939.

Holmes, Oliver Wendell. "Codes, and the Arrangement of the Law." *American Law Review* 5, no. 1 (1870): 1–13.

Holmes, Oliver Wendell. *Collected Legal Papers*. New York: Harcourt, Brace and Howe, 1920.

Honneth, Axel. *Freedom's Right: The Social Foundations of Democratic Life*. New York: Columbia University Press, 2014.

Hornberger, Julia. *Policing and Human Rights: The Meaning of Violence and Justice in the Everyday Policing of Johannesburg*. London: Routledge, 2011.

Hornberger, Julia. "Complicity: Becoming the Police (South Africa)." In *Writing the World of Policing: The Difference Ethnography Makes*, edited by Didier Fassin, 42–61. Chicago: University of Chicago Press, 2017.

Hornby, Donna. *The Social and Cultural Aspects of Small-Scale Agricultural Production in South Africa and the Implications for Employment-Intensive Land Reform*. Bellville: PLAAS, University of the Western Cape, 2020.

Hudson, Emily. *Drafting Copyright Exceptions: From Law in Books to Law in Action*. Cambridge: Cambridge University Press, 2020.

Hull, Matthew S. *Government of Paper: The Materiality of Bureaucracy in Urban Pakistan*. Berkeley: University of California Press, 2012.

Huskisson, Yvonne. *The Bantu Composers of Southern Africa*. Johannesburg: SABC, 1969.

Hutchison, Andrew. "Decolonising South African Contract Law: An Argument for Synthesis." In *The Constitutional Dimension of Contract Law: A Comparative Perspective*, edited by Luca Siliquini-Cinelli and Andrew Hutchison, 151–84. Cham: Springer: 2017.

Impey, Angela. *Song Walking: Women, Music, and Environmental Justice in an African Borderland*. Chicago: University of Chicago Press, 2019.

Ives, Sarah. *Steeped in Heritage: The Racial Politics of South African Rooibos Tea*. Durham, NC: Duke University Press, 2017.

Jacob, Marie-Andrée. "Form-Made Persons: Consent Forms as Consent's Blind Spot." *Political and Legal Anthropology Review* 30, no. 2 (2007): 249–68.

James, Deborah. *Songs of the Women Migrants: Performance and Identity in South Africa*. Edinburgh: Edinburgh University Press, 1999.

Janzen, John M. *Ngoma: Discourses of Healing in Central and Southern Africa*. Berkeley: University of California Press, 1992.

Jasanoff, Sheila. "Ordering Knowledge, Ordering Society." In *States of Knowledge: The Co-Production of Science and Social Order*, 13–45. New York: Routledge, 2004.

Jeffery, Anthea. "The New Constitution: A Triumph for Liberalism? Some Doubts." In *Ironic Victory: Liberalism in Post-Liberation South Africa*, edited by R. W. Johnson and David Welsh, 31–44. Oxford: Oxford University Press, 1998.

Kant, Immanuel. *Critique of Judgment*. Translated by Werner S. Pluhar. Indianapolis: Hackett Publishing Company, 1987.

Karaganis, Joe, ed. *Media Piracy in Emerging Economies*. New York: Social Science Research Council, 2011.

Karjiker, Sadulla. "Justifications for Copyright: The Economic Justification." *South African Intellectual Property Law Journal* 2 (2014): 13–41.

Kirby, Percival R. "Indigenous Music." In *Handbook of Race Relations in South Africa*, edited by Ellen Hellman, 619–27. Cape Town: Oxford University Press, 1949.

Kirman, Alan P. "Whom or What Does the Representative Individual Represent?" *Journal of Economic Perspectives* 6, no. 2 (1992): 117–36.

Klare, Karl E. "Legal Culture and Transformative Constitutionalism." *South African Journal on Human Rights* 4 (1998): 146–88.

Knorr Cetina, Karin. *Epistemic Cultures: How the Sciences Make Knowledge*. Cambridge, MA: Harvard University Press, 1999.

Koch, Grace. *We Have the Song, So We Have the Land: Song and Ceremony as Proof of Ownership in Aboriginal and Torres Strait Islander land Claims*. AIATSIS Research Discussion Paper No. 33. Canberra: AIATSIS Research Publications, 2013.

Kongolo, Tshimanga. *African Contributions in Shaping the Worldwide Intellectual Property System*. Abingdon, UK: Routledge, 2013.

Kraft, Timothy. *From Genesis to Cashing the Cheque: An Educational Resource on Music Production in South Africa*. Johannesburg: Academy of Sound Recording, 2010.

Kraut, Anthea. *Choreographing Copyright: Race, Gender, and Intellectual Property Rights in American Dance*. New York: Oxford University Press, 2015.

Kriegler, Anine, and Mark Shaw. *A Citizen's Guide to Crime Trends in South Africa*. Cape Town: Jonathan Ball, 2016.

Kruger, Loren. *The Drama of South Africa: Plays, Pageants and Publics since 1910.* London: Routledge, 1999.

Kruse, Corinna. *The Social Life of Forensic Evidence.* Berkeley: University of California Press, 2016.

Kymlicka, Will. *Multicultural Citizenship: A Liberal Theory of Minority Rights.* Oxford: Clarendon Press, 1995.

Lam, Anita. "Making Crime Messy." In *Actor-Network Theory and Crime Studies: Explorations in Science and Technology,* edited by Dominique Robert and Martin Dufresne, 51–65. Burlington: Ashgate Publishing, 2015.

Lametti, David. "The Virtuous P(eer): Reflections on the Ethics of File Sharing." In *New Frontiers in the Philosophy of Intellectual Property,* edited by Annabelle Lever, 284–306. Cambridge: Cambridge University Press, 2012.

Landes, William, and Richard Posner. "An Economic Analysis of Copyright Law." Journal of Legal Studies 18 (1989): 325–33, 344–53.

Larkin, Brian. *Signal and Noise: Media, Infrastructure, and Urban Culture in Nigeria.* Durham, NC: Duke University Press, 2008.

Latour, Bruno. "Drawing Things Together." In *Representation in Scientific Practice,* edited by Michael Lynch and Steve Woolgar, 19–68. Cambridge, MA: MIT Press, 1990.

Latour, Bruno. *Pandora's Hope: Essays on the Reality of Science Studies.* Cambridge, MA: Harvard University Press, 1999.

Latour, Bruno. "When Things Strike Back: A Possible Contribution of 'Science Studies' to the Social Sciences." British Journal of Sociology 51, no. 1 (2000): 107–23.

Latour, Bruno. *Politics of Nature: How to Bring the Sciences into Democracy.* Cambridge, MA: Harvard University Press, 2004.

Latour, Bruno. *Reassembling the Social: An Introduction to Actor-Network Theory.* New York: Oxford University Press, 2005.

Latour, Bruno. *On the Modern Cult of the Factish Gods.* Durham, NC: Duke University Press, 2009.

Latour, Bruno. *The Making of Law: An Ethnography of the Conseil d'État.* Cambridge: Polity, 2010.

Latour, Bruno. "A Plea for Earthly Sciences." In *New Social Connections: Sociology's Subjects and Objects,* edited by Judith Burnett, Syd Jeffers, and Graham Thomas, 72–84. New York: Palgrave Macmillan, 2010.

Latour, Bruno. *An Inquiry into Modes of Existence: An Anthropology of the Moderns.* Cambridge, MA: Harvard University Press, 2013.

Law, John. *After Method: Mess in Social Science Research.* New York: Routledge, 2004.

Lee, Benjamin. "The Subjects of Circulation." In *The Postnational Self: Belonging and Identity,* edited by Ulf Hedetoft and Mette Hjort, 233–49. Minneapolis: University of Minnesota Press, 2002.

Lessig, Lawrence. *Free Culture: The Nature and Future of Creativity.* New York: Penguin, 2004.

Lester, Toni. "Blurred Lines—Where Copyright Ends and Cultural Appropriation Begins: The Case of Robin Thicke Versus Bridgeport Music and the Estate of

Marvin Gaye." *Hastings Communications and Entertainment Law Journal* 36, no. 2 (2014): 217–42.

Lever, Annabelle, ed. *New Frontiers in the Philosophy of Intellectual Property.* Cambridge: Cambridge University Press, 2012.

Levinson, Jerrold, ed. *Aesthetics and Ethics: Essays at the Intersection.* Cambridge: Cambridge University Press, 1998.

Li, Tania Murray. *The Will to Improve: Governmentality, Development, and the Practice of Politics.* Durham, NC: Duke University Press, 2007.

Lipton, Merle. *Liberals, Marxists and Nationalists: Competing Interpretations of South African History.* New York: Palgrave Macmillan, 2007.

Lucia, Christine, ed. *The World of South African Music: A Reader.* Newcastle: Cambridge Scholars Press, 2005.

Luhmann, Niklas. *Kontingenz und Recht.* Frankfurt a. M.: Suhrkamp, 2013.

MacIntyre, Alasdaire. *After Virtue: A Study in Moral Theory.* 3rd ed. Notre Dame, IN: University of Notre Dame Press, 2007.

Madondo, Bongani. *Sigh, the Beloved Country: Braai Talk, Rock 'n' Roll & Other Stories.* Johannesburg: Picador Africa, 2016.

Magaudda, Paolo. "Popular Music, Technology, and the Changing Media Ecosystem from Cassettes to Stream." In *Popular Music, Technology, and the Changing Media Ecosystem: From Cassettes to Stream,* edited by Tamas Tofalvy and Emilia Barna, 23–41. New York: Palgrave Macmillan, 2020.

Maine, Henry. *Ancient Law: Its Connection with the Early History of Society and its Relation to Modern Ideas.* London: John Murray, 1861.

Malan, Rian. *My Traitor's Heart: A South African Exile Returns to Face His Country, His Tribe, and His Conscience.* London: Penguin, 1990.

Malan, Rian. "In the Jungle: Inside the Long, Hidden Genealogy of 'The Lion Sleeps Tonight.'" *Rolling Stone* no. 841 (2000): 54–66, 84–85.

Marcus, George E. "Contemporary Problems of Ethnography in the Modern World System." In *Writing Culture: The Poetics and Politics of Ethnography,* edited by James Clifford and George E. Marcus, 165–93. Berkeley: University of California Press, 1986.

Marshall, Lee. "The Recording Industry in the 21st Century." In *The International Recording Industries,* edited by Lee Marshall, 53–74. New York: Routledge, 2013.

Martin, Randy. "Artistic Citizenship." In *Artistic Citizenship: A Public Voice for the Arts,* edited by Mary Schmidt Campbell and Randy Martin, 7–26. New York: Routledge, 2006.

Marx, Karl, and Friedrich Engels. *Manifesto of the Communist Party.* Moscow: Progress Publishers, 1969.

Maton, Karl. *Knowledge and Knowers: Towards a Realist Sociology of Education.* New York: Routledge, 2015.

Matzukis, Nick. *South African Music Law and Contracts.* Johannesburg: Academy of Sound Recording, 2009.

Maurer, Bill. *Mutual Life, Limited: Islamic Banking, Alternative Currencies, Lateral Reason.* Princeton, NJ: Princeton University Press, 2005.

Mauss, Marcel. *The Gift.* Chicago: HAU Books, [1925] 2016.
Mazzarella, William. "Internet X-Ray: E-Governance, Transparency, and the Politics of Immediation in India." *Public Culture* 18, vol. 3 (2006): 473–505.
Mbembe, Achille. "The Banality of Power and the Aesthetics of Vulgarity in the Postcolony." *Public Culture* 4/2 (1992): 1–30.
Mbembe, Achille. *Necropolitics.* Durham, NC: Duke University Press, 2019.
Mbembe, Achille, and Sarah Nuttall. "Writing the World from an African Metropolis." *Public Culture* 16/3 (2004): 347–72.
Meierhenrich, Jens. *The Legacies of Law: Long-Run Consequences of Legal Development in South Africa.* Cambridge: Cambridge University Press, 2008.
Meintjes, Louise. *Sound of Africa! Making Music Zulu in a South African Studio.* Durham, NC: Duke University Press, 2003.
Meintjes, Louise. *Dust of the Zulu: Ngoma Aesthetics after Apartheid.* Durham, NC: Duke University Press, 2017.
Merry, Sally Engle. *The Seductions of Quantification: Measuring Human Rights, Gender Violence, and Sex Trafficking.* Chicago: University of Chicago Press, 2016.
Miller, Karl Hagstrom. *Segregating Sound: Inventing Folk and Pop Music in the Age of Jim Crow.* Durham, NC: Duke University Press, 2010.
Miller, Toby, and George Yúdice. *Cultural Policy.* London: SAGE Publications, 2002.
Miyazaki, Kirokazu, and Annelise Riles. "Failure as an Endpoint." In *Global Assemblages: Technology, Politics and Ethics as Anthropological Problems,* edited by Aihwa Ong and Stephen J. Collier, 320–32. Oxford: Blackwell Publishing, 2005.
Modiri, Joel M. "Transformation, Tension and Transgression: Reflections on the Culture and Ideology of South African Legal Education." *Stellenbosch Law Review* 24/3 (2013): 455–79.
Modiri, Joel M., ed. "Conquest, Constitutionalism and Democratic Contestations." *South African Journal on Human Rights* 34 (2018).
Moretti, Franco. *Graphs, Maps, Trees: Abstract Models for a Literary History.* London: Verso, 2007.
Morris, Jeremy Wade. "Artists as Entrepreneurs, Fans as Workers." *Popular Music and Society* 37, no. 3 (2014): 273–90.
Moss, S. P. *Charles Dickens' Quarrel with America.* Troy, MI: Whitston Publishing, 1984.
Mouffe, Chantal, and Ernesto Laclau. *Hegemony and Socialist Strategy: Towards A Radical Democratic Politics.* 2nd ed. London: Verso, 2014.
Muller, Carol. *Rituals of Fertility and the Sacrifice of Desire.* Chicago: University of Chicago Press, 1999.
Nattrass, Nicoli, and Jeremy Seekings. *Inclusive Dualism: Labour-Intensive Development, Decent Work, and Surplus Labour in Southern Africa.* Oxford: Oxford University Press, 2019.
Ncube, Caroline B. "Harnessing Intellectual Property for Development: Some Thoughts on an Appropriate Theoretical Framework." *Potchefstroom Electronic Law Journal* 16, no. 4 (2013): 369–95.
Ncube, Caroline B. *Intellectual Property Policy, Law and Administration in Africa: Exploring Continental and Sub-Regional Co-Operation.* New York: Routledge, 2015.

Ncube, Caroline B. "Decolonising Intellectual Property Law in Pursuit of Africa's Development." *WIPO Journal* 8, no. 1 (2016): 34–40.

Ncube, Caroline B. "Calibrating Copyright for Creators and Consumers: Promoting Distributive Justice and Ubuntu." In *What If We Could Reimagine Copyright?* Edited by Rebecca Giblin and Kimberlee Weatherall, 253–80. Acton: Australian National University Press, 2017.

Ncube, Caroline B. "Three Centuries and Counting: The Emergence and Development of Intellectual Property Law in Africa." In *Oxford Handbook of Intellectual Property Law*, edited by Rochelle Dreyfuss and Justine Pila, 1–22. Oxford: Oxford University Press, 2018.

Ndabeni, Esinako, and Sihle Mthembu. *Born to Kwaito: Reflections on the Kwaito Generation.* Johannesburg: Blackbird Books, 2018.

Neely, Abigail H. *Reimagining Social Medicine from the South.* Durham, NC: Duke University Press, 2021.

Nelken, David. "The 'Gap Problem' in the Sociology of Law: A Theoretical Review." *Windsor Yearbook of Access to Justice* 1 (1981): 35–61.

Neves, David. *Reconsidering Rural Development: Using Livelihood Analysis to Examine Rural Development in the Former Homelands of South Africa.* Cape Town: PLAAS, University of the Western Cape, 2017.

Niezen, Ronald. *The Origins of Indigenism: Human Rights and the Politics of Identity.* Berkeley: University of California Press, 2003.

Nwauche, Enyinna. *The Protection of Traditional Cultural Expressions in Africa.* Cham, Switzerland: Springer, 2017.

Ochiltree, Ian D. "'A Just and Self-Respecting System'? Black Independence, Sharecropping, and Paternalistic Relations in the American South and South Africa." *Agricultural History* 9, no. 2 (1998): 352–80.

Okorie, Chijioke Ifeoma. *Multi-Sided Music Platforms and the Law: Copyright, Law and Policy in Africa.* Abingdon: Routledge, 2020.

Oliphant, Lumka. "Lion King's Heirs in Painful Fight." *City Press*, June 21 (2019): 5–6.

Olsen, Kathryn. *Music and Social Change in South Africa: Maskanda Past and Present.* Philadelphia, PA: Temple University Press, 2014.

Oomen, Barbara. *Chiefs in South Africa: Law, Power and Culture in the Post-Apartheid Era.* Oxford: James Currey Publishers, 2005.

Oriakhogba, Desmond. *Copyright, Collective Management Organisations and Competition in Africa.* Cape Town: Juta, 2021.

Osborne, Richard, and Dave Laing. *Music by Numbers: The Use and Abuse of Statistics in the Music Industries.* Bristol: Intellect, 2021.

Osseo-Asare, Abena. *Bitter Roots: The Search for Healing Plants in Africa.* Chicago: University of Chicago Press, 2014.

Ouma, Marisella N. "Optimal Enforcement of Music Copyright in Sub-Saharan Africa—Reality or Myth." *Journal of World Intellectual Property* 9, no. 5 (2006): 592–627.

Patry, William. *How to Fix Copyright.* Oxford: Oxford University Press, 2012.

Perlman, Marc. "From 'Folklore' to 'Knowledge' in Global Governance." In *Making and Unmaking Intellectual Property: Creative Production in Legal and Cultural Perspective*, edited by Mario Biagioli, Peter Jaszi, and Martha Woodmansee, 115–32. Chicago: University of Chicago Press, 2011.

Perullo, Alex. *Live from Dar es Salam: Popular Music and Tanzania's Music Economy*. Bloomington: Indiana University Press, 2011.

Perzanowski, Aaron, and Jason Schultz. *The End of Ownership: Personal Property in the Digital Economy*. Cambridge, MA: MIT Press, 2016.

Petersen, Leif, et al. *What Price Cheap Goods? Survivalists, Informalists and Competition in the Township Retail Grocery Trade*. PLAAS Working Paper 59. Bellville: Institute for Poverty, Land and Agrarian Studies, University of the Western Cape, 2019.

Peyroux, Elizabeth. "City Improvement Districts in Johannesburg: An Examination of the Local Variations of the BID Model." In *Business Improvement Districts: ein neues Governance-Modell aus Perspektive von Praxis und Stadtforschung*, edited by Robert Pütz, 139–62. Passau: L. I. S. Verlag, 2008.

Pickering, Andrew. *The Mangle of Practice: Time, Agency and Science*. Chicago: University of Chicago Press, 1995.

Pietilä, Tuulikki. *Contracts, Patronage and Mediation: The Articulation of Global and Local in the South African Recording Industry*. New York: Palgrave Macmillan, 2015.

Pistorius, Tana. "The Imperial Copyright Act 1911's Role in Shaping South African Copyright Law." In *A Shifting Empire: 100 Years of the Copyright Act 1911*, edited by Uma Suthersanen and Ysolde Gendreau, 204–25. Northampton, MA: Edward Elgar, 2013.

Pollock, Anne. *Synthesizing Hope: Matter, Knowledge, and Place in South African Drug Discovery*. Chicago: University of Chicago Press, 2019.

Posey, Darrell A. *Traditional Resource Rights: International Instruments for Protection and Compensation for Indigenous Peoples and Local Communities*. Gland, Switzerland: International Union for Conservation of Nature and Natural Resources, 1996.

Posey, Darrell A., and Graham Dutfield. *Beyond Intellectual Property: Toward Traditional Resource Rights for Indigenous Peoples and Local Communities*. Ottawa: International Development Research Centre, 1996.

Pound, Roscoe. "Mechanical Jurisprudence." *Columbia Law Review* 8 (1908): 605–23.

Pouris, Anastassios, and Roula Inglesi-Lotz. *The Economic Contribution of Copyright-Based Industries in South Africa*. Geneva: WIPO, 2011.

Povinelli, Elizabeth A. *The Cunning of Recognition: Indigenous Alterities and the Making of Australian Multiculturalism*. Durham, NC: Duke University Press.

Power, Michael. *The Audit Society: Rituals of Verification*. Oxford: Oxford University Press, 1997.

Pratt, Mary Louise. *Imperial Eyes: Travel Writing and Transculturation*. New York: Routledge, 1992.

Priestley, Joseph. *Letters to the Right Honourable Edmund Burke, Occasioned by His Reflections on the Revolution in France*. 3rd corrected ed. Birmingham: Thomas Pearson, 1791.

Primo, Natasha, and Libby Lloyd. "Chapter 3: South Africa." In *Media Piracy in Emerging Economies*, edited by Joe Karaganis, 99–147. New York: Social Science Research Council, 2011.

Putman, Robert. "Tuning In, Tuning Out: The Strange Disappearance of Social Capital in America." *PS: Political Science and Politics* 28, no. 4 (1995): 664–83.

Radano, Ronald, and Philip V. Bohlman, eds. *Music and the Racial Imagination*. Chicago: University of Chicago Press, 2000.

Ramsden, Peter. *A Guide to Intellectual Property Law*. Cape Town: Juta, 2011.

Reckwitz, Andreas. *The End of Illusions: Politics, Economy, and Culture in Late Modernity*. London: Polity Press, 2021.

Reckwitz, Andreas. *Society of Singularities*. London: Polity Press, 2020.

Recording Industry of South Africa (RiSA). "The Investigation Process." *Enforcement Bulletin* no. 4 (January 2009): 6–7.

Reddy, Prashant T., and Sumathi Chandrashekaran. *Create, Copy, Disrupt: India's Intellectual Property Dilemmas*. New Delhi: Oxford University Press, 2017.

Reidel, Ivan. "The Taylor Swift Paradox: Superstardom, Excessive Advertising and Blanket Licenses." *New York University Journal of Law & Business* 7, no. 2 (2011): 731–810.

Rich, Paul B. *White Power and the Liberal Conscience: Racial Segregation and South African Liberalism, 1921–60*. Manchester: Manchester University Press, 1984.

Richards, Thomas. *The Commodity Culture of Victorian England: Advertising and Spectacle, 1851–1914*. Stanford, CA: Stanford University Press, 1990.

Rifkin, Jeremy. *The Age of Access: The New Culture of Hypercapitalism, Where All of Life Is a Paid-for Experience*. New York: Jeremy P. Tarcher/Putnam, 2000.

Riles, Annelise. "Representing In-Between: Law, Anthropology, and the Rhetoric of Interdisciplinarity." *University of Illinois Law Review* (1994): 597–650.

Riles, Annelise. *The Network Inside Out*. Ann Arbor: University of Michigan Press, 2000.

Riles, Annelise. "Property as Legal Knowledge: Means and Ends." *Cornell Law Faculty Publications*, paper 995 (2004): 775–95.

Riles, Annelise. "A New Agenda for the Cultural Study of Law: Taking on the Technicalities." *Buffalo Law Review* 53, no. 3 (2005): 973–1033.

Riles, Annelise. "[Deadlines] Removing the Brackets on Politics in Bureaucratic and Anthropological Analysis." In *Documents: Artifacts of Modern Knowledge*, 71–92. Ann Arbor: University of Michigan Press, 2006.

Riles, Annelise. *Financial Citizenship: Experts, Publics, and the Politics of Central Banking*. Ithaca, NY: Cornell University Press, 2018.

Roberts, Paul. "Renegotiating Forensic Cultures: Between Law, Science and Criminal Justice." *Studies in History and Philosophy of Biological and Biomedical Science* 44 (2013): 47–59.

Robins, Steven L. *From Revolution to Rights in South Africa*. Woodbridge, UK: James Currey, 2008.

Robinson, Dylan. *Hungry Listening: Resonant Theory for Indigenous Sound Studies*. Minneapolis: University of Minnesota Press, 2020.

Roitman, Janet. *Anti-Crisis*. Durham, NC: Duke University Press, 2014.

Rosa, Hartmut. *Resonance: A Sociology of Our Relationship to the World.* London: Polity Press, 2019.

Röschenthaler, Ute, and Mamadou Diawara, eds. *Copyright Africa: How Intellectual Property, Media and Markets Transform Immaterial Cultural Goods.* Canon Pyon, UK: Sean Kingston Publishing, 2016.

Rose, Nikolas, and Carlos Novas. "Biological Citizenship." In *Global Assemblages: Technology, Politics and Ethics as Anthropological Problems,* edited by Aihwa Ong and Stephen J. Collier, 439–63. Oxford: Blackwell Publishing, 2008.

Rottenburg, Richard, Sally Engle Merry, Sung-Joon Park, and Johanna Mugler, eds. *The World of Indicators: The Making of Governmental Knowledge through Quantification.* Cambridge: Cambridge University Press, 2015.

Sachs, Albie. *We, the People: Insights of an Activist Judge.* Johannesburg: Wits University Press, 2016.

SACO (South African Cultural Observatory). "The Mapping of the South African Creative Industry (CCI) and Creative Economy: A Baseline." 2017. https://www.southafricanculturalobservatory.org.za.

SACO (South African Cultural Observatory). "Employment in the Cultural and Creative Industries in South Africa." 2017. https://www.southafricanculturalobservatory.org.za.

SACO (South African Cultural Observatory). "Measuring the Impact of the Covid-19 Crisis on the Cultural and Creative Industries in South Africa: An Early Assessment." May 2020.

Said, Edward W. *Orientalism.* London: Routledge & Kegan Paul, 1978.

Sarat, Austin, and Thomas R. Kearns. "Beyond the Great Divide: Forms of Legal Scholarship and Everyday Life." In *Law in Everyday Life,* 21–61. Ann Arbor: University of Michigan Press, 1993.

Scarry, Elaine. *On Beauty and Being Just.* London: Duckworth, 2006.

Schmidt Campbell, Mary, and Randy Martin, eds. *Artistic Citizenship: A Public Voice for the Arts.* New York: Routledge, 2006.

Schmücker, Reinold. "Normative Resources and Domain-Specific Principles: Heading for an Ethics of Copying." In *The Aesthetics and Ethics of Copying,* edited by Darren Hick and Reinold Schmücker, 359–80. London: Bloomsbury, 2016.

Scott, Alan. "Modernity's Machine Metaphor." *British Journal of Sociology* 48, no. 4 (1997): 561–75.

Scott, Allen J. *The Cultural Economy of Cities.* London: SAGE, 2000.

Scott, David. "Culture in Political Theory." *Political Theory* 31, no. 1 (2003): 92–115.

Scott, James C. *Seeing like a State: How Certain Schemes to Improve the Human Condition Have Failed.* New Haven, CT: Yale University Press, 1998.

Seeger, Anthony. "Traditional Music in a Commodified World." In *Music and Copyright.* 2nd ed. Edited by Simon Frith and Lee Marshall, 157–71. Edinburgh: Edinburgh University Press, 2004.

Seeger, Pete. *Pete Seeger in His Own Words.* New York: Routledge, 2016.

SekelaXabiso. *Southern African Music Rights: SAMRO. Forensic Investigation Report into the United Arab Emirates Investment.* Johannesburg: unpublished, 2018.

Sen, Amartya. *Development as Freedom*. Oxford: Oxford University Press, 2001.
Serres, Michel. *The Parasite*. Minneapolis: University of Minnesota Press, 2007.
Shore, Cris, and Susan Wright. "Governing by Numbers: Audit Culture, Rankings and the New World Order." *Social Anthropology* 23, no. 1 (2015): 22–28.
Shore, Cris, Susan Wright, and Davide Però, eds. *Policy Worlds: Anthropology and the Analysis of Contemporary Power*. New York: Berghahn Books, 2011.
Simone, Abdel M. "People as Infrastructure: Intersecting Fragments in Johannesburg." *Public Culture* 16, no. 3 (2004): 407–29.
Sindane, Ntando. *The Call to Decolonise Higher Education: Copyright Law through an African Lens*. MA thesis, University of South Africa, 2020.
Sinnreich, Aram. "Ethics, Evolved: An International Perspective on Copying in the Networked Age." In *The Aesthetics and Ethics of Copying*, edited by Darren Hick and Reinold Schmücker, 315–34. London: Bloomsbury, 2016.
Skinner, Ryan. *Bamako Sounds: The Afropolitan Ethics of Malian Music*. Minneapolis: University of Minnesota Press, 2015.
Sonnekus, Jean. "Matrimonial Property Law and Reversionary Interest in Musical Composition. Legal Principles with a Southern Swing." In *Recht als Erbe und Aufgabe: Heinz Holzhauer zum 21. April 2005*. Edited by Saar, Stefan Chr, Andreas Roth, and Christian Hattenhauer, 500–526. Berlin: E. Schmidt, 2005.
Sonnekus, Jean. "Reversionary Interest in Musical Composition and the Administration of the Estate of a Deceased Composer." *South African Law Journal* 122 (2005): 464–80.
Special Issue Editors. "Law and Ideology." *Law and Society Review* 22, no. 4 (1988): 633
Spira, Laura F. *The Audit Committee: Performing Corporate Governance*. New York: Kluwer Academic Publishers, 2002.
Stahl, Matt. *Unfree Masters: Recording Artists and the Politics of Work*. Durham, NC: Duke University Press, 2013.
Star, Susan Leigh. "The Structure of Ill-Structured Solutions: Boundary Objects and Heterogeneous Distributed Problem Solving." In *Boundary Objects and Beyond: Working with Leigh Star*, edited by Geoffrey C. Bowker et al., 243–62. Cambridge, MA: MIT Press, 2015 (1988).
Steingo, Gavin. *Kwaito's Promise: Music and the Aesthetics of Freedom in South Africa*. Chicago: University of Chicago Press, 2016.
Stengers, Isabelle. *Cosmopolitics 1*. Minneapolis: University of Minnesota Press, 2010.
Stewart, Kathleen. *Ordinary Affects*. Durham, NC: Duke University Press, 2007.
Stobart, Henry. "Rampant Reproduction and Digital Democracy: Shifting Landscapes of Music Production and 'Piracy' in Bolivia." *Ethnomusicology Forum* 19, no. 1 (2010): 27–56.
Strathern, Marilyn. "From Improvement to Enhancement: An Anthropological Comment on the Audit Culture." *Cambridge Journal of Anthropology* 19, no. 3 (1996): 1–21.
Strathern, Marilyn, ed. *Audit Cultures: Anthropological Studies in Accountability, Ethics and the Academy*. London: Routledge, 2002.
Sundaram, Ravi. *Pirate Modernity: Delhi's Media Urbanism*. New York: Routledge, 2010.

Sunder, Madhavi. *From Goods to a Good Life: Intellectual Property and Global Justice.* New Haven, CT: Yale University Press, 2012.

Tadros, Victor. "A Few Thoughts on Copyright Law and the Subject of Writing." In *Intellectual Property and Ethics*, edited by Lionel Bentley and Spyros Maniatis, 127–46. London: Sweet & Maxwell, 1998.

Tamanaha, Brian. "The Lessons of Law-and-Development Studies." *American Journal of International Law* 89 (1995): 470–86.

Tamanaha, Brian. *Law as a Means to an End: Threat to the Rule of Law.* Cambridge: Cambridge University Press, 2006.

Tarantino, Bob. "Long Time Coming: Copyright Reversionary Interests in Canada." *Développements récents en droit de la propriété intellectuelle* 375 (2013): 1–18.

Taussig, Michael. *Shamanism, Colonialism, and the Wild Man: A Study in Terror and Healing.* Chicago: University of Chicago Press, 1987.

Taylor, Charles. "The Politics of Recognition." In *Multiculturalism: Examining the Politics of Recognition*, edited by A. Gutmann, 25–73. Princeton, NJ: Princeton University Press, 1994 [1992].

Terreblanche, Sampie. *A History of Inequality in South Africa, 1652–2002.* Pietermaritzburg, South Africa: University of Natal Press, 2002.

Thompson, Hunter S. *Generation of Swine. Gonzo Papers vol. 2: Tales of Shame and Degradation in the 80's.* New York: Vintage Books, 1989.

Tilley, Helen. *Africa as a Living Laboratory: Empire, Development, and the Problem of Scientific Knowledge, 1870–1950.* Chicago: University of Chicago Press, 2011.

Towse, Ruth, ed. *Copyright in the Cultural Industries.* Cheltenham: Edward Elgar, 2002.

Towse, Ruth. "Managing Copyrights in the Cultural Industries." *Semantic Scholar* (2005): 1–10.

Trebilcock, Michael. "Between Universalism and Relativism. Reflections on the Evolution of Law and Development Studies." *University of Toronto Law Journal* 66, no. 3 (2016): 330–52.

Trewhela, Ralph. *Song Safari: A Journey through Light Music in South Africa.* Scottsdale, AZ: Limelight Press, 1980.

Trubek, David, and Mark Galanter. "Scholars in Self-Estrangement: Some Reflections on the Crisis in Law and Development Studies in the United States." *Wisconsin Law Review* 4 (1974): 1062–1103.

Tsing, Anna Lowenhaupt. *Friction: An Ethnography of Global Connection.* Princeton, NJ: Princeton University Press, 2005.

Tsing, Anna Lowenhaupt. "On Nonscalability: The Living World Is Not Amenable to Precision-Nested Scales." *Common Knowledge* 18, no. 3 (2012): 505–24.

Tucker, Percy. *Just the Ticket: My 50 Years in Show Business.* Johannesburg: Jonathan Ball Publishers, 1997.

Uchtenhagen, Ulrich. *Copyright Collective Management in Music.* Geneva: WIPO, 2011.

UNESCO. *2019 Framework for Cultural Statistics.* Montreal: UNESCO, 2019.

Vats, Anjali. *The Color of Creatorship: Intellectual Property, Race, and the Making of Americans.* Stanford, CA: Stanford University Press, 2020.

Verdery, Katherine, ed. *Property in Question: Value Transformation in the Global Economy.* London: Berg Publishers, 1991.

Vigneswaran, Darshan. "The Contours of Disorder: Crime Maps and Territorial Policing in South Africa." *Environment and Planning D: Society and Space* 31 (2014): 91–107.

von Schnitzler, Antina. *Democracy's Infrastructure: Techno-Politics and Protest after Apartheid.* Princeton, NJ: Princeton University Press, 2016.

Wallis, Roger, Charles Baden-Fuller, Martin Kretschmer, and George Michael Klimis. "Contested Collective Administration of Intellectual Property Rights in Music: The Challenge to the Principles of Reciprocity and Solidarity." *European Journal of Communication* 14, no. 1 (1999): 5–35.

Wallis, Roger, and Krister Malm. *Big Sounds from Small People: The Music Industry in Small Countries.* New York: Pendragon, 1984.

Watson, Richard L. *Slave Emancipation and Racial Attitudes in Nineteenth-Century South Africa.* Cambridge: Cambridge University Press, 2012.

Watt, Richard. *Collective Management as a Business Strategy for Creators: An Introduction to the Economics of Collective Management of Copyright and Related Rights.* Geneva: WIPO, 2016.

Weheliye, Alexander. *Habeas Viscus: Racializing Assemblages, Biopolitics, and Black Feminist Theories of the Human.* Durham, NC: Duke University Press, 2014.

White, Bob. *Rumba Rules: The Politics of Dance Music in Mobutu's Zaire.* Durham, NC: Duke University Press, 2008.

Wilkins, Ivor, and Hans Strydom. *The Super-Afrikaners.* Johannesburg: J. Ball, 1979.

Williams, Pat. *King Kong: Our Knot of Time and Music. A Personal Memoir of South Africa's Legendary Musical.* London: Portobello, 2017.

Wirtén, Eva Hemmungs. *Terms of Use: Negotiating the Jungle of the Intellectual Commons.* Toronto: University of Toronto Press, 2008.

Wynberg, Rachel, and Roger Chennells. 2009. "Green Diamonds of the South: An Overview of the San-Hoodia Case." In *Indigenous Peoples, Consent and Benefit Sharing: Lessons from the San-Hoodia Case,* edited by Rachel Wynberg, Doris Schroeder, and Roger Chennells, 89–124. Dordrecht: Springer, 2009.

Wynberg, Rachel, and Sarah Laird. "Bioprospecting, Access and Benefit Sharing: Revisiting the 'Grand Bargain.'" In *Indigenous Peoples, Consent and Benefit Sharing: Lessons from the San-Hoodia Case,* edited by Rachel Wynberg, Doris Schroeder, and Roger Chennells, 69–86. Dordrecht: Springer, 2009.

Young, Hershini Bana. *Illegible Will: Coercive Spectacles of Labor in South Africa and the Diaspora.* Durham, NC: Duke University Press, 2017.

Young, James O., and Conrad G. Brunk, eds. *The Ethics of Cultural Appropriation.* Chichester, UK: Wiley-Blackwell, 2009.

Yúdice, George. *The Expediency of Culture: Uses of Culture in the Global Era.* Durham, NC: Duke University Press, 2003.

Yúdice, George. "Cultural Diversity and Cultural Rights." *Hispanic Issues On Line* 5, no. 1 (2009): 110–37.

INDEX

A2K. *See* Access to Knowledge (A2K)
Abbott, Andrew, 213
Abilene Music, 64–65, 92–93, 105–6, 321n5
Academic and Non-Fiction Authors' Association of South Africa (ANFASA), 137, 139
Access to Knowledge (A2K), 7, 45
actor-network theory (ANT), 57–58, 152, 231; following the actor, 194; infra-language, 193–94; in legal studies, 23, 51–52
ad fundandam jurisdictionem, 92
AEMRO. *See* Arab Emirates Music Rights Organization (AEMRO)
aesthetics: analog, 269; and beauty, 170–71; and citizenship, 158, 161–64; essentialism of, 171; and ethics, 161–62, 164, 166–73, 331n137; and judgments of taste, 162; and value, 332n143. *See also* citizenship; ethics; form and formalism
affect and affective, 116, 126, 128, 165, 169, 231, 242, 297–99
affidavit, 103–4, 198, 207–8, 211–12, 214–16
affordance, 4, 7, 55–56
African American music, 69–70, 97–99
African National Congress (ANC), 2, 4, 18–19, 141–42, 155, 226–27, 244–45; Legal Research Group, 19–20
African Regional Intellectual Property Organization, 137

Africa Umoja, 156
Afropolitanism, 17, 160
agency, 8, 21, 23, 46–48, 53–58, 67, 99–100, 121–22, 133, 158–59, 162–63, 169, 191–92, 252–53, 255, 290
agreements repository (AGM), 273, 286
AIDS. *See* HIV/AIDS
AlJabal, Yaser, 284–87, 290
Allingham, Rob, 77
Amazon, 19
American Society of Composers, Authors, and Publishers (ASCAP), 233
ANC. *See* African National Congress (ANC)
Anderson, John, 243–44
ANFASA. *See* Academic and Non-Fiction Authors' Association of South Africa (ANFASA)
Ansell, Gwen, 337n7
ANT. *See* actor-network theory (ANT)
anthropology: of auditing, 288–91; and crime, 177–78; and culture, 25; and economics, 261–62; and history of colonialism, 114–15, 129; and infrastructure, 281–82; in law, 9–13, 21–24, 33–34, 49, 302–3; legal, 9, 11, 25, 49, 52–53, 58–59, 66–67, 221–22; method, 12–13, 303–6; and ownership, 6–7; and statistics, 220–22, 335n70. *See also* economy and economics; ethnography; law

anti-piracy raids. *See* copyright law: enforcement; policing
apartheid, 2–6, 76–77, 143–45; and aesthetics, 166–69; and copyright, 22, 24–26, 65–66, 78, 95–96; and instrumentalism, 37–38; police violence during, 216–17; and urban geography, 181, 223–27
appropriation, 4, 72–73, 157, 169; cultural, 128, 131–32, 161, 331n137; and misappropriation, 128, 130–32, 135–36
Arab Emirates Music Rights Organization (AEMRO), 237, 284–88. *See also* Southern African Music Rights Organisation (SAMRO)
Arewa, Olufunmilayo, 97, 318n36
artist, 158–59, 161–63, 169–70. *See also* author and authorship
Asad, Talal, 222
ASCAP. *See* American Society of Composers, Authors, and Publishers (ASCAP)
Ash, Moses, 71
assemblage, 114, 117–18. *See also* network
attachment, 53–54. *See also* Latour, Bruno
Attali, Jacques, 161
audience, 169–70
audit: anthropology of, 288–91; audit function, 289; circularity of, 289–90; and compliance, 289; and populism, 291–95, 297–300; SekelaXabiso audit of SAMRO, 283–84, 286–89, 291–91; and transparency, 291–93. *See also* Southern African Music Rights Organisation (SAMRO)
author and authorship, 68–69, 96, 139–40, 157–58, 169, 253–54, 310, 327n14; and Orientalism, 72–73; and race, 97–98; Romantic ideal of, 33, 68–70, 158–59; and talent, 107. *See also under* copyright law
authority, 114, 149, 151–52, 162–63, 201, 228–29; competent, 124; interpretive, 11–12
autopoiesis, 56, 192

Ballantine, Christopher, 315n3, 316n15
Baloyi, Joel, 137, 253–54
Banks, Mark, 169
Barthe, Yannick, 33
Bateson, Gregory, 55
Bauman, Zygmunt, 136, 170
Bayart, Jean-François, 118

beauty. *See under* aesthetics
belonging, 3–4, 112, 139–40, 241–42; and citizenship, 116, 158–59, 162–66, 172–73; and indigeneity, 117–18. *See also* citizenship; community; indigeneity; worlding
benefit-sharing, 156–58; and hoodia, 145–46
Bentham, Jeremy, 22–23
Bentley, Kristina, 160
Berne Convention of 1886, 28, 75, 154–55, 266, 309
Bhe and Others v Khayelitsha Magistrate and Others, 91, 93
Bill of Rights. *See under* Constitution
biodiversity, 124–25, 144–46. *See also* knowledge
Biowatch South Africa, 144
Black Administration Act (Black Administration Act 38 of 1927), 91, 93, 110–11
black box, 23–24, 39–40, 49–50, 130–31, 152, 190, 192–93, 194, 231, 289
black economic empowerment, 4, 77, 90, 135
blanket licenses, 233, 247–48, 254–55, 264–66. *See also* collective management organization (CMO)
Bloom, Harry, 82–84
BMI. *See* Broadcast Music Inc. (BMI)
Boksburg North Police Station, 179–81, 194, 195–97, 201–5, 216–17. *See also* policing; South African Police Service (SAPS)
Bokwe, John Knox, 27
boundary objects, 207, 251–52, 302–8. *See also* classification
Bourdieu, Pierre, 158, 327n15
Bowker, Geoffrey, 207, 250–52, 280, 302–3
Bowman, Wayne D., 162–64
Boyle, James, 17, 124–25
Brackett, David, 98
British Copyright Act of 1911. *See* Imperial Copyright Act of 1911
Broadcast Music Inc. (BMI), 239, 285
Broederbond, 235–36. *See also* South African Broadcasting Corporation (SABC)
Business Against Crime South Africa (Business Leadership South Africa), 197
Business Software Alliance (BSA), 175, 229

Callon, Michel, 33, 61, 122, 263
CAPASSO. *See* Composers, Authors and Publishers Association (CAPASSO)

Cape Colony's Act No. 4 of 1854, 25
Cardozo, Benjamin, 34
Carmichael, Stokely, 72
CAS. *See* Criminal Administration System (CAS)
Chakrabarty, Dipesh, 260
Chanock, Martin, 24, 97
Chatterjee, Partha, 154–55
CIPC. *See* Companies and Intellectual Property Commission (CIPC)
CISAC. *See* Confédération internationale des sociétés d'auteurs et compositeurs (CISAC)
CIS-Net. *See under* Confédération internationale des sociétés d'auteurs et compositeurs (CISAC)
citizenship, 4, 9, 172–73; aesthetic, 158, 171–72; artistic, 161–65; civic-republican, 162–65; cultural theories of, 158–61; and ethics, 166–67; liberal-individualist, 162–65; and minority rights, 159–60
civil society. *See under* society
classification, 250–52, 302–3; interruptions, 305–6. *See also* boundary objects
Clegg, Johnny, 6, 119–20, 328n22
Clifford, James, 221
CMO. *See* collective management organization (CMO)
Cobussen, Marcel, 331n137
collecting society. *See* collective management organization (CMO)
collective management organization (CMO), 232–33, 239–40, 252–53, 339n49; and blanket licenses, 247–48, 264–66; as collectives of worlding, 241–42; "domaine publique" (DP), 238; economics of, 261, 268; efficiency of, 262–63; racial bias of, 234–36; research on, 240–41; solidarity function, 267–68. *See also* American Society of Composers, Authors, and Publishers (ASCAP); Broadcast Music Inc. (BMI); Composers, Authors and Publishers Association (CAPASSO); Gesellschaft für musikalische Aufführungs- und mechanische Vervielfältigungsrechte (GEMA); Société des auteurs, compositeurs et éditeurs de musique (SACEM); South African Music Performance Rights Association (SAMPRA); Southern African Music Rights Organisation (SAMRO)
colonialism, 47, 109–11, 154–55, 176, 261–62, 299, 302; and anthropology, 11, 114–15, 220; and copyright, 6–7, 22, 24–28, 41–42, 74–76, 91–94, 96–97, 125; and culture, 160; and indigenous knowledge, 127–31; and public sphere, 42–43; and urban geography, 224–25. *See also* apartheid; decolonialism and decolonization
Comaroff, John and Jean, 8, 25, 38–39, 177, 222
commodity, 18, 25, 31–32, 46, 133
common good, 23, 36–37
commons, 17. *See also* Creative Commons
community, 115–17, 140–41, 172–73; aesthetic, 156–64; and biodiversity, 124–25; communities of practice, 241–42; and cultural reproduction, 115; and economy, 191–92; indigenous, 114, 117–18, 126, 139–41, 145–46, 150–51, 164, 166–67, 297; and Intellectual Property Laws Amendment Act, 116–17, 118–21, 137–41, 150–51, 154–56, 166–67, 297; local, 32; and science, 212–13, 302–3; and worlding, 241–42. *See also* indigeneity
Companies Act (Companies Act 71 of 2008), 233, 287
Companies and Intellectual Property Commission (CIPC), 188–89
Company Gardens, 110
Competition Act (Competition Act 89 of 1998), 233
compliance. *See under* audit
Composers, Authors and Publishers Association (CAPASSO), 232, 296
Comprehensive Rural Development Programme, 41
Confédération internationale des sociétés d'auteurs et compositeurs (CISAC), 238, 266, 285; CIS-Net, 238, 273; Works Information Database (WID), 273
Congress of South African Trade Unions (COSATU), 271
Congress of Traditional Leaders of South Africa (CONTRALESA), 141

INDEX 373

Constitution: Bill of Rights, 5, 38, 91, 316n11; Chapter Nine Commissions, 160; Constitutional Court, 5, 37, 42–43, 91, 253; constitutionalism, 37–38; and politics of the particular, 4–5. *See also* Parliament
contingency, 54–56, 60, 113, 249–50
contracts and contract law, 47–48, 163, 263; colonial history of, 96–97, 109–10; fairness, 252
CONTRALESA. *See* Congress of Traditional Leaders of South Africa (CONTRALESA)
Convention of the African Intellectual Property Organization (1977), 123
Convention on Biological Diversity (1992), 124, 145
Conway's law, 252
Coombe, Rosemary, 16–17, 21, 25, 131
Coplan, David, 315n3
coproduction, 55, 122, 159, 194, 224, 260, 264, 320n120
Copyright Act (Copyright Act 98 of 1978), 76–78, 114, 137, 139, 157, 252–53, 309–13
Copyright Act of 1909, 98
Copyright Act of 1916, 25
Copyright Act 63 of 1965, 76, 337n7
Copyright Alliance, 296
Copyright Amendment Bill, 1, 8–9, 19–20, 107, 296, 301, 306, 315n2
copyright law, 1–2, 5–8; Africanization of, 7; and "articles," 209; assignments, 74–75, 79–95, 107, 249–50, 253–55, 304–5, 311, 323nn36–37, 324n49; and authorship, 253, 310; and citizenship, 310; colonial history of, 22, 24–25, 28, 66, 75–78, 96–97, 318n36; commercial bias in, 253–54; and cultural production, 4, 7, 16–18; and decolonialism, 320n101; and development, 40–42, 175–77; *droit d'auteur*, 253; duration, 311; enforcement, 184–91, 198–99, 203–4, 216–19, 229–31, 333n17; and ethics, 164–65, 331n137; exceptions, 19–20; exclusionary policies, 16–17; exclusive rights, 310–11; fair dealing exceptions, 312; and human rights, 41, 253–54; and indigeneity, 114; infringement of, 181–84, 187–88, 198, 312–13; and innovation, 40–41; instrumentalist logic of, 35–36, 48; and interest, 87–89; licensing, 311–12; materiality requirement, 139, 310; mechanical rights, 79, 232–33, 276, 323n35; and multisided music platforms, 317n16; originality requirement, 94, 137, 298, 310; performance rights, 79, 181, 232–33, 236, 253, 255–56, 273, 276–77, 311, 337n7; and personhood, 36, 315n7; protection, 309–10; and public, 41–43, 225, 297–98; and race, 5–6, 9, 95–100, 235–37; and (re)distributive justice, 44–45, 47, 65–66, 299–300; reversionary interest, 74–76, 81, 86–91; and "second economy," 32; and social planning, 4, 36; statutory presumptions, 214–16; tiered system of, 46; transfer, 311–12; *Urheberrecht*, 253; as Western imposition, 20–21. *See also* collective management organization (CMO); indigeneity; law
Copyright Review Commission Report (2011), 19, 107
corruption, 5, 121, 187, 234, 238, 284, 289, 294, 334n39
COSATU. *See* Congress of South African Trade Unions (COSATU)
Council for Scientific and Industrial Research (CSIR), 144–45
counterfeit, 188. *See also* piracy; trademark
Counterfeit Goods Act (Counterfeit Goods Act 37 of 1997), 187–88, 198–99
COVID-19 pandemic, 306–7
Creative Commons, 7, 44–45, 175
Creative Workers Union of South Africa (CWUSA), 179
creativity, 24–25, 40–41, 235–36
Crewe, Emma, 112, 289
crime: and crime dockets, 203–8; and statistics, 223–28. *See also* evidence; piracy; policing; statistics
Criminal Administration System (CAS), 203–5
criminal law: and Anton Piller order, 217; criminal procedure, 194, 198–201, 208, 214, 218–19, 230; search and seizure, 183–84, 186–87, 216–19. *See also* piracy; policing
Criminal Procedure Act (Criminal Procedure Act 56 of 1955), 194, 198–99, 208, 214, 218–19
critical development studies, 51
critical legal studies, 9, 13, 22–23, 34, 49–50, 67

critical policy studies, 122
critical race theory, 51, 67, 99–100
Cula Sibone (Let's See You Sing), 272, 274
Cullman, Sam, 107, 326n100
cultural appropriation. *See under* appropriation; culture
cultural industries, 1–2, 268–69, 340n68; and COVID-19 pandemic, 306–7; creative class in, 5, 269; economic impact, 319n75; and employment, 29–32; and entrepreneurship, 133, 270–71; equity and diversity, 271–72; and labor, 270–72; and scalability, 269–70
culture, 4; absorption in commodity relations, 30–31; cultural appropriation, 128, 131–32, 161, 331n137; cultural production and reproduction, 7, 16–17, 158–59, 169; "cultural values," 134–35; and citizenship, 159–61; and colonialism, 25–28; and economy, 191–92; hyperculture, 3; late-modern, 3; and law, 67; and nation-state, 123–24, 131–32, 154–55, 329n53; and racial justice, 5–6; and sovereignty, 155; spatiotemporal order of, 24–25; and traditional knowledge, 123–28, 131–33. *See also* appropriation; indigeneity; ownership
custody, chain of custody, 199–200. *See also* evidence
customary law, 90–91, 93, 95–96, 116, 126, 140–43; and copyright, 25–26, 124; and ubuntu, 45. *See also* copyright law; law
Customs and Excise Act 91 of 1964, 198–99
CWUSA. *See* Creative Workers Union of South Africa (CWUSA)

DAC. *See* Department of Arts and Culture (DAC)
DALRO. *See* Dramatic, Artistic and Literary Rights Organisation (DALRO)
data and databases, 21–22, 195, 209–11; in anthropology, 220–23; as "articulation work," 280–81; as boundary objects, 251–52, 302–3; at CISAC, 238, 297; and condensation, 149; at SAMRO, 241, 249–50, 257, 272–77, 280–83, 297. *See also* classification
Dean, Owen, 64–65, 77–78, 80–81, 84–88, 90–94, 97, 101–2, 104–6, 137–38, 155, 313, 323n37, 324n47
decolonialism and decolonization, 2, 7, 11, 22; and copyright, 253–54, 320n101; and science, 128–30
deindustrialization, 30–31
Department of Arts and Culture (DAC), 29–30, 105, 271
Department of Trade and Industry (DTI): Companies and Intellectual Property Commission, 147–49; Portfolio Committee on Trade and Industry, 22, 111
Designs Act 195 of 1993, 114
Desrosières, Alain, 222
development, 20–21, 28–32, 43; as freedom, 43–44; and instrumentalism, 39–44; in law and development studies, 39–40; in legal discourse, 39–40; rural, 41. *See also* Comprehensive Rural Development Programme; economy and economics; employment
Dewey, John, 101, 305
Dickens, Charles, 75
Dickens clause. *See under* Imperial Copyright Act of 1911
Digital Millennium Copyright Act (US), 214
Diplomatic Conference (1976), 123
Disney. *See* Walt Disney Company
Distant Echoes: Yo-Yo Ma & the Kalahari Bushmen (Yo-Yo Ma), 157
Dlamini, Sipho, 284–88, 290
dockets. *See under* crime; evidence
domaine publique. *See under* collective management organization (CMO); public domain (domaine publique; DP); Southern African Music Rights Organisation (SAMRO)
Drahos, Peter, 127
Dramatic, Artistic and Literary Rights Organisation (DALRO), 140, 296
DTI. *See* Department of Trade and Industry (DTI)
Dubow, Saul, 129–30
Dudula (Operation Dudula), 196–97, 227
Dugard, John, 82
du Plessis, Esmé, 113–14
Durkheim, Émile, 177, 261
Dutch East India Company, 96, 110
du Toit, Andries, 134
Dyer, Alison, 313

East Rand, 179, 182, 204–5
economy and economics: and access, 191–92; and collective management organizations (CMOs), 261–62; economies of scale, 261–62, 268–70; and externalities, 262–63; and indigenous knowledge, 127–28, 132–33; informal economy, 29, 225; law and, 22–23, 35, 188; and morality, 262, 340n63; national economy, 133–34; "platform economy," 31, 127; rural economy, 134; "second economy," 29–32; and transaction costs, 233, 264–65, 267–68, 300; unified economy, 126–27; and universalism, 261–62. *See also* black economic empowerment; law; wealth maximization
Egnos, Bertha, 156
Ekurhuleni, 181
employment, 29–32
entrepreneurship, 29, 40–41, 133, 270–71. *See also* cultural industries
environmentalism, 124–25; and "political ecology," 128
Ess, Charles, 166
Esselen Street City Improvement District (CID), 226–27
estate, 74–75, 99; intestate estates, 88–91; Solomon Linda estate, 65, 87–95, 102, 104–5. *See also* copyright law: and interest; copyright law: reversionary interest
ethics: and aesthetics, 157–58, 161–62, 166–73; and citizenship, 162–64, 166–67; consequentialist, 164–65; and copyright, 165–66; and cultural appropriation, 131–32; deontic, 163–65; of ethnography, 59–60; and ubuntu, 46; virtue, 163–64, 166. *See also* aesthetics; citizenship; culture
ethnography, 11–12; challenges of, 21–22; and governance, 21–22; and human action, 23–24; and intellectual property law, 320n107; as method, 50–61, 84, 103–4, 280–81, 290–91; performative critique, 307; and quantification, 220–22. *See also* anthropology; audit; infrastructure; relationality
ethnomusicology, 26, 70–71. *See also* musical scholarship

evidence: and criminal justice system, 203–4; chaining, 199–201, 204–5, 208–12, 214–16, 219; circulation of, 194; crime docket, 203–8; digital, 209–11; obviousness of, 200–201, 205, 211, 214–16, 219; pertinence of, 210–11; probative value of, 205, 210
experts: disembedding function of, 141–42; knowledge, 114, 142, 149–50, 152–53, 292–93; at parliamentary hearings, 136–41, 147–49, 152–54, 305; testimony of, 136–43, 147–49, 152–54, 211–12. *See also* knowledge
externalities, 262–65; and frames, 263–66; and overflows, 263–66

Faasen, Nicol, 138
facework, 142–43. *See also* experts
facts, issue statement, ratio, analysis, and conclusion (FIRAC), 78
fair use exceptions, 19–21, 165, 188. *See also* copyright law
Federation against Copyright Theft, 179
Ferguson, James, 31–32, 42, 135–36, 191, 225
FIC. *See* First Information of Crime (FIC)
Ficsor, Mihály, 266–67
file sharing, 8, 165–66, 216
FIRAC. *See* facts, issue statement, ratio, analysis, and conclusion (FIRAC)
First Information of Crime (FIC), 203, 207
First International Decade of the World's Indigenous Peoples (United Nations), 145
Fischer, Michael, 221
Fisher, William W., 35–36
folklore, 123–26, 154–55. *See also* traditional cultural expressions (TCE)
Folkways Music Publishers, 71, 74, 78–90, 92–94
forensics: and context, 212–13; epistemic culture of, 211–12; and jurisdiction, 213; at RiSA, 208–11, 213–16; at SAPS, 203–8. *See also* evidence
form and formalism, 59, 150, 153–54, 192; as technologies of inscription, 249–50
Foster, Laura, 146
Foucault, Michel, 33, 59, 165–66
Friedrich, Hanro, 104–5, 107, 324n46
frontier, 4, 112
fugitivity, 5, 100, 316n10

Gallo, Eric, 74, 236
Gallo (Gallo Africa, Gallo Recording Company, Gallo Records South Africa, Gallo Music Publishing), 69–70, 74, 76–81, 84–87, 90–92, 94, 97, 102, 156, 322n15
Gauteng, 30, 182, 255, 282
Gaye, Marvin, 99
GEAR. *See* Growth, Employment, and Redistribution (GEAR)
Geertz, Clifford, 49, 57, 103–4
GEMA. *See* Gesellschaft für musikalische Aufführungs- und mechanische Vervielfältigungsrechte (GEMA)
gemeinschaft. *See* community
genre, 97–98
Gesellschaft für musikalische Aufführungs- und mechanische Vervielfältigungsrechte (GEMA), 233
Giddens, Anthony, 141–43
gift and gift economy, 45–46, 291–92. *See also* benefit-sharing
Gilfillan, Graeme, 297
Gilroy, Paul, 2
globalization, 115, 134–35, 242–43
Gluckman, Max, 49, 57
Google, 19
gospel music, 46–47
governance: corporate, 239, 282, 287–89, 293–94; and data, 221–22; global systems of, 21–22, 154–55, 192; good, 33, 110; and governmentality, 221, 224, 288–89; liberal, 113, 122, 152
Greene, Kevin J., 97
Grey, George, 110
Griesel, Stephanus, 91–94, 102
Group Areas Act 41 of 1950, 110–11
Growth, Employment, and Redistribution (GEAR), 29, 77, 135, 145, 227
Guardian, The (newspaper), 144
!Gubi Tietei family, 156–57
Guthrie, Woodie, 70
Guyer, Jane, 31, 127

Habermas, Jürgen, 113
Habib, Adam, 160
Haffajee, Ferial, 4
Halbert, Deborah, 16–17
Hariman, Robert, 60
Haupt, Adam, 168

Hegel, Georg, 36, 45
Helmreich, Stefan, 55–56
heritage, 123–24, 152–55. *See also* tradition
Herzfeld, Michael, 18
Hesmondhalgh, David, 269, 340n63
Hetherington, Kregg, 290–92
HIV/AIDS, 68, 134, 227–28, 251
Hlongwane, Jabu, 156
Ho, Lok Sang, 44–45
Hobsbawm, Eric, 146
Hoernlé, Alfred and Winifred, 27
Holmes, Oliver Wendell, 34, 101
hoodia (*Hoodia gordonii*), 120, 143–46, 149
host and hosting, 56–57
Hottentot Proclamation of 1809, 110–11
How Far Have We Come (Pops Mohamed), 157
human rights, 41, 131–32. *See also under* copyright law
Huskisson, Yvonne, 236
Hutchison, Andrew, 47

identity: and anthropology, 51–52, 115; and colonialism, 129–32; and copyright, 25, 96, 99, 139–40; and citizenship, 162–63; and indigeneity, 131–32, 146, 160–61; postapartheid, 2–6. *See also* author and authorship; copyright law; culture; indigeneity
IFPI. *See* International Federation of the Phonographic Industry (IFPI)
IIPA. *See* International Intellectual Property Alliance (IIPA)
IKS (indigenous knowledge system), 118, 133, 134. *See also* indigeneity; knowledge
Imperial Copyright Act of 1911, 75–76, 95–96, 318n36, 322n26, 323n39; s5(2) (Dickens Clause), 75–76, 78, 81, 84–91, 93–96
Independent Communications Authority of South Africa, 298–99
Independent Music Performance Rights Association, 233
indigeneity: and citizenship, 166–67; defining, 150–52; and difference, 110–11, 329n55; and identity, 131–32, 146, 160–61; and indigenous communities, 20–21, 114–15, 117–20, 124–28, 132–33, 138–41, 164; indigenous knowledge systems (IKS), 19, 32, 112–13, 117–18, 126–36, 156; and indigenous modernities,

INDEX 377

indigeneity (*continued*)
143; and indigenous rights, 143, 145–46, 155, 160–61; and settlers, 129–30; and sustainable development, 299. *See also* knowledge; tradition

individualism, 24–25, 27, 31, 32, 35, 37, 38, 41, 45, 46, 47, 63, 70, 110, 113, 114, 115, 117, 126, 127, 132–33, 135–36, 159, 161, 163–65, 166, 169, 187, 195, 252, 254, 289, 327n14

information: materiality of, 249–51; information systems, 302–3, 341n82

infra-language, 193–94. *See also* language

infrastructure, 243, 281–82, 333n25, 341n80; and information, 51, 282–83; and service delivery, 282. *See also* data and databases; piracy; royalties

innovation, 40–41, 44

inscription and, 150, 194, 221, 250, 254–55, 281

Institute of Race Relations, 27, 38

instrumentalism: and anti-anti-instrumentalism, 23; and apartheid law, 37; and development, 39–44; failures of, 48–49; and legal fetishism, 13, 38–39; in legal scholarship, 22–23, 35–37, 38–39

intellectual property law: and citizen ethics, 164–66, 171–72; and cultural production, 16–17; and indigenous knowledge, 112–13, 118–24, 126–32, 143, 150–52, 158. *See also* copyright law; patent law

Intellectual Property Laws Amendment Act (Intellectual Property Laws Amendment Act 28 of 2013), 1, 8–9, 19–21, 32, 111–14, 116–19, 166–67, 172–73, 299, 305–6

Intellectual Property Laws Amendment Bill (B8-2010), 155–56; criticisms of, 136–42, 146–47

interest. *See under* copyright law; public interest

interested party information (IPI), 273

International Centre for Trade and Sustainable Development, 149

International Covenant on Economic, Social and Cultural Rights, 41

International Federation of the Phonographic Industry (IFPI), 194–95, 220, 228–29. *See also* Recording Industry of South Africa (RiSA); statistics

International Intellectual Property Alliance (IIPA), 228

International Telecommunications Union, ICT Development Index, 229

IP. *See* intellectual property law

IPI. *See* interested party information (IPI)

Ipi-Ntombi (Bertha Egnos), 156

isicathamiya, 62, 70, 156, 321n1

Jacob, Marie Andrée, 250

James, Wilmot, 155–56

Jeffery, Anthea, 38

Jenkins, Gordon, 71

Johannesburg, 133–34, 178–79, 181–82, 189, 200, 208, 223–26, 245

Johnnic Entertainment, 77, 91–92, 324n53

jubilee songs, 69

Ju/'hoansi people, 157–58

jurisdiction, 91–92, 118, 122, 212, 213

jurisprudence: and development, 40–41, 43–44; and instrumentalism, 35, 48; owner bias, 7–8; and pragmatism, 23; and prudence (*phronesis*), 60–61; and social and economic justice, 176–78; and "sweat of the brow," 68–69; and ubuntu, 45–46; utilitarian telos of, 58–59. *See also* copyright law; instrumentalism; law

justice, 5–6, 21, 101; and aesthetics, 170–72; and race, 5–6, 65–66, 99, 102–3, 106–7; (re)distributive justice, 44–45, 47, 65–66, 73, 159–60, 254, 299–300. *See also* copyright law; culture; ethics; law

Kant, Immanuel, 36, 162, 164, 168. *See also* ethics

Karaganis, Joe, 188

Karjiker, Sadulla, 19–20

Kearns, Thomas, 34

Khalaf, Hamzeh, 284–87, 290

Khoisan. *See* San people

Khuzwayo, Nkosi Vtuthuko, 141

King Kong (Bloom and Williams), 82

Kirby, Percival, 27–28

Klare, Karl, 37–38

knowledge: access to, 188; embedded, 291–93; epistemological condensation and rarefaction, 149–50, 153–54; expert systems, 141–43, 147–50, 152–53, 305; indigenous knowledge system (IKS), 19,

32, 112–13, 117–18, 126–36, 156; legal, 67; redefining, 8. *See also* experts; indigeneity; tradition; worlding
Koch, Grace, 173
Kruse, Corinna, 213
kwaito, 167–69
KwaZulu-Natal, 30, 140
Kymlicka, Will, 159

labor: creative, 5–6, 29–30; in cultural industries, 45–46, 269–70; immaterial, 128; and ownership, 25–26, 35–36, 310, 315n7; and precarity, 31–32; and race, 96–97, 110–11; and work for hire, 270. *See also* cultural industries; ownership
Laclau, Ernesto, 176
Ladysmith Black Mambazo, 28, 68, 156
Laird, Sarah, 146
Lametti, David, 166
Landes, William, 35
Langa, Pius, 37
language: as boundary object, 302–5; infralanguage, 193–94; legal, 58–59, 112, 135–36, 150, 207, 302
Larkin, Brian, 190–91
Lascoumes, Pierre, 33
Latour, Bruno, 53, 59, 103–4, 112, 128, 193, 203, 211. *See also* actor-network theory (ANT)
Lave, Jean, 241–42
law: and adverbial speech, 58–59; agency of legal form, 67; and behavior, 23–24; and class-action suits, 5; condensation strategies of, 150; constitutive view of, 34, 60; contingency of, 54–55; and cultural reproduction, 5, 17–18; and economics, 22–23, 35, 188; interdisciplinary study of, 22 23; law-in-action paradigm, 12, 95; legal-liberal model, 39; legal realism, 34–35, 101; as method, 303–6; minimalist versions of, 39–40; and objectivity, 318n57; ontology of, 59; poverty of social-analytical categories, 10, 34–35, 42–43; and public, 304; and relationality, 9–10, 103–4; Roman-Dutch, 25, 47–48, 96–97; rule of, 5, 8, 20–21, 33–34, 37–40; and science, 211–12; and society, 22–23; and transformative justice, 18–19; valence of, 57. *See also* anthropology; contracts and contract law; copyright law; criminal law; customary law; estate; law; instrumentalism; intellectual property law; language; patent law
Law, John, 9
Lee, Benjamin, 126
Legal Resource Center, 140
legal scholarship: and decolonization, 17; and instrumentalism, 22–23; is-ought binary, 17–18; method, 12–13, 21–22; and ownership, 6–7. *See also* decolonialism and decolonization; ethnography; law
legibility, 66, 98, 121, 143, 161, 250, 255, 264, 288, 305
Legos (game), 104–7
Le Roux, André, 232–33
Lessig, Lawrence, 44
Levinson, Jerrold, 169
Li, Tania Murray, 33–34
liberalism: and apartheid, 116, 176; and colonial project, 25–28, 176; and constitutionalism, 38; and development, 39–40, 43–44, 176; and indigeneity, 114–18, 122, 126–27, 131–32; and individualism, 4–6, 44–45, 114, 131–32, 135, 162–67, 187, 191–92, 251–52; limits of, 5–6; and racial justice, 65–66, 159–61; and ubuntu, 45–48; white, 69, 72, 81–82, 84, 102–3. *See also* neoliberalism
licensing, 243–49, 252–60; and capturing, 241–42, 249–50, 252–55, 257, 260, 264, 268, 294–95; license agreements at SAMRO, 241, 243–49, 252–53, 255–60, 264–65, 294–95; match and link, 241–42, 272–82; sociality of, 257–60. *See also* Southern African Music Rights Organisation (SAMRO)
Linda, Regina, 76, 81, 84, 86–89, 105
Linda, Solomon Ntsele, 19, 43, 62, 64–65, 67–70, 73, 76–82, 87, 90–91, 93–94, 97, 102, 105, 323n43. *See also* "Mbube" (Linda)
Lion King, The (Disney), 64, 92–93, 101, 321n5
Lion's Share, The (dir. Cullman), 107–8
"Lion Sleeps Tonight, The" (Disney), 64–65, 67–68, 93–94. *See also* "Mbube" (Linda); "Wimoweh" (Seeger)
"Lion Sleeps Tonight, The" (Weiss), 71, 76–81, 84, 93, 321n5, 323n39, 323n45, 326n87

Lion's Trail, A (dir. Verster), 107, 323n30
Locke, John, 35–36, 45
Lomax, Alan, 70
Lucia, Christine, 2
Luhmann, Niklas, 56

Ma, Yo-Yo, 157–58
Madondo, Bongani, 226
Mafokate, Arthur, 237
Maine, Henry, 11, 49
Maistry, Anjuli, 140
Makeba, Miriam, 72
Malan, Rian, 67–74, 76–77, 107–8
Malinowski, Bronislaw, 261
Mandela, Nelson, 2, 20
Marcus, George, 221
market: and crime, 187–88, 191–92; and culture, 3–4, 44, 135; and economy, 29, 31, 128, 187–88, 191–92, 239–41, 261–65; "educational marketing," 247–49, 254; free market ideology, 6, 44, 46–47, 252–53, 259–60; global, 115, 121, 221–22, 259–60; and indigeneity, 132; and market share, 46, 267, 270, 295–96; and piracy, 75; and politics, 142–43, 221–22; and race, 96–98, 127, 296; and social planning, 36, 118, 176–77; in South Africa, 4, 7–8, 27, 40, 267, 270, 295–96; and valorization, 3–4. *See also* economy and economics
Martin, Randy, 162
Marx, Karl, 81
Marxism, 112, 116, 269, 272, 281
MASA. *See* Musicians Association of South Africa (MASA)
maskanda, 267, 328n22
Master and Servants Act 15 of 1856, 110–11
Maton, Karl, 149
Maurer, Bill, 53
Mauss, Marcel, 46, 261
Maweni, Nicholas, 293–94
Mbeki, Thabo, 20, 68
Mbembe, Achille, 115
"Mbube" (Linda), 19, 43, 62, 64–65, 67–73, 76–81, 84–87, 90, 92–94, 101–8, 305, 321n5, 323n36, 324n49, 325n86, 326n87, 326n95; as boundary object, 304–5. *See also* "Lion Sleeps Tonight, The"; "Wimoweh" (Seeger)
Mbuli, Mzwakhe, 196

McAdoo, Orpheus, 69–70
Mcinga, Lusanda, 197
McLennan, John, 11
media, 29, 144; and affordance, 55–56; consumption, 257; and crime, 177, 179–80, 188, 190–91, 223; multinational, 65, 90, 102–3, 197; and race, 30, 168
mediator and mediation, 10, 49–50, 68–69, 115, 120–21, 123, 152, 164–65, 169, 249–50, 291–92; immediation, 250, 255; intermediary, 207, 240–41, 249, 281, 305. *See also* actor-network theory (ANT)
Meintjes, Louise, 167, 169, 171, 315n5, 316n24, 322n20
Merry, Sally Engle, 222
metadata, 210–11, 213–14, 216, 317n16. *See also* data and databases
Mhlaba, Hlengiwe, 238, 297–98
Mhlophe, Gcina, 140
Migogo, Nothando, 237–38, 286–87, 293, 297–98
Mill, John Stuart, 191
Ministry of Trade and Industry, Standing Advisory Committee on Intellectual Property, 113–14
minority group rights, 116, 143, 159
Mkhize, Boyce, 289
Mkhize, Lindelani, 156
Model Provisions. *See under* United Nations Educational, Scientific and Cultural Organization (UNESCO)
modernity, 141–42, 249; indigenous, 143; late, 3, 115; pirate, 190–93
modernization theory, 39
Moeketsi, Kippie, 156
Mohamed, Pops, 156–58
morality, 37, 45, 47, 60, 101–8, 120–21, 161–71, 177–78, 253, 262–64, 281–82. *See also* ethics; jurisprudence; ubuntu
Moretti, Franco, 280
Morgan, Lewis, 11
Motion Picture Association of America (MPAA), 77
Motsatse, Nicholas, 104, 107, 138
Motsoeneng, Hlaudi, 298–99
Mouffe, Chantal, 176
Mowles, Chris, 289
MPAA. *See* Motion Picture Association of America (MPAA)

MPASA. *See* Music Publishers Association of South Africa
Mthembu, Sihle, 168
Mthethwa, Nathi, 175, 178–79
musical scholarship, 1–2; and anti-anti-essentialism, 2; and ownership, 6–7; post-apartheid, 2–3
musical works information (MWI), 273
Musicians Association of South Africa (MASA), 296
music industry, 1–2; and colonialism, 26–27; and copyright law, 6–7; history of, 26–28; as market-oriented, 46–47; and race, 97–98; recording industry, 322n22; in US, 70–73. *See also* Recording Industry of South Africa (RiSA); Southern African Music Rights Organisation (SAMRO)
musicology. *See* musical scholarship
Music Publishers Association of South Africa, 296
MWI. *See* musical works information (MWI)

Namba, Mthunzi, 156
National Development Plan 2030 (NDP), 271–72, 340n67
National House of Traditional Leaders, 136
nationalism, 32, 115–17, 160–61; anticolonial, 154–55; cultural, 130–32
National Trust Fund, 137–38, 150–51
Native Lands Act (Native Lands Act 27 of 1913), 96, 110–11
Natural Justice (NGO), 149
Ncube, Caroline, 44–47, 320n101
Ndabeni, Esinako, 168
N'Dour, Youssou, 270
NDP. *See* National Development Plan 2030 (NDP)
necropolitics, 115
needle time, 232–33, 236, 248, 311–12, 337n7
neoliberalism, 8, 20–21, 39, 47, 54–55, 203, 261. *See also* liberalism
Netshitenzhe, MacDonald, 113–14
network: and assemblages, 112–15, 117–18, 224, 299; network effects, 207, 219, and piracy, 190–94; and statistical evidence, 220. *See also* actor-network theory (ANT)
Neves, David, 134
ngoma, 166–67, 169–70, 322n20. *See also* aesthetics; ethics

Ngubane, Sihawukele, 137
Nkabinde, Mzwakhe Reginald, 290
Nollywood (Nigerian film industry), 270
Ntsele, Elizabeth, 62–63, 101–2, 105–6
Nu-Metro Cinemas, 102, 321n5
Nussbaum, Martha, 191

objectivity, 34–35, 52, 54, 205, 291, 318n57
Old Slave Lodge (Slaven Loge), 109–10
Operation Dudula (Operation Eradicate). *See* Dudula (Operation Dudula)
organization studies, 12, 51
Oriakhogba, Desmond, 240
Oriani-Ambrosini, Marco, 148
Orientalism, 72, 322n20
originality. *See under* copyright law
Ouma, Marisella, 188–89
ownership, 35–36, 52–53, 139–40, 270, 311–12; as analytic paradigm, 3–6; and body, 3; and colonialism, 25–26, 72–73, 74–76, 96; and indigeneity, 117–18, 124–25, 144–45, 151–52, 297; and race, 65–66, 96, 254. *See also* author and authorship; copyright law; labor

Parliament, 109–10, 136; and legislative process, 111–12; Portolio Committee on Trade and Industry, 111; and portfolio committees, 111–12, 114
PASA. *See* Publishers Association of South Africa (PASA)
patent law, 124–25, 176–77; and benefit-sharing, 143–46; and development, 40–41; and *hoodia*, 120–21, 143–46. *See also* copyright law; innovation; law
Patents, Designs, Trade Marks and Copyright Act 9 of 1916, 76
Paynter, Geoff, 77, 97
Performance Rights Society (PRS), 233–35, 339n55
performative critique, 59–61, 307–8. *See also* ethnography
Performers' Organisation of South Africa, 232–33
Performers' Protection Act 11 of 1967, 312
Performers' Protection Amendment Act (Performers' Protection Amendment Act 8 of 2002), 19, 114

performing rights organization (PRO). *See* collective management organization (CMO)
Perlman, Marc, 126
personhood, 36, 167–69. *See also* identity
Perullo, Alex, 228–29
Pfizer, 144–45. *See also* hoodia (*hoodia gordonii*); patent law
phronesis (prudence). *See under* jurisprudence
Phytopharm, 144–45. *See also* hoodia (*Hoodia gordonii*); patent law
Pickering, Andrew, 55, 320n120
piracy, 20–21, 75, 177–78; and apartheid urban geography, 179–82, 223–27; biopiracy, 144; as creativity, 190–91; and global pricing, 188; and jurisprudence of copyright, 176; and networks of information-sharing, 190–91; and statistics, 175–76, 178–79, 220, 227–30; war on, 174–75, 178–81. *See also* crime; evidence; infrastructure; network; policing
platform economy. *See under* economy and economics
pluralism, 26–28, 33, 106–7, 159–60. *See also* liberalism
policing: and Anton Piller order, 217; and hotspots, 223–27; and paperwork, 203–7; by public-private partnerships, 194–98, 228–31; public resentment of, 216–17; by SAPS, 201–3; search-and-seizure operations, 216–19; and urban geography, 223–25. *See also* crime; piracy; South African Police Service (SAPS)
policy, 118–19, 121–22, 133–36; circularity of, 152–53; policy studies, 51
Policy Framework on the Protection of Indigenous Knowledge through the Intellectual Property System (2004), 32
Policy on Indigenous Knowledge Systems (IKS), 118
politics: and aesthetics, 167–73; and audits, 291–93; and economy, 28–32, 44; and governance, 111–18; and infrastructure, 281–82; and instrumentalism, 36–37; and law, 4–5, 37–38, 53, 66–67, 103–4, 150, 152–54, 302; and liberalism, 27–28; and ownership, 4; and postapartheid, 4–5, 9, 106–7, 160–61; and populism, 292–95, 297, 299; and race, 95–96, 126–32, 146; and science, 128–29; and statistics, 221. *See also* copyright law; development; economy and economics; law; liberalism
portfolio committee. *See under* parliament
Posner, Richard, 35
postcolonialism, 17, 21, 51–52, 130, 171; limits of, 22
postcolony: and community, 116–17, 241–42; and copyright law, 60, 75–76, 106–7, 252–53; and cultural production, 6–8, 240–41; and governance, 113; and legacy of colonial law, 110–11; and piracy, 190, 192–93; and public interest, 42–43; and social, 47; and subjectivity, 38–39; and West, 72, 146, 242
Pound, Roscoe, 34
Power, Michael, 289
pragmatism, 34, 39, 52, 56, 101, 169, 305–6. *See also* jurisprudence
precedent, 74, 78, 86, 303
Prevention of Organised Crime Act 121 of 1998, 198–99
Priestley, Joseph, 129
property, 3; and anthropology, 52–53; "property clause" of South African Constitution, 137–38. *See also* labor; ownership
protestant work ethic, 26, 289
PRS. *See* Performance Rights Society (PRS)
prudence. *See under* jurisprudence
public domain (*domaine publique*, DP), 45, 238, 296–98. *See also* ubuntu
public interest, 23, 41–48, 164–65, 231, 254, 304; local versions of, 48
public sphere, 42–43, 139. *See also* society
Publishers Association of South Africa (PASA), 138
Putnam, Robert, 117

race: and class, 116; and intellectual property, 5–6, 9, 65–66, 95–100, 110–11, 235–36, 254; and "Mbube" case, 65–66, 95–96; "racial scripts," 99–100; at SAMRO, 234–36; scientific racism, 129. *See also* copyright law; indigeneity
Radebe, Mark S., 27–28
Radio Bantu, 235–37
ragtime, 69. *See also* syncopation; vaudeville

rainbowism, 5, 70, 106–7, 109, 159–60
Ranger, Terence, 146
Rawls, John, 171
RDP. *See* Reconstruction and Development (RDP) Programme
realism, legal. *See under* law
Reckwitz, Andreas, 3, 115
recognition, 5–6
Reconstruction and Development (RDP) Programme, 29, 145
recording industry. *See under* music industry
Recording Industry of South Africa (RiSA), 22, 181–83, 194–97, 205, 217–18, 232, 296, 334nn48–49, 335n62; Affidavit in terms of the Copyright Act, 214–16; Audio Visual Licensing, 232; *Enforcement Bulletin*, 229–31; forensics lab at, 208–11, 213–16; *The Investigation Process*, 184–87, 190, 200–201; relationship with IFPI, 194–95, 214, 220, 228–30; and statistics, 220, 223–30. *See also* Southern African Music Rights Organisation (SAMRO)
Reidel, Ivan, 265–66
relationality, 9–12, 51–52, 55–56, 100, 171–72, 241–42, 249–50, 281–82
relativism, 39–40, 48, 52, 158, 211–13, 260
Rens, Andrew, 175
reproduction, cultural. *See under* culture
Restitution of Land Rights Act 22 of 1994, 140–41
Return of Sara Baartman, The (dir. Maseko), 157
reversionary interest. *See under* copyright law
Rheder, Angus, 195–96, 208–11, 213–14, 217–18, 224, 226
Rhodes, Cecil, 110
Richmond, Howard, 71
Richmond Organization, 71
Rifkin, Jeremy, 191
Riles, Annelise, 50, 53, 55, 67, 192
RiSA. *See* Recording Industry of South Africa (RiSA)
risk society, 223, 336n78
Roberts, Paul, 212
Robins, Steven, 146
Robinson, Dylan, 173
Roitman, Janet, 307
Rolling Stone, 67–68, 74
rooibos, 120–21
Roos, Gideon, 235–37

Rosin, Mark, 290, 293
royalties, 21, 138, 150, 232–34, 236–37, 261, 275–77, 282–83, 295–97, 311–12, 337n7. *See also* Southern African Music Rights Organisation (SAMRO)

SABC. *See* South African Broadcasting Corporation (SABC)
SACEM. *See* Société des auteurs, compositeurs et éditeurs de musique (SACEM)
Sachs, Albie, 24
SACO. *See* South African Cultural Observatory (SACO)
SAFACT. *See* South African Federation Against Copyright Theft (SAFACT)
SAFCA. *See* South African Society of Composers, Authors and Music Publishers (SAFCA)
Said, Edward, 72
SAMPRA. *See* South African Music Performance Rights Association (SAMPRA)
SAMRO. *See* Southern African Music Rights Organisation (SAMRO)
San people, 143–46, 156–58. *See also* hoodia (*Hoodia gordonii*); indigeneity
Sanscapes (Mohamed), 156–58
SAPS. *See* South African Police Service (SAPS)
Sarat, Austin, 34
SARS. *See* South African Revenue Service (SARS)
scalability, 268–72; economies of scale, 233, 242, 258, 268; nonscalability, 269–70
Scarry, Elaine, 170–72
Schmücker, Reinold, 166, 331n137
science: "colonial science," 129–30; and decolonialism, 128–29; and forensics, 211–13; and indigenous knowledge, 130–31; and law, 54; and politics, 128; and social engineering, 121. *See also* indigeneity; statistics
science and technology studies, 12, 51, 55, 121, 211–12, 221–22, 241–42
Scott, James, 121
second economy. *See under* economy and economics
Seeger, Pete, 70–74, 78–80, 82, 84, 323n39
Sen, Amartya, 43
Serres, Michel, 56
Shabalala, Joseph, 28, 68, 156

Shuttleworth Foundation, 175
Sibiya, Abe, 284–88
simplification, 121–22
singularities and singularization, 3–4, 9, 115, 158, 192–93, 211–12, 221–22, 280, 303, 307, 327n14; "singularity capital," 4. *See also* anthropology; ethnography; individualism
Sithole, Sipho, 238
Skyline Film and Television Productions, 157
Slaven Loge. *See* Old Slave Lodge (Slaven Loge)
slavery, 3, 69. *See also* colonialism; spirituals
Smith, Adam, 37, 45, 191
Société des auteurs, compositeurs et éditeurs de musique (SACEM), 233
society, 176; as analytical construct, 34–35; and capital, 117, 327n15; civil society, 33, 42–43, 121, 230–31; and cohesion, 21; and order, 47; and planning, 36; and poetics, 18, 257–60, 294; and reproduction, 3; of singularities (Reckwitz), 3; social Darwinism, 37; as Western construct, 23
socio-legal studies, 67; "gap problem," 48–49
Solomon Linda Trust Fund, 104–5
Sonnekus, Jean, 88–89, 324n50
sound studies. *See* musical scholarship
South African Broadcasting Corporation (SABC), 234–36, 247–48; and Copyright Act 63 of 1965, 236; local music quota, 298–99; non-payment of licensing fees, 238, 247–48; Radio Bantu, 235–37. *See also* Southern African Music Rights Organisation (SAMRO)
South African Cultural Observatory (SACO), 29–30, 270–72
South African Federation Against Copyright Theft (SAFACT), 77, 179–81, 183, 196, 201–4, 213, 334n39
South African Music Performance Rights Association (SAMPRA), 138, 183–84, 194–97, 208–9, 213, 232, 296
South African Observatory (SACO), 29, 271–72
South African Police Service (SAPS), 22, 178–79, 183, 197; anti-piracy operations, 174–75, 178–81, 216–19

South African Revenue Service (SARS), Customs and Excise Division, 179
South African San Council, 145
South African Society of Composers, Authors and Music Publishers (SAFCA), 234–37
Southern African Music Rights Organisation (SAMRO), 22, 104–5, 137–38, 232; audit by SekelaXabiso, 283–84, 286–89, 291–94; and authors, 253–54; corporate ethics of, 299–300; corruption, 232–34, 237–38, 283–88, 293–94; distribution of royalties, 275–81; efficiency of, 263, 277–81; and domaine publique (DP) scheme, 297–98; financial disclosures, 261; forms, 249–51, 338n39, 254–56; grudge purchases, 247–48, 252, 254–55, 260; licensing and sales, 241, 243–49, 252–53, 255–60, 264–65; membership, 266–67; natural monopoly, 233–34; and race, 234–37, 337n4, 337n7; SAMRO Foundation, 299; tariffs, 233, 243–44, 247–59, 265–66; UNDOC, 295–96, 298; written-back royalty distribution, 295–97; Zeus platform, 272–75, 281–83. *See also* Recording Industry of South Africa (RiSA)
spaza, 255, 259
spirituals, 69. *See also* jubilee songs
Spivak, Gayatri, 146
Star, Susan Leigh, 207, 241–42, 250–52, 280, 302–6
state-function, 54, 57–58
statistics: in anthropology, 220–22, 335n70; circulation of, 222–23; and crime, 223–28, 306; and governance, 221–22; and hotspots, 233–27; and indicators, 221–22, 261; at RiSA, 195, 220, 224–31. *See also* anthropology; crime; piracy
Steingo, Gavin, 167–68
Stengers, Isabelle, 54
Stewart, Kathleen, 242
Strathern, Marilyn, 291
subjectivity: colonial, 25–27; indigenous, 113, 133. *See also* ethics; identity
Sundaram, Ravi, 191
Sunder, Madhavi, 16, 28, 43, 44, 124–25
sustainability, 299
Swift, Taylor, 265–66

syncopation, 69–70. *See also* ragtime; vaudeville

Tabane, Rapule, 4
Tadros, Victor, 165–66
Tamanaha, Brian, 36–37, 39
Taylor, Charles, 159
Taylor, Matthew, 191
TCE. *See* traditional cultural expressions (TCE)
termination rights, 76, 107, 307
Theron, Johan (Joe), 156
thing theory, 51
Thompson, Hunter S., 297
Tilley, Helen, 130
Token Music Publishing Company, 79–80
Tokens (band), 71, 79
Towse, Ruth, 261
trademark, 188. *See also* copyright law; counterfeit; piracy
Trade Marks Act 94 of 1993, 114
Trade-Related Aspects of Intellectual Property Rights (TRIPS) Agreement, 19, 137, 145, 187–88, 227–28, 266, 309
tradition, 2, 4–5, 19, 21, 24–25, 27–28, 145–46, 150–52; and invented tradition, 146
traditional cultural expressions (TCE), 126–28, 132–34, 137–39, 143, 154, 156, 158, 165, 170, 170–73. *See also* indigeneity; knowledge
traditional knowledge, 32, 118–21, 123–32, 137–38, 143, 156. *See also* indigeneity; knowledge
traditional resource rights, 158
transduction, 55
transparency, 222, 290–94. *See also* statistics
Trebilcock, Michael, 39–40
TRIPS. *See* Trade-Related Aspects of Intellectual Property Rights (TRIPS) Agreement
Tshwane (Pretoria), 181–82
Tsing, Anna, 22, 239, 269–70, 272
Tucker, Raymond, 81–84, 324n46
Tunis Model Law on Copyright (1976), 118–19, 124–25

ubuntu, 7, 20, 44–45, 159; and definitions of public good, 45–48; essentializing categories of, 45–47; and liberalism, 45–48
UNCTAD. *See* United Nations Conference on Trade and Development (UNCTAD)

UNESCO. *See* United Nations Educational, Scientific and Cultural Organization (UNESCO)
Unilever, 144–46
Union of Southern African Artists (USAA), 82
United Nations Conference on Trade and Development (UNCTAD), 135
United Nations Educational, Scientific and Cultural Organization (UNESCO), 123, 125, 135, 154; *Framework for Cultural Statistics*, 132–33; Model Provisions (UNESCO-WIPO), 123–25, 138
United States Trade Representative (USTR), 227–28, 336n86
Universal Copyright Convention (1985), 123
Universal Declaration of Human Rights, 138
USAA. *See* Union of Southern African Artists (USAA)
user: and collective management organizations (CMOs), 233–34, 239–41, 248–50, 252–56, 259–60, 264–65; and copyright, 7–8, 138–39, 164–65, 311–12; disadvantaged, 254–55; and networks, 191; rights, 41
USTR. *See* United States Trade Representative (USTR)
utilitarianism, 22–23, 35–36, 46, 58, 163, 165–66, 304

valence, polyvalence, 57–58
value, aesthetic, 157–58
van der Merwe, Charmaine, 146–48
Vats, Anjali, 99–100
vaudeville, 69. *See also* ragtime; syncopation
Verdery, Katherine, 52
Verster, François, 107
Vilakazi, Strike, 235, 300
violence, 174–75, 183; colonial, 126–27, 166–67; during police raids, 183; at SAMRO, 296; sexual, 168; structural, 109
Virginia Jubilee Singers, 69
Visser, Coenraad, 1, 301–2
von Schnitzler, Antina, 282

Walt Disney Company, 19, 43, 62, 64, 77, 92–94, 101, 105–6, 321n5, 324n47
wealth maximalization, 23, 35
Weber, Max, 26
Weheliye, Alexander, 6

Weiss, George, 71, 74, 321n5, 323n39
Wenger, Étienne, 241–42
Williams, Pat, 82
"Wimoweh" (Seeger), 70–71, 74, 78–84, 323n39, 323n45. *See also* "Lion Sleeps Tonight, The"; "Mbube" (Linda)
WIMSA. *See* Working Group of Indigenous Minorities in Southern Africa (WIMSA)
WIPO. *See* World Intellectual Property Organization (WIPO)
Working Group of Indigenous Minorities in Southern Africa (WIMSA), 145, 157
Works Information Database (WID). *See under* Confédération internationale des sociétés d'auteurs et compositeurs (CISAC)
World Forum on the Protection of Folklore (1997), 125
worlding, 241–43, 251–52, 298–99. *See also* community
World Intellectual Property Organization (WIPO), 42, 123, 125, 137, 188–89; Intergovernmental Committee on Intellectual Property and Genetic Resources, Traditional Knowledge and Folklore (2000), 118–19, 125; Revised Provisions for the Protection of Traditional Cultural Expressions/Expressions of Folklore, 126, 154
World Trade Organization (WTO), Intellectual Property Division, 149
Wynberg, Rachel, 144, 146

Zulu: guitar music, 267; kingship, 73; orientalism, 322n20
Zuma, Jacob, 5, 20

www.ingramcontent.com/pod-product-compliance
Lightning Source LLC
Chambersburg PA
CBHW050158240426
43671CB00013B/2174